The
Berlin Area

Berlin, Pennsylvania
1777 1977

The Berlin Area

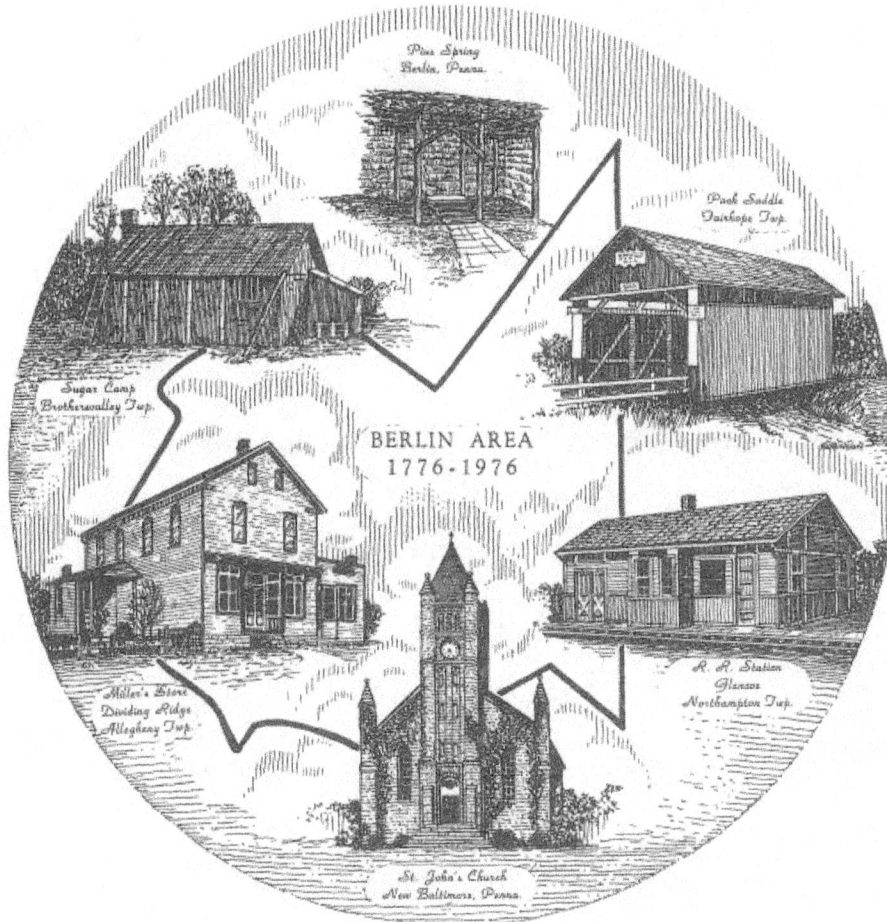

BERLIN AREA
1776-1976

Pine Spring
Berlin, Penna.

Pack Saddle
Fairhope Twp.

Sugar Camp
Brothersvalley Twp.

Miller's Store
Dividing Ridge
Allegheny Twp.

R. R. Station
Glencoe
Northampton Twp.

St. John's Church
New Baltimore, Penna.

which includes

Berlin Borough	New Baltimore Borough
Brothersvalley Township	Northampton Township
Allegheny Township	Fairhope Township

Published by the Berlin Area Historical Society
1977

Fifth Printing
ISBN: 978-0-9886458-6-8

Scanning and cover services provided by:
Beggs Printing
472 Latrobe Avenue
Confluence, PA 15424
beggsprinting.com

Pius Spring

References

Berlin Borough Ordinance Book of 1853
Old Berlin Newspapers
      The Berlin Record
      The Berlin Gleaner
      The Berlin Bulletin
Two Centuries of Brothersvalley by H. Austin Cooper
History of Bedford, Somerset, & Fulton Co., Waterman & Watkins & Co., 1884
Beers Atlas of Somerset County - 1876
Pastors and People of Somerset Classis
History of the Allegheny Evangelical Southern Synod, 1918
Meyersdale Republican
Hillcrest Grange 1966—50th Anniversary Publication
Pioneer Simon Hay Brochure written by Edward R. Hay
Laurel Messengers of Somerset County Historical and Genealogical Society
Old Home Week Booklet of 1908
Berlin Centennial Booklet, 1937
One hundred years of Somerset County History
      by Paul C. Trimpey
Holy Trinity Lutheran Church Records
United Church of Christ Church Records
Dr. Ezra C. Saylor Records
Penna. Clocks and Clock Makers
      by George Eckhardt
Western District of Brethren
      by Jerome E. Blough, 1916
Annuals of Southwestern Penna.
      by Lewis Clark Walkin Shaw, 1939

The above picture appeared in the Sunday Roto Section of The Pittsburgh Press dated November 19, 1961. Press staff writer, William Gill, wrote: "The only walls in Berlin, Pennsylvania, are built around lawns and gardens. Here Mrs. Anna Walbert chats over her garden wall off Main Street with her neighbor, Mrs. Marie Beachley."

During this past year, it became even more evident to me there were no walls in the Berlin Area except around our lawns, gardens, and fields as a truly dedicated group of people came together in this our national Bicentennial year and formed the Berlin Area Historical Society, Inc.

I would be remiss if I didn't use this opportunity to express my personal and the area's gratitude to these people for their dedicated effort, hard work, and the vision they've shown in bringing the Berlin Area Historical Society to a reality. Those involved in this effort and the areas they represented are:

Allegheny Township
    Mrs. Ray E. (Thelma) Boyer
    Mrs. Lee D. (Lorene) Hoppert
Berlin Borough
    Mr. Samuel C. Engle (elected Treasurer)
    Mrs. Charles A. (Elizabeth) Merrill, Jr.

Brothersvalley Township:
    Mrs. Richard F. (Helen) Croner
    Mrs. James L. (Dorothy) Killius (elected Secretary)
Fairhope and Fairhope Township:
    Mrs. James R. (Jeannine) Cummins
    Mrs. George A. (Cinda) Emerick
New Baltimore Borough:
    The Rev. Father Robert C. Flaherty
    Mr. John J. Will
Northampton Township and Glencoe
    Mrs. Carl A. (Marjorie) Hay
    Mr. Carl A. Hay

The Rev. Ralph E. Mills was elected our Vice-President.

The roses are still growing and blooming on the wall pictured above for all to enjoy even though the one who planted them is no longer here. It's my sincere prayer the seeds planted by the above group of people will grow and mature so those coming after us can have a better understanding of their heritage and their roots.

We have attempted to be accurate in our presentation of the information in this book. However, it is only as good as its sources. We regret any errors or omissions and would appreciate being advised where they exist.

               John O. Ream, Jr.
               President

Woodrow Wilson wrote: "A nation which does not remember what it was yesterday does not know what it is today, nor what it is trying to do. We are trying to do a futile thing if we do not know where we came from or what we have been about."

The Berlin Area is full of memories on the road from yesterday to tomorrow. What follows on these pages is an attempt to preserve those memories, to show the people and the institutions who have contributed to every phase of human activity in our community.

From this section went forth soldiers who fought in the Revolutionary War and succeeding wars. From this community have gone forth ministers of note, lawyers, physicians, and professors of whom the community has been proud.

We have attempted to compile a book which may be read with pleasure and excitement, a book which will create a sympathetic understanding of the problems confronting our forefathers and the institutions which helped to make this place which we call HOME.

It is an attempt to implant a more lively concern for the lessons of the past. A reader who relives our history will have a deeper appreciation for the hardships and contributions of the men and women who built Berlin and the surrounding country's rich historic lore.

We offer our book, not as a literary achievement, but as a souvenir warm with interest for the area we love.

It is our way of reminding you that our community is fortunate in having numbers of men and women who are interested in collecting and preserving the history of Berlin and the surrounding territory.

The Berlin Area Historical Society, chartered in Pennsylvania, is dedicated to this endeavor. We found it heartwarming to discover that those who live here feel a oneness with us in the accomplishment of this goal. We ask that the tradition of cooperation, the spirit of helpfulness, so evident in our history, continue so that the Berlin Area Historical Society may perpetuate recognition and appreciation of our heritage.

Rev. Ralph E. Mills,
Vice-President

Berlin Borough

Pius Spring
Berlin, Penna.

Berlin Committee

Elizabeth L. Merrill - Co-chairman
Samuel C. Engle - Co-chairman
Eleanor M. Engle
Margaret Shober
Thelma Saylor
John Lichvar
Robert Brant - Photographer
Garner Pritz

Contributors

Rev. D. C. White
Miss Hazel R. Baker
Mrs. Gilbert McQuade
Mrs. Mabel (Dudley) Dunbar
Albert Philson
Ralph Groff
Mrs. Marie Beachley
Ben F. Walker
Mrs. Betty June (Dively) Wymer
Robert L. Miller
Thomas Gerber
Mrs. Myrtle Harding
William Brown
Mrs. John O. Ream, Sr.
Eugene C. Johnson
Walter A. Johnson
Mrs. Jacob Stutzman
Mrs. Samuel Miller
Mrs. Wm. E. Scurfield
William Flamm
Thomas Croner
Miss Bertina Layding

Pius Spring

Berlin, Pennsylvania, named after Berlin, Germany, situated high on top the Allegheny Mountains like an eagle with its wings outspread reaching into the distance is the oldest town in Somerset County. It seems to have been settled around 1784, as there were settlers in this locality as far back as 1763 or perhaps even earlier and was discovered purely by accident.

About the year 1770, three men were sent over the Allegheny Mountains by a number of Calvinistic or Reformed and Lutheran settlers of the east to locate a settlement west of the mountains. Having arrived at a point near the old depot, the horse of one of them threw his rider, breaking his leg. They found they could go no farther and decided to locate at that spot. After the settlers arrived they decided to move up the hill and build their first buildings close to the Pius Spring. This spring is the source of the Stony Creek River, which flows into the Conemaugh, Allegheny, Ohio, Mississippi, thence into the Gulf of Mexico.

The first record is that on April 4, 1786, the supreme executive council of the Commonwealth of Pennsylvania, granted Jacob Keefer, in trust, for the Calvinistic and Lutheran churches, for the support of schools, a tract of land, comprising forty and one-half acres of land, on the headwaters of the Stony Creek, upon which tract said Calvinistic and Lutheran congregations had laid out a town, calling it Berlin.

The town was laid out by Jacob Keefer in trust on a warrant dated July 27, 1784, a year or two previous to the time this grant was made. Shortly after the original forty-acre plot was laid out in lots a dispute arose among Jacob Keefer, Jacob Fisher, and Francis Hay as to the ownership of the tract of land lying immediately west of Berlin, designated in the deed as the "troublesome" tract. The dispute was finally settled by agreeing to donate this property to the Lutheran Church of Berlin to be laid out in town lots for the benefit of the church. The land was not to be sold but was to be rented and the sum of one Spanish milled dollar was to be paid to the Lutheran Church of Berlin annually, forever, by the holder of each lot.

The first deed recorded in the Somerset County deed record is for lot 56 in the town of Berlin, sold to Adam Miller for fifteen shillings and an annual ground rent of one Spanish milled dollar. Among other things, this deed states that Jacob Keefer in 1789 conveyed to Jacob Glassner in trust for Lutheran and Calvinistic churches, one half of the tract of forty acres, and that they have laid out the town of Berlin on this half and further that the deed is recorded in Book C, page 226, of the Bedford County records. As Jacob Keefer joined in the deed to Adam Miller, we must assume that he made the deed to

15

Glassner as a co-trustee, who would represent the Reformed Church. On this half are plotted the seventy lots that are referred to in the indenture.

The beginnings of Berlin are quite interesting, showing how the community spirit manifested itself in these early days. The following interesting document, translated from the German, has been recorded in the Bedford County records:

"KNOW ALL MEN BY THESE PRESENTS: That this indenture and instrument was made the 2nd day of June in the year of our Lord and Savior one thousand seven hundred eighty-four, for a piece of land in Brothers Valley Township, Bedford County, State of Pennsylvania, which was used by Jacob Keffer, Joseph Johns, and Jacob Gut (Good), and was taken up by the following men, for church and school land and this land was afterwards laid out by the owners into lots for the City of Berlin and the following articles shall be binding upon the owner, Lutherans and Reformed, namely between Jacob Glassner, Jacob Fischer, Jacob Keffer, Jacob Giebeler, Philip Wagerlein, Walter Heil, Peter Kober (Cober), Heinrich Glassner, Valentine Laut, Franz Hay, Frederick Alfatter, Johannes Eideneier, Peter Schweitzer, Nicolaus Miller, Godfried Knepper, Nicolaus Faust, Michael Beiger, Peter Loeble and Peter Glassner, the several owners of the City of Berlin.

..1st. That both owners of the City of Berlin, Lutherans and Reformed, agreed to divide the lots and began with number one. Number one was apportioned to the Reformed and Number two to the Lutherans and so forth, with the exception of the church lots. The money for the purchase of lots or from lottery, or from lots still unsold shall be evenly divided by both owners.

"2nd. That three lots shall be laid out for every church and school for both parishes as numbers, 61, 62, 63 and numbers 34, 35, 36. The numbers 61, 62, 63, shall fall to the lot of the Lutheran parish, and to the Reformed 34, 35, 36, or the old Church and school plot by the spring. So is the old school house by the spring by both owners, Lutherans and Reformed, taxed to the amount of twenty pounds and shall be maintained by both sides. In the event of the parish separating, the Reformed must pay to the Lutherans ten pounds of the above mentioned twenty pounds and this money shall be paid from the first revenue that comes from the City of Berlin. It has seemed good to both communities to lay out a meadow to every church and school house.

"3rd. That each and every descendant of the undersigned owners of the City of Berlin, as Lutherans and Reformed, shall forever possess the right to church and school, if he depart not from his religion, but should one or the other depart from his religion, so has he lost his right to church and school, and it shall be forbidden him to sell his right.

"4th. That each and every possessor of a lot in the City of Berlin shall build a house with a frontage of at least 22 feet which shall have stone chimney so that there may be no danger of fire, and thereby must in every possible way, as city be covered with shingles, and each and every possessor or owner of a lot must pay to the owners One Spanish Dollar of Seven Schillings and Six Pence Ground Rent.

"5th. That each and every lot, if the owners thereof abide not by the above written condition, shall be forfeited to the several owners of the City of Berlin for Church and School and the owners shall take the money from the forfeited lots and apply it to the Churches and Schools in the City of Berlin; so that all the revenues of the City of Berlin from purchase and Quit Rents be applied to the same object as the above mentioned forever and ever.

"6th. It is agreed by the owners of the City of Berlin that no tannery shall be built at the spring other than Martin Daubele's (Diveley's) tannery and no noxious trade shall be established.

"7th. Each year, on a definitely set day, as the day before the New Year, shall the accountants (which shall consist of men of each side, so that each parish can conduct its own accounts) further each year upon the above mentioned day, before the New Year, render their accounts, and if necessary, elect others. The men who are elected as accountants are empowered to receive all purchase monies and ground rents from each and any possessor and owner of lots in the City of Berlin.

"8th. The lots from Number 1 to 12 are eleven rods in length and four rods in width, and from Number thirteen to Number twenty-four, are ten rods in length and four rods in width, and from Number twenty-five to thirty-six fourteen rods in length and four in width, and from Number thirty-seven to forty-eight twelve rods in length and four in width; forty-nine to sixty, twelve rods in length and four in width; from Sixty-one to seventy, twelve rods in length and four in width.

"9th. We, the owners, promise each and every one who draws or buys a lot, a lawful right thereto. We, the owners of the City of Berlin, as Lutheran and Reformed bind ourselves and our heirs, executors and administrators in the sum of One Thousand Pounds good and lawful money of Pennsylvania to keep the above articles as they are set forth.

"Witness our hands and seals:

Jacob Geibeler	Peter Glassner
Jacob Keffer	Friederich Alfalthr
Johann Nickelhous	Johannes Edynger
Peter Kober	Jacob Fischer
Valentine Laudt	Frantz Hay
Peter Loeble	Godfried Knepper
Walter Heil, his mark	Peter Sweitzer, his mark
Jacob Glassner	Michael Beyer
Heinrich Glassner	

"The above written, dated, signed and sealed in our presence,

"JACOB HAETCHL,
"GEORGE RAUCH.

"BEDFORD COUNTY, PA., SS: Personally appeared the whole number of the subscribers within mentioned and signed before me, one of the Justices of the Peace and Common Pleas for said county, and one and all acknowledged the foregoing instrument in writing to be their act and deed and they all desired that the same might be recorded as their act and deed, as witness my hand and seal the twenty-first day of March in the year of our Lord one thousand seven hundred and eighty-eight 1788.

"ABRAHAM CABLE (Seal)"

In the 1760's the land west of the Alleghenies was opened by a treaty with the Indians and soon afterwards settlers began arriving. They followed the streams to their source and found Pius Spring, which is now in the center of Berlin. Here they built a town which was at that time part of Bedford County. They named it after their fatherland in Germany. They were religious people and soon afterwards built a church which was also a school.

Berlin was a wooded area, and a large ravine extended from Division street to Fifth Avenue between Mulberry and North Streets. A wood pump well with a water trough for horses existed for many years prior to 1920 at the corner of Fifth Avenue and Mulberry Street. At Vine Street, between Mulberry and North Street, was a low field with a big ditch that was fed by water from a marsh area on South Main Street between Vine and Fifth Avenue. The National Bank of Western Pennsylvania occupies this area today. The water from the marsh flowed across Main Street and down Vine through Saint John's Canal. This canal was walled with large stone along each side and was about eight feet high, and had stones five feet by two feet as a cover and was actually a sidewalk for 75 years before Vine Street was paved by the W.P.A. in 1940. If it were uncovered today, you would find the stones intact, otherwise the street would have collapsed.

The portion of Berlin west of Division Street is on twenty-five acres of land that Jacob Keffer, John Fisher, and Francis Hay bought from Joseph Johns and plotted into fifty-five lots, the first addition to the new town. These lots were also subject to the annual ground rent of one Spanish milled dollar but for the use of the Lutheran Church only, with its school and the poor. The article of agreement concerning these lots was made August 25, 1787, and recorded at Bedford, while the deed by Johns was not executed and recorded until 1796. The town of Berlin was first incorporated as a borough on February 27, 1821, by the legislature, but it did not function as such very well until 1837, when the Somerset County court granted a full decree of incorporation. There were two little villages adjoining, which later were added to the borough: Vietersburg, laid out by Jacob Kimmel and surveyed by A. H. Philson in 1888; and East Liberty, otherwise known as Hinkelstadt or Chicken Town, to the eastward, also added in 1888. With this religious setup as between the Lutherans and the Calvinistic Reformeds, there is little wonder that the later Brunerstown, renamed Somerset, was chosen as the county seat. Some of Berlin's disappointed citizens must have been responsible for one story that when the commissioners appointed to fix the county seat reached Somerset, they were wined and dined by its people; and another, that while Berlin had better taverns and whiskey, there was not enough water there to care for the horses, were it selected as the county seat.

Berlin was a place of militia mustering, and the settlement of difficulties between citizens that did not care to take the issue to court. It was also a place of holding one of the earliest fairs in western Pennsylvania. From the reminiscences of Henry J. Lang has come the following account of the first fair held in Somerset County:

"Great crowds of people from all parts of the county were in attendance during its continuance of three days. There were no exhibits of any kind at the fair, which was held on a farm later owned by Herman Brubaker. A race track of a mile around was in front of where the house now is. Four horses ran a race, which was won by a horse from Ligonier known as the Ligonier Pony. There were fiddling and dancing in all the taverns from morning till night and from night until morning. Among the fiddlers were Peter Lavie, John Laire, and Peter Troutman, the latter an old Revolutionary soldier who lived in Southampton Township. Each of these fiddlers had his own place where he held forth. In short, in those days horse racing and frolicking constituted a fair. This one wound up with a foot race for the whiskey between Ludwig Baer and Valentine Lout, who weighed 250 pounds apiece and were 70 years old. After running a couple of rods Lout tripped Baer, both falling to the ground in a heap to the great amusement of the spectators." Such were the amusements of our forefathers when they went out for the purpose of having a good time.

Most of Berlin west of 7th Avenue was developed by Mr. John Fletcher.

For a number of years, Berlin was the only trading place of consequence in the county or, in fact, west of Bedford in southern Pennsylvania.

At the time of Berlin's settlement in 1784 the surrounding community was one of gigantic growth of virgin timber interposed with sections of grasslands called the "Glades." There were no passable roads—just a few Indian trails for foot travel and packhorses. Transportation to and from the Eastern manufacturing cities was impossible. Consequently the struggling little community was forced to depend on her own skill and ingenuity to furnish her with the bare necessities of life as well as with clothing and implements.

Berlin was soon dotted with shops that housed the various embryo industries necessary for the existence and growth of a tiny, isolated settlement on the summit of the Allegheny Mountains.

1763—Jacob Fischer owned a mill on Miller Run and later sold it to Mr. Isaac Stoner. Later on it was the Calvin Hay Mill.

1770—Martin Dively came to this section and established the first tannery. His tanyard was located on the northern end of Marie Beachley's lot. When the inhabitants of Berlin drew up a paper concerning the lots deeded by Jacob Keffer, they specified that no tannery

Berlin Drum Corps, organized 1782

except Martin Dively's would be allowed in town. An agreement, drawn up on June 2, 1784, and acknowledged before Abraham Cable on March 26, 1788, was later broken, for Jacob Gull established a tannery soon after Dively's opened.

1771—As Harmon Husband traveled through here, he found Peter Wagerline settled nearby what is now Berlin.

1771—Schmidtbarndt—the first blacksmith whose shop was on Main Street near the place where the First National Bank was later located. A short distance across the street was the Reformed Church Cemetery. Ghostlike figures were said to have been seen flitting from the shop into the graveyard. The people of that day were very superstitious; therefore the blacksmith shop soon became a place to be shunned. Robert Philson finally investigated the matter and found that the "ghosts" were caused by light reflecting through the windows of the shop onto the tombstones.

1777—A union worship and school was built on Mulberry and Fifth. Services were held by the Reformed and Lutheran denominations, and so infrequently that they did not conflict. The ministers came from the east at regular intervals.

1782—George Johnson, Henry Close, and George Platz organized the Berlin Fife and Drum Corps.

1784—Of the seventeen signers of the document establishing the town of Berlin, all but two could write their own names.

1784—Christian Evel built the first pottery, located on the corner of Main and Vine in the building where Mr. Robert L. Miller's office now stands. The articles were fired in kilns which were located along Vine Street.

1785—John Fletcher, Robert Philson, and Adam Miller operated the first stores. The goods was first brought in for these stores by packhorses and about 1790 wagons began hauling the merchandise to Berlin.

1786—Methodist Society was organized by George Johnson, who came here from Shepherdstown, West Virginia. A small church was erected costing about four hundred dollars. This was later sold to the Disciple Denomination.

1787—Frederick Gary, who settled in Berlin, was the first carpet weaver in the county. Later weavers were: John Atchinson, John Lane, Fred Knepper, Jacob Sheetz, and Cornelius Gary.

1787—An agreement recorded at Bedford on the land purchased by Jacob Keffer, John Fisher, and Francis Hay from Joseph Johns and platted into fifty-five lots as the first addition to the town of Berlin. It is west of Division Street. These lots were also subject to the annual ground rent of one Spanish milled dollar, but for the use of the Lutheran Church only, its school and the poor. There must have been a misunderstanding of some kind and eventually there was both contention and litigation about them.

1789—Jacob Keefer conveyed to Jacob Glassner, in trust for Lutheran and Calvinistic churches, one half of the tract of forty acres, that have been laid out for the town of Berlin. This deed is recorded in Book C, page 226, of the Bedford County records. Since Keefer joined in the deed to Miller, it is assumed that he made the deed to Glassner as a co-trustee representing the Reformed Church. On this half were plotted seventy-two lots. This indenture makes no reference to the lots on the eastern half of the Pius Spring tract.

1790—Berlin had a severe winter with deep snow.

1790—Charles Zorn came to Berlin from Lancaster and was a potter. One grade of pottery clay was obtained from along the Will's Church road from the farm presently owned by Edwin Landis. For the other grade of pottery, clay was brought from the farm now owned by John Croner.

1790—John Kimmel, storekeeper.

1790—Lucwick Baker, blacksmith.

1790—The Brallier's Drug Building on the lower diamond, built between 1785 and 1790, was torn down in 1905 and rebuilt with brick.

1791—Dr. John Kimmel, a graduate of medicine, came to Berlin from York County and spent the remainder of his life in Berlin. He was a colonel in the militia and an associate judge of Somerset County and also owned a store and a tavern, the sign of which was a black horse. When he first arrived he built a small log cabin out near a place called Chicken Town, or in later years East Berlin. Here he and his wife, Elizabeth Ulrich, lived the first years of their married life. They had a cow and no stable the first winter, so in inclement weather they drove the cow into the kitchen to milk. They had to go to Hagerstown for flour and supplies, a distance of more than one hundred miles, in the absence of roads, on an Indian trail on horseback. The price of everything was most exhorbitant; think of calico at $1.00 per yard, coffee at $1.00 a pound, etc. It was likely the milk which the cow gave as she was being milked before the open fireplace was more frequently called for than the coffee pot. The doctor prospered in the practice of medicine and also farmed and built a hotel on the southeast corner of the upper diamond in Berlin where the large brick hotel now stands. They had eleven children who were all born in Berlin.

1794—A Dr. Boerstler who came from Funkstown, Maryland, told of his arriving in Berlin on August 31, 1794, when everything was in an uproar on account of the new excise tax. He tried to keep out of politics, but it was impossible. His wisdom told him to join the party of the government but he spoke to the people and explained to them about the great danger they were in. An army was marching on our country to suppress the revolt, but on their arrival everything was quiet. Later he was called to Bedford to appear before Judge Peters as a witness, in order to report what he knew about Robert Philson and Harmon Husband in respect to insubordination against the excise and the state. He was compelled by $500 bond, under his signature, to appear in Federal Court if called. He told the judge that "the people are quiet and peaceloving and the only thing against them is ignorance. When the first troop of the army arrived here Oct. 24, 1794, they distinguished themselves excellently in their politeness and humanity and deserved to be publicly praised on that account. The following day Gov. Thomas Mifflin, his nephew, John M. General Morris, General Ross, Lawyer Hamilton and Mr. Read took their quarters in his house (although there were much larger and nicer houses). They comported themselves very well; all paid. The Governor

gave me his hand as he went off and said that he hoped I would visit him if I got to Philadelphia." Later in the spring of 1795 he told of being taken to Philadelphia with many others to be a witness against the leaders of the mob accused of high treason. He left home with seventy dollars and expected to receive another sixty dollars for his services. With this he planned to buy medicine to bring back to Berlin. But he did not get the sixty dollars and after paying traveling expenses he had only two dollars left. Two of the prisoners (Philson and Husband) were liberated, two were hanged, and he was disgusted with the way the trial was handled. (Taken from the November, 1970, issue of *Laurel Messenger*.)

1795—Jacob Gulls operated a tannery.

1795—Adam Stull had a blacksmith shop on the John C. Philson lot on the corner. He had learned his trade from Philip Wegley.

1795—The old barracks in Berlin, where the National Bank of Western Pennsylvania now stands, were said to have been built in 1795 and part of it was the Schmidtbarndt blacksmith shop. During the war of 1812 they started calling it "The Barracks." After this, the building was used as a wheelwright shop for the manufacture of chairs, and a German named Deusch manufactured powder horns for the hunters. Then it was a residence until Fred Groff bought it and built his store here and used the barracks as a warehouse until it was sold to the bank.

1795—Reverend Heinrich Geise came to Berlin as a resident pastor and taught German in the old log school on the north bank of the spring on the Reformed burying ground. It stood for many years. This was the building in which Spangenburg killed Glessner. Previous to that time the Reformed congregation had been served for several years by Cyrianus Spangenburg. During a quarrel he stabbed Elder Jacob Glessner and inflicted mortal wounds. He was tried, convicted, and was awaiting execution in the Bedford jail. Berlin was under the shadow of this awful event when the five-man commission viewed the town as a possible choice for the county seat. We do not know how all this may have affected their decision, but we do know they moved on to survey Brunerstown and when their choice was announced on September 12, that was the chosen site.

1795—Somerset County was created by an act of the general assembly out of Bedford County from the land lying west of the Allegheny Mountains.

1795—The first deed on the Somerset County deed record was recorded on June 20, 1795. It was for lot 56 in the new town of Berlin, sold to Adam Miller for fifteen shillings and an annual ground rent of one Spanish milled dollar to be paid to the Calvinistic congregation for the use of its schools. It further provides that, within three years, the purchaser shall build a substantial house of at least twenty-two feet front, with a good shingle roof and a stone chimney, under penalty of forfeiture of the lot. The deed was executed before James Wells, justice of the peace, April 3, 1792.

1796—In this year the deed for the land purchased from

Joseph Johns was made. It was for the land west of Division Street, being the west part of town and consisted of twenty-five acres and was platted into fifty-five lots as the first addition to the town of Berlin. The article of agreement for this land had been made in 1878, and recorded at Bedford.

1796—Jacob Cumer's house in Berlin was purchased by Doctor Boerstler for 130 pounds. On April 9, 1796, he sold his house to John Russel for 163 pounds. Later on in April he moved to Cumberland, Maryland, from Berlin.

1800—The Lutherans built a log school and church on the corner of Fletcher and Vine streets. This was on the northeast corner of the Lutheran burial ground and was during the pastorate of Reverend Frederick Lange. At this time the union building was taken over by the Reformed congregation. These buildings were built with a large fireplace at one end and a partition through the middle, one story with the attic floored. It was the rule for the teacher of the school to live in the rear room where the divine services were also held. These partitions were later taken out and the buildings were used for school purposes only.

1800—The Reformed congregation took over the union building for themselves.

1800—Berlin now had fifty-four houses, two churches, and three taverns.

1800—Henry Young, who came to Berlin in 1800 at the age of ten, mentioned in his reminiscences a rifle company commanded by Captain Robert Philson. The exact date of this is uncertain.

1801—Alexander H. Philson was born in Berlin. He was a surveyer and merchant who was also justice of the Peace for thirty years and performed many of the early Berlin marriages, most of them in German. He was also the first burgess of Berlin. His father, Robert Philson, had come here from Ireland along with his uncle John Fletcher in 1785. Robert Philson was the first congressman from this district, associate judge for twenty years, a member of the state legislature in 1795, and a brigadier general of the militia of Bedford, Somerset, and Fayette counties for a number of years. Alexander wore a patch on his right eye.

1808—This was the date of the first fair to be held in Somerset County. Great crowds of people from all parts of the county were in attendance during its continuance of three days. There were no exhibits of any kind at the fair held on a farm later owned by Herman Brubaker and now across from the James Broderick residence. A racetrack a mile around was in front of where the house now is. Four horses ran a race won by a horse from Ligonier known as the Ligonier Pony. There was fiddling and dancing in all the taverns from morning till night and from night till morning. Among the fiddlers were Peter Lavie, John Lave, and Peter Troutman, the latter an old Revolutionary soldier who lived in Southampton Township. Each of these fiddlers had his own place where he held forth. In short, in those days horse racing and frolicking constituted a fair. This one wound up with a foot race for the whiskey between

Ludwig Baer and Valentine Lout, who weighed 250 pounds apiece and were seventy years old. After a couple of rods, Lout tripped Baer, both falling to the ground in a heap to the great amusement of the spectators. Such were the amusements of our forefathers when they went out for the purpose of having a good time.

1809—Francis Hay, Simon Hay, and Jacob Keffer, as trustees of the Reformed Church, executed a deed to the trustees of the Lutheran church for the ground rents for the forty-five lots in the addition, specifying the numbers of the lots. The deed states that, in order to settle all the disputes and litigation that had arisen, a suit had been brought in the circuit court of Somerset County. It was in the nature of a replevin, in the name of John Kimmel, and had been decided in favor of the plaintiff.

1813—Frederich Goeb, an early printer who was born in Germany and came to Philadelphia in 1804, later settled in Chambersburg. He sold his paper there in 1808 and soon afterwards moved to Somerset. A number of the articles, calendars, and publications he printed have been found in the Berlin Area. These are all in German and we have several among which are the Goeb Bible, a ponderous volume more than a foot high, bound in leather over heavy oak board, and two and one-quarter inches in thickness. This is the first German translation of the Bible published in western Pennsylvania. It is quite rare. It belonged to a Gumbert family near Berlin.

A year after publishing the Bible, Goeb published a small edition of the New Testament. One of these has also been found near Berlin.

A Frederich Goeb baptismal certificate of a John Hefle married to Barbara Swartz on the birth of their daughter, Drusylla Hefle, who was born in Berlin in the year 1818, is still preserved as it was found glued inside the lid of a blanket chest.

Around 1820 he sold his home in Somerset and moved to Schellsburg, Bedford County, where he continued in the printing business. One of the articles he then printed found its way back to Berlin, his Allgemeines Vieharzneibluch—or General Veterinary Science Book published in 1823. A few of the remedies printed in the back of the book are printed in both German and English. He died in Schellsburg in 1829 at the age of forty-seven, and is buried beside his wife, Catherine, and a daughter in the old church cemetery at Schellsburg.

1818—John Heffley, a native of Berks County, settled in Berlin and was a tanner by trade. He and his sons took over Dively's Tannery in 1830, which was at the site of present-day Marie Beachley's residence at 543 Main.

1819—At this time there was a company of riflemen at Berlin commanded by Captain John Brubaker. This company and one in Milford Township commanded by Captain Gephart were expected to celebrate the anniversary of Perry's victory on Lake Erie.

1823—The first brick house in Berlin was built on the northeast corner of Division and Main streets by Jacob Lowery. Today it is the residence of Mr. and Mrs. Clarence Gindlesperger at 401 Main.

1825—The first Sunday school in Berlin was established by John Fletcher and Jacob Crigler.

Johnson and Son first hearse—a 1918 Pierce Arrow

1825—The Reformed congregation erected a stone building to take the place of the old union house and about the same time the Lutheran congregation erected a frame building near the site of the old high school building or what is known today as Cedar Heights. This was known as the red schoolhouse.

1828—Mr. Levi Shoemaker was sexton of both the Lutheran and Reformed churches in 1828 and 1829 and among the duties imposed were ringing the bell, scrubbing the floor, cutting wood, furnishing the candles, keeping the burial ground in order, the compensation from each congregation being $2.50 per annum.

1830—The minute books of the Lutheran church were written in German until this time.

1830*—The Johnson and Son Furniture Store and the Johnson and Son Funeral Home are the results of five generations of family effort and dedication. The firm was established in 1830 by John Johnson, making it one of the oldest businesses in the area. John Johnson was a cabinetmaker who also made wood coffins in a log building erected at 701 Main Street; this is the location of the Walter Johnson home. That first log building burned down and was later rebuilt at the site of the present funeral home. At the close of the Civil war, John Johnson was joined in the business by his son, Aaron Krissinger Johnson; together they continued as cabinetmakers for the community. About 1890, John Nelson Johnson entered the business with his father,

Johnson and Son Funeral Home

A. K. Johnson and family

Aaron, as a cabinet and coffin maker; later they not only made their own caskets but also manufactured concrete vaults at the lower end of their property. Under John N. Johnson, the funeral business was established at its present location in 1937, and in that same year the furniture store was moved to its present location at 522 Main Street. In 1963, J. Theodore Johnson joined his father, Eugene, and his uncle, Walter, in the partnership. In 1964 The Johnson and Son Furniture Store was changed from a general furniture store into a Colonial Gallery, featuring five major lines of furniture. In May 1968, the furniture store became an Ethan Allen Gallery, which it is at the present time (1976).

1832—The first heating stoves for coal came into use about this time and were called cannon stoves.

1835—The Hathaway cooking stove was introduced in 1835. It was a superior wood-burning stove which sold for fifty dollars and upwards.

1836—The first free school was established in Berlin. Buildings for public school use were successively erected on Diamond Street, in 1837, 1857, and 1876, which later on was the Fogle Cigar Factory.

1837—Since all transportation was by means of wagons, the business of making and repairing buggies and wagons was an important one. The blacksmiths constructed the metal parts, and the wagon makers made the woodwork and assembled the wagons and buggies.

1837—At this time there were three blacksmiths, four wagon makers, and one wheelwright in Berlin.

1837—Martin Diveley, William Conrad, Frederick Swope, Jacob Kimmell, Michael Zorn, and Alexander H. Philson were chosen as school directors.

1837—The town now had six tailors and six shoemakers.

1837—John Lane was weaving carpets and coverlids at this time. Later weavers were Fred Knepper, Jacob Sheetz, Cornelius Gary, and John Atchinson.

1837—The manufacture of hats, an important industry at this time, was carried on by George Lower, Henry Lower, George Johnson, Michael Ream, and Isaac Miller. Isaac Miller's shop was later the location of Dr. I. C. Miller's residence and presently George Groff's. The hats were carried to Pittsburgh on wagons or packhorses and then shipped down the Ohio River on flatboats and sold to Southern planters. Imagine a member of the old Southern aristocracy proudly strutting around with a high silk hat bearing the label "Made in Berlin." A Mr. Heiner had an extensive hat industry where Bowser's Garage was later located.

1837—Berlin incorporated as a borough.

1838—An addition to the borough known as Vietersburg was laid out by Jacob Kimmel and surveyed by Alexander H. Philson, but this was not incorporated into the borough limits until 1888, when the present lines were surveyed by George P. Brubaker and what is now known as East End (then Chicken Town) was also taken in. In Hinklestadt or Chicken Town it was said that the people baked their bread on one side only as there were houses on only one side of the street.

—The first two-story house in Berlin was built on the northeast corner of the lower diamond. It was first a tavern and afterwards a store was kept in it. It was at one time Bralliers Drug Store and presently is Western Auto.

1842—Charles Stoner, a blacksmith, decided to open the first foundry in Somerset County. His establishment was located behind the spot where Collin's Drug Store later stood, and today Anchor Real Estate is located. During the first half of the nineteenth century all the houses had open fireplaces. For cooking purposes the cooking pots were suspended over the fire by means of a crane. After opening the foundry, Mr. Stoner designed the Hathaway Cooking Stove which was designed to burn wood and

Berlin Foundry - C. Stoner

had a door on the side where the fuel was put in. This was a great improvement over the crane, and it met with the instantaneous approval of the housewives of the community. Once a woman had tried the modern stove, she would not go back to the old method of cooking; consequently, Mr. Stoner had two teams busy hauling stoves throughout the community. His drivers would take along pipe, pots, and pans, and set up the stoves for a trial. A great many stoves were sold, and because there was little money in circulation, Mr. Stoner was often forced to accept meat, potatoes, and other produce in exchange for his products. He would then pay his employees with these articles of barter which he had received.

When coal was later discovered in this community, Mr. Stoner designed the William Penn Coal Stove. Pig iron for the foundry was hauled from Cumberland and Bedford. Mr. William Bender remembered the time when the sight of six or more covered wagons drawn by six horses and laden with pig iron for the foundry was a common one. The coke used in the foundry was made on the farm where John Stoner now lives. Edward McQuade and Jacob Millhouse made the coke. The remains of two coke ovens could be seen many years later. Pots, kettles, sugar pans, threshing machines, and plows were among the articles made at the foundry.

1842—John Oliver Kimmel was elected Register of Wills, Recorder of Deeds, and Clerk of the Orphan's Court of Somerset County. He then moved to Somerset.

1843—The third Reformed church was built at a cost of $3,000.

1845—Mr. Henry Floto manufactured cigars in a barn belonging to Daniel Heffley on Meadow Street.

1845—On April 6, 1845, a fire occurred that threatened to destroy the town. Over 40 buildings were on fire at one time but by vigorous work on the part of the citizens, all were saved but three. These were the dwelling and shop of Samuel Hofford, the dwelling and store of Samuel Philson, and the stable of widow Fletcher.

1850—The Berlin foundry began making the William Penn Cooking Stoves, a coal-burning stove.

1850—Alex Brubaker had a tannery on the north side of

RESIDENCE & STORE OF
S. PHILSON - BERLIN

Lower diamond looking east

the borough parking lot on North Street. Many years later while some men were working in the ditch on North Street, they dug up several feet of tanbark from this tanyard.

1850—The Hagner Brewing Company was founded in the 1850's, and was housed in a two-story building on Vine Street across from the Samuel Engle residence.

1850—Early tanneries of Berlin were Heffleys, Brubakers, Hiram Miller, and Martin Weimer's, which stood where Don Kimmel lived for many years and presently is owned by Harold Bittner at 219 Broadway.

1850—Weavers at this time were Fred Knepper, Jacob Sheetz, and Cornelius Gary.

1850—John Hook owned a chair factory near the site where the National Bank of Western Pennsylvania stands today at 538 Main.

1850—John Ham had a shop where Lane's stable later stood.

1850—The Brallier Pharmacy was located on the lower diamond on the site of the present-day Western Auto Store at 507 Main.

1851—A. Greenwalt established a chair factory and from his advertisement in the Somerset Weekly Visitor for December 3, 1851, it is evident that he was an accomplished workman. His ad read as follows:

"The undersigned would respectfully inform the citizens of Berlin and the public generally that he has rented the shop adjoining the residence of W. F. Dively, Esq., where he has commenced the Chair Making Busi-

W. F. Philson Store, started 1858

ness, and where he will consistently keep on hand and manufacture to order all kinds of chairs. Persons desirous of purchasing had better give me a look before they buy elsewhere, as I can and will sell on such terms as will suit all Berlin. A. Greenwalt."

1851—The second Methodist church was built.

1852—On January 9 the Odd Fellows Lodge was organized. Two of the charter members were Daniel Heffley and Henry Brubaker.

1853—The second Lutheran church was built under the pastorate of Rev. Elias Fair.

1853—The Albright Seminary was established under

Philson National Bank 1866

Evangelical Association and was later changed into a college.

1856—The Farmers' Store of Berlin was managed by Samuel A. Philson, who had previously taught school in the old stone schoolhouse which was located on the site where the Swartzendruber Mill later stood. Later on he taught school at Hays Mills in Brothersvalley Township. Next he attended Gettysburg College, returned to Berlin to be a clerk in the Old Stoner Foundry, and later on to manage a store at Summit Mills. After about a year, he and his uncle, Samuel Philson, erected a sawmill on a large tract of timber at Philson's Station along the B & O Railroad near Sandpatch.

1858—He now went to Roxbury and started a store, remaining there for three years, and then moved to Berlin to go into partnership with his brother, Jacob C. Philson, after which they opened a General Store where the Cook Block stood, as it was called in the early days. Much later it was known as Collin's Drug Store and presently is Anchor Real Estate. After three years they moved to the corner of the upper Diamond until 1884 when the partnership was dissolved and turned over to the two sons of Samuel A.—or John A. and William F. Philson—the father retiring from business. Later John A. sold out his share to William F., who conducted a general store on the same site until 1920.

1860—The Walker map of this year showed several toll gates on the outskirts of Berlin on the main roads. One was located near the present home of Eugene Johnson, where there was a pole across the road. This gate was tended by a lady. Those who lived on the farm just below did not have to pay toll but had to wait until she unchained the pole and swung it across the road. The toll to Wellersburg was five cents.

1865—Hoffman Brewing Company founded.

1866*—Samuel Philson and Charles A. M. Krissinger established the banking house of S. Philson and Co. at 313 W. Main Street, which is now owned by Robert Zorn. Present location is on the lower diamond at 518 Main.

1870—Theodore H. Floto manufactured cigars on Main Street in a building beside the present-day home of Dr. Paul Klose. His son Austin (Bud) continued the business for many years. They made the Berlin Toby.

1870—From the White Horse Tavern to Altfather's Mill was a wilderness. Besides running the mill, Altfather kept the Buck tavern, the sign being a buck.

1870—Walter Hoyle sold his farm to Jacob Wingart for a bushel of salt.

1870—The tract of land east of Berlin where the Platt coal mine was located was owned by Valentine Keffer.

1870—The Herman Brubaker farm, now the site of the James Broderick residence, was earlier owned by Jacob Weyand.

1870—Jacob Good, Sr., lived on the farm still known as the Good farm, presently owned by Edwin Landis. This was earlier the John Zug (pronounced Zook) farm.

1872—Emanuel Meyers and Ephraim Cober built the first gristmill in Berlin. It was run by steam and was later destroyed by fire.

1874—The Berlin Water Company was incorporated April 29, but no lines were laid until 1902.

1874—The construction of the Buffalo Valley Railroad was an enterprise undertaken by the citizens of Berlin and Brothersvalley Township. It connected with the Pittsburgh division of the Baltimore and Ohio Railroad at Garrett.

1875—A shoemaker who made leather boots had his shop where Frank Groff later had a store. Today it is Gardner's 541 Main.

1875—Thomas Price is credited with opening the first coal mines in a commercial way. This was down near the station. In a few years he sold to Morgan Reese & Co. who employed sixty-five men and shipped a large amount of coal. John Stoner bought these workings in 1888.

1875—Cyrus Musser established a blacksmith shop at the corner of Diamond and Washington streets which was until recently the location of the home of Mr. and Mrs. Bert Walker. Later his son Joseph B. Musser operated the blacksmith shop. Cyrus Musser lived on the northwest corner of Diamond and Washington streets, and Joseph Musser lived across the street on the property owned later on by the Harry Dickey family.

1876—Our oldest school building, still standing at the top of the station hill, was built in 1876 at a cost of $5,700. It was later used as a cigar factory and more recently

"Berlin Orchestra"—standing, left to right: Harvey Dively, Fred Krissinger; seated: Wesley Garey, Harmon Riehl, Harvey Hay, W. F. Philson, S. P. Brubaker; front row: Warren Fogle, H. B. Philson, Don Kimmel, John Brallier

Buffalo Valley Railroad (1874)

Oldest school still standing (1876)

as a glass factory which made beautiful church windows which were shipped all over the country.

1876—The Standard or Adams coal mine was opened around this time. It also was not operated very extensively.

1878—The Berlin Bulletin, a Berlin newspaper, was printed at its office in the Mansion House, a large hotel on the upper diamond at the present site of Lafferty's used car lot. This paper was printed partly in German. Several of the advertisers were:

Mrs. J. H. Knepper, Berlin, Pa., Dealer in Millinery goods, Ladies Neckwear, Zephurs, Perfumery, Hair Oil, Lilly White, Sewing Machine Oils, and Needles etc. etc.

N. Garey & Son, Stove, Tin & House Furnishing Store, manufacturers in Tin, Copper, and Sheet ironware, Sugar pans, Hollow ware, Stamped & Japanned ware, Cook stoves, Parlor stoves, Heating stoves, House furnishing goods, Roofing, Spouting, Repairing, etc. Attended to at short notice.

Berlin Marble Works, R. H. Koontz, Proprietor, (formerly of the firm of Runyan and Koontz.) All work executed in the most artistic manner and satisfaction guaranteed.

National Hotel, S. S. Shaffer, Proprietor. Day and Week boarders can have good accommodations at reasonable rates. Good Stabling and abundant supply of feed for stock.

J. Poorbaugh and Son.

1880—Charles Krissinger began operating a foundry in the southwest part of the town. It was located beside Martin Weimer's tannery on Broadway and was smaller than Stoner's.

1880—The Philson Iron and Coal Company opened its mines two miles southwest of Berlin.

1881—The Berlin Brethren Church members began their building on Main Street

1882—A gristmill was erected by Solomon Spangler.

1882—A planing mill was built by Atchison & Pile.

1882—C. D. Floto bought out the cigar factory of his father, A. D. Floto.

Denner Heffley and Joe Evel (1884)

1882—Samuel S. Shaffer operated the National Hotel and when he retired, in 1882, E. H. Fiscus from Westmoreland County came to Berlin to manage it.

1883—The present Reformed or United Church of Christ building was erected in 1883 and 1884 at a cost of more than twenty thousand dollars.

1884-1930—Joe Evel had a repair shoe shop in the rear of Denner Heffley's Hardware Store.

1885—The Berlin Record's first issue was published Nov. 25, 1885, with F. G. Chorpenning, editor. It was housed then in parts of what today is the residence of William Scurfield on the upper diamond at 226 Main.

1885—The Will Engle Box Factory, located between the present-day Robert Croner and Harold Zorn residences on East Main Street, made boxes for cigars, cardboard for tobies, and wooden boxes for the more expensive cigars, for the many stogie factories in Berlin.

1885—During the period from 1885 to 1890 Dan Brubaker and Sam Engle, who were partners in contracting, had a shop on the same lot as the present home of Robert Croner at 822 E. Main Street. Mr. Brubaker lived there. Both were carpenters.

1885—D. J. Reitz founded the Reitz Manufacturing Company that had a two-story building on the corner of Vine and Mulberry and another two-story building in the shape of an "L" across the street to the east. This was a woodworking shop which was destroyed by fire July 1, 1910. It made flour mill machinery, and employed 21 people.

1889—This marked the beginning of the first two-year high school course, with S. D. Elrick as principal.

1889—Ida Grace Garman, daughter of Doctor William A. Garman of Berlin, was a victim of the Johnstown Flood. She was in charge of the telegraph office there at the time, and sent out the last dispatch prior to the destruction of the building in which the office was located. Her body was buried with the unknown dead, but five months later was identified by her father and was brought to Berlin where she is buried in the I.O.O.F. Cemetery. She was a beautiful young lady who at the time of her death was twenty-two years of age.

1890—Prior to 1900 Charles Floto had his cigar factory on Main Street on the site now known as the Dr. Robert Heffley residence. His cigars cost ninety cents for a box of 100. This building still stands on Fletcher Street where it became a residence when moved and was later occupied by Mr. and Mrs. Chester Musser.

1890—Samuel Beam flew his balloon from the Stoner Grove, located on the road to the John Stoner Farm. This was around the year 1890.

Ida Grace Garman (1889)

Berlin Record Printing Office (1889)

Samuel Beam (1890)

C. A. Floto Cigar Factory (1890)

1890—Reams Meat Market was started in 1890 and operated until 1945 when it was sold to William Crowe.

1890—Electric power was manufactured in Beaver Hollow behind the Robert Croner property. Electricity was made only at night.

1890—The Reitz Manufacturing Company, whose specialty is the building of roller mills and the manufacture of roller mill machinery, was incorporated in 1890 with a capital of $18,000. D. G. Reitz, president; Albert Heffley, secretary; Jacob J. Zorn, treasurer.

1891—Fred Groff's Store. On the inside corner of his store ledger is written "I started my store May 25, 1891 with a capital of 1 horse and buggy valued at $125.00." This was first located on the lower diamond at the present-day location of Appleyard's T.V. Shop. Later he moved down to the present-day location of the National Bank of Western Pennsylvania at 534 Main Street.

1892—The Eclipse Wood Pulley Works was organized in February, 1892. The corporation had a capital stock of $30,000 and was under the management of D. G. Reitz. In 1900 the company was reorganized and pulleys, silos, porch swings, gliders, and brooder houses were among the articles manufactured by the Berlin Wood Products Co., Inc. This company had previously been the Eureka Wood Pulley Company which had gone into receiv-

Fred Groff's Store (1891), lower diamond looking west

R. C. Heffley Hardware (1899)

Berlin Shoe Factory (1892)

Brant Brothers Store & Restaurant (1900)

ership. It was located at the site of the late Harold Miller residence on North Street. Ralph Engle states he helped to build a wooden pulley at Eclipse Wood Pulley Factory in Berlin in 1904 that was the largest ever built there, which was then sent to Germany. It was 25 feet in diameter and between two and three feet in width.

1892—W. J. Gardner operated a flour mill.

1892—Garman's Hall opened. This was located on the lower diamond at 500 Main Street, where Gardill' Drug Store is today. It was destroyed by fire in 1903.

1893—A. C. Dively had a blacksmith shop next to the flour mill.

1894—G. E. Fogle and George Long Cigar Factory were located in the house on Diamond Street and Mulberry across from Dr. Prugh's. Later they moved to the old schoolhouse on the top of the station hill. Cliff Dively had a cigar shop between the New National Hotel and Herman Schellers' Service Station.

1894—Samuel Reihl had a cabinet shop on Broadway across from the Bunn Philson home, now occupied by Albert Philson.

1894—Frank Heffley operated a box factory at this time.

1895—The Floto (A.C.) Creamery was established around 1895 at a location on North Street where the old Brothersvalley Township building later stood. Today it would be adjoining the residence of Mrs. William Gindlesperger. Newton Berkebile operated the creamery for A.C. Floto. About the year of 1912, the creamery was moved to Fletcher Street at 5th Avenue, and that building is now a private garage on the property of Jess M. Hillegas. In fact, the Hillegas house was the A.C. Floto residence. The creamery made tub butter, and this was sold in the cities and was shipped from Berlin by the B&O Railroad. A John Sheets gathered the cream throughout the country using a horse and wagon for this creamery.

1898*   —The Co-operative Mutual Fire Insurance Company of Berlin was incorporated in March, 1898. It insures town and farm property on the premium note plan. It has been highly successful in giving its patrons cheap insurance. It has outstanding risks exceeding one and a third million dollars. Its officers from the start have been William H. Ruppell, of Somerset, president; C. A. Floto, vice-president; Frederick Groff, treasurer; and Jacob J. Zorn, secretary. After Mr. Zorn's death in February, 1914, Jacob B. Schrock was elected secretary. In the year 1921, Jacob B. Schrock resigned in order to be manager of Pine Hill Fuel Co., and Allen C. Miller was elected secretary. At the annual meeting of the insurance company, January, 1929, Robert L. Miller was

First National Bank (1901)

Lower Diamond (1908)

elected secretary, after his father, Allen C. Miller, expressed his wish to retire.

1899—R. C. Heffley Hardware Store was in the I.O.O.F. Building. Denner Heffley—so called because he once had stated he was a Dennercrat!

1899—An electric power plant was built by Scott Matthews.

1899—George Brubaker operated the East End Dairy.

1899—Electric streetlights were installed in the town.

1899—The mines of the Pine Hill Coal Co. opened. The company had 2,200 acres of coal land in Brothersvalley, and Isaiah Good, Norman Knepper, and Daniel Zimmerman of Somerset were the principal stockholders.

1900—Gus Floto had a butter factory in the hollow back of the present residence of Harold and Catherine Croner at 810 E. Main Street. Butter was packed in wooden containers and packed in ice and stored in buildings at rear of lot where Jesse Hillegas now lives on Diamond Street. Mr. Floto lived in the home now occupied by Jesse Hillegas at 310 Diamond St. This was around 1900.

1900—At this time, before the fire, the Garman Opera House was upstairs in the present location of the Philson Bank Building, 518 Main Street.

1900-1928—Donner's Restaurant was owned by Mr. and Mrs. Harry Donner. Their last restaurant was in the Wilkows location, 429 Main.

1900-1940—Berlin Bottling Works was run by Clarence Tipton.

1900-1910—William Menges, Henry Menges's father, made shoes.

1900-1910—Brant Brothers restaurant and Groceries was located where Anchor Real Estate is today.

1901*   —National Bank of Western Pennsylvania had its beginning as the First National bank of Berlin on September 17, 1901. Dr. William A. Garman was president and J. B. Schrock, cashier. On July 12, 1966, a branch office was opened at Shanksville, and on November 18, 1968, a merger with the First National Bank at Stoystown resulted in a name change to the First National Bank of Somerset County. Two years later on October 29, 1970, the Meyersdale office was opened, and two years after that the New Centerville office was opened on September 14, 1972. July 19, 1974, brought about the present change in name to National Bank of Western Pennsylvania due to a consolidation with The First National bank of Confluence and its two branches of Old Trails at Markleysburg and Indian Head.

1901—The Mansion House, a large hotel located on the upper diamond where Lafferty's Garage and Used Car Lot is today located, burned down in 1901.

1901—The Disciple Church, which was beside the Mansion House, also burned at this time, plus a stable belonging to Lewis Esken, which was behind the Mansion House. The townspeople got the water to fight these fires from a well that is now under the street to the left of Lafferty's Car Lot. This had a hand pump and was covered with boards. When a fire occurred, the firemen came running to the pump, pulling the two-wheeled fire cart, and then filled it with water. Another stable belonging to the Mansion House containing many fine horses which could not be rescued also burned. The owner of the hotel was Mr. James Trent.

1901-1945—Dudley's Barber Shop. First located below Hotel Berlin in the block that was burned in 1929. Next it moved across the street where Horning is located today, then down into the Central Hotel, where Dudley ran the pool hall and had a barber shop. Finally he moved to the northeast corner of lower diamond at present-day Appleyard T.V. location, 441 Main.

1902—Albert Swartzendruber purchased the flour mill from his father, Jacob Swartzendruber, who had operated a gristmill for many years. This was located on the corner of Mulberry and Fifth streets. Today it would be directly behind the post office and on the same lot as the old Reformed Cemetery.

1902—T. H. Floto moved his cigar shop from the upper diamond to East Main Street in a building which was finally torn down. It was located beside the home of Doctor Paul Klose at 738 Main.

1902—The Garman Drug Store, Frank Collins Store, and Gus Floto General Store were located in the block now occupied by Johnson and Son Furniture Store and the Philson Bank.

1903—Another early Sunday morning blaze took place in 1903. This started in a stable belonging to Frank B.

Floto's Store (1902)

Old Berlin Scene (1902)

Collins. The fire could not be checked until it had destroyed the drugstore, public hall, and a brick residence belonging to Dr. John S. Garman, Frank B. Collins' store building, a log house occupied by A. B. Cober as a clothing and men's furnishing store, the brick residence of F. B. Collins, the frame store building occupied by the dry goods store of A. C. Floto, the residence of Dr. W. A. Garman, and restaurant of W. C. Emery had all been destroyed. Some of the contents of the houses were saved; a part of others which had been

taken out of the buildings burned in the street. By the superhuman efforts of the bucket brigades, the flames were confined to these buildings, but other buildings were badly scorched.

1903—Fogle and Long built a cigar shop on Diamond Street, next to the Evangelical Church, or today across from the residence of Dr. Prugh.

1903—Berlin's Electric Light plant was purchased and greatly enlarged.

1903—A Berlin Hose Company was organized.

1903—The Berlin Hospital started. This was sold to Harry DeHaven in 1906.

1903—John Brallier had a drugstore at the present site of Western Auto Store and lived in the home occupied by the George Gindlesperger family on Main Street.

1903—John Ream operated a livery stable where the Food Rite store now stands, 540 Main Street.

1903—William McLuckie and Wesley Hartman established a paper box factory. Since the shoe factory was closed, they made cigar boxes and shipped them to Uniontown, Connellsville, and other cities. The factory was sold to various individuals and was later moved to Meyersdale.

1903—Names of people who operated businesses in Berlin at this time were:

Barbers: A. L. Dudley and William Williams
Blacksmiths: H. K. Hay, W. H. Millhouse, John Musser, Jos. B. Musser, and F. E. Straul
Books and Stationery: Charles F. Cook
Contractors and Builders: Cyrus Musser & Son
Dentists: Ronald B. Colvin and L. F. Miller
Department Stores: Frederick Groff
Druggists: George W. Brallier and Jacob S. Picking
Dry Goods and Notions: C. E. Pile
Electricians: E. H. Allen, C. H. Blough, Charles F. Blough, Frank Cam, J. L. Minick, and Zell Uncapher
Fire Insurance Agents: Robert M. Walker and J. J. Zorn
Furniture: B. J. Bowman and A. K. Johnson & Son
General Merchandise: J. C. Philson and W. F. Philson
Hardware: C. W. Krissinger
Grocers: Charles F. Cook & Co. and Thomas Reuben
Hotels: Ferdinand Bizold, J. C. Brady, A. B. Falkner, P. J. McGraph, and Andrew McQuade
Jewelers: A. H. Dorn and Joseph Hauger
Livery and Sales Stables: John O. Ream
Marble Dealers: Robert W. Ross
Milliners: Lizzie Masters
Newspapers: Record
Painters and Paper Hangers: George W. Buckman, Elmer E. Heffley, John A. Long, and J. J. Reidt
Physicians: W. H. Garman, Henry Garey, Robert J. Heffley, John A. P. Murray, and W. P. Shaw
Plasterers: John H. Glessner, Frank Powell, Homer Zorn, Milton Zorn

Restaurants: M. M. Dively and W. G. Emory

Stone Masons: Obediah Brant, Andrew Glessner, and Edward Glessner

Surveyors: D. B. Burns

Tailors: R. P. Rolly

Tinners: Nelson Gary, Wesley C. Gary, and Ralph Suder

Undertakers: B. J. Bowman and John H. Johnson

Variety Stores: Frank Rankin

Veterinary Surgeons: Peter Fogle

Ministers: L. H. Hazlett, M. F. Kelley, R. S. Patterson, E. P. Sykles, and W. C. Sykes

Justices of the Peace: D. J. Brubaker, Robert C. Heffley, and H. W. Knepper

Constables: J. J. Sidel

Notaries Public: Alexander Brubaker and Albert Heffley

1904—Samuel Engle and son, Ralph, had a livery stable on Fletcher Street on lot now owned by Ben Donner; followed by Saxon and Chalmers Auto Agency operated by Samuel Engle and son, George.

1904—Floto's Store was located in the building which houses Johnson and Son Furniture Store at the present time at 522 Main. Smith, Francis & Co., Groceries and Dry Goods, was in the Hillegas Building, now the Larry Gardner property at 629 Main Street.

1904—Ben Bowman operated a furniture store on Main Street, had a post office in the store, and was postmaster. Ralph Engle, Worley Fogle, Harvey Logue, and Harvey Hay were rural mail carriers at that time, annual pay $600. Ed Levy Jewelry Store and Albright Hotel stood in this block prior to its burning in early 1900's.

1904—A cider press and apple butter addition were added to Swartzendrubers' flour mill.

1904—The Berlin Mercantile Store opened at this time and closed in 1909. It was built after the fire of 1903. Prior to that it was the Collin's General Store and now is the Philson National Bank Building at 518 Main. Several of the officers were C. W. Krissinger, George P. Brubaker, and C. W. Saylor.

1904—Bessie Bennett, aged twelve years, daughter of Frank Bennett; and Willie Millhouse, aged nine years, a son of Daniel Millhouse, were burned to death in a fire that destroyed the house of Frank Bennett on the night of February 2, 1904.

1904—A public water supply is furnished by the Berlin Water Company. The plant was installed in 1904 and is a gravity system, deriving its source of supply from mountain streams.

1905—Shoe factory closed.

1905—A three-year high school course was begun.

1905—A group of local men organized a shoe factory in the plant of the pulley works. The machinery was bought at Rowena, Pa., and a number of people were brought along to run it. At the time the factory closed in 1907, the output was approximately 300 pairs of shoes daily.

1905-1969—Ralph Landis plumbing shop.

1905—I. A. Engleka entered the general store business in March 1905 when he bought out the stock of Albert

Brallier Pharmacy (1903), lower diamond looking east

John Ream's Livery Stable (1903)

Berlin Mercantile Co. (1904)

Hillegas who had a store in the building later known as the Lafferty Building, 629 Main Street.

There was a little old store building in the east end of Berlin which he rented and moved his stock there in March 1907. In 1908 he bought the building and went into the general store business in earnest.

In 1910 he erected a new building much larger than the first one. By that time there were 1,000 people in or near Macdonaldton.

The mines were running full blast and business was booming.

Mr. Engleka had the agency for the Austin Powder Company, Pittsburgh, Pa., for many years. He would get 100 kegs or 2,750 pounds at a time. At first the powder cost $500 a carload but by the time of World War I the price had increased to $2,000 per carload. The railroads brought him five carloads at a time.

In 1913, Mr. Engleka was Berlin's first automobile dealer handling the Metz Auto which was made in Waltham, Mass. He was not satisfied with the results of the trade nor with the car. The mechanism of the Metz operated somewhat similarly to a saw in a sawmill. In those days most people were still suspicious of the automobile business, thinking that autos were not here to stay. They thought the companies would quit making cars, that there would be no place to get them repaired and no place to buy gasoline. Also, there were only a few roads over which to drive.

1903 Ford "Model A"
One of first assembly line cars. 2 cylinder. 8 h.p. Cranked on side.
2 speeds forward, 1 reverse. $750

I. A. Engleka, Ford dealer and merchant (1903)

1911 Ford "Model T"
15 million were produced over a 19 year period.
Prices ranged from $850. in 1909 to a low of $290. in 1924.

Model T

Berlin's First Ford Agency: In 1914, Mr. Engleka secured the privilege of selling the Ford automobile. E. A. Stahl of Somerset had all the territory of Cambria and Somerset counties. He gave Mr. Engleka the Berlin territory and he ordered 60 cars the first year. Stahl sent the Fords to him so fast that he had 28 autos on hand while this section was still snowbound. There were also no snowplows. Besides that, you couldn't drive a Ford in the winter then because you couldn't start it. But as soon as the weather changed the Fords sold fast and he soon sold the 60 cars. Fords came six in a carload. Next he ordered 100 cars and easily sold them. He increased his orders and sold more and more each year for the next several years.

Mr. Engleka also carried on a good trucking business for 20 years, delivering truckloads of potatoes, apples, etc., to regular customers in Cumberland, Md.; Keyser, W.Va.; and many Pennsylvania counties. He played a very important part in building up a market for the Somerset County potato and other produce all over the tri-state area. His wife was the former Lucy Fisher.

East End Antiques is presently in the old Engleka Store Building in East End of Berlin at 1400 E. Main.

1905—Marshall's operated the Berlin Post Office.

1907—The first movie theater was in a small room next to George Groff's brick residence on Main Street and was called Dreamland. It is presently Appleyard's T.V. Repair. This was the Poorbaugh Block.

1907-1965—Buckman Signs.

Old Home Week, 1908

August 9-15, 1908, was a gala week for the residents of Berlin and surrounding community, for this was the time of the Old Home Week celebration. The town was gaily decorated for the occasion and arches of concrete were erected on the upper and lower diamonds. People came from far and near, and had great difficulty finding housing.

Special programs were planned for each day with large parades featuring elaborate floats drawn by white horses. Miss Minnie Snyder, the queen of Old Home Week, and her court rode on a float. There were many free acts on the ball diamond. To climax the whole affair, an ox roast was held on the lower diamond.

1908—A newspaper called "The Berlin Gleaner" was published. Its office was on the second floor of the First National Bank Building, 538 Main Street.

1908—Berlin had four good hotels and 31 stores.

1908—Cable and Suder Store was located in the Harris Bakery Building in 1908.

1908—Vincent's Restaurant was where Kinetic Inn is located today. He sold it to Harry Donner, and Donner sold it to Mellot and went to Pittsburgh in 1928. In 1929 Harry Donner returned from Pittsburgh and started a restaurant in the McGrath Hotel. This building burned in 1929.

1908—Brallier's Drug Store was located at the today's Western Auto location, 507 Main Street.

1908-1916—Bake Shop, 1000 E. Main Street.

1909—A Chinese laundry was located at the site of Dr. Prugh's home. Later a cobbler named Steer lived there.

1909—Diveley's Lunchroom was located next to Marie

Scenes from "Old Home Week," 1908

Adolph Abbey Photographer (1909), building on left

Present location of Croner Hardware (1912)

Central Hotel (1910)

John Ream's Market (1916)

Beachley's. It was only a counter where he sold cheese, crackers, and candy.

1909—The Opera House, built by Albert Dively, who was a plasterer by trade, was situated on the South Side of Main Street, west of High Street.

1909—Adolph Abbey, a photographer, had his shop on Broadway about where Lafferty's Garage is today.

1910-1927—The Variety Store, W. H. Dively, Prop.

1910—Norman and Henry Brant operated Brant Brothers grocery before Fred Krissinger had his hardware at 411 Main Street. Later Croner Hardware, Collins Drug, Robertsons Drug, and now Anchor Real Estate were located there.

1910—Fred Krissinger's Hardware, 411 Main Street.

1910—Bill Bridegum's Shoe Repair Shop.

1910—E. H. Miller Company, 621 South Street.

1911—Weldon Knepper had a blacksmith shop on Washington Street between Broadway and Division streets at the rear of a dwelling where Sammy Miller lives today, 519 Division Street.

1912-1948—Croner Hardware—across the street from present-day Croner Bldg. Homer Croner purchased the Fred Krissinger Hardware Store and stayed at this location seven years, after which he moved to present-day location. After the fire of 1929 he started in business

again in the newly built Croner Building and continued until 1948 at 410 Main Street.

1913—The Pastime Theater was in the Old Mercantile Building. The owners were F. B. Collins, Richard Gould, and A. R. Dallam.

1916—Jake Ross' Shoe Repair Shop, North Broadway.

1916-1936—John Ream's Bake Shop was in the rear of his meat market on Main Street and was enlarged in 1924.

Chautauqua

1916-1932—The years of Chautauqua in Berlin. Sometimes a week in July, sometimes in August, the big tent with its stage up front and its rows of folding chairs drew large crowds. A season ticket for the week was $2.00 and without a season adult ticket the cost for the week would be $7.00. There were morning, afternoon, and evening sessions and early morning programs for the young folks.

A typical week's program would include:

The Filipino Collegians—a group from the Philippines with a great variety of native instruments.

Arthur Walwyn Evans—a distinguished Welsh orator speaking on "What American Means to Me."

Louise L. McIntyre—with delightful humor and

Chautauqua (1916)

Collins Drug Store (1919)

practical suggestions Mrs. McIntyre emphasized the great importance of good health. She is the author of the book "How's Your Health?"

"A Message from Mars"—a play on the remaking of a selfish man.

Gypsy Revelers—an exceptional group of vocalists offering a costumed production featuring songs of the vagabonds.

A play, "The Patsy," an exceptional comedy, famed for its brilliant dialogue.

Conservatory artists—a compnay of fine instrumentalists and vocalists.

Major John J. Hill tells of his experiences and thrilling adventures of 18 years with Cecil Rhodes in Africa or of primitive life on the dark continent.

These were some of the programs in the year 1927.

The prices of the tickets varied according to the programs ranging from 35¢ in the afternoons for adults to $1.00 in the evening.

For children the afternoon prices were sometimes 20¢ and ranged up to 50¢ in the evening for the most expensive ticket, more often costing 35¢.

Chautauqua was owned and operated by the Redpath-Brockway Chautauqua System of Columbus, Ohio.

1918-1922—Hillegas & Stutzman - Flour and Feed. They bought it from A. B. Cober, who had earlier bought it from John Groff. Located at 526 Main Street.

1918—Levy purchased his building from Ben Bowman. It was located east of the Croner Building and after the fire moved down Main Street to present-day location of Gardner's Barber Shop, 629 Main Street.

1919—The post office was near the present-day Painter Barber Shop when Croner's started their Hardware Store at 420 Main Street.

1919—Collin's Drug started where Anchor Real Estate is today at 411 Main Street.

1919—W. S. Lane and Sons bought the old log house on the lower diamond which is called the Gardill house and remodeled the first floor and started a meat market.

1920—The W. F. Philson Store was purchased by John Ream.

1920-1929—Frank Robinson who came from Europe had a barber shop where the Croner Bldg. is today, 410 Main Street.

1920-1944—C. E. Van Order Monuments, Fletcher Street.

1920—Collins' Drug Store, Philson Collins, 411 Main Street.

1920-1932—Keystone Store at Hornings location, run by Edgar Sarver, 405 Main Street.

1921—National Lincoln Service Station, Robert L. (Coxy) Groff and family, 501 Broadway.

1921—Landis Hat Shop, operated by Mrs. Roy Landis.

1921-1929—Salvia's Fruit Market.

1922-1945—Stutzman's Groceries, Flour, and Feed. Jacob Stutzman, 526 Main Street.

1922—A cooperative store was started by a group of Berlin residents, run by Edgar Sarver, and located where Hornings is presently at 405 Main Street.

1922-1965—Berlin Feed Company, John Glessner and Robert Hillegas, Fourth Avenue.

1923-1961—Myrtle Walker Dress Shop. This building at this time was owned by Clarence Fisher. She rented from him for 38 years at 511 Main Street.

1923—Goldsteins' Store, men's and boys clothing. Located at 507 Main Street.

1924-1948—Crawford's Store, 538 Main Street. Had earlier been Fred Groff's Store.

1924-1967—J. Wesley Ross, contractor and builder, worked for the Pulley Works until 1924 when he went into business for himself.

1924* —Berlin Publishing Co., 312 Division St. Rev. Levi and Paul Wilson bought the **Berlin Record** in 1924 and sold it to the Somerset Daily American in 1932. Since then they have been doing only job printing under the name Berlin Publishing Co.

1924—Adolph G. Weyand opened a 5 & 10 at the Western Auto location at 507 Main with Robert G. Van Meter as manager. Then Van Meter took it over from 1926 to 1931.

1925-1971—at the depot. Jay Hauger was a director of this for 21 years. Meadow Gold Dairies, Inc., receiving plant in Berlin.

1925* —Robert L. Miller, Insurance, 603 Main Street.

1925-1930—Gross (Levi) moved to location of present-day poolroom. Before this he had a store where Johnson & Son Furniture is located today, 522 Main Street.

1926-1929—Irvin Gillfillin's Coffee & Gift Shop.

1926-1945—Evergreen Nurseries - Howard Reed. Later the office was added to and made into a residence. It was owned by Mr. and Mrs. James Edwards and today is owned by Dr. and Mrs. Paul Klose, 701 Division Street.

1926   —The Berlin Feed Company was located in the Central Hotel at that time, 423 Main Street.

1926-1974—Harry Driggs Barber Shop, East Main St.

1927-1955—Taylor Motor Company - R. M. Taylor, North Broadway.

1927-1929—The A & P, located in Hotel Berlin and managed by Leroy Dively, was located on the southwestern corner of Main and Division streets or at the location of the Richard Coughenour property. The fire of 1929 started in this basement at 400 Main Street.

1927-1946—Dabby Baldwin's, 631 Main Street.

1927-1929—Hotel Berlin—new name given to Albright Hotel by new owner, P. J. McGraph, 400 Main Street.

1927-1958—Clarence Altfather Trucking, 905 E. Main Street

1928-1937—C. E. McClintock's Garage, North Broadway.

1928-1947—Lew Shockey owned the Central Hotel at 423 Main Street.

1928*   —Painters Beauty & Barber Shop first was located on the lower diamond at 501 Main. Later he moved and built a home and shop beside the Croner Building at 420 Main Street.

1928-1931—Frank Robinson came back after the fire and continued his barber shop in the Croner Building.

1929-1975—Arthur Scheller's Garage, Stewart Street.

1929-1970—Groff's Dept. Store - Ralph Groff, 541 Main Street.

1929-1942—National Lincoln Service Station #2 - Robert (Coxy) Groff and family, 1401 E. Main Street.

1929—Wilkow's Restaurant and News Stand on the side of the street where Keidel Hardware is today burned in 1929. After the fire it was moved across the street where Kinetic Inn is today, 429 Main Street.

1929—Donner's Restaurant. Harry Donner returned from Pittsburgh in early 1929 and opened a restuarant in the McGrath Hotel or on the corner where Doc. Forney later built after the 1929 fire at 400 Main Street.

1929—Blatt Brothers Theater run by Terrance McGary. For a short time Harold and Wilfred Miller operated this theater and after this it closed until 1931 when Clyde Donner operated it and called it the Blue Ridge Theater.

1930-1942—Mrs. Theodore Schrock had a restaurant and store in James Cassel's house. She had a hat shop there first, at 1000 East Main Street.

1930-1966—Modern Beauty Shop was operated by Mrs. Lloyd Hauger behind the present-day Doris Fogle Beauty Shop at 525 Main Street.

1930-1939—Bill Martin's Shoe Repair Shop was located west of Appleyard's, 439 Main Street.

1930-1931—The Serve-U-Shop, dressmaking, Tillie Engle, 511 Main Street.

1931-1966—Miller Electric, run by William J. Miller, 510 North Street.

1931—Mountain View Nursery, Frank Boyer, owner, Broadway.

1931—1945. Evergreen Nurseries, owned by Howard Reed.

1931—Keystone Store - at Hornings location and run by Edgar Sarver, 405 Main Street.

1931   —Coca-Cola Plant, managed by Russell Gill, Broadway.

1931-1944—Gene's Barber Shop, Croner Building. He was lost in the service of our country in 1944.

1932-1955—The A & P was located at the present-day Western Auto location and run by William Griffith.

1932-1959—American Store in Croner Building, run by Edgar Sarver, 410 Main Street.

1933-1967—Berlin Battery Mfg. Co. - John Mothersbaugh, 215 Main Street.

1934-1938—Jeff Hewitt operated the Denner Heffley Hardware Store, 535 Main Street.

1936-1939—A. J. Potter Lumber Co., North Street.

1937—Walter Lane sold his meat market to his sons John and George, 501 Main Street.

Gross' Store (1925)

Hotel Berlin (1927)

1937-1959—George P. Bauer - harness maker, 203 Broadway.

1937*   —Schrock's School Bus Garage owned by Charles and Larry Schrock, East Main Street.

1937—The Centennial of our town was celebrated July 27, to 31 in 1937. A pageant was presented called "The Story of Berlin." This was produced by the John B. Rogers Co., rehearsed and directed by Dorothy M. Rowland.

Some of the scenes from the pageant were:

Early Indian Life and the Visit of George Washington and a Party of Traders; Early White Settlers; An Early Wedding; The Whiskey Insurrection; The First Church; Berlin, Incorporated; Tableau of the Wars; Judge Jeremiah Black; and the Masque of Nations.

The program for the week had a religious day, Sunday, July 25, 1937.

> Monday - Historical Day
> Tuesday - Trades Day
> Wednesday - Farmers' Day
> Thursday - Firemen's Day
> Friday - Pennsylvania Day
> Saturday - Youth Day

There was a parade every day except Sunday when a cantata, "The Holy City," was presented in the Berlin Brothersvalley High School building in the afternoon and a Community Sing was held on the Centennial Grounds in the evening.

A souvenir book was published which today is treasured by those fortunate enough to have one.

1938-1957—Norman Brant's Garage, North Street.

1938-1955—Glodfelty Hardware, 535 Main Street.

1939*   —Edna Mae's Beauty Shop. First in upstairs of house on Main Street in front of present-day Food Rite, next in New Central Hotel, and today in her home at 208 Broadway.

1939-1966—Modern Dairy Co. - 506 South Street. Elkins Deeter and Clyde Imhoff.

1939-1941—Dickey's Shoe Store. First located in east side room of Kinetic Inn. Moved across street to 426 Main. In 1946 until November 1962. Clyde Dickey,

owner. He was in the service from 1941 to 1943.

1939-1945—Shultz and Wetmiller were located on lower diamond at old restored log house called the Gardill house. It was purchased from Dickey and Imhoff.

1940-1950—Sam Miller Shoe Repair was in the basement of the Shockey Hotel, presently Lishia's, 423 W. Main.

1940-1945—Deist Cleaner's at Hornings Superette location, 405 Main.

1940-1951—Crawford's Store, Fred Crawford, 538 Main Street. This was purchased from Fred Groff.

1941-1941—Bennett's Meat Market on lower diamond. Operated by John Bennett, 501 Main Street.

1941*   —Ben Donner & Son Lynn - Nationwide Insurance Company, 723 South Street.

1941-1965—Harry Zimmerman Restaurant, 631 Main Street.

1942*   —John Thomas Trucking, 607 Meadow Street.

1942-1957—Zorn and Good bought the New National Hotel, 302 Main Street.

1944—Earl Austin bought the C. E. Van Order Monument plant and moved it to Somerset.

1945-1947—Wetmiller's Market was in the Gardill house on the lower diamond.

1945-1975—Llewellyn's Groceries & Gas, 190 Broadway.

1945-1946—Eleanor's Beauty Shop - Eleanore Krissinger, 428 Main Street.

1945-1967—Ralph Stuck's East End Garage, 1401 E. Main Street.

1945*   —Highland Gardens, Donald Heffley, 200 High Street.

1945-1960—Crowe's Super Market, owned and operated by William Crowe at 531 Main Street.

1946-1955—Broadway Motors was owned and operated at this time by Ernest Landis and John Scheller.

1946*   —Janet's Beauty Shop, Janet Gindlesperger, 511 Main Street.

1946-1949—Hern's Bakery (behind George's Barber Shop), Diamond Street.

1946-1957—B. F. Goodrich moved in at this location,

West Main Street (1928)

Shultz & Wetmiller later were located in the old log house which is being restored

526 Main Street, or where the Harris Bake Shop is today. They stayed here until 1957, when they moved across the street to the corner building where Western Auto is located today, 507 Main Street.

1946* —George's Barber Shop, George Walters. At first this was located in the Croner Building on Main Street, to the west of present-day location of Latshaw's, 410 Main Street. Today is at 449 Main.

1946* —Herman Scheller's Grocery & Service Station, Broadway.

1946-1960—Keystone Shoe Repair. Peter Bongivini had his shoe repair shop at 441 Main Street, where Appleyard's T.V. Repair is presently located.

1946-1953—Dick Johnson's Restaurant, 631 Main Street.

Snyder's Potato Chips of Berlin

On February 12, 1947, the 24,000-square-foot Snyder's Potato Chip factory went into operation at Berlin, Pennsylvania. The Snyder family decided to build a plant in the area where high-quality potatoes were grown. The Berlin-Brothersvalley Industrial Association was formed under its president, Sherman Berkley. The association sold bonds to people in the community. By 1956, the Sterner family repaid all the bonds. The growth of Snyder's of Berlin has been amazing, from the first hand-filled bags of chips to completely automated packaging. June 9, 1972, the Sterner family sold the 78,000-square-foot facility to Pro-Fac Cooperative through a merger with Curtice-Burns, Inc., of Rochester, New York. Once again the local community, through the potato farmers in the area, coupled with other Pro-Fac members throughout the United States purchased the local facilities. Through the past several years, Curtice-Burns has continued to carry the Snyder tradition in quality and growth. Today, the facility boasts 114,000 square feet and 165 employees.

1947-1975—Luterie's Restaurant, 1026 East Main Street.

1947-1949—Whiting and Glessner had a grocery store and meat market in the Gardill house.

1947-1950—Mary Margaret Maust's Beauty Shop.

1947—William Dahl purchased the Central Hotel, 423 W. Main Street.

1947-1959—Smith's Service Station - Harry Smith, owner. A smaller wooden building at location of Saylor's Superette, 301 Cumberland Street.

1948-1958—Berlin Hardware (John Thomas of Johnstown), Robert Miles, manager, 410 Main Street.

1949*—Croner, Inc. The office is presently located at 1038 E. Main Street.

1949-1956—McKinley's Store. Dale McKinley located where National Bank of Western Pennsylvania is located today, 538 Main Street.

1950-1951—John Haines Hobby Shop, 423 Main Street.

1950* —Berlin Lumber Co., 701 North Street, Jack Brant & Son, purchased from H. F. Ball.

1950-1960—Ruth & Alma Boyer's Beauty Shop, 428 Main Street.

1951-1952—Vella's Ice Cream Bar, Vella Bockes, 531 Main Street.

Snyder's Chip Plant (1947)

A&P (1955), present-day post office

1951-1959—Wetmiller's Market, owned and run by Richard Wetmiller at John O. Ream's meat market location on Main Street, which today is the parking lot in front of the Food Rite Store, 540 Main Street.

1951* —Will Brothers, 405 Vine Street.

1952-1956—Deeter (Mrs. Robert) had a small shop beside the Lutheran Church on Main St. on the western side of the Crowe Bldg. beside Hersheys 5 & 10, 531 Main Street.

1953*—Tipton's Jewelry, located beside Appleyard's T.V. Repair Shop on west side in 1953; later moved to 807 East Main St. in 1971; presently is at 603 Division Street.

1953* —Harris Bakery, 526 Main Street, Lois and Victor Harris.

1953* —Bingman's, Robert Bingman, Jr., Fifth Avenue.

1953-1957—Earl Miller Shoe repair shop at the Jake Ross location and later in the Lishia Hotel basement, 423 W. Main Street.

1955-1967—Landis & Lafferty, located at 413 Broadway, Ernest Landis and Kenneth Lafferty.

Western Auto (1958)

Lishia Hotel (1955)

Somerset County Home for the Aged (1965)

1955—Brown's Hardware, 535 Main St., William J. Brown.

1955—The A & P moved to the location of the present-day post office, 531 Main Street.

1955* —The present owner of the Central Hotel, Tony Lishia, purchased it in 1955 from his brother, James Lishia, 423 W. Main Street.

1956* —George Horning's Grocery or Superette, 405 Main Street.

1957* —East End Tavern, 1310 East Main Street, was purchased from Robert Zorn and John Good in 1957 and sold to George Glessner and John Woytek in 1958.

1957-1959—James Lishia purchased the New National Hotel at 302 Main Street.

1957-1965—Berlin Variety Store - Guy Gardner.

1957* —Appleyard's T. V. Service, 441 Main Street.

1958-1970—Vaughan Shoe Repair located in his home at 511 10th Avenue.

1958-1973—B. F. Goodrich was changed to Western Auto and was owned and operated by Anthony Taterelli. He had bought this building from Jacob Schrock and Ed Fogle, 507 Main Street.

1958-1971—Joan Bush and Kathryn Christner operated the B & C Diner on the lower diamond at 501 Main Street.

1958* —Keidel Hardware and Electric, Robert Keidel, owner, 410 Main Street.

1958-1969—Herbert Smith Service Station & Groceries, 301 Cumberland Street.

1959- —William Farber bought the New National Hotel, 302 Main Street.

1959-1960—Wetmiller's Market, owned by Elfreda and George Wetmiller, was at the John O. Ream Meat Market location at 540 Main Street.

1960-1967—Wetmiller's Market moved across the street to the Crowe Building and was run by Elfreda and George Wetmiller.

1960-1965—Clover Farm at present Food Rite location, 540 Main Street.

1960—Al's Body Shop - Alfred Queer, 515 W. Main St.

1961—Stewart's Cleaners - Herb & Alice Stewart, North Street.

1961-1961—Mary Austin's Dress Shop at this location for a short time, 511 Main Street.

1961-1964—Austin's Fashions, Mary and Earl Austin, 410 Main Street.

1962* —Hay's Office Supply, 1201 East Main Street, Karl Hay, owner.

1963-1969—Karen Kimmel's Beauty Shop, 1210 East Main Street.

1964-1974—Ruth's Dress Shop - Ruth Gindlesperger, 410 Main Street.

1965-1975—A & P moved across the street to Food Rite location, 540 Main Street.

Somerset County Home for the Aged

The Somerset County Home for the Aged, built in 1965, was designed to care for the growing need of our county people. The Home is located at the edge of Berlin Borough on a knoll commanding the view of thousands of acres of Pennsylvania scenic farmland.

There has been very little physical change other than

41

Main Street (1972)

drapes, spreads, and repainting. No major buying of equipment has been done since the opening of the Home.

Most changes have been in the upgrading of nursing care. Patients today need more nursing care. This has changed the Home into more of a nursing home than a residential home.

In keeping with the new state and federal regulations to improve the total patient care, two new departments have been added. They are Therapy and Recreation.

1965* —Croner Cartage, East Main Street.

1966* —Gardner's Barber Shop, 629 Main Street.

1966* —Doris Fogle Beauty Shop, 625 Main Street.

1967* —Krause Hardware, 535 Main Street. Later it became Krause True Value Home Center, Blair Krause, owner. He built a new building and moved to the present location on 219 in 1971.

1967* —Landis Service & Sales, 311 Cumberland Street, owned and operated by Ernest Landis.

1968* —Lafferty Chevrolet, 413 Broadway, Kenneth Lafferty, owner.

1968—Estelle G. Moore bought the I. A. Engleka Store (a Church of God preacher), 1400 E. Main Street.

1969-1976—Saylor's Hillside Superette, 301 Cumberland Street, Elbert Saylor, owner.

1970* —Harold Konhaus - Clean Corner Laundromat, 1401 E. Main Streeet.

1970* —North American Protective Services, Inc. (Clark Security), 405 Main Street.

1970-* —Gardner's Store, 541 Main Street.

1970* —John F. Long—Carpet and Contracting, Fletcher Street.

1971-* —Fogle Engineering, 602 Diamond Street.

1971-* —Custer A T V Sales, 1218 East Main Street.

1971-* —The pool hall on the upper diamond was sold by Zorn and Good to Lynn Custer in 1971, 305 Main Street.

1972-* —Novilla, Inc., Estates - mobile trailer park, Robert and Gregory Croner.

1972-* —Berlin Kinetic Inn, 429 Main Street.

1972-* —East End Antiques, Paul and Rose Saylor, 1400 East Main Street.

1973-* —Paul Miller, son-in-law of Tony, purchased this business and is presently running it. It is called Western Auto Associate Store, 507 Main Street.

1973-1975—Hazel Clark's Hobby Shop, 411 Main Street.

1973-1976—Malletts Restaurant, 535 Main Street.

1974-1975—Pat's Boutique - Pat Wojnaroski, 410 Main Street.

1974-* —Berlin Pharmacy, 500 Main St., Tom Gardill.

1975-* —Latshaw's Dairy Store, 410 Main Street.

1975-* —Berlin Food Rite, 540 Main Street.

1975-* —Joyce's Restaurant, owned and run by Joyce Knotts, 1026 East Main Street.

1976-* —Shelva's Restaurant, Shelva Miller, 535 Main Street.

1976-* —Anchor Real Estate, Inc., 411 Main Street.

1976-* —Lynda S. Chalk's Beauty Shop.

1976-* —Roy Ogburn, law office, 411 Main Street.

1976* —Boyer's Corner, 301 Cumberland St., Scott Boyer.

1976* —Tacy Scheller's Beauty Shop, 425 South Street.

*Still in business today.

Births and Baptisms

of

Somerset Co., Pa.

Reformed and Lutheran Church Records,

of

Berlin, Somerset County, Pa.

Translated from German Script

by

E. C. Saylor, Berlin, Pa.

1929

Volume I.

Copyright 1929

by

E. C. Saylor

Historical

During the early months of 1924, while searching for some data on my own family, I was kindly given possession of the old church records of the Reformed and Lutheran churches of the town of Berlin, Somerset Co. Pa. and found them of great historical value. I translated them, the original being German. Acknowledging the very valuable assistance of Mrs. Emilie Pollnow Wilkow of Berlin, Pa. lately from Goldap East Prussia, Germany. Also the translation of several abbreviations by the assistant chief of manuscript division of the Library of Congress, Washington, D.C.

These churches are the oldest of these denominations west of the Alleghenies, with the possible exception of one "HAROLDS" near Greensburg, Westmoreland Co., Pa.

We have reason to believe that these churches were organized prior to 1777; however, the baptismal records begin in that year, and contain names of people who lived as much as twenty miles distant, and the territory now supports forty or fifty churches of these two denominations and the descendants of the people here baptized have migrated to practically every state in the union.

These two volumes, the oldest, dating from 1777 to 1837 containing 1489 baptisms, some marriage records, was used jointly from 1777 to 1788. After that each congregation kept their separate records. Volume two from 1788 to 1856 contains 1330 births and baptisms, 327 marriages and 115 burials; these records are of the Lutheran Church.

Realizing the historical importance of these records I have endeavored to do the best I could, taking into consideration the age of the manuscript, some of which is almost illegible, and somewhat torn and the use of obsolete abbreviations and phrases, we feel that it can be relied upon as being as nearly correct as is possible to get. In doing this we hope we have rendered some service of historical value.

E. C. Saylor, Berlin, Pa.

Church Book of Both Congregations

The Evangelical Lutheran and the Evangelical Reformed, situated in Bedford County, Brothersvalley Towsnhip, Province of Pennsylvania

Containing

I. Births and baptisms.

II. Confirmation and communion records.

III. Marriages.

In the year of Christ 1777

(3) In the name of God, the Father, Son and spirit. Jesus says in Mark the 10th. chapter, let the little children come unto me and forbid them not, for such is the kingdom of God. As Moses the husband of Zippocah, spake to the people while he cast away the circumcision of his son, so may God own all the children recorded in this book, now and in eternity. Only to the glory of God, to God alone be glory. One by me a teacher and preacher of the Evangelical Lutheran Church, holding to the Augsburg Confession.

M. J. W. Lizel

The above mentioned brother congregations have united themselves together in the above mentioned year, 1777. To build a respectable church house, for the purpose of instructing the children in the word of God, and in grace, and besides at certain times to hold religious worship as well as to read a sermon, on the scriptures on Sunday by their lay leader, or among themselves, to do the same thing by a man who is a member of the congregation, as also at appointed times to hold preaching services by some appointed preacher of the highly honored coetus and ministerium, to visit the members and also to administer the Holy Sacraments, until the congregation is able to build a church building, such as is suitable for the Christian Church, in the above mentioned school house. The members of the two congregations are as follows.

(Note) No names appear, was never completed.

December 17, 1789, a meeting of the congregation was held and it was agreed to collect some money to build a new Reformed church and the following elders were elected as collectors, Jacob Glessner and John Peter Graef, and one third of the money promised to the collectors for their trouble. The above stated collectors have authority to collect the money in February 1790, and when they returned after taking off their wages they brought the congregation cash money the sum of—
-----Pounds---------Schillings-------Pence.

August 27, 1791,the following settlement was made of the collections of the church, according to the last settlement, Nov. 4, 1789. The collections amounted to 5 pounds, 2 shillings and 5 pence. From Nov. 4, 1789 to Aug. 27, 1791 the money in the treasury remaining was 8 shillings. The whole amount was 5 pounds, 10 shillings, 5 pence. There was expended 2 pounds, 12 shillings, 9 pence, leaving a balance of 2 pounds, 17 shillings, 8 pence. This amount is now in the hands of Elder Altfather; we certify that this settlement is correct and accordingly we have signed our names, New Berlin, Brothersvalley Twp. Pa. Aug. 27, 1791.

April 7, 1792, Anna Marie Brant, a widow, after having given offense to the congregation by the sin of being a whoar and having acknowledged before the church council, the deed and having promised to do better, and in accordance with this promise she was again received into the congregation and admitted to the communion of the first Easter following.

Peter Graeff presented the trustees with $4.00 to buy a communion cup.

On Mar. 31, 1791, after being made acquainted with our form of belief the cathechism, which he promised to learn by heart, and by it to live and die, and never to leave the Reformed church, confirming the same with an oath, and under the same circumstances after the ten commandments were read, which he likewise promised to learn by heart and to live as far as possible according to them, he was received into the fellowship of God, his church, being baptised in the church of Berlin, after prayer in the presence of the whole congregation. This nigger (colored man) belonging to Peter Winger of Berlin, and called Peter Schwarty, about 21 years old, having himself made a covenant with God did not need baptismal witnesses. To the great goodness of the Lord be praised and thanks forever, that to this poor heathen has been given a hearty desire for baptism, and by the same, the promised of grace has been made over to him and the kingdom of heaven opened. Amen.

This same grace made by the Lord, was made this day to another person by the name of Barbara Burck, the parents being Mennonites, she made the promise to the minister, to learn the commandments as soon as she can read, and elder Zigler was to assist her in keeping this promise, and so it is that after being instructed by short interviews about the sorrows and fears of baptism, no objections being brought forth she was baptised in John Hubers house in the presence of the Church Council of Berlin as witnesses. April 10, 1791.

As it has pleased God to unite the hearts of the whole community and in as much as Pastor Weber has removed to such a distance that it is impossible for him to serve the Glades the latter urged the people to secure a pastor for themselves because this was necessary. After I had preached for some time and was liked by the congregation, I was hired in writing Nov. 28, 1788 for the pastor to work against the tricks of the devil by the grace of God. I began the work Aug. 10, 1788, with a willing heart and by the words of Jeremiah 4-23. I will set a watch over them.

Cyriacus Spangenberg of Reidmeister
Pastor

(Note)

This man stabbed Elder Jacob Glessner during a congregational meeting, March 19, 1794, from the effects of which he died March 21. Spangenberg was arrested convicted and hanged in Bedford, Pa. Sept. 11, 1795. Reference Bedford and Somerset County History 1906. Volume 1, page 85. Also Vol. 11, page 535.

Be it so and may it remain that this is the rule of the congregation. The following was assumed Jan. 4, 1789. By the united action of the congregation, after services when it was read to them, and after it had been explained to them and urged upon them and to this they all agreed.

In the name of the Triune God, Amen. God is a God of order, as Paul says in I Corinthians 14:40: Let all things be done decently and in order.

We have at the end signed our names, the preacher, and consistory and all the members present of the Evangelical Reformed congregation in Brothersvalley Township, Bedford Co. Pa. It has become our duty in order to show honor and obedience to God and thereby subserve the everlasting welfare of our congregation to make the following church ordinances and to establish a guard for our congregation, in the presence of all the members of the congregation and with one voice accepting for a rule, to regulate ourselves thereby without dispute, these laws were undertaken. Namely.

I. If the congregation is in need of a preacher, a man of known fitness with good testimonials, after an election, having received a majority of votes shall be called. He shall stand in connection with the Coetus (Synod).

II. Each and every preacher whether Lutheran or Reformed shall make sure and establish the righteousness of his teachings and good behavior, and shall hold our church to the services of God.

III. Every member of the congregation shall according to his ability be bound to contribute to the support of the preacher, as also for the building of a church, this is right since each one will be benefited, also each one is to help bear the expense in love, whoever refuses to do this shall no longer be considered a member of the congregation and all services of the preacher shall be withheld.

IV. Whoever shall work on Sundays or on the Festal days, if such is unneccessary and not a work of love, or gets drunk, dances or gambles or allows any sinful or wicked company in his house, or is present at any time when the name of God is insulted or profaned and thus cause trouble in the congregation, and brings many innocent souls into sin and punishment, shall for the first offense be brought before the preacher and consistory, and shall be admonished in love and affection not to commit in the future at all such gross profanation of the name of God. If however such a one does not improve he shall according to Mathiew 18-15, and Timothy 3-10, be again admonished, and if again he shall continue in open sin, he shall upon order of the consistory through the office of the keys, according to I Cor. 5-13, be locked out of the communion of Jesus Christ, and he shall remain outside until he shows repentance and promises to lead a better life.

V. Even so it shall be with those who openly follow a loose life and who live in open sin and lust, and who dishonor the public service of God, and the holy sacraments and the name of God, who refuses to send their children to school or to bring them to a knowledge of Jesus Christ and there start gross offenses and sin in the church.

VI. We wish these beautiful formulae and other good regulations of our church council to rest upon us in love, and we wish to do our best that the honor and duty to God in our congregation shall be supported and that sins, offenses and open bad behavior shall be placed under a ban and eternally hid and that inward conver-sion and virtue among us may improve and also among us a clear and true Jesus Christ may be possible, we pray to God to give us grace and that his spirit and help and strength from heaven may truly come upon us.

This compact is the rule of our church, made this day, all the church council, and all the members present willingly signing the same, and so also it was established afterwards by a public reading of these church rules in the presence of the signers of the church council, Sept. 13, 1789.

> Jacob Glessner, Elder
> Arndt Grissing, John Zigler, Deacons

On April 14, 1793. Before this date there were 2 Elders and 2 Deacons, and now the congregation decided to elect more officers on account of the increase in the congregation and on account of the building of the church, this causing more work and the congregation agreed to elect 4 additional officers, Jacob Glessner and Frederick Altfather remained in office as Elders and John Ziegler and Dillman Schutz were elected Elders, and Simon Schunck and John Knepper and Jacob Gunderman and George Frey Deacons, and on May 12, these were installed, and in case of death or need the following should serve, Jacob Huber and George Burckler had the most votes as Elders and John Huber and Jacob Glessner, Jr. as Deacons.

Trinity United Church of Christ

Trinity United Church of Christ, Berlin, was one of the earliest congregations of the Reformed faith to be organized west of the Alleghenies. The first church record book, dated 1777, written in German, states that the Lutheran and Reformed congregations have "united themselves together to build a respectable church-house" to instruct their children and to use as a church until such time as they are "able to build a church building." It was financially expedient that the two congregations share the same building until they were able to build a church and school of their own. Schoolmasters, itinerant preachers, or lay readers served the Reformed congregation for a number of years. The first regular minister, Rev. John Weber, arrived in 1783, but he had such a large territory to cover as a pastor that he was not able to be present very often for Sunday worship services.

The first school-church building was a log structure located in the northeast section of a plot of ground bounded today by North Street, Fifth Avenue, Mulberry Street, and Vine Street. When the town of Berlin was laid out, Jacob Kepper had deeded approximately twenty acres of land to Jacob Glessner in trust for the Reformed congregation. The money from the sale of these lots to home builders or shopkeepers was used to help maintain the church, and each landowner continues to pay a yearly sum of one dollar (quit rent) to the church. In 1793, the Reformed congregation built a stone house of worship, and in 1824 a stone schoolhouse. These buildings were located near the old log building. A brick church was erected in 1843, and stood on the southwest corner of the original square of land. The present church building, erected in 1883 on the

German Reformed Church

Present-day United Church of Christ

been three women who were commissioned into the missionary service while they were members of the church. Five young men have gone into the Christian ministry, and another one is presently in his final year at Lancaster Theological Seminary.

The Sunday school was organized in 1836; and in 1847, through the money bequeathed to the Sunday school by Mr. John Fletcher, the first "Fletcher" Bibles were given to those students eligible under the stipulation of the will. Each year, since that date, boys and girls in the third-grade class of the Sunday school have received a Bible.

The church cemetery is located on the corner of North Street and Fifth Avenue. An endowment fund was established in 1927 for the continued upkeep of the grounds and stones. No one has been buried in the cemetery since 1883.

The records of the church from its beginning down to the present are intact and remarkably well kept, considering the difficulties and scattered labors of the early pastors, the change of ministers from time to time, and the many different lay people who have served as secretary of the consistory, or treasurer, during these years. The earliest records are in German, but have been translated into English.

Trinity Church, with a membership of 575, began as part of the German Reformed Church, and since then has been part of the Reformed Church in the United States, the Evangelical and Reformed Church in 1934, and the United Church of Christ since 1957. The congregation provides its members with a strong music program, a vital youth program, and task forces to provide fellowship, spiritual development, and long-range planning.

In 1977, Trinity United Church in Berlin will celebrate its two-hundreth anniversary, at which time a detailed history of the church will be published.

corner of Main and Vine streets, was completely renovated in 1964 in order to preserve the building, modernize it, and make it more attractive. In 1968, a parsonage was built to the rear of the church on the corner of Vine and Fletcher streets.

Twenty ministers have served the congregation. The longest pastorate was from 1795 to 1832. There have

Pastors of Trinity United Church of Christ

This is the oldest Reformed congregation west of the Alleghenies.

A church historian has written that Rev. John W. Weber was the first minister of the Reformed faith to cross the Alleghenies. When he came to Berlin in 1783, he found an organization six years old. There are in existence records as early as the year 1777, when the congregation was first organized. Prior to that date there must certainly have been religious worship, although no congregation had been formed.

The following named pastors have served this congregation.

Visiting ministers and laymen	1777-1783
Rev. John W. Weber	1783-1788
Rev. Cyriacus Spangenberg	1788-1794
Rev. Henry Giese	1795-1832
Rev. Jacob S. Regnier	1833-1834
Rev. S. K. Denius	1834-1841
Rev. William Conrad	1841-1859
Rev. Francis A. Edmonds	1860-1863
Rev. Frederick Wahl	1864-1866
Rev. William Rupp, D.D.	1866-1877
Rev. S. R. Bridenbaugh, D.D.	1877-1885
Rev. Abner R. Kremer, D.D.	1886-1901
Rev. W. C. Sykes, D.D.	1901-1912
Rev. D. S. Stephen, D.D.	1912-1941
Rev. John N. Bethune, Ph.D	1941-1944
Rev. Herman C. Snyder	1944-1946
Rev. Ira R. Harkins	1947-1954
Rev. Edwin O. Wenck and	
Rev. Mary E. Wenck	1961-1963
Rev. Randall L. Heckman	1964-1972
Rev. Charles W. Sigler	1972

Reformed Cemetery

Situated in Berlin borough, Somerset County, Pa. One block north of Main Street. This record of burials put together by Dr. E. C. Saylor. Appears here as taken from burial stones.

HIER RUHEN DIE GEBEINE DES HR. JOHANNES KNEPPER, GEBOHREN I MARZ. 1765 ER HINTER LAST EINE BETRUBTE WITWE MIT 12 KINDER DIE UHNBETRAUEN, ER STARB IHM IARH 1817. ER WAR ALT 52 JAHR 4 MONAT 7 TAGE.

HIER RUHE GEBEINE VON JOHANNES FLICK, GEBOHREN 25, JULY 1763. GESTORBEN DEN 3 ten JUNE, 1831, ALT 67 IAHR, 10 MONAT 10 TAGE.

PETER SCHWEIZER, BRACHT SEIN ALTER AUF 77 IAHR (Died about 1817)

HIER RUHEN IN GOTT JOSIAH GEBHART, GESTORBEN DEN 23 ten JUNI 1830, ALT 1 IAHR 9 MON. 26 TAGE.

HIER RUHEN DIE GEBEINE VON ELIZABETH DEN 27, FEBRUAR 1825 IM EINEM ALTER VON 27, JAHR 2 MONATH.

ANA MARIA HOHHEN, STARB DEN 19ten MARZ 1818, ALTER WAR 63 IAHR IND 3 MONAT. WAR CHRISTUS DER IST MEIN LABEN. (Note: wife of Simon Hay)

HEIR RUHT IN GOTT, MICHAEL WILD, IST GEBOHREN DEN 24 JANUARI 1817. ER STARB DEN 5ten JENNER 1818, er BRACHT SEIN ALTER AUF I IAHR. LESS 19DAYS.
(Date not legible) D.9 MEY, P.G.S.B.N.GBD. 22 A. 1724.

JACOB SAHLER IST GEBOHREN DEN 23ten JENNER 1818. EHR STARB DEN 6ten SEPTEMBER 1818.

HIER RUHEN DIE GEBEINE SIMON SCHUNK, GEBOHREN DEN 3ten MAY 1749, STARBEN DEN 7ten OCTOBER 1828, NUN WAN DUE EIN STOLEBENS FURST DIE GARBER MACHTIC, NEN WIRST DAN SAS MICH FROILICH AYFFER STEHN, UN DAN DIE MANTLITZ EWIG SEHEN, A MEN SANFT RUHET SEINN ASCHE. FAREWELL DEAR FRIEND A LONG FAREWELL FOR WE SHALL MEET NO MORE, TILL WE ARE RAISED WITH THEE. (Revolutionary soldier)

HEIR RUHEN DIE GEBEINE DES JOHANNES HAGER, GEBOHREN 1749, GESTORBEN DEN 6ten DEC. 1813, EHR HINTER LAST EIN BELIEPT WITWE MIT 7 SOHNE UND 2 TOCHTER, SEIN ALTER WAR 64 IAHR.

ES IST MEINEN TOCHTERIN GEBOHREN 26ten MARZ 1818. JOHN MILLER, ALT. 3 MONAT 21 TAGE.

ANNO, 1779, DEN 29ten JULY IST CHRISTIAN BOGER GESTOBREN SEIN ALTER IST 31 IAHR UND 7 MO.

DIELMAN SCHUTZ, GEBOHREN den 6ten DECEMBER 1734, GESTORBEN DEN 2ten JULI 1821. ALTER WAR 76 IAHR MONAT 15 TAGE.

ELIZABETH CATHERINE SHUTZEN, IST GEBOHREN DEN 5ten MAY 1735 SIE IST GESTOBREN DEN 17ten FEBRUARY, 1813.

HIER RUHEN GEBEINE DES JACOB GLESNER, GEBOHREN DEN 21 SEPTEMBER 1732. GESTOBREN DEN 21ten MERTZ 1794. SEIN LEICHT TEXT WAS APOSTE GESECHTE, CAPITAL 7, V 58, 59 SEIN GANSES ALTER WAR EIN UND SECHEZIG IAHR UND SEX MONATHE. (Revolutionary soldier)

HIER RUHEN DIE GEREINE DER CATERINA ELIZABETH GLESNER, GEBOHREN DEN 25ten JULI 1734 STARB DEN 23ten SEPTEMBER 1807. (wife of Jacob.)

HIER LIET BEGRAWEN CATERINA LISBET RIME, MICHAEL RIHM SINE FRAW SIE WAR GEBOHREN 1771, D 23 MERTZ, GESTORBEN 1799, NOV. 17, ALTER GEBRACHT AUF 28 IAHR UND 19, TAGE SIE WAR JACOB KLESSNER SEIM TOCHTER CATERINA.

HIER RUTHEN DIE GEBEINE DSE JOHANN ENGLE GLESNER, GEBROHEN DEN 14ten SEPTEMBER 1762, ERTRANK IMMUHL DAM DEN 14ten MAY 1783, ER HAT SEIN GANSFS ALTER GEBRACHT AUF 21 IHAR UND 8 MONATH. WER WEIS WIE NAHE MIR MEIN ENDE.

MARIA ELIZABETH GLESSNERIN, GEBOHREN DEN 3ten NOV. 1779, GESTORBEN 17ten MAY 1786. SIE LEAPT 7 IAHR.

ANNA ELIZABETH GLESNERIN, GEBOHREN 1740, GESTORBEN DEM 12ten MERTZ, 1802. ALTER WAR 63 IAHR 9 MONAT UND 19 TAGE (?) (Note: Wife of Henry Glessner)

HIER RUHET IN GOTT ESTHER SUTTER, TOCHETER VON FREDERICK SUTER WAR GEBOHREN DEN 12ten. FEBRUARY, 1794, SIE STARB DEN 24ten. NOVEMBER 1809.

HIER RUEN DIE GEBIENE DES JACOB BAUMAN, IST GEBOHREN 1755 IST GESTORBEN DEN 26ten,

FEBRUARY 1819, SEIN GANSAS ALTER WAR 63 IAHR, EHR HINTER LAST WITWE, MIT 6 SOHNE UND 2 TOCHER. (Revolutionary soldier)

HIER RUHEN GEBEINE DES ELIZABETH SUTTER, GEBOHREN DEN 26ten OCTOBER 1799, GESTORBEN DEN 29ten AUGUST 1815, SIE HINTER LAST EIN BELIEPT GATTEN MIT 4 SOHNE.

GEORGE BEILER, GEBOHREN DEN 18 OCT. 1725, GESTORBEN DEN 19ten DECEMBER 1812.

HEINRICH GLIEFELT, GESTORBEN DEN MAY 14, 1814, ALTER 80 IAHR.

HIER RUTH IN GOTT, SAMUEL WILD, IST GEBOHREN DEN 26ten SEPT. 1825, EHR STARB DEN 18 MARZ, 1826, ALT 5 MONAT 22 TAG.

VERONICA SCHWEIZERIN BRACHT IHR ALTER AUF 74 IAHR.

HIER RUHEN IN GOTT ELIZABETH KEFFERIN, EINE GEBOHREN IACHMENIN 1777 STARP DEN 5ten MARZ, 1815, SIE HINTER LAST EIN BETRUBTE GATTEN 2 SOHNE UND 2 TOCHTER, BRACHT IHR ALTER AUF 37 IAHR.

SALE (SALLY) GEBHARDEN IST GEBOHREN DEN 3ten MAY 1777, ES STARB DEN 25ten. AUGUST 1818 (Note: Probably wife of John Musser)

HIER RUHEN DIE GEBEINE DER ELIZABETH MUSSER STEINERIN, GEBOHREN DEN 25ten AUGUST 1778 5 IE STARB DEN 16 APRIL, 1817, SIE BRACHT IHR ALTER AUF 38 IAHR 7 MO. 21 TAGE (Note: Stone removed from Oscar Miller place, cemetery being destroyed)

HIER LEBT IN GOT SALOMON ANAWALT, IST GEBOHREN DEN 22ten FEBRUARY, 1818 STARBEN DEN 26ten AUGUST 1818.

HIER RUHEN DIE GEBEINE DER SEBASTIAN GRAFF, WAR GEBOHREN 31 JENNER, 1747, STARB DEN 19ten FEB. 1822. ER HINTER LAST EIN BETRUBTE WITWE MIT EINEN SOHN UND 4 TOCHTER. ALTER BRACHT ER AUF 75 IAHR UND 19 TAGE (Note: Revolutionary soldier)

HIER RUHT IN GOT MARIA GERTRAUT GRAFEN, GEBOHREN DEN 11ten FEB. 1752. GESTORBEN DEN 11ten. DECEMBER, 1830, SIE BRACHT IHR ALTER AUF 77 IAHR UND 10 MONAT. SANFT BUHT IHR ASHCE. (Note: Wife of Sebastian Graff)

JOHANNES MILLER, IST GEBOHREN DEN 17ten JULI, 1774, ER STARB DEN 1ten MEI, 1816. (Note: Stone removed from Oscar Miller farm, cemetery destroyed)

IN MEMORY OF AARON JEROME, SON OF CHARLES AND MARIA L. KRISSINGER, BORN MARCH 2, 1840, DIED NOV. IST. 1842, AGED 2 YRS. 7 MO. 29 DAYS.

SACRED TO THE MEMORY OF PETER HAY, BORN APRIL 18, 1790, DIED MAY 4, 1845, AGED 55 YRS. 16 DAYS.

MARY ATCHESON, DIED AUG. 28, AGED 9 MONTHS 10DAYS. BUT WHY SHOULD I LAMENT AS DUST, MY CHILD BEFORE ME GONE. YET A FEW MORE MOMENTS AND I TRUST, THE SAME WAY FOLLOW ME.

IN MEMORY OF THOMAS ATCHESON, WHO DEPARTED THIS LIFE THE 16 DAY OF MARCH 1812. AGED 73 YRS. (Revolutionary soldier)

THOMAS ATCHESON DEPARTED THIS LIFE 1809, AGED 10 MO. 12 DAYS.

SACRED IN MEMORY OF CHARLOTTE, DAUGHTER OF JAMES & ELIZABETH DUNCAN, DIED JAN. 10, 1835. AGED 3 YRS. 8 MO. 15 DAYS.

IN MEMORY OF LUDWICK BAKER, BORN APRIL 4, 1766, DIED MAY 2, 1840, AGED 74 YRS. 28 DAYS.

IN MEMORY OF CATHERINE DAUGHTER OF DANIEL & HARRIETT LANDIS. DIED JUNE 6, 1846. AGED 1 YR. 2 MO. 1 DAY.

LEONARD REAM, DIED NOV. 26, 1826, AGED 5 YRS. 6 MO.

IN MEMORY OF MARTHA JANE, CONSORT OF LEWIS JOHNSON, BORN OCT. 24, 1821, DIED JULY 8, 1845, AGED 23 YRS. 8 MO. 15 DAYS.

IN MEMORY OF DR. WILLIAM MCGOWAN, DEPARTED THIS LIFE AUG. 6, 1837, AGED 7 YRS. 6 MO. 12 DAYS. (Stone is broken and the first figure of his age is missing)

IN MEMORY OF GEORGE HAAS, DIED SEPT. 3rd, A.D. 1838. AGED 3 YRS. 8 MO. 14 DAYS.

ELIZA COLEMAN, DIED MAY 6, 1840, AGED 1 YR. 6 DAYS.

IN MEMORY OF ANNA MARIA KNEPPER, DIED MAY 12, 1847. AGED 78 YRS. 10 MO. 7 DAYS. (Wife of John)

HERE LIES THE BODY OF MARGARET KNEPPER, CONSORT OF JACOB KNEPPER, WHO WAS BORN THE 6th DAY OF APR. 1803, AND DEPARTED THIS LIFE 13th JUNE A.D. 1826. AGED 23 YRS. 2 MO. 7 DAYS.

HERE LIES THE BODY OF JACOB STONER, SON OF JACOB STONER. DEPARTED THIS LIFE 20th OF JUNE 1827 AGED 2 YRS. 2 MO. 6 DAYS.

PHILIP REAM, DIED 13th OF JULY 1822 AGED 4 YRS.

IN MEMORY OF ISAAC STONER, DIED JUNE 6, 1845. AGED 7 YRS. 3 MO. 10 DAYS.

IN MEMORY OF SUSANNA SHUNK, DIED MARCH 19th, 1844. AGED 87 YRS. 2 MO. 3 DAYS.

IN MEMORY OF WILLIAM SHUNK, BORN OCT. 24, 1784, DIED DEC. 22 1852. AGED 68 YRS. 1 MO. 28 DAYS.

ELIZABETH WIFE OF WILLIAM SHUNK, DIED DEC. 27, 1848, AGED 57 YRS. 6 MO. 15 DAYS.

IN MEMORY OF ANNA MARIA GEETING, BORN APR. 5, 1766, DIED OCT. 1, 1835. AGED 67 YRS.

IN MEMORY OF HENRY GEETING, BORN OCT. 8, 1762, DIED MAY 12, 1848. AGED 85 YRS. 7 MO. 4 DAYS.

IN MEMORY OF PETER GLESSNER, BORN OCT. 17, 1764. DIED JAN. 23, 1836. AGED 71 YRS. 3 MO. 6 DAYS.

CATHERINE GLESSNER, BORN SEPT. 14, 1774. DIED NOV. 19, 1834 AGED 60 YRS. 2 MO. 5 DAYS. (Maiden name Wegerline)

HERE LIES THE BODY OF FANNY GLESSNER, DAUGHTER OF PETER GLESSNER, BORN APR. 2, A.D. 1815 AND DEPARTED THIS LIFE SEPT. 7, A.D. 1816.

HERE LIES THE BODY OF JACOB WEYAND, SEN. BORN THE 6th DAY OF FEB. 1746, DIED THE 19th DAY OF DEC. 1811. (Revolutionary soldier)

IN MEMORY OF CATHERINE WEYAND, WHO DEPARTED THIS LIFE SEPT. 26th. IN THE YEAR OF OUR LORD 1830, AGED 79 YRS, 5 MO. 19 DA.

HERE LIES THE BODY OF SAMUEL KERSHNER, WEYAND, SON OF JACOB WEYAND SR. BORN THE 2ND OF MARCH 1801. DIED THE 25th DAY OF APRIL 1803.

VALENTINE HAY, WHO WAS BORN THE 26th DAY OF JUNE 1774, DEPARTED THIS LIFE THE 27th DAY OF AUG. 1833. AGED 54 YRS. 2 MO. 1 DAY.

IN MEMORY OF SIMON HAY WHO DEPARTED THIS LIFE FEB. 3rd, 1842, AGED 99 YRS. 9 MO. 15 DAYS.

IN MEMORY OF CONRAD BRANT, BORN SEPT. 14, 1763, DIED JULY 22nd. 1845, AGED 81 YRS. 10 MO. 8 DAYS.

IN MEMORY OF BARBARA BRANT, BORN NOV. 11, 1767, DIED OCT. L 1855. AGED 87 YRS. 10 MO. 20 DAYS.

IN MEMORY OF ELIZABETH BRANT, WIFE OF JOHN S. BRANT, BORN JAN. 27, 1797, DIED DEC. 14, 1856. AGED 60 YRS. 10 MO. 17 DAYS.

IN MEMORY OF CAROLINE, DAUGHTER OF JACOB & ELIZABETH BRANT, DIED JULY 15, 1845. AGED 18 YRS. 1 MO.

SACRED IN MEMORY OF ANA ELIZABETH, CONSORT OF FREDERICK SCHWAB, DIED JULY 18, 1842. AGED 53 YRS. 9 MO. 22 DAYS.

IN MEMORY OF PINEINAS SON OF FREDERICK SCHWAB, DIED MAR. 19, 1846, AGED 4 MO. 16 DAYS.

IN MEMORY OF JACOB SMITH, DIED NOV. 19, 1840, AGED 74 YRS. 10 MO. 7 DAYS

IN MEMORY OF ELIZABETH SMITH, CONSORT OF JACOB SMITH, DIED JUNE 13, 1829, AGED 56 YRS. 2 MO.

IN MEMORY OF FREDERICK SUDER, WHO WAS BORN 10 OF NOV. 1755, DEPARTED THIS LIFE 17th OF APRIL, 1829. AGED 74 YRS. 5 MO. 7 DAYS. REV.

IN MEMORY OF CHRISTINA SUTER, WHO WAS BORN 3rd. OF APRIL A.D. 1794, DEPARTED THIS LIFE 22nd. OF MARCH A.D. 1831. AGED 36 YRS. 11 MO. 17 DAYS.

HERE LIES THE BODY OF MARGARET SUTTER, DAUGHTER OF FR. SUTTER, SHE DEPARTED THIS LIFE THE 12th DAY OF MAY 1816, AGED 15 YRS. 9 MO.

HENRY SUDER, WHO WAS BORN JAN. 8, 1813, DIED MAY 7 A.D. 1826.

SACRED TO THE MEMORY OF JOHN KUHNS, DIED OF SAMUEL KUHNS, DIED AUG. 21, 1851, AGED 45 YRS. 8 MO. 15 DAYS.

IN MEMORY OF JOHN KUNTZ, DEPARTED THIS LIFE DEC. 10, 1824 AGED 23 YRS. 4 MO. 2 DAYS.

HERE LIES THE BODY OF ADAM MILLER, WHO WAS BORN 14th OF MAY A.D. 1750, AND DEPARTED THIS LIFE 2nd OF FEBRUARY A.D. 1827. AGED 76 YRS. 8 MO. 26 DAYS. (Revolutionary soldier)

SACRED IN MEMORY OF ROSANNA CONSORT OF ADAM MILLER, BORN JUNE 22, 1765, AND DEPARTED THIS LIFE FEB. 24th. A.D. 1839. AGED 73 YRS. 8 MO. 2 DAYS.

HERE LIES THE BODY OF ELIZABETH, DAUGHTER OF JACOB G. MILLER WHO WAS BORN 3rd. OF MARCH, 1811, DEPARTED THIS LIFE 25th. DAY OF JAN. 1818.

IN MEMORY OF MATILDA, DAUGHTER OF JACOB G. MILLER, AND SUSANNA HIS WIFE, WHO WAS BORN ON THE 16th. OF NOVEMBER 1826, AND DEPARTED THIS LIFE ON THE 28th. OF JUNE 1833.

HERE LIES THE BODY OF HENRIETTA MILLER, DAUGHTER OF JACOB G. MILLER, DEPARTED THIS LIFE 26th OF JAN. AGED 1 YR. 1 MO. 19 DAYS.

HENRY FOUST, DEPARTED THIS LIFE 30th. OF MARCH, 1824, AGED 50 YRS. 2 MO. 6 DAYS.

IN MEMORY OF CATHERINE FOUST, DIED MAY 26th. 1847, AGED 66 YRS. 5 MO. 3 DAYS.

IN MEMORY OF HENRY FOUST, DIED MAR. 30, A.D. 1833. AGED 7 YRS. 5 MO. 10 DAYS.

IN MEMORY OF JACOB SON OF C. & M. L. CRISSINGER, BORN JAN. 5th. 1845, AND DIED APRIL 22nd. 1849. AGED 4 YRS. 3 MO. 17 DAYS.

IN MEMORY OF _____ KRISSINGER, BORN MARCH 2nd. 1840 DIED NOV. 1, 1845 AGED 5 YRS. 7 MO. 9 DAYS.

IN MEMORY OF ROBERT PHILSON, DIED JULY 25, 1831, AGED 72 YRS. (Revolutionary soldier)

IN MEMORY OF JUDITH PHILSON, DIED NOV. 19, 1853, AGED 83 YRS. 5 MO. 25 DAYS.

IN MEMORY OF JOHN PHILSON, BORN OCT. 20, A.D. 1793. DIED JAN. 10, 1813, AGED 19 YRS. 2 MO. 20 DAYS. (1812 soldier)

AGNES CONRAD, DIED MAY 22nd. 1840. AGED 23 YRS. 9 MO. 2 DAYS.

IN MEMORY OF ELIZABETH PHILSON, DEPARTED THIS YEAR AUG. 17th A.D. 1837, AGED 25 YRS. 2 MO. 16 DAYS.

IN MEMORY OF JAMES PLATT PHILSON, BORN DEC. 21, 1840, DIED MAY 7th. A.D. 1841.

SACRED IN MEMORY OF JUDITH PHILSON, BORN OCT. 23, A.D. 1805, DIED FEB. 27, A.D. 1814. AGEd 8 YRS. 4 MO. 5 DAYS.

IN MEMORY OF SARAH CONRAD, DIED JULY 31; 1859, AGED 76 YRS. 15 DAYS.

IN MEMORY OF ISAAC STONER, DIED JUNE 5th. 1845, AGED 74 YRS. 3 MO. 10 DAYS.

GEORGE, INFANT SON OF JONA AND MARGARET KNEPPER, DIED DEC. 1841.

SACRED IN MEMORY OF ELIZABETH BOWMAN, DIED JUNE 15th A.D. 1837. AGED 75 YRS. 1 MO. 6 DAYS.

IN MEMORY OF JOHN BOWMAN, AGED 77 YRS. 8 MO. DIED JULY 3, 1847. (1812 soldier)

ANJULINE BRUBAKER, WHO DEPARTED THIS LIFE 7th. OF JUNE 1825, AGED 3 YRS. 5 MO. 28 DAYS.

UNDERNEATH THIS STONE LIES THE BODY OF JOHN SHAVER, WHO WAS KILLED ACCIDENTLY BY HIS OWN MILL, DECEMBER 25th, 1794. AGED 25 YRS. 9 MO. 14 DAYS. IN JUVENILES WHILST IN YOUR BLOOM SECURE A FRIENDSHIP WITH THE TOMB, AND BY MY DEATH, AND SUDDEN FALL, BELIEVE THE FATE AWAITS YOU ALL, BUT SHALL I NOW PROCEED AS THOSE, WHO NUMBER DEATH AMONGST OUR FOES, NO O; FOR DEATH IS VIRTUES FRIEND, TRUE LIFE BEGINS WHERE DEATH DOTH END, O: WHY WILL MEN BE FOOLS AND DARE, ON AMES DELUSIONS AND WHAT NOT. O: WHY PREFER THE BILLOWS ROAR TO SOLID BLISS OF EDENS SHORE.

DENA BEAR, DIED AUG. 5th. 1848, AGED 49 YRS. 7 MO. 6 DAYS.

IN MEMORY OF MARGARET, WIFE OF LUDWIG BAKER. DIED MAR. 29th 1839, IN THE 54th YEAR OF AGE.

IN MEMORY OF WILLIAM GELLERT, SON OF S. K. AND MARY ANN DENIUS, BORN JAN. 31, 1831. DIED JULY 14, 1838, AGED 7 YRS. 6 MO. 12 DAYS.

IN MEMORY OF JACOB LORE, DEPARTED THIS LIFE 25th OF MAY 1827, AGED 2 MO. 26 DAYS.

IN MEMORY OF MARY ANN, WIFE OF BENJAMIN WALKER, DIED DEC. 5th, 1847, AGED 20 YRS. 2 MO. 17 DAYS.

IN MEMORY OF HENRY MESSERSMITH, BORN OCT. 15, A.D. 1764, DIED DEC. 16th. A.D. 1832.

DAUGHTER OF M. REAM, DIED 1876, AGED 5 WEEKS.

IN MEMORY OF HARRIET, DAUGHTER OF JAMES

AND CATHERINE BLACK, BORN SEPT. 31st. A.D. 1820, DIED FEB. 24th. A.D. 1846.

IN MEMORY OF TOBIAS FLOM, WHO DEPARTED THIS LIFE OCT. 11, 1835, AGED 1 YR. 11 DAYS.

IN MEMORY OF GEORGE STAHL, SEN. DIED MAR. 2nd. 1844. AGED 73 YRS. 15 DAYS.

HERE LIES THE BODY OF HENRY LOUT, DEARTED THIS LIFE 12th OF APRIL 1828. AGED 2 YRS. 9 MO. 12 DAYS.

ELIZABETH, WIFE OF JAMES FERRELL SEN., DIED DEC. 24th. 1831 IN THE 77 YR. OF HER AGE.

IN MEMORY OF WILLIAM BALDWIN, DIED APRIL 17, 1840. AGED 58 YRS. 8 MO. 9 DAYS.

HERMAN, SON OF WILLIAM LONG, BORN JAN. 22nd. 1832, DIED AUG. 9th, 1833. AGED 1 YR. 7 MO. 7 DAYS.

HERE LIES THE BODY OF REBECCA JOHNSON, DEPARTED THIS LIFE 21 OF JAN. 1826. AGED 1 YR. 11 MO.

HERE LIES THE BODY OF HERMAN ALTFATHER, SON OF DANIEL ALTFATHER, DEPARTED THIS LIFE THE 14th OF FEB. 1830, AGED 8 YRS.

IN MEMORY OF CHRISTIAN SWARTZENDRUBER, BORN NOV. 19, 1798, DIED OCT. 7th, 1851, AGED 52 YRS. 10 MO. 18 DAYS.

MICHAEL W. BOWER, DIED MAR. 26th. 1832, AGED 1 YR. 10 MO. 12 DAYS.

MARIA BARBARA HAGER, WHO WAS BORN 5th OF APR. 1749, AND DEPARTED THIS LIFE 11th. OF MAY 1826, AGED 77 YRS. 1 MO. 5 DAYS. (Wife of John)

IN MEMORY OF DR. J. H. STOASSNER, BORN FEB. 2nd 1790, DIED MARCH 16th. A.D. 1840. AGED 50 YRS. 1 MO. 14 DAYS. AND THOUGH AFTER MY SKIN, WORMS DESTROY THIS BODY, YET IN MY FLESH SHALL I SEE GOD, WHOM I SHALL HOWEVER SEE FOR MYSELF, AND MINE EYES SHALL BEHOLD AND NOT ANOTHER, MY REMAINS BE CONSUMED WITHIN.

NICHOLAS SMITH, DIED MAR. 25, 1864, AGED 68 YRS. 8 MO. 9 DAYS.

ELIZABETH, WIFE OF NICHOLAS SMITH, DIED DEC. 1, 1862, AGED 66 YRS. 14 DAYS.

IN MEMORY OF PETER MARTIN, DIED FEB. 24, 1847, AGED 86 YRS. 4 MO. 24 DAYS.

IN MEMORY OF CATHERINE, WIFE OF PETER MARTIN, BORN OCT. 13, 1772, DIED OCT. 28, 1855, AGED 83 YRS. 15 DAYS.

IN MEMORY OF SARAH, WIFE OF HENRY SUDER, BORN APR. 22, 1797, DIED JULY 7th, 1859 AGED 61 YRS. 2 MO. 15 DAYS.

SARAH, WIFE OF HENRY BRANT, DIED FEB. 26, 1883, AGED 74 YRS. 9 MO. 13 DAYS.

IN MEMORY OF CHARLES, SON OF HENRY BRANT, BORN APR. 7th, 1853, DIED OCT. 23, 1861, AGED 8 YRS. 6 MO. 16 DAYS.

IN MEMORY OF DINAH, DAUGHTER OF HENRY AND SARAH BRANT, BORN JULY 23, 1834, DIED JUNE 21st, 1853. AGED 18 YRS. 10 MO. 28 DAYS.

CHANCEY, SON OF HENRY BRANT, DIED JUNE 3rd, 1849, AGED 13 YRS. 3 MO. 25 DAYS.

IN MEMORY OF ANN BREWSTER, BORN NOV. 1806, DIED JAN. 8, 1867, AGED 60 YRS. 1 MO. 20 DAYS.

IN MEMORY OF ROSE ANN, WIFE OF JOSIAH BRANT, BORN JUNE 18, 1836, DIED JUNE 17, 1857, AGED 20 YRs. 11 MO. 19 DAYS. FAREWELL MY FRIENDS OF EVERY NAME HOWEVER NEAR OR DEAR, MAY WE A NOBLER FRIENDSHIP CLAIM, THAN DEATH IN TWAIN CAN TAIR.

IN MEMORY OF HENRY BRANT, DIED MAR. 30, 1833, AGE 7 YRS. 5 MO.

Inscriptions on old tombstones lying on Mrs. Herman Divelys lot which were likely moved from the Reformed Cemetery and later replaced with modern stones, Nov. 11, 1933.

ANNA MARIA, WIFE OF JOSEPH WILD, DIED FEB. 9, 1863, AGED 36 YRS. 5 MO. 19 DAYS.

ELIZABETH BALSER, WIFE OF JOSEPH WILD, DIED FEB. 7, 1868, AGED 65 YRS. 2 MO. 5 DAYS.

M. ELIZABETH RIEHL, DIED AUG. 29, 1831, AGED 6 YRS. 10 MO. 11 DAYS.

JACOB G. MILLER, D. DEC. 14, 1865, AGED 80 YRS. LESS 1 MO.

SUSANNA ZIMMERMAN, WIFE OF JACOB G. MILLER, B. JUNE 26, 1790, D. JULY 30, 1852 AGED 62-1-4

Total: 143 graves

These are the original papers of Holy Trinity Lutheran Church, Berlin, Pa. For many years these papers and the original Bible (published in Germany in 1765 in High German) were missing.

The summer of 1976 they were found in the basement of the Philson National Bank. Age of these documents required that they be taped. When photo-copied, the tape comes out black.

53

A
Record
of
Pastors, Church Officers, Church Members
Births, Baptisms, Marriages
Deaths and Burials
Communion Seasons,
and an
Annual Summary:
also,
A Record of Interesting and Important Events,
Occurring from time to time in the history of

The Evangelical Lutheran Church
Berlin, Somerset County, Penna.

Baltimore
T. Newton Kurtz,
151 W. Pratt St.
1873

Rev. R. S. Patterson was called to become pastor of Holy Trinity Evangelical Lutheran Church Nov. 26, 1899. He began his labors on Jan. 1st, 1900. His resignation was tendered to Council Feb. 4, 1906.

During his pastorate the present parsonage on Main St. was built at a cost of $3300.00. The pipe organ and other improvements at the church were made costing about $2500.

During pastorate of Rev. H. B. Burkholder which began Sept. 15, 1911, and ran to Sept. 15, 1918, a grand piano was placed in the Sunday school room.

The exact time of the organization of a Lutheran Church in Berlin is not known. The earliest record in existence shows that Rev. J. W. Lizel preached in Salisbury, Northampton County, Pa., from 1765 till 1769. Nothing more is said of him there. It is likely that he moved to what is now known as Somerset County upon leaving Northampton County. This may have been as early as 1770. The earliest record we have of him preaching for the Lutherans in Berlin was in 1777. There is no record showing when he came or when he left.

In 1789 Rev. John Michael Steck (German, Steg) came to this county and preached in Berlin till 1792 or 1793 and moved to Greensburg, Westmoreland County. In 1793 Rev. Frederick William Longe began to preach in Berlin. He died in Somerset in the fall of 1811 or spring of 1812.

In 1813 Rev. Ernest Henry Tiedeman became pastor and remained till 1818.

In the spring of 1819 Rev. Jacob Crigler took charge of the Berlin pastorate and remained till April 1, 1834.

See history of the Berlin Evangelical Lutheran Church written by Samuel Philson for the succeeding pastors. The old bell now hanging as a relic in the Sunday school

vestibule of the new church was purchased in 1801 by Mr. Fletcher and Mr. Philson at a cost of $122. 1 shilling and 10 pence. It was in service till it was replaced by the new one at the time of building the new church. The inscription on the bell is as follows: "Me Fecit Ciprianus Crans Iansz Amstilodami Anno 1753." It is said to have been an old ship bell and was purchased secondhand by the Berlin Lutheran congregation.

The present Lutheran Church was built in 1889 and 1890 with J. J. Zorn, contractor. Cost of lot, $1,400.00; cost of building and furnishing complete, $12,230.61. Total $13,630.61. The stone foundation was laid by

Evangelical Lutheran Church

George Fogle. The framework for church and steeple were erected by Samuel Engle and Daniel Brubaker, contractors.

Church Book
and
Baptismal Register
Belonging to the Evangelical Lutheran Congregation of Berlin, Bedford County, Pa. Containing the Births of Children and the Time of Their Baptism, From the Year 1788, and the Following Years, Entered and Registered as
Follows

Volume II.
Copyright 1929
E. C. Saylor

Rules adopted for the newly built Lutheran School House in Berlin, Somerset Co. Pa.

So that no mistake may be made to preserve unity & peace in the congregation it becomes necessary to adopt the folloing rules to guide the Trustee's and meetings of the congregation.

The Trustees and the congregation shall have oversight over the new school house and no one shall preach or teach school in it without permission of the majority of the members.

When there are several applicants for the position of teacher the applicant who is a regular member of our church shall have the preference.

The teacher shall be able to teach the German and English language.

The teacher shall agree to teach the children to sing and pray and shall attend to it.

The Trustees and members of the church shall visit the school and see that good order is kept and the children are properly instructed.

When the majority of the members and Trustees become dissatisfied with the teacher they shall notify him in writing at least two weeks before when he shall leave and the scholars shall not pay longer than the two weeks time.

The teacher shall have the necessary knowledge to be a teacher.

The teacher shall be a good character, shall not be a scoffer at religion, shall not be a drunkard, shall not be a gambler, shall not use profane language, shall not break the Sabbath, shall not be a liar (etc.).

Resolved and adopted by the officers and members of the congregation on Sunday Nov. 5, 1827. Witness, Jacob Crigler, Evangelical Lutheran preacher of Berlin, Pa.

On the 10th of Sept. 1826, at a meeting of the Western Pennsylvania Synod the name of the Holy Trinity Church was given to the Berlin Church in the presence of the preacher, President of Synod, Mr. Schmucker, and the other officers and the rest of the preachers by their official consent. Wilhelm Schultz, Secretary of the Ministerium.

A record of all the people single and married who were confirmed and instructed, and communed in the year 1789, registered in the church book by Michael Steg. Confirmation and communion record.

In the year 1789 by preacher Michael Steg record of married and single persons who were confirmed and communed all together 79.

Trinity Evangelical Lutheran Church

The history of this congregation covers a period of 200 years. The oldest church record extant was purchased for both the Lutheran and Reformed congregations. This is also the oldest church record in Somerset County. On the first page is written:

"Church book for both congregations: Evangelical Lutheran and Evangelical Reformed, in the Glade, Bedford County, Province of Pennsylvania; [then interlined] Brothers Valley Township; Written in the year of our Redeemer, Jesus Christ, 1777."

This is followed by an account of the first building erected for educational and religious purposes: "Both the above-named congregations have in the above-named year united together to build a good schoolhouse to have their children instructed in the word and grace of God! Also, on certain days, to hold public worship in it, as well as reading of sermons on Sunday by the school teacher; or other religious books by a person who is a member of one of the congregations; also at certain times to preach in it by certain ministers of the honora-

ble Reformed Classes and Ministerium, who pay us a visit and also attend to the sacrament until either congregation is in condition to build a comfortable church."

The record contains an entry signed by Rev. John Wolf Lizel, who was the first Lutheran minister of the Allegheny Synod. He remained here until sometime in the eighties. The record continues:

"On April 1, 1786, the Supreme Executive Council of Pennsylvania granted to Jacob Keffer, in trust for the Calvinist [Reformed] and Lutheran Churches for the use of schools, a tract of land containing forty and one-half acres, on the headwaters of Stonycreek, upon which said Calvinistic and Lutheran congregations had laid out a town calling it Berlin; the name of the tract of land was Pious Springs."

On April 22, 1789, a charter was obtained from the Commonwealth of Pennsylvania, signed by Governor Thomas McKean, for the addition to Berlin, whereby the proprietors of said addition gave the ground rent of one Spanish milled dollar yearly, to the Evangelical Lutheran congregation of Berlin, forever. From this provision an annual income of $94 is obtained.

In the office of the Recorder of Deeds of Bedford County is found the record of the division of the church property between the Lutheran and Reformed churches of Berlin. This was effected by lot. Lots numbered 61, 62, and 63 fell to the Lutherans, while the Reformed received lots 34, 35, 36. By this method the old schoolhouse came into possession of the Reformed. It was estimated to be worth twenty pounds. Both congregations were to hold possession until the Reformed paid the Lutherans ten pounds.

During the ministry of Rev. Frederick William Lange the first Lutheran Church was built in 1800. It was a two-story log building with a gallery on three sides. The bell then in use was cast in Amsterdam in 1753. In 1808, Jacob Fisher, Jacob Keffer, and others of this congregation emigrated to Sherwood, Canada, and established a Lutheran Church, a child of this congregation.

On January 1, 1825, Rev. Crigler and John Fletcher, with a few other persons, organized a Sunday school in the Lutheran Church—the first Sunday school of a denomination in Somerset County. Mr. Peter Lane was the first superintendent. From its organization Mr. Fletcher took a very active part in the Sunday school, and at his death he bequeathed the sum of $2,140, the interest of which is to be used to purchase Bibles, New Testaments, and sacred literature for the Sunday school. Every scholar attending is presented with a Bible. By an act of the Legislature, $800 of this bequest was used, in 1846, to erect the brick Sunday school room.

The meeting of the West Pennsylvania Synod in the Berlin Church on September 9, 1826, was the first synodical meeting held on what is now the territory of the Allegheny Synod. The minutes record the sum of $7.50, which the Berlin congregation contributed at the Chambersburg meeting in 1825.

The second Lutheran Church was built during the pastorate of Rev. Elias Fair. The cornerstone was laid, and the church was dedicated in 1853. At the meeting of the Allegheny Synod in the Berlin Church in 1880, the Synodical Woman's Home and Foreign Missionary Society was organized. At the same time the local organization was effected. In the winter of 1908-1909 the Young Women's Home and Foreign Missionary Society was organized. A little later a Mission Band came into existence. The Lutheran Church now standing was built during the pastorate of Rev. Charles B. Gruver. The cornerstone was laid June 8, 1889, and the church was dedicated June 29, 1890. The church was free of debt although costing, including furnishings, $13,630.61.

January 22, 1893, a congregational meeting was held to determine whether the Berlin congregation was to become a separate pastorate. The vote was: yeas, 100; nays, 30. The Rev. S. J. Taylor, D.D., became the first pastor of the Berlin Church as a separate pastorate.

It was during the time that Rev. R. S. Patterson headed the church that the present parsonage was built at a cost of approximately $3,000 and that the pipe organ was installed. In 1907 an addition of twenty-five feet was

Present-day Holy Trinity Lutheran Church

built to the Sunday school room, at a cost of $2,000. In 1916 this room was again enlarged.

During the week of January 18, 1925, the Trinity Lutheran Sunday School celebrated the one hundredth anniversary of its organization. The elaborate program consisted of special music and addresses by outstanding clergymen. The present enrollment of the Sunday school is 523, and the confirmed members of the congregation number 552.

Rev. C. P. Bastain served the congregation the longest from 1919 to 1942. He was very active with the young people of the church.

Rev. Robert S. Naugle served from 1942 to 1951. The first Christmas Eve candlelight service was held.

Rev. John Heller served from 1951 to 1956. Two young girls entered the service of the church as full-time parish workers. They were Miss Shirley Mason and Miss Eleanor Dively.

In the spring of 1969, under the leadership of Mr. Ernest E. Landis, chairman of the Property Committee, work was begun on excavating beneath the main auditorium of the church. Mr. Landis personally drew up the plans and supervised the work for five classrooms, a secretary and pastor's office—a very welcome addition.

The 150th anniversary of the Sunday school was held with three elaborate programs celebrated from May 4 through May 8, 1975.

This concludes with 200 years of services for Holy Trinity Lutheran Church.

Roster of Pastors

Rev. John Lizel	1777—	Rev. J. W. Poffenberger	1875—1885
Rev. Michael Steg	1788—1792	Rev. C. B. Gruver	1885—1893
Rev. Frederick Lange	1792—1813	Rev. S. J. Taylor	1893—1899
Rev. Ernest Tideman	1813—1819	Rev. R. S. Patterson	1899—1906
Rev. Jacob Criegler	1819—1834	Rev. A. J. Rudisill	1906—1911
Rev. Geo. Leiter	1834—1835	Rev. H. B. Burkholder	1911—1918
Rev. Chas. Reese	1835—1840	Rev. C. P. Bastian	1919—1942
Rev. Louis Gustinian	1840—1842	Rev. Robert S. Naugle	1942—1951
Rev. Chas. Reese	1842—1843	Rev. John Heller	1951—1956
Rev. Jesse Wincoff	1843—1846	Rev. Donald R. Yost	1956—1959
Rev. Charles Young	1846—1851	Rev. Walter L. Brandau	1959—1967
Rev. Elias Fair	1851—1856	Rev. Robert A. Miller	1967—1972
Rev. Philip Sheeder	1856—1864	Rev. George Buechner	1973—1976
Rev. Jesse Wincoff	1864—1872	Rev. Kenneth S. Swanson	1976—
Rev. A. M. Strauss	1872—1875		

1825   Historical Sketch of the   1977
Evangelical Lutheran Sunday School
Berlin, Pennsylvania

After reviewing all available records for a history of the Holy Trinity Lutheran Sunday School of Berlin, Pa., from its organization, Jan. 1, 1825, to its fiftieth anniversary, held Jan. 1, 1875, it was decided that the historical sketch, compiled and read by Samuel Philson at that time, is more interesting than anything we might be able to present, so we will not attempt to do more than offer the account of that service, as entered in the Sunday school minutes by the secretary, Jacob C. Philson.

"At a meeting of the officers of the society, held in Dec. 1874, it was suggested and resolved to hold a Semi-Centennial Anniversary of the Lutheran Sabbath School.

"Accordingly on the evening of Jan. 1, 1875, a large assemblage of citizens gathered together in the Evangelical Lutheran Church in Berlin. The Church was handsomely decorated, having in front of the pulpit a beautiful tree, which had been used on Christmas eve for the enjoyment of the children of the school.

"The Anniversary meeting was opened by an appropriate anthem by the choir. The Throne of Grace was addressed by Rev. Wm. Rupp, of the Reformed Church, followed by singing from the 'Echo,' page 142. An address by Rev. A. M. Strauss, pastor, of the Evangelical Lutheran Congregation.

"Singing from the 'Carmina Ecleasia,' followed by an historical sketch of the school written and read by Samuel Philson, who was the oldest member of the school at the present time and who was an attendant of the school when established in 1825.

"Rev. Jacob Crigler, the faithful pastor of the Evangelical Lutheran Church at Berlin, Pa., from 1819 to 1834, was always active in establishing any measure conducive to the interest of the church of his choice. Thus finding

Sunday Schools being established in the United States, to train the rising generation in the way they should go; he expressed his views to a few faithful members of his Church, together with some of the citizens of the place, whose aid and influence were very desirable to make it a success.

"On Jan. 1, 1825, the Evangelical Lutheran Sabbath School was organized, and continued to the present day.

"Mr. Peter Lane was the first superintendent who served in the same capacity for several years, faithfully admonishing the children and teachers, ever impressing upon them the importance of early piety.

"Mr. John Fletcher, an active and energetic co-worker in this Sunday School, after becoming aged and feeble in body, delighted to sit at the window on Sabbath morning, and watch with delight, the passing of the children to the Sabbath Schools.

"Feeling that his days were few upon earth and deeming the Sunday School as a great advantage to the Church, he in the largeness of his heart, in the year 1838, devised and bequeathed of his estate, the sum of $4280.00, to be divided between the Evangelical Lutheran Church and German Reformed Sunday Schools in the place at that time. The bequest reads as follows:

" 'The interest of said fund to be annually collected and appropriated to the purchase of Bibles, testaments, and other religious books for the use of said school, and for furnishing each child attending aforesaid schools, with one Bible as a present, as soon as it is able to read.'

"The privilege of attending a Sunday School having the advantage of funds provided by a liberal bequest cannot be too highly prized and appreciated, and we should feel thankful for the rich provision made for us by our deceased friends."

We now reach the second period of the school's history from 1875 to 1925.

At this time there were 14 male and 17 female teachers and 115 female and 123 male scholars for a total enrollment of 271.

At a meeting held March 4, 1879, a committee was appointed to report a plan with an estimate of the cost of same for the alteration of the Sabbath school room to provide an infant department.

On March 2, 1880, a committee was appointed to consult with a committee from the Reformed congregation in regard to building a monument to the memory of and repairing the grave of the late John Fletcher.

July 20, 1887, at a meeting of the officers of the Society, the question of continuing two sessions a day was dicussed and on motion there was a meeting of the officers and teachers called after the morning session on July 31, and a vote was taken for or against the continuation of two sessions of school as in the past. At this meeting there was a motion offered that the afternoon session be dispensed with, which was agreed to without a dissenting voice.

At this point, it might be well to state why the school held two sessions a Sunday, and why they were finally discontinued.

When the school was organized, there were no public schools and the subscription schools were held only a few months of the year and were costly and poorly attended at that. Hence, two hours of schooling a week for fifty-two weeks a year meant much to our forefathers. Besides, at that time, there was never more than one church service on Sunday and frequently none at all.

On March 4, 1845, it was resolved that the school be opened as follows: during the summer at half past eight o'clock and in the afternoon at half past twelve, and in winter, at nine in the morning and half past twelve in the afternoon, so that each session could continue one hour.

On March 7, 1847, the Book Committee reported that the school was not supplied with sufficient ABC books in both languages and also recommended that English and German hymnbooks be purchased.

Since 1875, the following persons have served as superintendents and assistant superintendents, some of them serving at different times: Alex Brubaker, Jacob J. Zorn, Charles A. M. Krissinger, B. F. Rayman, J. M. Berkey, J. C. Speicher, S. J. Ball, Robert Philson, S. P. Brubaker, C W. Krissinger, W. P. Brant, W. H. Dively, J. A. Heffley, A. C. Miller, Grover C. Dively, G. A. Hoffman, H. E. Stuck, N. R. McClellan.

The present enrollment is 9 officers, 20 teachers, 427 pupils, for a total of 456.

In 1902, an addition of 25 feet was added to the Sunday school room at the cost of $2000.

By the summer of 1916, the Sunday school had again outgrown its quarters, so another addition was added to the Sunday school room. This was done by widening the room to the west 100 feet at a cost of $1700. The enrollment of the Sunday school at that time was 425.

The 100th anniversary was held from January 18 to January 25, 1925, with an eight-day celebration, which was very well attended.

Now we reach the third period of the Sunday school: "History from 1925 to 1975."

In 1933, Mr. H. Wallace Walker was superintendent during the Depression, and the Sunday school was in need of new hymnals, and even though he was not a member of the church, he contributed the last $18 so that the books could be purchased.

In 1950, the Sunday school purchased the "Red Devotional Hymn Book."

In 1953, the church and Sunday school was recarpeted, and the Sunday school donated $500 toward this project.

In 1959, the Sunday school room was remodeled, and a new lighting system installed. The two hinged doors on rollers that were lowered to separate the church from the Sunday school were removed, as were also the doors on the east side, which had been the former primary room, and that room was converted into the present Kurtz Parlor.

Later a 10 foot addition was added on the east side of the Sunday school, consisting of a room leading to the basement, a six-foot stairway, and a nice-sized library all for a great improvement.

Now go with me to the basement and see if you can remember what improvements were made. A new concrete floor which was covered with tile block, and the walls all painted, and new rest rooms installed, new chairs and tables, coat racks, and folding curtains.

In 1969, we needed more room for our Sunday school, so plans were made to excavate under the church nave. We started to dig, and through the efforts of Mr. Ernest E. Landis, who came up with a blueprint of the layout, we now have five new classrooms, a pastor's office, and a church secretary's office.

The Sunday School Association was dissolved on Jan. 11, 1957, and all monies were turned over to the Sunday School Treasury. Then in September 1963, the Sunday school was taken over by the Church Council, and the Sunday school funds were all placed in the Church Treasury. There were no more elections for Sunday school officers. The Church Council appoints the superintendent, and he then asks the other officers to serve with him.

The following persons served as superintendents: Robert Philson, P. P. Baker, H. Ed. Stuck, H. Wallace Walker, R. L. Miller, Frank Eckman, R. Wayne Suder, Wilfred Smith, Mrs. E. C. Johnson, Kenneth Martz, Thomas Gerber, Ruth Engle, Paul E. Pritts, Dwayne Hittie, Richard Shipley, Dale E. Letdig, Carl Walker, John O. Ream, and the present superintendent, Francis W. Maust.

The present officers of the school are:

General supt.	Francis W. Maust
Children's Supt.	Mrs. Jean Ferguson
Secretary	Otis O. Bockes
Pianist	Debra Cober
Pianist Children's Dept.	Meg Pugh

The present enrollment is two officers, 19 teachers, 269 pupils, for a total of 291.

Mr. John Fletcher and Rev. Jacob Crigler organized the Sunday school in 1825, and upon Mr. Fletcher's death, he willed the Sunday school the sum of $2140, the interest to be used to purchase Bibles for all the children attending Sunday school regularly. The first Bibles were given out on Jan. 2, 1848, and since that time 2,473 Bibles have been distributed, 1,121 to males, 1,352 to females. In this connection, it might be well to state that while Mr. Fletcher died in 1838, his bequest was not available until the death of his widow, who was to have the use of the money during her lifetime, and her death occurred in 1846.

We now have five former pastors living since the last anniversary and our present pastor: George Buechner, Robert S. Nagle, John Heller, Donald R. Yost, Walter L.

Brandaud, and Robert A. Miller.

One of the most interesting historical facts in connection with the school is that 150 years after its organization by Rev. Jacob Crigler two of his great-great grandchildren are members of the Sunday school. We refer to Mrs. Marie Beachley and Mrs. Betty Musser.

Holy Trinity Lutheran Sunday School was the first organized Sunday school of any denomination in Somerset County.

The following persons are responsible for compiling this historical sketch of our Sunday school:

Samuel Philson 1825-1875
H. Bunn Philson 1875-1925
Paul E. Pritts   1925-1975

Lutheran Cemetery

Situated in Berlin, Brothersvalley Township

CATERINA GUNDLEN
ist Gebohren 1789
sie Starb den 19ten Nov. 1817
Alt 9 Iahr 10 mo. 19 Tag

Hier Ruhen die Gebeine von
ANNA MARIE KURZEN
ist Gebohren 6 ten July 1738
Starb den 15—1821

Heir Ruht in Gott MARIEN WITT
Gestorben den 30 ten
April 1830
Alt 2 Iahr und 6 Tag

Hier Ruhiet Dem Liebe Mag
Died DOROTHEA HERRE, dem
John Herre Seine, Frau,
Sie ist Gebohren 24 Octr. 1748
Gestorben 28 Julius 1792
alt 44 Iahr 9 mon.

Gebohren ist Christof Sauer
D 6, E. E. 1726 D 9 AG 1794

Hier Ruhen die Gebeine Von CARL HEFLE
Gebohren den 2ten Juni 1762
Starb den 10 ten Dec. 1816
alt 53 Iahr 6 monat 8 Tag

IN MEMORY OF ELIZABETH
Wife of Philip Coleman
Died Dec. 1, 1851

IN MEMORY OF ABRAHAM LANDIS
Born A.D. 1789
Died March 9, 1839
Aged 50 yrs.

Here lies the body of
BARBARA HEFLE
Who was born Jan. 20, 1793
and departed this life the
21 of June 1823
aged 30 yrs. 5 mo. 19 days

Here lies the body of CHARLES WALTER DEPARTED THIS LIFE 8TH OF Dec. 1822. Age 17 days

In memory of CHARLES R.
Son of Daniel Kautz
Born April 30, 1830
Died May 12, 1848
Aged 18 yrs. 12 days

IN MEMORY OF CATHERINE
Wife of John Atcheson
Died July 10, 1846
Aged 58 yrs. 7 mo. 14 days

DANIEL LANDIS
Died June 29, 1848
Aged 77 yrs. 9 mo. 2 days

IN MEMORY OF SUSANNA
Wife of Jacob Coleman
Died Dec. 25, 1847
Aged 25 yrs. 6 mo. 1 day
(Daughter of John A. Miller)

IN MEMORY OF ELIZABETH
Consort of John Flick
Born May 26, 1763
Died May 1, 1843
Aged 79 yrs. 11 mo. 6 days.

MARY
Wife of Pete Lane
Died Dec. 27, 1866
Aged 79 yrs. 8 mo. 19 days

PETER LANE
Died June 14, 1864
Aged 82 yrs. 4 mo. 27 days
(Capt. of War of 1812)

IN MEMORY OF JONATHAN KNEPPER
Died March 30, 1840
Aged 1 yr. 1 mo. 3 days

CHARLOTT KNEPPER
Died April 25, 1834
Age 12 days

CHARLOTTE
Dau. of Peter and Mary Lane
Died Oct. 8, 1831
Aged 17 yrs. 4 mo. 10 days

Sacred to Memory of
Elizabeth
Dau. of Charles and Catherine Refs (Reese)
who departed this life June 23rd, 1840
Aged 9 yrs. 8 mo. six days
Farewell parents, brothers and sisters dear,
I am not dead but sleeping here,
My Peace was made, my grave you see,
Prepare for death and follow me.

In memory of
CHARLES SCHMUCKER HAZELIUS
Son of Catherine and Charles Reese
Died Feb. 18, 1838
Aged 2 yrs. 5 mo. 8 days

In memory of
LOVES
Consort of John P. Lane
Died April 23, 1835
Aged 22 yrs. 9 mo. 21 days

In memory of
WILLIAM BENDER
Died March 28th, 1835
Aged 2 yrs. 10 mo. 13 days

Here lies the body of
CHARLES WALTER
Who departed this life 28th of Dec. 1822
Aged 17 days

SILASS
Son of P. & M. Lane
Died Jan. 5, 1851
Aged 27 yrs. 1 mo. 11 days

In memory of
DAVID COLEMAN
Died Oct. 16th. 1835
Aged 27 yrs. 4 mo. 14 days

In memory of
OLIVER
Son of Benj. Walker
Died Dec. 7, 1859
Aged 5 yrs. 9 mo. 12 days

In memory of
JUDITH ENGLE
Died 1842 Feb. 19th.
Aged 36 yrs. 5 mo. 23 days

MICHAEL UMBERGER
In honor of service in the war of 1812

In memory of
KATHERINE JANE
Daughter of Rev. Jacob Crigler & Nellie his wife who
departed this life Nov. 4th. 1829 aged 5 yrs. 10 mo. 4 dys.
Farewell dear child, a long farewell,
for we shall meet no more,
Till we are raised with thee to dwell,
in Zions happier shore.

In memory of
JACOB FLICKINGER
Died April 5th, 1840
Aged 73 yrs. 10 mo. 19 days

In memory of
WILLIAM G. WALKER
Born May 28th, 1805
Died April 6th, 1843
Aged 37 yrs. 1 mo. 9 days

In memory of
CATHERINE
Wife of Benjamin G. Walker
Daughter of John Miller
Died Dec. 16th, 1845
Aged 20 yrs. 11 mo. 23 dys.

CAROLINE A.
Dau. of William Long
Born Sept. 25th, 1829
Died June 20th, 1839, Aged 9 yrs. 8 mo. 28 days

In memory of
MATILDA
Dau. of John Miller
Died Dec. 15th, 1848
Aged 15 yrs. 10 mo. 29 days

SAMUEL P. LANE
Died Dec. 20, 1833
Aged 25 yrs. 3 mons.

MATILDA HOUPT
Aged 13 yrs. 5 mons. 20 days

REBECCA HEIPLE
Died March 9th, 1849
Aged 71 yrs. 5 mo. 7 days

In memory of
CASPER BAKER
Died Sept. 17, 1857 (or 1837)
Aged 61 yrs.

In memory of
MARTIN LUTHER
Son of Samuel and Martha Hufford
Born Oct. 10, 1829
Died May 4th, 1837, Aged 7 yrs. 7 mo. 6 days

SAMUEL HUFFORD
Died Dec. 31, 1848
Aged 47 yrs. 29 days

Sacred to memory of
SUSANNA RAUCH
Born April 11th, A.D. 1815
Died July 6th, A.D. 1836
Aged 21 yrs. 2 mo. 22 days

In memory of
WILLIAM
Eldest son of M. King who was born 17th of March 1822
Departed this life 6th of June, 1824
Aged 2 yrs. 2 mo. 19 days

Sacred in memory of
ANN MARY DIVELY
Deceased Dec. 15th, 1836
Aged 72 yrs. 10 mo. 13 days

In memory of
JESSE LONG
Died Sept. 26, 1845
Aged 6 months 1 day

In memory of
ELIZABETH
Consort of John N. Coleman
Born Jan. 5 A.D. 1778. Died Oct. 7th, A.D. 1834
Aged 56 yrs. 8 mo. 2 days

In memory of
CATHERINE
Wife of John Berns
Born Feb. 9th, 1822. Died May 9th, 1840
Aged 28 yrs. 3 mo.

In memory of
MARGARET BENDER
Died Feb. 16th, 1834. Aged 11 yrs. 12 days

In memory of
CHRISTIAN
Son of John and Mary Finrock
Died Feb. 10, 1837. Aged 5 yrs. 1 mo. 2 days.

In memory of
C. J. ANN
Dau. of Philip and Ann Auman
Died Sept. 14, 1834
Aged 28 days.

Anna Margaret
Trufrock
Died Mar. 10, 1851
Aged 74 yrs. 3 mo. 4 dys.

In memory of
CHARLOTTE LANE
Dau. of John P. and Loves, his wife
Died Dec. 23, 1838
Aged 4 yrs. 7 mo. 15 days

ELIZABETH
Dau. of Daniel and Harriet Landis 1840

In memory of
MATILDA KUHNS
Was born Feb. 25, 1820. Died April 9th, 1843
Aged 23 yrs. 1 mo. 14 days

In memory of
SARA
Dau. of J. A. Probst
Died Mar. 15th, A.D. 1839
Aged 25 yrs. 6 mo. 8 days

HENRY HEIPLE Sr.
Died May 16th, 1849
Aged 75 yrs. 7 months 14 days

In memory of
HENRY GROSS
Died Nov. 18th, 1842. Aged 1 yr. 7 mo. 10 days

In memory of
MARY GROSS
Died Oct. 4, 1836. Aged 1 yr. 9 mo. 14 days

In memory of
LYDIA
Wife of Jesse Long
Died July 4th, 1847. Aged 30 yrs. 4 mo. 14 days

In memory of
GEORGE WASHINGTON
Son of John and Caroline Baldwin
Died Aug. 25, 1847

In memory of
MARIAH LANE
Died Feb. 19, 1833. Aged 8 mons. 26 days

Here lieth
SIMON McBEE
Departed this life 8th of Marz 1828, aged 48 years.

In memory of
MARIA BARBARA HEILEN
Departed this life 6th, of Marz, A.D. 1830
Aged 89 yrs. 11 mo. 6 days. (Wife of Walter)

In memory of
MARTHA HOFFARD
Born Mar. 4, 1805. Died June 9, 1844

HENRIETTE
Wife of S. J. Bittner
Died April 12, 1872. Aged 27 yrs. 10 mo. 12 days

BARBARA
Wife of W. Hoffman
Died Oct. 23, 1871. Aged 56 yrs. 6 mo. 9 days

In memory of
JACOB HAMM
Born Nov. 11, 1786. Died June 2, 1866.
Aged 79 yrs. 6 mo. 21 days

In memory of
ELMER
Son of Joseph and Elizabeth Mason
Died Mar. 30, 1867. Aged 10 mo. 19 days

ANNA BARBARA
Wife of C. Baker
Died Mar. 1, 1864. Aged 82 yrs.

J. JOHN BALDWIN
Died April 15, 1855. Aged 45 yrs. 7 mo. 14 days.

In memory of
ABRAHAM LANDIS
Born A.D. 1789. Died Mar. 9, 1839. Aged 50 yrs.

HENRY BALDWIN
Died April 15, 1857. Aged 8 yrs. 7 mon. 10 days

In memory of
MARTIN LUTHER
Son of J. & L. Krigler
Born May 19th, 1826. Died May 12,
Aged 5 yrs. 11 mo. 23 dys.

In memory of
CATHERINE
Wife of Michael Umberger
Born Mar. 9th, 1790. Died May 30th, 1853.
Aged 63 yrs. 2 mo. 21 days

In memory of
MICHAEL UMBERGER
Born Sept. 29th, 1783. Died Oct. 8th, 1856.
Aged 73 yrs. 9 days

In memory of
CASPER PALER
Died Sept. 17, 1857. Aged 61 yrs.

In memory of
HENRY ESKEN
Born Nov. 10th, 1827. Died Sept. 10th, 1863
Aged 38 yrs. 10 mo.

In memory of
B. F. EWALT
Died Mar. 28th, 1853. Aged 25 yrs. 4 mo. 15 days

HARRIETT LANDIS
Died Nov. 14th, 1871. Aged 69 yrs. 6 days

MARGARET
Dau. of E. & I. Mosholder
Died Feb. 27th, 1862. Aged 12 yrs. 6 mo. 23 days

HEIL KNEPPER
1851

Total 80 graves   (E.C.S. May 5, 1930.)

The Will of John Fletcher

Filed 15th of June, 1838

In the name of God Amen: I, John Fletcher of Berlin, Somerset Co., Penna., considering the uncertainty of this mortal life, and being in sound mind and memory (blessed by Almighty God for the same) do make and publish this my last will and testament,—in manner and form following to wit: Principally, and first of all, I commend my immortal soul into the hand of God, who gave it, and my body to the earth to be buried in a decent and christian like manner, at the discretion of my executor, hereinafter named, and as to such worldly estate wherewith it hath pleased God to bless in this life, I give and dispose of the same in the following manner: to wit: First, I give and bequeath unto my wife, Susanna, the house and lot No. 22 in the addition to Berlin aforesaid, which I now occupy with all the appurtentances, thereto belonging all the beds, and bedding, carpeting, household and kitchen furniture remaining in the house at my decease, together with all the stock such as cows and hogs. And also that tract of land containing fifteen acres and three quarters, strict measure adjoining land of John Rauch on the east and South and on the north, adjoining the town of Berlin and on the west, the land of Phillip Wegley, together with the sum of one thousand dollars in lawful money, arising from the sale of the two tracts of land adjoining each other now in the occupancy of Peter Zimmerman, which two tracts shall be sold at public outcry at the discretion of my executor hereinafter named. The aforesaid thousand dollars to be paid to her out of the first monies arising from such sale. And I also give and bequeath to my wife Susanna the sum of one thousand dollars out of the monies arising out of the sale of that tract of land now occupied by George Zimmerman, situation in Somerset Twp., and county aforesaid, which tract shall also be sold at public outcry at the discretion of the executor, said money to be paid as the thousand dollars, aforesaid. And likewise all my stock and interest in the bank of Brownsville, Penna. together with three lots, numbered in the general plan of the town of Berlin Nos. 25, 26 and 27. And also I give and bequeath unto her, my library together with the one-fourth of the money arising from the sale of a tract of land situated on a branch of Wills Creek below the Elk Lick in Londonderry Twp., County aforesaid. Which tract of land to be sold to the highest and best bidder at public sale at discretion of my executor. And likewise, I bequeath to her the one-third of the monies arising from the sale of a certain house and two lots situated in Brownsville, Pennsylvania. All the above legacies and bequests, all and singular, I bequeath as above stated to my wife, Susanna forever. I bequeath to Isabella Parker my three lots, situated in the Borough of Somerset, County aforesaid, to have and hold forever. I bequeath to Alexander H. Philson and Samuel Philson a certain tract of wood adjoining lands of John P. Brubaker, William Long, and others, to be equally divided between them, out of which bequest each of them shall pay to the aforesaid Isabella Parker in lawful money, the sum of one hundred dollars. I also bequeath to my beloved niece, Margaret Patterson, the sum of fifteen hundred dollars lawful money to be paid out of my estate. I bequeath to Jane Zimmerman all the horses and cows and farming utensils which she has already received. I bequeath to Harriet Ankeny, now residing in Millersburg, Homes County, Ohio, the sum of three hundred dollars lawful money. I bequeath five hundred dollars lawful money to the Lutheran Sunday School, to be vested in the hands of the trustees of the Lutheran Church, which sum shall be put out on interest secured from mortgages, which interest shall be annually collected and appropriated to the purchase of Bibles, Testaments and other religious books. Exclusively for the use of the Lutheran Sunday School of Berlin, moreover, each child attending aforesaid Sunday School shall receive one Bible as a present soon as it is able to read. I likewise bequeath five hundred dollars lawful money to the German Reformed Church, which sum shall be put out on interest secured by mortgage which interest shall be annually collected and appropriated to the purchase of Bibles, Testaments, and other religious books, exclusively for the use of the German Reformed Sunday School of Berlin, moreover each child attending aforesaid Sunday School, shall receive one Bible as a present as soon as it is able to read. After the foregoing bequest, and legacies are well and truly distributed as above directed, the residue of balance of my estate all and singular to be divided between the German Reformed Sunday School and the Lutheran Sunday School, as aforesaid. I give and bequeath to my beloved wife, Susanna, all of my outstanding book accounts—and lastly, I nominate, constitute and appoint Alexander Philson of Berlin, Somerset County, to be executor of this my last will and testament, hereby revoking all other wills and testaments, by me heretofore made, and declaring this and no other to be my last will and testament. I have hereunto set my hand and seal this twenty-first day of April, in the year of our Lord, One Thousand eight hundred and thirty-eight.

John Fletcher

Witnesses:

J. E. Steffer   Filed June 15, 1838
Charles Reese   Typed April 11, 1936

The Berlin Brethren Church

This year marks the 95th anniversary of the organization of the Berlin Brethren Church. At a council meeting in the Beachdale Church, Jan. 1, 1881, an organization was formed which named W. H. Menges as clerk.

On January 29, of the same year, the Brethren met in council, in the Disciple Church, which had been the Methodists first church house, and unanimously agreed to build a new church in Berlin.

A plot of ground was purchased on Main Street from Samuel Forney for $350, with brother Forney agreeing to contribute $100 toward the new building. The white frame church was dedicated on Dec. 4, 1881. It still stands at the rear of the present building, and was used by the Berlin borough for many years, and presently owned by the Brethren, is used for Scout purposes only.

Down through the years 22 men have served as pastors. During the pastorate of Rev. C. W. Benshoff, a new church was built. The church observed its 40th anniversary in 1921. The need for more space was becoming quite apparent. A 12-member finance committee was elected and a committee of three, A. B. Cober, J. H. Landis, and F. H. Meyers, was appointed to investigate the matter of building a new church.

Lewis Keiper was given the contract on March 30, and the cornerstone was laid May 31, 1925, with Pastor Benshoff officiating. Rev. C. H. Ashman, pastor of the Johnstown First Church, gave the address. The evening sermon was delivered by Rev. H. L. Coughenour, pastor of Meyersdale Brethren Church.

The new red brick church was dedicated on April 25, 1926, with Dr. W. H. Beachler of South Bend, Ind., as the dedicatory speaker. A community service was celebrated in the afternoon with a choir of 60 voices assisting. Short addresses of good wishes were given by local pastors. Cash pledges in the amount of $33,500 was raised against a dedication cost of $67,000. Sixteen years later, during the last year of Rev. N. V. Leatherman's ten-year pastorate, the Berlin Brethren ceremonially burned the last note of indebtedness, on January 4, 1942.

Several notable additions to the church plant have been made since that time. In 1946, during the pastorate of Rev. S. M. Whetstone, a gift of chimes was dedicated. The gift was from the J. H. Glessner family in honor of their daughter, Sara Jane. In this same year the church celebrated the 25th anniversary of the present building.

In 1960 a new brick parsonage was erected next door to the church. Two adjacent properties were acquired for paved parking. The Cable property and the original white church were used for more than thirty years as the Borough Building. A carillon was dedicated, the gift of Paul J. Coleman, in memory of his mother, Mrs. Mary Esken Coleman.

In recent years the Sunday school has been renovated. A gas furnace was installed. A new church organ, pew cushions, and public-address system throughout church and Sunday School have been added.

Other highlights include supporting two missionaries, Reginea Hendershot Rowsey, in Argentina, and Mrs. Richard Sarver Winfield, in Africa, both daughters of the congregation.

Fourteen men have been called to the ministry from the Berlin Brethren Church. Three women have been called to be missionaries and three other men received training at the Brethren Church, prior to entering the ministry.

The 50th anniversary of the church and the 95th anniversary of the congregation was observed in 1976, with Rev. Lyle Lictenberger and Rev. Percy Miller, former pastors, bringing messages, and W. S. Benshoff, son of a former pastor, also attending. There were more

Old White frame Brethren Church

64

Berlin Brethren Church and Parsonage

than 400 present at a luncheon served at the school cafeteria.

It is interesting to note that the pulpit Bible, bought in 1880, by H. R. Holsinger, founder of the church, was still being used at the time of the 95th anniversary. The four oldest members of the church are Mrs. H. W. Menges, 97; Rev. D. C. White, 92; Mrs. J. C. Werner, 90; and Frank Boyer, 90. All are still active in the church.

Members of the church are grateful to God, for without His Spirit and presence their labors would have been in vain. To God be the glory, great things He has done.

Ralph E. Mills, Minister

Highlights of Our History

1881—Church organized January 1
1881—Church dedicated December 4
1881—Rev. H. R. Holsinger begins pastorate
1882—Rev. J. H. Knepper begins pastorate
1883—Rev. A. D. Gnagey begins pastorate
1883—Rev. Alvin Cober begins pastorate
1884—Rev. S. W. Wilt begins pastorate
1885—Rev. J. H. Knepper begins pastorate
1891—Rev. J. D. McFaden begins pastorate
1894—Rev. B. C. Mumau begins pastorate
1894—Rev. J. H. Knepper begins third pastorate
1898—Rev. M. C. Meyers begins pastorate
1900—Rev. P. M. Swinehart begins pastorate
1902—Rev. L. A. Hazlett begins pastorate
1903—Rev. J. L. Bowman begins pastorate
1908—Rev. David Flora begins pastorate
1910—Rev. I. O. Hubbard begins pastorate

1913—Rev. C. E. Kolb begins pastorate
1915—Rev. J. F. Watson begins pastorate
1918—Rev. I. B. Trout begins pastorate
1920—Rev. W. C. Benshoff beings pastorate
1921—Fortieth anniversary, December 4
1925—Laying of cornerstone of new church
1926—Dedication of new church
1929—Rev. Albert Lantz begins pastorate
1932—Rev. N. V. Leatherman begins pastorate
1942—Burning of last note
1943—Rev. S. M. Whetstone begins pastorate
1948—Rev. Percy C. Miller begins pastorate
1951—70th anniversary of church organization
1951—25th anniversary of dedication of present edifice
1953—Rev. Lyle Lichtenberger
1956—Rev. Ralph Mills

Little White Church

Little White Church within the dell
Your history I have tried to tell,
In 1881 you were white and new,
The faithful few had builded you,
They gathered to hear the Word so dear,
Sang songs of praise, for God was near.
These faithful few your presence knew,
Did worship here, God's Word to do,
God led them and they followed on,
And now they wear the victor's crown.

Little White Church so small and plain,
In you, they received much spiritual gain,
Through life you lifted their heavy loads,

They walked with God down the troubled road,
The faithful few each in their regular place,
Adorned each service with humble grace.
The pastor back of the walnut pulpit stood,
For God, and right, and what was good.

Little White Church you were moved to the back,
To make room for the new brick edifice,
But you still stand as proud as ever,
With your steeple pointed towards heavens
May the echo of your glorious past,
Remain in the hearts of those who held fast,
The doctrines of the church until the last,
One of the faithful shall answer the triumphant blast.

Rev. D. C. White

Methodist Episcopal Church, Berlin

The first Methodist Society was organized in Berlin in 1786 by George Johnson, who came here from Shepherdstown, West Virginia. Somerset County was then a part of Bedford County. The record kept by Cornelius Garey, who writes of his inability to find any class records of earlier date than 1834, says that Father Johnson was at that time a member of the German Reformed Church. He always gave shelter and entertainment to the Methodist missionary preachers who traveled the country. He would also throw open his house for preaching, as there was no other place because of the opposition to those Methodist preachers who were even believed to have power to bewitch persons. Preaching services were first held in Mr. Johnson's home which is now known as the Donner building. The first preaching services were conducted by Methodist itinerants who visited this part of the country in their long weary journeys over immense circuits.

Brother Johnson became a class leader and a local preacher and kept his house open for public religious services for years. He was a hatter by trade but turned his shop into a place of worship, where services were held from 1822 to 1835. In 1834 James Platt donated a building lot to the Society. A small church was erected, costing about four hundred dollars. This was later sold to the Disciples Denomination and a brick church was built in 1851, the lot being donated by Mrs. Sarah Platt. The bricks were made and put up by Jacob Zorn. The carpenter work was done by Michael Shafer under the supervision of Samuel Philson, one of the Building Committee. Father Johnson died in 1837 and was buried in the Reformed Church graveyard.

The church was partly destroyed by fire on March 21, 1925. It was repaired and was ready for the reopening exercises held on April 18, 1926.

The ministers who served the church are: Lock and White, 1835-1836; J. White and Walter Chalfant, 1837-1838; Dunlap and Erwin, 1839-1840; Samuel Wakefield, 1840-1842; Covert and Long, 1842-1843; Sawhill and Raygor, 1843-1844; Williams and Coleman, 1844-1845; J. Dennison, 1845- ; Robert Laughlin, 1851-1852; Beacon, 1852-1853; Jordan and Stewart, 1853-1854; G. D. Keener, 1854-1855; Griffith and Green, 1855-1857; Crook and Marrow, 1857-1858; Crook, 1858-1859; Walter Brown, 1861-1863; Fairall, 1863-1964; Endleys and Kerr, 1864-1868; Norcross and Mitchell, 1868-1870; Freshwater, 1870-1871; William Steward, 1872-1874; J. B. Taylor, 1874-1877; N. Loccock, 1877-1878; M. L. Weekley, 1878-1879; George Holmens, 1879-1880; M. L.

Methodist Evangelistic Church built in 1851

Weekley, 1880-1881; A. Freeman, 1881-1882; O. W. Hutchinson, 1882-1883; W. A. Rutledge, 1883-1884; J. N. Pershing, 1884-1886; N. L. Brown, 1886-1887; W. P. Harmon, 1887-1888; W. H. McBride, 1888-1889; G. H. Flinn, 1889-1891; L. S. Wilkinson, 1891-1892; P. C. Brooks, 1892-1893; J. H. Lancaster, 1893-1896; R. M. Fowles, 1896-1897; H. N. Cameron, 1897-1902; R. B. Cuthbert, 1902-1904; P. C. Dalladay, 1904-1905; S. W. Bryan, 1905-1910; Newell, 1910-1911; H. H. Hofelt, 1911-1912; G. G. Gallegher, 1912-1913; R. L. Aitken, 1913-1914; Frederick Edmons, 1914-1915; L. H. Thomas, 1915-1916; Wagner, 1916-1919; G. W. Ringer, 1919-1922; L. F. Athey, 1922-1923; H. M. Coughenour, 1923-1928; N. L. Brown and C. A. Tracey, 1928-1929; Trimpey, 1929-1930; Whipple, 1930-1932; Ronald Moseley, 1932-1933; Nordham, 1933-1934; F. M. Bennett 1934-1936; L. J. Wallis, 1936- .

This church site was not occupied after the Methodist charter was dropped but remained in a good state of repair. In 1953 the Christian and Missionary Alliance Church was organized by Rev. D. A. Breegle, who was its first pastor. Following the death of Rev. Breegle in 1965, Rev. Donald B. Ansell became pastor and has remained in this capacity to date.

Christian Alliance

The United Evangelical or Albright Church

The Albright Church was located at 405 Diamond Street in Berlin. In the year 1919 the Harrison Company, who built the Berlin-Garrett State Road, leased the property and installed lights, heat, water, and telephone, and used it for office purposes. Then in 1924, Mr. John Ream remodeled it into a duplex. The old church bell was removed and installed on top of Reams' Auditorium to use as a fire alarm, with a rope hanging down to about six feet from the sidewalk.

Albright Church

Berlin Schools, 1777-1976

The purpose and need of schools for the children came with Berlin's first settlers. The primary obligation was assumed by the churches of the community, supplemented by the subscription, or private schools, of pioneer history. The town of Berlin maintained schools from a very early date. In the year 1777 a union schoolhouse was built near the site of the present gristmill (Mulberry Street and Fifth Avenue). In 1800 the Lutheran congregation erected a log church on the northeast corner of their burial ground (Fletcher and Vine Streets). The Lutheran congregation used this for both church and schoolhouse and the union building was taken over by the Reformed congregation. The schoolhouses and churches were built of crude, round logs. The benches were made of slabs and tables or desks of rough boards. A high chimney and fireplace adorned one end of the schoolroom, and the low attic and a small rear room afforded living quarters for the lonely schoolmaster.

In 1825 the Reformed congregation erected a stone building to take the place of the old union house, and about the same time the Lutherans built a frame schoolhouse near the site of the present high school building. This was known as the "Red Schoolhouse."

The Pennsylvania free school law of 1834 was promptly accepted by the people of Berlin and the first free school was established in 1836. This advance step on the part of the town was the primary cause of its organization as a borough and a separate school district. The surrounding township, however, also established free schools in 1849. Buildings for district public school use were successively erected on Diamond Street, present site of Fogle Cigar Factory, in 1837, 1857, 1876. In 1889 the school district purchased the Lutheran Sunday school building for a primary building. This building was used for primary work until 1905 when an extra story was added and then used as a four-room elementary building until 1915.

In 1853 John Frederick Eberhart was principal of the Albright Seminary under the auspices of the religious

Teacher's Provisional Certificate

Union School Building built in 1777

Berlin public school built in 1837

The Red School House

Vine Street School under construction

Present-day Berlin-Brothersvalley School

Vine Street School completed

denomination known as the Evangelical Association. This seminary was located on the William H. Menges property, North Broadway. Professor Eberhart was very successful, but there seemed to be no one to take up the work after he was gone.

The first high school was organized in 1889 with a two-year course. In 1905 a three-year course was adopted, followed by a four-year course in 1924.

A new school was built in 1914 at Vine and Fletcher streets and was used for forty-seven years for the elementary and high school.

In 1937 Berlin and Brothersvalley Township consolidated and a new high school was erected on East Main Street. This building contains classrooms, a gymnasium, an auditorium, a home economics department, and industrial arts and agricultural shops.

In 1960 a new elementary school was built adjoining the high school. This building contains twenty classrooms, one kindergarten room, a special education room, a multipurpose room, an agriculture room and shop, a health room, an office, faculty and service facilities and a kitchen and cafeteria.

In 1970 an addition to the high school was constructed. This contains a new band room, administration offices, enlargement of the commercial department. An addition to the elementary building was added consisting of six classrooms and a music and art room.

Berlin borough and Brothersvalley Township consolidated in 1937, making one school district. In 1952 New Baltimore, Allegheny Township, and Northampton Township joined the consolidation. In 1969 Fairhope Township was added to the district.

The first school in Berlin was started in 1777. Now, 200 years later, we have a modern elementary school with an enrollment of 1,151 pupils for the year 1975-76.

Pennsylvania Clocks and Clock Makers

In the book "Pennsylvania Clocks and Clock Makers" by George H. Eckhardt (page 214) the following were listed under clock makers outside of Philadelphia:

HEFFLEY, ANNANIAS   Berlin
Born 1817, died 1876   Somerset County

Annanias Heffley made the same kind of clocks as Daniel Heffley, in Berlin, and worked about the same time. His clocks bear his name on the dial.

HEFFLEY, DANIEL   Berlin
Born 1813, died 1887   Somerset County

He was apprenticed to Samuel Hoffard and continued to make the clocks, which bear his name, until 1867.

HOFFARD, SAMUEL   Berlin
Born 1801, died 1845   Somerset County

He made the same kind of clocks as those made by Michael Hugus in Somerset (not Berlin).

The following was taken from the "Laurel Messenger," published by Somerset County Historical Society, Volume VI, number 1, dated February 1965 (page #8):

"The name Hofford appears in the Mayflower Index, found at University of Pennsylvania Library.

"The Hofford family Bible, in possession of Mrs. Anna Lane Menges, Berlin, contains this record: Samuel Hofford was born 2 Oct. 1801 son of Martin Hofford; died 31 Dec. 1845 aged 44 years, 2 months, 29 days. Martha (Thomas) Hofford was born 1 March 1805, baptized Sept. 1828. Died June 1844; maiden name of Thomas of Lancaster Co Penn; her parents buried in a Quaker Cemetery near Phila. Samuel Hofford and wife Martha both buried in Berlin."

Lutheran Cemetery (Berlin, Pa.) records show that Samuel Hufford died on Dec. 31, 1848, aged 47 years, 29 days. Martha Hoffard was born on Mar. 4, 1805, and died June 9, 1844.

There does not appear to be any recorded information on where Hoffard and Heffley clocks were made in Berlin. Early residents who had this knowledge advised

the generations that followed them that both men lived in and built their clocks in what is known as the William Philson home, Main Street. This a large two-story brick in good condition and stands on north side of upper diamond in Berlin. We quote from a letter dated July 24, 1976, and written by Charlotte Lane Imhoff, great-great granddaughter of Samuel Hoffard to Barbara Miller Croner of Berlin. "I remember Aunt Annie (Menges) telling how grandfather Hoffard would make enough clocks to fill a wagon, then deliver them to Pittsburgh. The home was the "Old Philson Home" on the northeast corner of the upper diamond. A large old brick building, remodeled since, I believe, into apartments.

Again we quote the Laurel Messenger (page 8) February 1965 issue. "The research department of the Library of Congress of Washington reports that the moon attachments to clocks was first used in England about 1740 and became very popular about 1760. It continued in style until 1820, since which time it has been used less frequently."

George H. Eckhardt continued:

The late Dr. Edwin Miller Fogel collected many of the beliefs of the Pennsylvania Germans, and published them. It may be well to present a few of the beliefs regarding the moon so that the importance of the lunar phases to these people be appreciated:

Sweep the house in the dark of the moon (new moon)

The house in which the Hoffard and Heffley clocks were made

RES OF W.F. PHILSON, BERLIN, PA.

Samuel Hoffard Clock

Daniel Heffley Clock

and you will have neither moths nor spiders.

Shingle the roof in the decrease of the moon (between full moon and next new moon) so that the shingles are put on when the horns of the moon are turned down, and they will work and rise up. The same holds good for boardwalks.

The number of snows during winter is indicated by the number of days from the first snow in fall to the following full moon.

Trees planted in full moon will bear very well.

Plant peas and potatoes in the increase of the moon.

The meat of animals slaughtered in the increase of the moon will not shrink in the pot or in curing.

A clock, made by Samuel Hoffard, Berlin, Pa., is engraved B.C. on face under name. This means before Somerset County. It was bought by Capt. Albert Heffley for his wife after the Civil War. It was made of solid cherry and owned by Blanche Heffley Kimmel, Berlin, Pa. It was willed to Walter A. Johnson, Berlin, Pa.

Another clock was made by Daniel Heffley, apprentice of Samuel Hoffard, May 16, 1831. It was sold to Aaron K. Johnson on Dec. 5, 1881. The original date was written under the face of clock on bottom strip. The present owner is Walter A. Johnson, Berlin, Pa.

71

Early Gunmakers - Gunsmiths, Berlin Area

JOHN ALLFATHER—Near Berlin (no dates or data given).

WILLIAM BLAIR—Brothersvalley Township, tax list 1823.

HENRY BOWSHINGER—Brothersvalley Township tax lists 1820, 1823.

SAMUEL CONRAD—Brothersvalley Township tax lists 1832, 1833, 1834; Berlin Township tax lists 1837, 1840, 1843, 1850, 1853. He was an excellent riflemaker.

PHINEAS M. COMPTON—Berlin. Gunsmith and tinner. Born June 1, 1804, near Brunswick, N.J. Grandparents came from France. Father came to Berlin in 1813. Died July 4, 1858.

SAMUEL COMPTON—Son of Phineas. Entered his father's shop at age 13. Died Nov. 27, 1902.

JACOB PAINTER—Allegheny Township tax lists 1805, 1806.

The above taken from "Laurel Messenger," Volume XII, number 4.

Survey was made by Vaughn E. Whisker, Bedford County, who named 30 gunmakers and gunsmiths in Somerset County. He indicated that a gunsmith did not make guns. November 1971 issue.

Doctors

The approximate years they practiced

1791—Dr. John Kimmel came into the county as early as 1791 and was a graduate in medicine. He came from York County and located in Berlin, where he spent the remaining years of his life. He also kept a tavern and store and was a colonel in the militia and an associate judge of Somerset County. After practicing medicine here for over fifty years, he died in 1839.

1800—Dr. John Groner was born in 1779. It was said that he traveled all over the mountains and glades collecting herbs and flowers for his medicines. It is said that he practiced "blood-letting." He died in 1848.

1817—Dr. Lucas Gibbs located in Berlin in 1817 and held a diploma from the University of Pennsylvania granted in 1791. He was probably the first physician in Somerset County to advertise his claims to public patronage. He carried a three-column advertisement in the Somerset "Whig" in 1818.

1827—1877 Dr. John P. Cober of Brothersvalley Township practiced medicine for over fifty years. He was also an elder in the Buechley-Beechdale Church. In 1884 he died and is buried on the Edwin Landis farm on the edge of Berlin.

1843—Dr. Michael Berkey.

1845—1864 Dr. John Beachley or Buechley. He is said to have built the lower house on the present-day Calvin Will farm in 1838.

1850—Dr. William A. Garman, physician and surgeon, Berlin, Pa., was born in Stoystown June 9, 1829, a son of John and Sara Hite Garman. He received his early education in the public schools of Stoystown and at the Normal School taught by Professor Stutzman. After teaching school at Shadetown one winter, he began the study of medicine under the direction of Robert H. Patterson, M.A., of Stoystown. He received his medical degree at the University of Pennsylvania in 1850 and was also a graduate of the Baltimore College of Physicians and Surgeons. He began practicing medicine in Stoystown in 1851 and moved to Berlin in 1857 where he remained for the rest of his life. He was also the father of Ida Grace Garman, who was the telegraph operator from Johnstown who was drowned in the flood of 1889.

1851—Dr. Henry Brubaker began the study of medicine in 1848 under Dr. J. H. Reidt of Berlin. He attended Jefferson Medical College in Philadelphia and graduated in 1851. He first located in New Lexington, where he remained eighteen months, after which he returned to Berlin where he remained until 1856. Afterwards he moved to Somerset. The degree of M.A. was conferred upon him by Allegheny College in 1879. He died in 1899.

1851—Dr. J. H. Reidt.

1854—Dr. Christian G. Stutzmen practiced in Sand Patch.

1861—Dr. Henry Garey, born in 1828, was educated at Cumberland, Md., high school. In 1859 and 60 he attended Jefferson Medical College and afterwards joined the Southern army and served as assistant surgeon in the fourth regiment, Mississippi Cavalry. After the war he practiced two years at Coalmont, Huntingdon County, Pa., three years in Memphis, Tennessee, and five years in Greenleaf, Mississippi. He came to Berlin in 1872 where he began practicing medicine.

1867—Dr. Jeremiah K. Miller practiced for twenty-two years and was a student of Dr. Brubaker's.

1878—Dr. John S. Garman, son of William A. Garman, was born at Southampton Mills, in this county, and educated in the public schools of Berlin and in the County Normal School and then taught several terms in Brothersvalley and Allegheny townships. From 1872 to 1876 he studied medicine with his father, and upon graduating from the Baltimore College of Physicians and Surgeons in 1878, was engaged in practice with his father. He was also the local physician for the B & O Railroad Company, was burgess of the borough of Berlin, and a member of the Board of Health.

1878—Dr. W. R. Krissinger, the son of Charles Krissinger, was born and educated in Berlin. In 1876 he entered the Baltimore College of Physicians and Surgeons from which he graduated in 1878. He then began practicing medicine in Berlin and in 1880 started a drugstore.

1879—George B. Masters, born in 1856, received his early education in the public and normal schools in Berlin, Pa., and this was supplemented by a course at Mount Union College, Ohio. After teaching at Pine Hill one term, and in Bedford County, he began the study of medicine under the direction of William A. Garman, M.D., of Berlin, Pa., and received his medical degree in 1879 from the Medical College of Ohio, at Cincinnati. He practiced in Somerset one year, 1 ½ years at Shanksville, and then moved to Illinois, where he practiced until 1885 when he returned to Pennsylvania to live and practice medicine in Rockwood. For a number of years he served as local surgeon for the Baltimore and Ohio Railroad and had an office in Macdonaldton, Pa.

1885—Dr. Harry Kimmel Stoner was born in Berlin, Pa., in 1859 and attended the public school which is presently known as the Fogle Cigar Factory. He went to Chambersburg Academy, then to Allegheny College in Meadville, and received the Doctor of Medicine Degree from Jefferson Medical School in Philadelphia. He practiced in Cleveland, Ohio. His death occurred in 1946.

1890—Dr. Jessie Boggs Stoner was one of four children reared near Zanesville, Ohio, and was born in 1866. She attended Muskingum College and the Chicago School of Medicine, where she received her Doctor of Medicine Degree. She practiced in Cleveland, Ohio. She died in 1939. Dr. Stoner and Dr. Boggs were married about 1900. Both retired from practice and moved to Berlin to operate the farm and mine. Their son is John O. Stoner II, who now operates the farm and continues the direct line of descendants from the original settler, Philip Wagerline.

1895—Dr. W. P. Shaw was born in Maryland in 1865 and came to Somerset County as a tot of two years. He spent the remainder of his years in Berlin. His medical studies were pursued at the University of Maryland, where he received his degree in 1895 after which he came to Berlin to practice.

1900—Dr. Robert J. Heffley was born in 1871. In 1895 he lived with his mother and sister in Master's house in Berlin where Keidel's Hardware now stands. In 1902 he married Geneva Height from New Jersey, at which time he and Mrs. Heffley moved into the property on the southwest corner of the lower diamond, now owned by Mrs. Jay Hauger. Here Dr. Heffley was a general practitioner for many years. A familiar sight was to see Dr. and Mrs. Heffley in their horse-drawn carriage making calls into the country. Later Dr. Heffley went to New

Dr. Jeremiah K. Miller

Dr. and Mrs. Heffley and Rev. Burkholder

York City and took a course in eye, ear, nose, and throat. When they returned to Berlin they built the brick house at East Main Street, where he practiced only this phase of medicine and only from his office. He died in 1949.

1903—Dr. John A. P. Murray.

1916—Irving C. Miller, was born in Northampton Township, May 18, 1884, the son of John H. and Mary O. Miller. After attending public school, he attended Normal School and devoted four years to teaching. He then graduated from Franklin and Marshall Academy in 1908 and studied two years at Franklin and Marshall College. Dr. Miller then attended Medico Chirurgical College in Philadelphia where he graduated with the degree of Doctor of Medicine in 1914. After an internship at Allegheny General Hospital in Pittsburgh, he began practicing medicine in Berlin, where he spent the rest of his life. He was very active in school affairs, having served as president on both the Berlin School Board and later on the Berlin-Brothersvalley School Board. He was a member of the Somerset County and Pennsylvania Medical Societies and the American Medical Association.

He had worked his way through school by a series of interesting positions. In the summer of 1910, he worked as a carpenter on the Sand Patch Tunnel, traveling by horse ten miles each way, getting up at four-thirty a.m. and getting home at nine at night. The $2.50 per day wage he received was considered to be good. Other summers, in addition to teaching normal school, he worked on his father's farm, where his father had retired after selling the Johnsburg Store.

Beginning to practice, he traveled at first by horse and buggy and later by a Model T Ford. He was one of the first to travel by auto in winter in the Berlin area.

Doctor Irving Cleveland Miller was honored for his services to the community with a "Doctor Miller Day" on August 17, 1952, at Berlin Community Grove. John O. Stoner headed the general committee for the day; Rev. John Heller was master of ceremonies. The blessing was invoked by Rev. H. Austin Cooper and the main speaker of the afternoon was Dr. J. T. Bowman of Somerset, who gave an interesting history of Dr. Miller's life as a doctor. At one point in his long career, he proudly estimated that the children he had assisted into the world would populate a town larger than the one he had chosen as his home. His wife, the former Violet C. Clark of Meyersdale, who had followed the teaching profession for thirteen years, was also presented gifts.

Judge Thomas Lansberry offered brief remarks following the doctor's response. More than 1000 residents were on hand to voice their appreciation of the physician's thirty-six years of service to the community. A fund designed to finance construction of a building on the Berlin playground was raised in his honor. Dr. Miller died two years later at the age of 71.

1923—Dr. Harold G. Haines, a native of Warren, Ohio, came to Berlin to open a medical practice in 1934. He was a graduate of the University of Pittsburgh School of Medicine and had practiced in Warren for about eleven years before moving here. Dr. Haine's wife, the former Anna Marie Rubright, was a daughter of Mr. and Mrs. William Rubright of Berlin. They both died in a fire in their apartment in 1958. He was aged 63 and she was 58.

1932—Dr. John Miller was located in the house owned by Robert Zorn or where Dr. Haines later had his office.

1937—Dr. Glen Brant had his office on Broadway in the house later owned by Wilson Boyer. Then he moved to Dr. Shaws location or in the present day house of Clarence Gindlesperger at 401 Main Street.

1949—Dr. James L. Killius was born in Johnstown, Pa., March 1, 1923, the son of James and Clarise (Heiner) Killius. He attended Johnstown public schools and graduated from the University of Pittsburgh School of Medicine in 1946. He served a sixteen-month internship at Mercy Hospital in Pittsburgh, after which he served two years in the Army of Occupation in Japan, from 1947 to 1949. In September of 1949 he started practicing medicine in Berlin. He is married to Dorothy Williams and is the father of Martha and David.

Dr. W. C. Wolford

1954—Dr. Paul L. Klose, originally from Pittsburgh, Pa., the son of Lester A. and Mary C. Klose, started general practice in Berlin in 1954. After service as corpsman in the U.S. Navy in World War II, he received a B.S. and M.D. Degree from the University of Pittsburgh. He served two years in the U.S. Navy during the Korean Conflict as a physician. He is affiliated with the Somerset Community Hospital and the Meyersdale Community Hospital, where he served as chief of the medical staff in 1971 and 72. His wife, Marian, is the daughter of the late Harry E. Landis, who served the National Bank of Western Pennsylvania for 52 years and the doctor has served as director since 1968. He has also served as Director of Highlands Professional Review Organization from 1975 and as medical director of the Somerset County Home for the Aged. He is a member of the Pennsylvania Medical Society and the American Medical Association.

Dentists

—Dr. Ingrum.

—Dr. Wolford came to Berlin from Confluence and lived in the house presently occupied by Robert L. Miller.

—Dr. Williams.

—Dr. Colvin—Dr. Ronald B. Colvin was born in Schellsburg and studied dentistry at the University of Maryland at Baltimore, which conferred upon him his degree. He practiced in Berlin until 1913, when he moved to Somerset. While in Berlin he lived in the present-day home of Miss Thelma Saylor.

1905—Dr. E. C. Saylor was born near Meyersdale, Pa., on June 18, 1881. He attended school in Summit Township and the normal school in Meyersdale, Pa. After teaching school for two years, he entered Baltimore school of Dental Surgery and graduated in 1905. He practiced dentistry in Frostburg, Md., and Salisbury, Pa. In 1914 he moved to Berlin, where he practiced dentistry for forty years. He died on June 9, 1954. He was married to Edith M. Glessner on June 6, 1906. Their children are Thelma, Berlin, Pa.; Kathleen S. Buckman, Johnstown, Pa.; and John, Carlisle, Pa. Dr. Saylor was interested in genealogy and collected many family records and other historical data. He translated the old German birth and baptismal records of the Reformed and Lutheran churches in Berlin, Pa. These two volumes have been copyrighted and placed in libraries throughout the country. He also compiled about 48,000 tombstone records from old cemeteries in Somerset County.

—Dr. Harry R. Forney, a native of Rockway, graduated from New Castle High School in 1914 and took the dental course at the University of Pittsburgh School of Dentistry, getting his degree in 1917. He was commissioned a first lieutenant in the United States Army on August 4, 1917, and entered the service October 23, 1918. He served as a dental surgeon at the American University Chemical Warfare station in Washington, D.C., until February 7, 1919. After the war he held a commission in the active reserve and had a captain's commission after 1924. He practiced dentistry in Berlin and built the brick house on Main Street presently owned by Richard Coughenour.

1935—Dr. Harry C. Prugh is a graduate of Homer City High School, Homer City, Pa., and the University of Pittsburgh School of Dentistry, class of 1935, with the degree of Doctor of Dental Surgery.

After graduation from college he practiced dentistry in New Castle, Pa., until November 1936 when he moved to Berlin.

During World War II he served 2 ½ years in the U.S. Air Force at which time he was in both the American and the Philippines theater and was discharged in 1946 with the rank of captain.

Dr. Prugh is a member of Trinity United Church of Christ, Berlin, where he has served as deacon and elder. He is also a charter member and a past president of the Berlin Lions Club. He and his wife, Amelda, live at 410 Diamond Street in Berlin.

Dr. Ronald Colvin

List of Cemteries Cared for by Harry Fisher Post Number 445

	Flags				
Pine Hill	13	Mt. Lebanon	27	Mt. Zion	26
Hays	16	Johnsburg	3	Glen Savage	4
Fritz	11	Fiehtner	4	Mountain	4
Walker Farm	2	Glencoe	1	Sarver	3
Peter Hay Farm	3	Harvey Emerick Farm	1	Brotherton	8
Beachdale	4	J. T. Leydig Farm	1	Croner Farm	2
Ridge	9	Dog Hill-Holly Farm	1	New Baltimore	18
Flickinger	1	Mance	1	Berlin IOOF	170
Dan Landis Farm	1	Kammerer	5	Berlin Reformed	18
Simon Foust Farm	1	Shaffer	1	Berlin Lutheran	5
				Total	365

Early Military History of Berlin Area

Information in this article is from "History of Bedford and Somerset Counties" by Wm. H. Welfley, "The Somerset County Outline" by John C. Cassady, and early history of Bedford, Somerset, and Fulton counties.

The people who have come into this area since its early beginning have taken part in gaining its independence and preserving freedom.

At the time of the French and Indian War of 1754-59, Somerset County had as yet no settlements and therefore no military history. However, it is known that some of the people participating in the war later became settlers here.

The Revolutionary War period (1775-1783) found a number of settlers located in the area and records show that during the war the militia was regularly organized and when in service the men were mostly employed as rangers for the defense of the pioneers. In 1777 the territory of Somerset County was divided into three companies. The third company included some men from the Brothersvalley area, namely, Captain Henry Rhoads, First Lieutenant Jacob Glessner, Ensign Phillip Cable, Court Martial Men, Jacob Fisher and George Countryman.

In the year 1778 these companies were commanded as follows: Brothersvalley Company, Captain Henry Rhoads, First Lieutenant James Hendricks, Second Lieutenant Jacob Walker, Ensign John Bowman, Court Martial Men, George Countryman and Robert Estop.

In 1779 we find the following participants: William Tissue, Christopher Ankeny, George Bruner, and George Shaffer.

While their services were on the frontier and largely for their own protection, they were, nevertheless, as much soldiers of the Revolutionary War as if they had served under Washington himself.

At an early date the borough of Berlin had a strong militia which was active for many years. Some of the early captains were Captain Clement Engle, Captain

Samuel Philson, Captain Lohr, Captain Martz and Captain Long.

Annual occasions of great importance to the townfolks as well as the militia were the annual "musterings" which attracted huge crowds to the town from all over the district. The fourth day of May was set aside for "The Little Mustering" when the militia of every township and borough paraded and displayed its strength to the public.

Two weeks later was the occasion of the "Big Mustering" invariably held in Berlin. These included militia men from the entire county. The afternoons were spent in foot races, horse races, and sports of all kinds for the militia as well as the visitors.

It was also no uncommon thing for quarrels and disputes to be deferred to the day of the "Big Mustering" at which time the parties were to meet and fight the quarrel to the finish, and, having first taken a few drinks of whiskey, they often did so.

A number of Tories had emigrated from eastern counties of Pennsylvania into what is now Somerset County in 1777-1778. They settled in Brothersvalley Township and opposed the war for freedom. Later they were compelled to flee to Canada.

There was another group of settlers in the area who would take no part in the war for independence because of their religious beliefs. They believed that all wars were wrong. They were unlike the Tories. They were not sympathetic to the British. They wished to be loyal to their country, but they took no active part in the conflict for liberty.

Three other men from Brothersvalley Township, who were on the pension rolls, were John Lowry, Michael Lowry, and Jacob Lowry. The last two served in the Pennsylvania Militia. The nature of John Lowry's service we do not know. It is quite probable that these men were brothers, or at least closely related.

Adam Miller was a sergeant in Captain Daniel Clapsaddle's Company of the Maryland Militia. Miller afterwards located in Berlin. He represented Somerset County in the Assembly five successive terms and also served as justice of the peace.

Another event in the early history of the area was the Whiskey Rebellion or Insurrection.

One of the principal products of the farm in those days was rye and much of it was used for making whiskey.

In 1791 Congress passed an act that placed an excise tax on every gallon of whiskey distilled. As soon as this became known it raised a great storm of opposition. The opposition became widespread and soon led to resistance to the officers of the government whose duty it was to enforce the law and collect the tax. In many instances these officers were maltreated and even their houses and property destroyed by fire.

Finally the situation became so acute that military forces were sent in to suppress the insurrection.

Leave of absence and Commutation documents from 1864 and 1865

Headquarters, Provost Marshal,

Sixteenth District, Pennsylvania:

Chambersburg, March 29th, 1865.

No. 2246.

Leave of absence for *Sixteen* days is hereby given to *Henry Coler*, a drafted man, who will report at the expiration of that time or be deemed a deserter.

Geo Eyster

Capt. and Provost Marshal,
16th District, Pa.

(Fa Cm 1864. N. C.)

READ THE FOLLOWING CAREFULLY!

NOTE 1.—A violation of the terms of this furlough will deprive the drafted man of the privilege of furnishing a substitute.

NOTE 2.—The day of the date of this furlough, as well as the day on which it expires, are counted as a part of the total number of days for which the furlough is given. Furloughs are deemed to have expired at four o'clock on the evening of the last day.

NOTE 3.—When a furloughed drafted man returns he must have this paper with him and present it to the Board as evidence of his authority to be absent. Other evidence of authority to be absent will not be received.

No. 35

Office of Receiver of Commutation Money,

16th District of Penna

186

Received at *Somerset* on the *15th* day of *October* 1864, from *Henry Cober* of *Brothersvalley Tp Somerset Co Pa*, who was drafted into the service of the United States on the *26th* day of *September*, 1864, from the *16th* Congressional District of the State of *Pennsylvania* the sum of Three Hundred Dollars ($300.) to obtain exemption, under section 13 of the "Act for enrolling and calling out the National forces, and for other purposes," approved March 3d, 1863, and section 10 of the amendments thereto, approved *July* 24th, 1864.

Ed Scull

Receiver of Commutation Money.

77

It was deemed of sufficient importance to cause the arrest of Harmon Husband and General Robert Philson. The latter was one of the principal citizens of Berlin. Philson is supposed to have raised a liberty pole in front

Early scene of militia in the Berlin area

of his house and also did too much talking. To effect these arrests it is said an entire regiment was detached from the main body of the military force and marched to Berlin. His house was surrounded and his surrender demanded. Philson was the only person arrested in Berlin.

When they left Berlin Philson was riding a fine black mare of his own. They waited on top of the mountain for another party. While there Philson told his captors that if they would give him a good stick two feet long and his black mare he would whip the entire party, whereupon he was placed on a slow horse under strong guard all the way to Philadelphia. They were later jailed in Bedford.

Somerset County responded to President Lincoln's calls for men to defend the Union. Among them were men from the Berlin area.

The Soldiers' Monument, which was erected in Somerset near the courthouse, lists the names of 412 Somerset County men who gave their lives for their country during the Civil War. Some of these dead heroes gave their lives on the battlefields, while others died of wounds and disease and the horror of Southern prisons.

110 Reg. Band and Company C's entry in the 1919 Memorial Day Parade on May 31

Same parade—different view

Soldiers Enlisted for War of 1812 at Berlin

From the "Berlin Record," April 23, 1926. The newspaper clipping is through the courtesy of Rev. D. C. White, Berlin, Pa. It was reproduced by "Laurel Messenger," May 1973, page 6.

Recently Dr. E. C. Saylor of Berlin was able through the courtesy of Hon. S. A. Kendall to secure from the War Department at Washington photostatic copies of the payrolls of the two companies of soldiers who enlisted in Berlin for the War of 1812. Finding these documents very interesting historically, he very kindly consented to give them for publication feeling that many more would be interested to know just who the men were who served from this district, comprised of the

following townships: Brothersvalley, Stony Creek, Allegheny, Northampton, Southampton, Larimer, Fairhope, Greenville, Elk Lick, and Summit.

To his knowledge it is the only complete list in Somerset County, at least there is none given in local histories, and if in existence, is filed away among some private papers and is not generally known. The only list known is only partial, from the reminiscences of Henry Young, published in "Bedford and Somerset County History" by Welfley.

These two companies in question were commanded by Captain Casper Keller and Captain Peter Lane. Captain Keller's company was known as the Allegheny Blues and the men were required to furnish their own equipment while Captain Lane's company were furnished their equipment.

These two companies left Berlin on Saturday, Sept. 12, 1812, escorted on their way by a number of citizens for several days. The first day's march was as far as Somerset, where they were quartered with the citizens. The second day they marched as far as Stoystown, where they were again lodged with the citizens and where they were joined by Captain Richard McGuire's company of Cambria County. The third day or Monday they proceeded as far as Laughlintown, Westmoreland County, thence to Greensburg, Turtle Creek, and Pittsburgh. Near Greensburg they were joined by Captain Jonathan Rhoads' company, partly from Somerset and partly from Jenner Township. From there they went to Buffalo, N.Y., by way of Meadville, where they did the duties assigned them, until finally they were ordered to seek winter quarters, which they did in their old homes in Somerset County enduring great hardships in doing so. Due to the deep snows encountered on the way and the sparsely settled country, they encountered some difficulty in securing food and shelter.

It is believed that many of these soldiers are buried in Somerset County and do not have proper recognition by having the flag they so gallantly defended placed on their graves on Memorial Day. Some may lie in unmarked graves, while others are sadly neglected. Anyone knowing of such graves should communicate the fact to the proper authorities that they may have due recognizion for their patriotic services at this late date.

The following salaries were paid the different classes as shown by the payrolls: captain, $40.00; lieutenant, $30.00, ensign, $20.00; sergeant, $8.00; corporal, $7.33; while the privates received the magnificent sum of $6.66, and then were paid only two months' salary for practically four months' service.

Following is a copy of a payroll for Captain Peter Lane's company for the period from Sept. 25 to Nov. 24, 1812. This company was attached to the Second Regiment (Purviance's) Pennsylvania Infantry.

P100001

Name	Rank				
Peter Lane	Captain	George Coleman	musician	William Troutman	Private
William Atcheson	1st Liet.	Daniel Bowman	Private	Peter Shumaker	Private
Michael Keefer	2nd Lieut.	James Meheffe	Private	Peter Mosholder	Private
Samuel Lane	1st Sergeant	Henry Shumaker	Private	Jacob Mowry	Private
John Walker	2nd Sergeant	Benjamin Brubaker	Private	Michael Mull	Private
John Harden	3rd Sergeant	Nicholas Shultz	Private	Henry Ware	Private
William Knepper	4th Sergeant	Philip Brown	Private	Abraham Shaver	Private
Andrew Pletcher	1st Corporal	William Welch	Private	George Mull	Private
John Ulm	2nd Corporal	Jacob Hiner	Private	Peter Boyer	Private
Aquila Wiley	3rd Corporal	John Close	Private	Charles Corns	Private
Hiram Pendelton	4th Corporal	Benjamin Rhemer	Private	Frederick Coleman	Private
Jacob Hyle	Musican				

The following is a copy of a payroll of Captain Casper Killer's company for the period from September 25 to November 24, 1812. This company was attached to the Second Regiment (Piper's) Pennsylvania Riflemen.

Name	Rank				
Casper Keller	Captain	Samuel Wigle	Private	Henry Marker	Private
John Brubaker	1st Lieut.	Henry Young	Private	Jonathan Camp	Private
John Crawford	Ensign	Jeremiah Morgan	Private	Abraham Brant	Private
Michael Dively	1st Sergeant	George Cassel	Private	Jacob Glass	Private
John Rouch	2nd Sergeant	John Miller	Private	John Philson	Private
James Ferrel	3rd Sergeant	Peter Gibler	Private	George Swartz	Private
John Faidley	3rd Sergeant	Christian Wingert	Private	Nicholas Gibler	Private
Micharl Werley	1st Corporal	Henry Menges	Private	Frederick Wible	Private
George Coleman	2nd Corporal	Peter Rhoads	Private	Nicholas Wertz	Private
Peter Haldeman	4th Corporal	Adam Quier	Private	Jeffe Ringler	Private
Jacob Haldeman	4th Corporal	Daniel Hamelton	Private	Thomas Flenn	Private
Conrad Antibus	Hornblower	John Lowrey	Private		
Jacob Dively	Drummer	Jacob Lowrey	Private		

Robert Philson of Berlin served as a brigadier general in this war.

The following names, dates, and inscriptions are taken from burial stones in Old Lutheran Cemetery, Berlin. The information gives all that is legible.

Thomas Baldwin Rev.
dr Peter Fuinfrick Rev.
James Ferrell 1812
Peter Lane 1812
Michael Umberger 1812 SWC

The following names, dates, and inscriptions were taken from burial stones in Old Reformed Cemetery, Berlin, Pa.

Frederic Suder Rev. S.S. 1755
William Atchesin 1812-No-ST-S.S.

John Brant 1812 S.S. Died 1882
William Shunk 1812 S.S. 1784
John Philson 1812 N.S. 1793
Jacob Glessner Rev. N.S. 1732
John Groff 1812 W.S. 1776
Thomas Atchison Rev. Center
John Bowman 1812-S-corner-died 1847
Sabastian Groff Rev. W-S 1747
Jacob Bauman Rev. Center 1755
Jacob Weyand Rev. center 1745
Adam Miller Rev. E-S 1750
Jamaher Hauger Rev. E.S. 1749 (first name not legible ?)
John Brant 1812 W.S. 1766
Simon Shunk Rev. N.S. 1749
Robert Philson Rev. N.S. 1756
Jacob Anawalt 1812 No-S-S.S.

Farm Graves and Plots

Farm	Name	War
Brothersvalley Township:		
Boyd Burial Plot	George Kimmel	Revolutionary
Joe Croner Farm	John Mosholder	Revolutionary
Newt Saylor Farm	Jacob Walker	Revolutionary
Robert Glessner Farm	Christian Brant	Revolutionary
Black Burial Plot	James Black	Revolutionary
Jacob Glessner Farm	Peter Brubaker	Revolutionary
Peter Hay Farm	George Countryman	Revolutionary
Northampton Township		
Jacob Emerick Farm	Philip Burbach	Revolutionary
Glencoe	Benjamin Kritchfield	Revolutionary
Allegheny Township		
Deeter Burial Plot	John Deeter	Revolutionary
Fairhope Township:		
Burkett Burial Plot	Jacob Burkett	Revolutionary
Cober Burial Plot	Jacob Good	War 1812
Brothersvalley Township		
Musser Burial Plot	Jacob Meyers	War 1812
Brothersvalley Township		
Mary Werner Farm	Benjamine Boyer	War 1812
Northampton Township		
Peter Hay Farm	Jacob Countryman	Militia
Brothersvalley Township		

Deceased Veterans of All Wars in Rural Cemeteries

Veteran	Inscription	War
BROTHERTON BLACK		
James Black	1803	Revolutionary
BROTHERTON PIKE		
Moses Yoder	4-20-1838 9-7-1911	Civil War
Solomon J. Baer	1827—1885	Civil War
Leroy C. Landis	8-7-1932—10-21-1973	Korean
Kenneth Piell		WW II
Ephram C. Walker	1847—1919	Civil War
Charles F. Rayman	3-10-1842—2-4-1899	Civil War
John H. Martens	2-28-1830—9-7-1924	Civil War
Edward R. Kabina	1931—1950	Korea
Wm. P. Stahl	1901—1950	U.S. Peacetime
Floyd F. Beeghley	-20-1897—8-18-1964	WW I
Harrison Hoffman	1889—1967	WWI
Earl R. Lambert	1895—1973	WW I
Henry Earle Zerfoss	12-23-1918—7-3-1962	WW II
Hilton B. Mosgrave	1892—1946	WW I
Oscar Mosgrave	1894—1918	WW I
David Rayman	6-24-1812—12-20-1862	Civil War
Henry Snyder	7-2-1865 21 yrs.	Civil War
CRONER CEMETERY		
Jeremiah P. Hartman	9-13-1893	Civil War
MACDONALDTON		
Joseph G. Krepelka	3-7-1920—12-7-1960	WW II
Karl Krepelka	1896—1974	WW I
RUSSIAN ORTH. GREEK PINE HILL		
Mike Turko	10-6-1890—12-29-1953	WW I
FRITZ CEMETERY		
Henry W. Saylor	3-10-1853—5-21-1928	Civil War
Herman Fritz	Died Dec. 14, 1862	Civil War
Franklin Enos	1830—1912	U.S. Peacetime
Franklin Bittner	not legible	Civil War
Charles Bittner	3-19-1840—7-24-1907	Civil War
John Gary	1846—1925	Civil War
Jacob Sipe	3-21-1899	Civil War
Grave—fence	not legible	Civil War
Zachariah Walker	1834—1904	Civil War
Mack Reich	not legible	WW I
James Young Nedrow	8-23-1900—5-20-1962	WW II
Bruce B. Ackerman	1916—1972	WW II
Henry C. Wahl	1842—1929	Civil War
Stanley R. Nedrow	1918—1968	WW II
PINE HILL LUTHERAN		
Ralph C. Goodman	1901—1950	WW II
Jonathan Walker	—5-17-1874	Revolutionary
Russell R. West	1896—1956	WW I
Joseph P. Samuel	1890—1921	WWI
Ralph Blubaugh	1921—1945	WW II

Veteran	Inscription	War
? Coleman	17—1830	Revolutionary
Not legible	Not legible	Revolutionary
John N. Roil	Not legible	Revolutionary
Earl W. Shaffer	19-17-68	WW II
Not Legible	Not legible	Revolutionary
Andrew Eckman	3-21-1897—8-2-1965	WW I
Not legible	not legible	Revolutionary
Alvin C. Turney	1891—1943	WW I

HAY'S CHURCH

Veteran	Inscription	War
Simon Hay	?—9-12-1903	Civil War
Benjamin Hay	?—2-8-1874	Civil War
? Walker	?—2-25-1862	Civil War
Augustus Madary	5-5-1824—8-5-1883	Civil War
Samuel Arnold	7-10-1884—4-30-1905	Civil War?
Ralph F. Lyons	1936—1968	Vietnam
Joseph Walker	1842—1923	Civil War
Conrad P. Baker	3-15-1825—5-12-1894	Civil War
Herman Boger	8-3-1843—9-27-1905	Civil War
Samuel D. Brant	1835—1921	Civil War
William Dickey	?—1-24-1900	Civil War
Chauncey Bowman	1837—1904	Civil War
Henry C. Hay	1844—1932	Civil War
Uriah Fritz	1—10-19-1864	Civil War
R. Earl Dickey	9-8-1892—1-18-1961	WW I
Preston J. Firl	1923—1944	WW II
Samuel M. Saylor	10-22-1840—11-6-1912	Civil War
Benjamin G. Hay	1840—1923	Civil War
Herbert G. Walker	1887—1965	WW I
Edward P. Broeseker	1888—1964	WW I
William F. Braeseker	1892—1965	WW I
Gus A. Broeseker	1896—1970	WW I
George D. Brant	6-2-1832—3-30-1901	Civil War
Norman B. Werner	1897—1918	WW I
Lloyd S. Hoover	1892—1936	WW I
Charles F. Wright	1876—1941	USA Cuba
James H. Wright	8-10-1928—1-4-1951	Korea

BEECHDALE—

Veteran	Inscription	War
John Orn Jackson	Feb. 8, 1900—Aug. 9, 1962 Pvt. US Army	WW I—WW II
Guy F. Gardner	1-17-25—7-20-65 S. Sgt. US Air Force	WW II—Korea
Milton W. Cover	1893—1949 Pvt. Mtr. Trans. Corp	WW I
Earl M. (Rooky) Sivits	1899—1967 Pvt. Co C Inf. Div AEF	WW I
J. P. Henghon	not legible 42 Co NY Inf.	Civil War
Abraham M. Sevits	1838—1913	Civil War
James P. Lynch	1879—1967 Cpl USS Iowa, USS Pierrie Panama	Spanish-American
Charles E. Fogle	1889—1975	WW I
Harvey F. Kendall	1895—1939 Co C 110 Inf 103F Sig Bn	WW I
Floyd C. Caler	2-13-97—10-3-65 Cpl. Qt. M Corps Md	WW I

Veteran	Inscription	War
Donald G. Stayrook	12-14-46—10-24-67 AO 2 US Navy	Vietnam

CAMERON CEMETERY—FAIRHOPE TWP.

Veteran	Inscription	War
Jacob Smith	Co. F. 138 Pa. Inf.	Civil War
Franklin L. Beck	Pvt. 28 Inf. 1st. Div. 5-28-1918	WW I
Simon Smith	5-7-1815—10-20-1917	Civil War
Esta Boyer	Co. D 3 P.H.B. Md. Inf.	Civil War

MT. OLIVE CHURCH

Veteran	Inscription	War
Benjamin R. Meyers	1891—1954 Sgt. Co. A. 15th Reg. Engineers	WW I

SARVER I—ALLEGHENY TWP.

Veteran	Inscription	War
William J. Custer	Pvt. Alien Enemy Int. C.P.	WW II
Benjamin R. Glessner	1887—1950 Pvt. Co. B 133rd Inf.	WW I
Frederick Dupont	Pvt. G. 1 21st. Reg. Inf. No marker	Spanish-American

SARVER

Veteran	Inscription	War
George Sarver	—	WW I

GLEN SAVAGE

Veteran	Inscription	War
Alvin G. Bruck	1923—1969	WW II
W.O. Gus E. Kern	1915—1943 1st Armored Div.	WW II
George Shaffer	not legible	Civil War
Carl A. Oberg	died 5-2-1897 66 yrs. 4 mo. 14 dys	Civil War

MT. ZION CEMETERY

Veteran	Inscription	War
Amos Ware	1837—1923	Civil War
Franklin D. Manges	Co. D. 133 regt. Pa. Vol.	WW I
Wm. G. Shaffer		Civil War
Benjamin Frazer		Civil War
James A. Deeter	Pvt. Btry. B 97 AAA Gun Bn.	Vietnam Korean Conflict
Jeremiah Keller	Dec. 22, 1862 Aged 31 yrs. 15 days.	Civil War
James P. Glessner	1847—1932	Civil War
Henry Suder	Col 3rd Pa. Vol. 1830—1871	Civil War
William Kelley	Died Aug. 5, 1915 Co O 49th Reg Pa.	Civil War
Lester H. Foust	1891—1934 Sgt. CO 24th C.O.T.S.	WW I
Clyde R. Foust	CY US N R F 5-3-1890—10-18-1962	WW I
Joseph Sarver	Died Dec. 26, 1913 71 yrs. 8 mo. 14 dys.	U.S. Peacetime

Veteran	Inscription	War
George Foust	Died 5-31-1900	Civil War
John Flamm	Born 9-11-1894	WW I
John R. Burkhart	1895—1970	WW I
Oliver Meyers	8-9-1841—2-11-1923	Civil War
Warren Ray Clites	Cpl 5th Armd Div. 1914—1943	WW II
Roy S. Browning	Pfc. 14 Inf. 8-13-1908—9-7-1947	WW II
William D. Browning	1900–1964	WW II
Clyde E. Logsdon	Pvt. 45 Engrs 6-1-1890—12-28-1947	WW I
Ralph E. Groft	1-3 Co. 153 Depot Brig. Feb. 16, 1894- May 24, 1969	WW I
Kirby Robb Deeter	1949—1975	Vietnam
Dalton Sheirer	1911—1950 Sgt. 387th FTR. S.Q.	WW II
Solomon F. Bittner	1897—1964	WW I
Clark G. Robb	2nd Lt. Co A 4 Sup & Trans Bn Jan 14, 1943—Jan. 24, 1965	WW II
John Mowry	1836—1925	Civil War
Thomas B. Bent	Died Aug. 1875, 29 yr 6 mo 5 dys	Civil War
Names unknown	Killed in old South	Civil War
Two Negro	Penn RR Tunnel now Allegheny Tunnel	

MILLER CEMETERY—Ralph Miller Farm—Present Owner Chas. Miller

Mahlon R. Miller	Pvt. 333 I.N.F. Born 4-29-1911 Died 10-16-1948	WW II
Fred W. Chaney	TEC/5 US Army 1941 to 1945	WW II
Daniel A. Miller	Pvt. Comm H171 GAR 1861 to 1865 Died 4-14-1896 Age 56 yrs.	Civil War

Farm Graves and Plots

Brothersvalley Township—		
Flickinger Farm	Tony Flickinger	Civil War
Landis Farm	Samuel Stahl	Civil War
Simon Foust Farm	Chauncey Queer	Civil War
Croner Burial Plot	Jeremiah P. Hartman	Civil War
John Snyder Farm	David Rayman	Civil War
John Snyder Farm	Henry Snyder	Civil War
Francis Maust Farm	Jeremiah J. Brant	Civil War
Francis Maust Farm	Herman W. Lape	Civil War
Northampton Township—		
Walter Emerick Cemetery	John J. Smiley	Civil War
Fichner Burial Plot		
Lewis Hartman Cemetery	Adam Cook	Civil War
	Daniel Canton	Civil War
	Reuben Moser	Civil War
	John Crosby	Civil War
Johnsburg Cemetery	George Markel	Civil War

Johnsburg Cemetery	William Hittie	Civil War
Johnsburg Cemetery	Jones Brown	Civil War
Dog Hill-Holley Farm	John Kennel	Civil War
Mance Cemetery	Daniel Bauman	War of 1812
Allegheny Township		
Old Sarver Burial Plot	George Sarver	Civil War
Henry Miller Farm	Daniel A. Miller	Civil War
Fairhope township		
Burkett Burial Plot		
½ mi. W. Grenke Farm	Noah Tipton	Civil War
Kammerer Burial Plot	Esta Boyer	Civil War
Kammerer Burial Plot	Jacob Smith	Civil War
Kammerer Burial Plot	Simon Smith	Civil War

Deceased Veterans of All Wars in Rural Cemeteries

Lot No.	Veteran	War
MT. LEBANON CEMETERY		
74	John M. Stief	Civil War
7	Herman Hinemayer	Civil War
21	Dennis Leydig	Civil War
23	William Mobley	Civil War
88	Dennis Landis	WW II
28	Samuel Mishler	Civil War
40	John S. Miller	Civil War
42	Gidion Mull	Civil War
108	Charles Lane	WW II
44	Dennis Ackerman	WW I
56	Wilbur C. Brant	WW II
56	Simon Bauman	Civil War
69	William Crosby	Civil War
59	Willis Schrock	Spanish-American
22	Irene Werner	Spanish American I
231	Charles Shipley, Jr.	WW II
227	Merle Sayler	WW II
134	Frederick Jones	WW II
232	Jerry Saylor	WW I
217	Lee E. Imler	WW II
201	Carl Raupach, Jr.	WW II
188	Ray Miller	WW II
157	Adam Sembower	WW II
160	Lee Deist	WW II
3	Herman B. Coughenour	Civil War
2	Melvin Close	WW I
1	Edwin Petinbrink	WW II
149	Wesley Shipley	WW I
14	J. E. Deal	Civil War
36	Jehu Bauman	Civil War
47	Joel Bauman	Civil War
61	Jesse Cook	Civil War
64	Herman Martz	Civil War
136	E. H. Deal	Civil War
65	George Keefer	WW I
66	Alfred Bittner	WW I

Lot No.	Veteran	War
66	Herman Bittner	Civil War
197	Blasien Burkhart	WW I
167	Charles Smith	WW II
168	William Broadwater	WW I
133	Henry William Deist	WW I
129	George Bittner	Civil War
106	George Lantz	WW II
65	Harry A. Keefer	WW I
58	Raymond Mull	WW II
227	Charles Bowman, Jr.	Korean War
169	Henry Franklin Hyde	WW II
99	Alvey Martz	WW I
117	Harry H. Deist	Korean War
275	Lewis W. Hartman	WW II
21	Carl C. Miller	Vietnam

Veteran	Inscription	War
NEW BALTIMORE—OLD CEMETERY		
Frank Foller	1860-1929	GAR
Lewis Wambaugh	1836-1922	GAR
Jacob Harbrant	1842-1905	GAR
John Hochard	1843-1922	GAR
Thomas Hachard		WW I
Augustine Engbert		WW I
Louis Wambaugh	1789-1887	GAR
Robert R. Roddy		GAR
Andrew Werner		GAR
Henry Burkett		GAR
Michael Zellers	1834-1915	GAR
Jacob Wambaugh	1812-1895	GAR
John Connor		WW I
John Fisher	1856-1944	GAR
Richard Restley		WW I
Unknown		WW I
NEW BALTIMORE—NEW CEMETERY		
Tom Hillegass		WW I
Paul Housel		WW II
Louis Rudolph		WW II
Joaquin Coderich		WW I
Russell Topper		WW I
John T. Long		WW I
Michael Jordon	1839-1921	GAR
Cyril Straub	Killed in Action	WW II
John J. Will	Killed in Action	WW II
Joseph L. O'Brien		WW I
Mark Wolfhope	Killed in Action	WW II
Joseph P. Wolfhope		WW II
Irvin M. O'Brien		WW I
Edward Buratty		WW I
William A. Will	Killed in Action	Vietnam
Vincent Hickey		Korea
John Driggs		WW II
Robert Smith		Vietnam
Harold Grasser	Killed in Action	Vietnam
George Topper		WW II
John Fisher		WW I
Merle T. Barnett		WW II

Veteran	Inscription	War
Paul Zellers		WW II
Paul Fochtman		WW II
Edmund Felten		WW II
Blanch E. Straub	Gold Star Mother	WW II
Verge Will	Gold Star Mother	WW II
Irene Grasser	Gold Star Mother	Vietnam

Deceased Veterans, I.O.O.F. Cemetery, Berlin

Section	Veteran	War
#A	Andy Hummel	WW II
13	Harry J. Pritts	WW II
14	Paul L. Landis	WW II
19	Clyde M. Bruck	WW II
24	John V. Chutis	Vietnam
26	Chester E. Keith, Sr.	WW II
-	John J. Harrison	WW II-Korea-Vietnam
-	Myron L. Queer	WW I
#B		
-	Maurice Strawn	WW I
11	Joseph A. Deitz	WW II
13	Devon E. Landis	WW II
14	Paul H. Robley	WW I
15	Archibald R. Underwood	WW I
-	Richard C. Deitz	WW II
-	William V. Harris	Vietnam
#C		
1	J. D. Gumbert	Korean
-	Richard Hittie	Korean
6	Ferris Deeter	WW II
11	David Lawson	WW II
-	William Schaeffer	WW II
-	Harry D. Maust	Vietnam
-	Ross Hendershot	U.S. Peacetime
-	Harvey E. Lohr	WW I
-	William W. Schrock	Korean
#1		
3	Simon Hoffman	Civil War
9	William Johnson	WW II
10	Samuel J. Brant	Civil War
11	Thomas Miller	Civil War
19	Wm. A. Brant	Civil War
22	Joseph Landis	Civil War
24	Marques E. Steere	Civil War
#2		
3	Charles A. Floto	Civil War
6	Augustus W. Hoffman	WW I
7	Samuel S. Forney	Civil War
14	John Baughman	Civil War
16	Abner Schrock	Civil War
18	John O. Sarver	WW I
23	James Graham	WW I
-	Ralph E. Floto	WW I
-	Leonard E. Sarver	WW II
#3		
1	Michael Ream	Civil War

Section	Veteran	War
7	Rev. Ephriam Dickey	Civil War
7	John M. Schrock	Civil War
13	Joseph Gindlesperger	Civil War
14	Frederick Platt	Civil War
15	Richard Stull	WW II
15	Elijah Stull	Civil War
19	William S. Dively	Civil War
19	Harry Fisher	WW II
20	Howard B. Cober	Spanish-American
28	Ira Harding	WW II
#4		
1	Emanuel Atcheson	Civil War
7	Isiah Wechtenheiser	Spanish-American
8	Henry Stuck	Civil War
9	Josiah D. Brandt	Civil War
11	Tobias Fisher	Civil War
26	Arthur Eisenhower	WW I
27	Orville Adams	WW II
28	Emanuel Custer	WW I
-	Leopold Albright	Civil War
#5		
4	Stanley Poorbaugh	Spanish-American
5	Eugene P. Caton	WW II
16	Thomas W. Philson	WW I
17	Levi Lease	Civil War
17	Donald E. Platt	Korean
18	Fred W. Berkebile	WW I
27	Howard W. Latta	WW I
28	Harry L. Walker	WW I
-	Edgar B. Philson	WW I
#6		
2	William P. Atchison	Civil War
2	Joseph B. Atchison	Civil War
13	Peter M. Hauger	WW I
17	Joseph Baldwin	Civil War
19	Harry P. Hay	U.S. Peacetime
22	Levi Queer	Civil War
25	Walter M. Brown	WW II
28	George E. Hummel	Korean
-	Howard S. Engleka	WW I
#7		
9	Chester Louis Odell	WW II
12	Jeremiah Zorn	Civil War
13	Henry Schockey	WW I
14	Abraham Murset	Civil War
16	Joseph Imhoff	Civil War
20	Charles H. Miller	Civil War
20	Herman A. Miller	Spanish-American
21	Henry Ringler	Civil War
27	Michael James Duskin	U.S. Peacetime
#8		
1	Dr. J. K. Miller	Civil War
2	Michael A. Zorn	Civil War
7	Benjamin Brubaker	War of 1812
7	Mark Collins	Civil War
8	John Brubaker	War of 1812
11	Frederick H. Buckman	WW I
11	Menery Muhlenberg	Civil War
22	Leroy Diveley	WW I

Section	Veteran	War
24	Richard Driggs	WW II
27	Robert McIntyre	WW I
28	Graham Hamilton	WW I
28	John Holland	Spanish-American
#9		
3	J. G. Cardill	Civil War
10	Dan M. Ball	Civil War
12	Chauncey Long	Civil War
13	Eli Ball	Civil War
14	Lewis Cope	Civil War
14	Ephraim Fremmd	Civil War
15	Edward D. Cassel	WW I
16	William Rubright	Civil War
19	John Bridegum	Civil War
25	Ralph E. Baker	WW I
#10		
2	Jacob Krissinger	Civil War
3	Aaron Johnson	Civil War
5	William Bender	Civil War
9	J. P. Dively	Civil War
11	Augustus Floto	Civil War
14	William Johnson	Civil War
14	Joseph Johnson	Spanish-American
16	Solomon Grine	Civil War
18	Benjamin Philson	WW I
18	Robert Philson	WW I
18	Samuel Philson	WW I
19	John Groff	Spanish-American
28	William Matthews	WW I
29	Andrew J. Barwatt	WW II
#11		
2	William Knepper	U.S. Peacetime
17	William J. Penn	Civil War
18	Eugene K. Bowman	WW I
19	Glenn Bingner	WW I
19	Lewis Miller	Civil War
21	Robert L. Henderson	WW II
29	William Merrill	WW II
28	John J. Holliday	WW I
-	Harry Dively	WW I
-	Carl Gindlesperger	WW II
-	Oscar Coleman	WW II
-	William D. Maul	WW II
-	Bert Walker	WW I
-	Floyd W. Everett	WW I
#12		
3	Charles Dively	Civil War
6	C. P. Heffley	Civil War
8	Jack Hiner	War of 1812
10	William H. Landis	Civil War
23	Bert Z. Stuck	WW I
28	Jerome Dickey	Civil War
#13		
1	Casper Esken	Civil War
5	Jacob Kimmel	War of 1812
13	James McQuade	Civil War
13	Solomon Brant	Civil War
15	George Kossel	Civil War
15	David T. Brooks	WW I

Section	Veteran	War
18	Sylvester K. Landis	Spanish-American
19	Harry J. Thomas	WW II
#14		
1	George Fogle	Civil War
2	Joseph Heffley	Civil War
5	George Johnson	War of 1812
5	Peter Heffley	War of 1812
6	Henry Glessner	Civil War
7	Samuel Imhoff	Civil War
12	Frank McQuade	WW II
14	Warren Fogle	Spanish-American
15	Richard L. Pugh	WW II
22	Lorene C. Berkley	WW I
28	Vernon O. Troutman	WW II
32	John Hoyle	WW I
-	Paul R. Berkey	WW II
#15		
6	Herman Dively	Civil War
7	John A. Groff	Civil War
8	Zac T. Heffley	Civil War
9	John C. Helf	Civil War
11	Jeff M. Ringler	Civil War
13	John Ginder	Civil War
16	Joseph E. Mason	Civil War
22	Frank C. S. Ream	WW II
27	Paul Evans Bills	WW I
29	Dalton E. Foust	WW II
30	Paul Edward Moore	WW II
-	Elmer A. Leecy, Sr.	WW II
#16		
1	Samuel Ferrell	Spanish-American
2	William M. G. Stoner	Civil War
3	Edward Zorn	Civil War
4	Albert Heffley	Civil War
7	Clement Engle	Civil War
7	Frank McGinness	WW I
9	John Henry Shumaker	War 1812
20	Stuart Heffley	WW I
27	Robert E. Bingner	WW I
27	Harry O. Binger	WW I
29	Charles E. Blubaugh	WW I
29	Frank R. Blubaugh	WW I
29	Norman Miller	WW II
31	William Keller	WW I
-	George W. Bender	WW I
-	Roy A. Blubaugh	WWII
	Glenn O. Kimmel	WW II
-	Donald F. Buckman	WW II
-	Harvey C. Cameron	WW II
-	Richard C. Bingner	WW II
#17		
6	Henry Young	War of 1812
9	Conrad Hochstetler	Civil War
10	Chauncey Yutzy	Civil War
15	Josiah Meyers	Civil War
20	Jacob J. Zorn	Civil War
24	Emile Barr	WW I
29	Henry Dickey	WW I
32	Harry M. Zorn	WWI

Section	Veteran	War
#18		
1	James Green	Civil War
2	Joseph Mosholder	Civil War
3	John C. Weimer	Civil War
3	David C. Meyers	Civil War
6	Dr. John Kimmel	War of 1812
11	Henry J. Baer	Civil War
15	John Lester Wilhelm	Vietnam—WW II
15	J. Lester Wilhelm	WW I
#19		
1	Robert R. Griffith	Civil War—no marker
2	Adam Queer	War of 1812—no marker
2	Fred Houdux	Mexican War—no marker
3	John Baker	Civil War
4	Peter Bearl	Civil War
8	Boyd E. Bowers	WW I
29	Charles Gindlesperger	WW I
#20		
1	Elwyn B. Mays	WW I
4	Howard Deist	WW II
9	John Hummel	WW II
13	John Arthur Smith, Sr.	WW II
15	Lewis E. Wetmiller	WW I
15	George G. Cross	WW I
19	John H. Glessner	WW I
20	Dorothy E. Hoerr	WW II
24	John A. Miller	Civil War
28	Carl Lynn Walker	Vietnam
31	Lewis L. Gartner	WW II
-	Curtis Lafferty	WW II
#21		
1	Eugene Coleman	WW II
13	J. Edward DeHaven	WW I
16	Walter Sorber	Grand Army Republic
17	Iris H. Miller	WW I
20	Homer Hay	WW I
-	Freeman Tipton	WW I
#22		
1	Frank A. Swanson	WW I
7	Mildred J. Forney	WW II
7	James C. Forney	WW II
9	Ray D. Kimmel	WW II
14	Walter L. Reitz	WW I
-	Harry R. Forney	WW I, WW II, Korean
#23		
1	Charles Foor	U.S. Peacetime
3	Alfred Brocht	WW I
6	Elmer Walker	WW I
11	Merle Boyer	WW I
12	Bruce Boyer	WW I
15	Harry Weld Neesham	WW I
-	Ancel W. Painter	WW II
#24		
3	George A. Seibert	World War I
15	Philip Austin Shaffer	Spanish-American—WW I
21	Byron J. Hay	WW I
21	W. Gordon Hay	WW I
21	M. Edgar Coughenour	WW I
-	John A. Custer	WW II

Section	Veteran	War
#25		
7	Karl Nelson	Korean
9	Philson D. Collins	WW I
10	Donald Musser Kimmel	WW I
12	Howard E. Weller	WW I
20	Hayes S. Ayers	Spanish-American
-	Harry M. Glessner	WW I
-	George Sheavley	WWI
#25		
1	Milton E. Weimer	Spanish-American
3	Ira Ferner	WW I
5	Claude A. Shelbauer	WW II
8	Paul S. Castner	WW II
-	Merle G. Custer	WW II
-	Charles R. Brown	WW II
#27		
7	George I. Lafferty	WW II
8	Floyd E. Beal	WW II
9	Harry J. Boehm	WW I
-	George I. Lafferty	WW II
28	Charles B. Sproull	WW II
-	Frank A. Boucher	WW I

NOTE: This listing is maintained by Harry Fisher Post, Number 445, American Legion, Berlin, Pa. Any omissions or corrections can be directed to them. Prepared for book form 6-24-76. Their records cover all wars for Allegheny, Fairhope, Northampton, and Brothersvalley Townships and New Baltimore and Berlin Boroughs.

Levi Shoemaker

Copied from the "Berlin Record," Volume 28, Berlin, Somerset County, Pa., 1-12-1912:

The first citizen of this county to reach the century mark in life celebrated his 100th birthday anniversary on Tuesday. Almost the whole town and community turned out in the teeth of a fierce blizzard to do his honor by attending special anniversary exercises held in the Reformed Church of Berlin, of which he has been a life long member. While many called at his home during the day and evening to pay their respects and tender congratulations, Mr. Shoemaker was also the recipient of a number of congratulatory letters and telegrams from all over the country. Among them was a message conveying congratulations and best wishes from Governor John K. Turner of Pennsylvania, which the centenarian prizes very highly.

Other messages were from relatives and former Berlin citizens residing at a distance and who were unable to be here on this important occasion.

Levi Shoemaker was born on Jan. 9, 1812, his birth being recorded in German text in an old book or record of the Reformed Church, which dates back to the year 1777. In this old book, which is remarkably preserved, is also recorded his baptism in March of that year, stating that the child was named Levi. His name has appeared ever since in the church records for many years as elder, deacon or Sunday school superintendent. He was always an active worker in the church and a regular attendant upon all the services, even at his advanced age making it a point to be out on communion Sundays.

Last Sunday, Jan. 7, however, on account of severe weather, a special communion service was held at the Shoemaker residence, which was a very impressive occasion.

Being a member of the Reformed Church for almost a century, the fact suggested to Rev. W. C. Sykes, the pastor, the holding of a suitable testimonial on the anniversary of Mr. Shoemaker's 100th birthday, in which the people of the community should be invited to participate, and along this line the anniversary exercises of Tuesday were carried out.

Mr. Shoemaker awoke on his hundredth birthday in good health and fine spirits, keen with delightful anticipation of the pleasant events of the day. About nine o'clock, while a severe blizzard was raging, the old gentleman stepped from his home into an open sleigh and was conveyed to the Reformed Church. He shook the snow from his great coat and blew a hearty breath into his hands, rubbed them, and beamed a wonderful smile upon the reception committee of little girls.

A prayer by the Rev. John Brubaker, D.D., a native of Berlin opened the services. The Rev. W. C. Sykes read the

Standing, left to right: Dr. W. A. Garman, W. A. Powell, Alex Musser, J. J. Ross, William Ream. Seated: Dr. H. Garey, Charles Ream, Levi Shoemaker (with cane), Emil Masters, J. S. Heffley. Levi Shoemaker was 97 at the time of this photo. The others were all in their eighties.

recollections and reminiscences of Mr. Shoemaker, which the centenarian had related to him:

I was born either in the house opposite the Methodist Church, which stood between where the station and the Miller barn now stand, or the house this side of the Nelson Gary property. I attended the common schools of the town, at that time pay schools. The first day I attended school I got a paddling because I would not say my A & B & C's. My father was a tailor and I learned that trade. My mother sometimes wove cloth. In 1832 I was a member of the Lafayette Cavalry Co., which drilled on the area now occupied by the cemetery. Clement Engle was the First Captain of the company; Samuel Philson was Second Captain; I was First Sergeant; Daniel Weyant of White Horse was one of the company.

I was the first man in Berlin to own a buggy. It was without a top and was bought from Judge Black's father.

The ordinary means of travel was by stage coaches, which ran from Cumberland to West Newton. When eight or nine years of age I saw at Somerset a large parade of soldiers from Westmoreland County and from here. I remember of visiting Stoystown when I was about sixteen and Mt. Pleasant when I was about twenty years old. At Meyersdale there was a log house, a grist mill, and a saw mill.

In 1839 I made a trip on horseback through Ohio, where I saw a few Indians and a railroad near lower Sandusky, the rails of which were of wood. My first ride on a railroad was from Garrett to Confluence when I was about sixty years old. My earliest recollection of Berlin is that all told, big and little, young and old, there were here 200 people. In extent the town was not half of its present size. The buildings were constructed of round logs and contained a living room and a kitchen, between the two being a large fire place five or six feet long. The Gardill and Hillegass houses are among the oldest. Another old one is the Donner house, where the restaurant now is, and was owned by George Johnson, a great great grandfather of the misses Irene and Barbara Johnson, and was a preaching place for Methodists and Albrights.

My father owned and repaired the Hillegass house on the south side of east Main street. The next house towards the east stood where Stewart Cable now lives, and on the other side of the street was the last house where Peter Miller lives. The cemetery was then a grove. On the west of town, the last house was where widow Landis lives, and on the site of the L. J. Esken home there stood a tavern. While a little beyond, near the Somerset road, there was a small house owned by widow Crawford. On the north of the town there were small log houses where William Spencer now lives, owned by Philip Daum, father of Jacob J. Zorn's mother; also, where Albert Swatzendruber and John Musser now live were small houses. There was no Beulah road at that time. On the south side of town there was a small house on the site of the old Lutheran parsonage, then the residence of the Lutheran minister.

On Spring avenue there was a house where O. O. Cook now resides and a spring house in the rear of what is now the Jefferson Altfather home. Back of where Ed. Walker lives was a large tract of timber.

In the country the first farm houses south of town were those on the properties now owned by J. O. Stoner and Warren Mason. At Frank Glessner's, a Mr. Greeting then lived.

The Brubaker farm, now owned by Daniel Zimmerman, then belonged to John Kuhns, great grandfather of William Koontz, who cleared the land. There was also a small house on what is now the George P. Brubaker farm.

The first store was kept where Falkner's Hotel now stands. There was a tavern and store where Brallier's drug store is now located. In these stores maple sugar sold for four and five cents a pound and white sugar sold in the form of loaf sugar.

For fuel our fathers burned pine knots and punk, which they lit striking steel on flint. For light, dirty lard was used. Flour was ordinarily made by grinding grain in coffee mills. Sometimes flour and salt were brought from eastern cities. The journey occupied a week or more. The vegetables raised were largely cabbage, potatoes and turnips. A large amount of beef and pork was eaten.

There were a large number of tanneries in town. Where Samuel Heffley lived was a tannery and two others were located where the willow tree stands. Nearly all the leather was used at home. There was a weaving mill owned by Stern and Lane where Peter Miller now lives. And there was also one on the site of the Berlin Hotel, owned by Squire Miller.

Fuller mills were operated at Hay's Mill and below where Wesley Hay now lives. The women carded and spun wool at home.

Benjamin Brubaker, father of the late Alex Brubaker, was a blacksmith and carried on at Garman's corner. Jacob Lowery built the first brick house where Dr. Shaw now lives and had a blacksmith shop on the rear of the lot. Casper Keifer was a carpenter and built the first house were A. K. Johnson now lives. Jacob Kimmel, father of the late John O. Kimmel, was squire, the jail being at Somerset. We voted where widow Gardill now lives. I cast my first vote for Andrew Jackson.

I think the people now are better than formerly, the result of more moral education.

There were a few Indians in this section. The first family that improved the farm beyond J. O. Stoner's had an experience with Indians. One evening, when the father was away from home, looking out through a small window, the mother saw two Indians prowling around. She extinguished the lights and when the Indians went to the rear of the house she took her children and went out by the cellar way, hid under the nearby road bridge and stayed there till morning.

Formerly there were two school houses in town, one at the Reformed Cemetery at the line fence between the mill and the cemetery, inside the fence. This was built of logs. It was about 30 x 30, had two or three windows and a large open fireplace which would hold a log six feet long. The school teacher lived upstairs and had his kitchen in the rear of the school house. The other school house was on the site of the present primary school building.

At times schools were taught where George P. Brubaker and Harvey Hay now live. Jacob Shober, grandfather of Madison Shober, was one of the first teachers. Others whom I remember were Cyrus Krin-gler, Josiah Shaw from Westmoreland County, Mr. Brisco and daughter Mary. The school teacher was the best man they could get. Three months constituted a term and pupils paid $2.00 to $2.50 apiece. When free schools were established the term was six months and the teacher was paid $20.00 per month. The U.S. spelling book was a text book, arithmetic and mental arithmetic were emphasized, and the Bible was considerably used in the schools.

The first minister whom I remember was Rev. Geisey. In those days it was customary to hold an early prayer meeting on Sunday, most of the church members being praying members. Among those who took an active part were Aaron Miller, John Musser, Josiah Poorbaugh, Peter and Valentine Hay. One year when I was about sixteen, I was sexton of both the Reformed and Lutheran churches. I received $1.50 a year from the Reformed and $3.00 from the Lutherans, because the latter had more services. Then the sexton had to chop the wood, make candles, top the candles, scrub the church once a year, keep up the fences and clean the grave yard.

It was with some hesitancy that Mr. Shoemaker left the church, as he desired to linger a while longer to mingle with the people who came to pay him homage. But a birthday dinner had been prepared at the home of his son-in-law and daughter, Mr. & Mrs. Cyrus Musser, and he was wanted there as the honored guest. The table was surrounded by some of his children, grandchildren, great-grandchildren, and one great great granddaughter, besides a few close friends. On the table was a huge birthday cake adorned with a hundred small candles, which was cut and presented to relatives and friends as favors. All during the afternoon Mr. Shoemaker was in high spirits, being delighted with the events of the day. Much of his time was devoted to inspecting his presents, reading messages and letters of congratulations, and conversing with friends.

After all the excitement of the day he retired and slept well, awakening the next morning refreshed and none the worse for the pleasant ordeal through which he passed the previous day. Among his progeny who came from a distance were his son J. K. P. Shoemaker and wife of Homestead, and their children, Mr. & Mrs. Houghton Robson, of Charleston W. Va., and their grandchild, Betty Jane Nelson; Mrs. Ralph Davis of Homestead; Mr. Daniel Shoemaker of Donora; Mr. Oden Shoemaker and wife, and Miss Kate Carns, of Pittsburgh.

Mr. Shoemaker enjoys remarkably good health for a person of his age and retains his mental faculties to an astounding degree. His vision is good and he spends much time in reading, but of late his hearing has become somewhat impaired. He gets about quite spry and when the weather permits may be seen walking about doing some little odd jobs in his yard and garden.

This account on Berlin and vicinity was given to R. Mognet by Mr. Oran Kister of Somerset. Mr. Mognet, Somerset, Pa., provided this copy.

Berlin Borough

Early history taken from records in Berlin Borough office. Certificates of the oaths and affirmations of the borough officers required.

"We the subscribers duly elected Chief Burgess and Town Council do severally swear or affirm that we will support the Constitution of the United States and the Commonwealth of Pennsylvania and to perform the duties of our respective offices with fidelity.

"Sworn and subscribed before me the 26th day of March 1833."

Ordinances of Berlin Borough, April 2nd, 1833.
Pursuant to adjournment members of corporation met at the house of W. P. Carrol, Chief Burgess, at which time and place the following ordinances was passed.

S. A. Philson, clerk

The original ordinances, shown in first minute book were in long hand, written and adopted from time to time as needed. Not all are legible and some were not copied. A revised copy of ordinances was made in 1885, numbering one to thirty-four and some of interest were reproduced here.

The following ordinances revised and enacted by the Burgess and Town Council of the Borough of Berlin, for its proper government, are published for the information of all concerned; and all former ordinances are hereby repealed:

#6. That a fine of one dollar shall be imposed on the owner or owners of any horse, mare, gelding, or jack, who shall suffer any of them to run at large within the limits of the Borough.

#7. It shall be the duty of the Burgess to collect a license of five dollars from the keeper or owner of any and each stallion, kept for the service of mares within the Borough limits, such service only allowed in a close stable or barn, arranged for that purpose. Said license to be collected at the beginning of the season.

#8. That if any owner or keeper of any stallion kept for the service of mares shall suffer such stallion to stand hitched in any street or alley of this Borough more than five minutes at any one time, or any such person shall exhibit or train such stallion in any street or alley of said Borough, the owner, keeper, or person so offending shall be liable to a fine of $5.00 together with cost of suit for each and every such offense.

#9. It shall not be lawful for any person or persons to hitch a horse or horses in or on any street or alley for any unreasonable time, under a penalty of one dollar for each offence.

#10. It shall not be lawful for any cows or cattle to run at large within the Borough limits after dark, under a penalty of 50 cents for each offence.

#14. The owner of any dog within the Borough limits, shall be personally responsible for all damages or accidents caused by such dog in any way whatsoever.

#17. It shall be unlawful for any person or persons to ride or drive faster than a trot, within the Borough limits, under a penalty of $1.00 for each offence.

#23. It shall not be lawful for any person or persons to congregate or loiter about the outside of any church, during services, within the limits of the Borough, under a penalty of one to five dollars for each offence.
Enacted and subscribed this 24th day of February, A.D. 1885.

Jac. J. Zorn,
Burgess
C. A. M. Krissinger
Wm. H. Menges
George Fogle
Council

M. A. Collins,
Secretary
March 11, 1885

These ordinances with amendments remain in effect today, numbers one to thirty-three.

NOTE: We have learned that the W.P. Carrol home is presently occupied by Olive Baughman on Main Street.

A "Cesspool Committee" was appointed by Burgess and Town Council of Borough of Berlin to enforce requirements on construction and use of privy vaults. Violators liable for fine of not less than $25.00 or more than $100.00 plus costs.
Passed this 19th day of September 1904.
Attest: Don Kimmel, Secretary
Approved this 26th day of September A.D. 1904.
R. P. Collins, Burgess

Economy Telephone Stock Company Franchise

An ordinance was granted to the Economy Telephone Stock Company of Somerset County, Pa., the privilege of erecting its poles on the streets of the Borough of Berlin, Pa.

Twelve sections cover the ordinances enacted by the Burgess and Town Council of Berlin, Pa.

Passed the seventh day of December, 1903.
Attest: Don M. Kimmel, clerk
Attest: L. J. Esken, Pres.

Approved the first day of February, A.D. 1904.
R. P. Collins, Burgess

An ordinance granted certain rights to the Pennsylvania and Maryland Street Railway Company or assigns

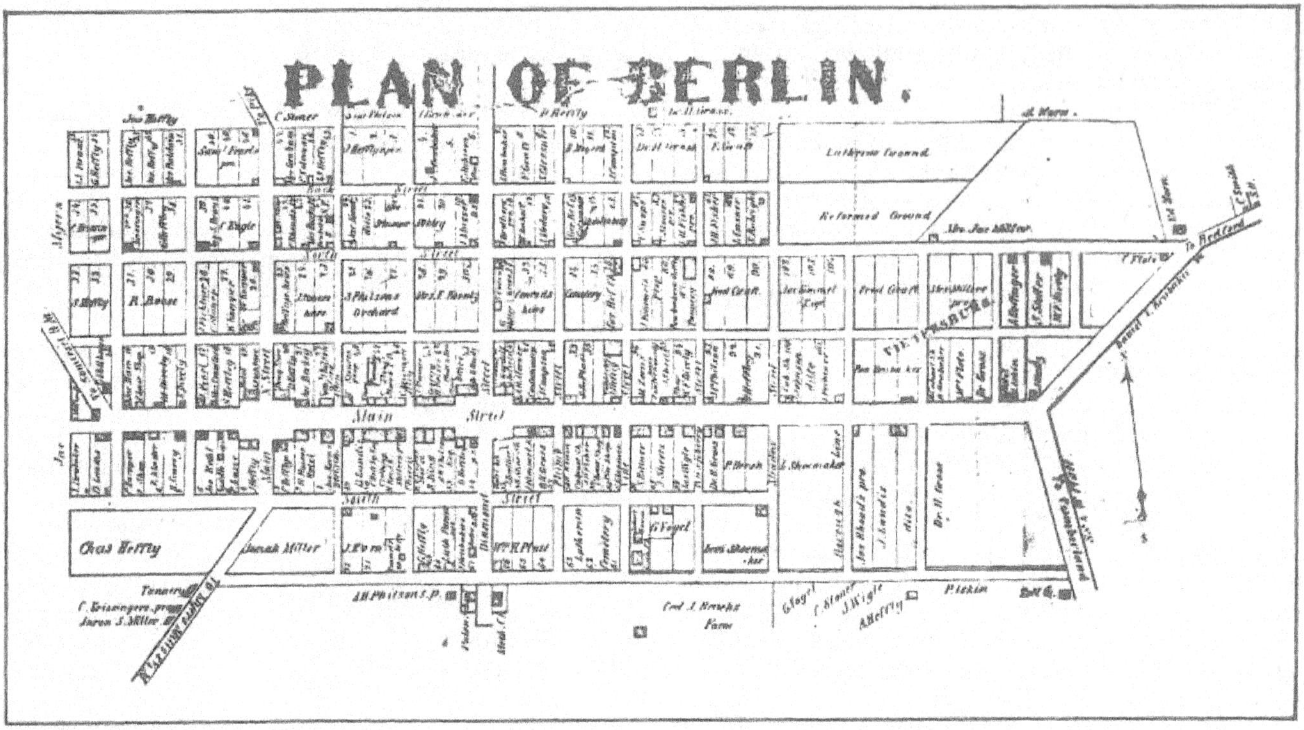

Map of Berlin Borough

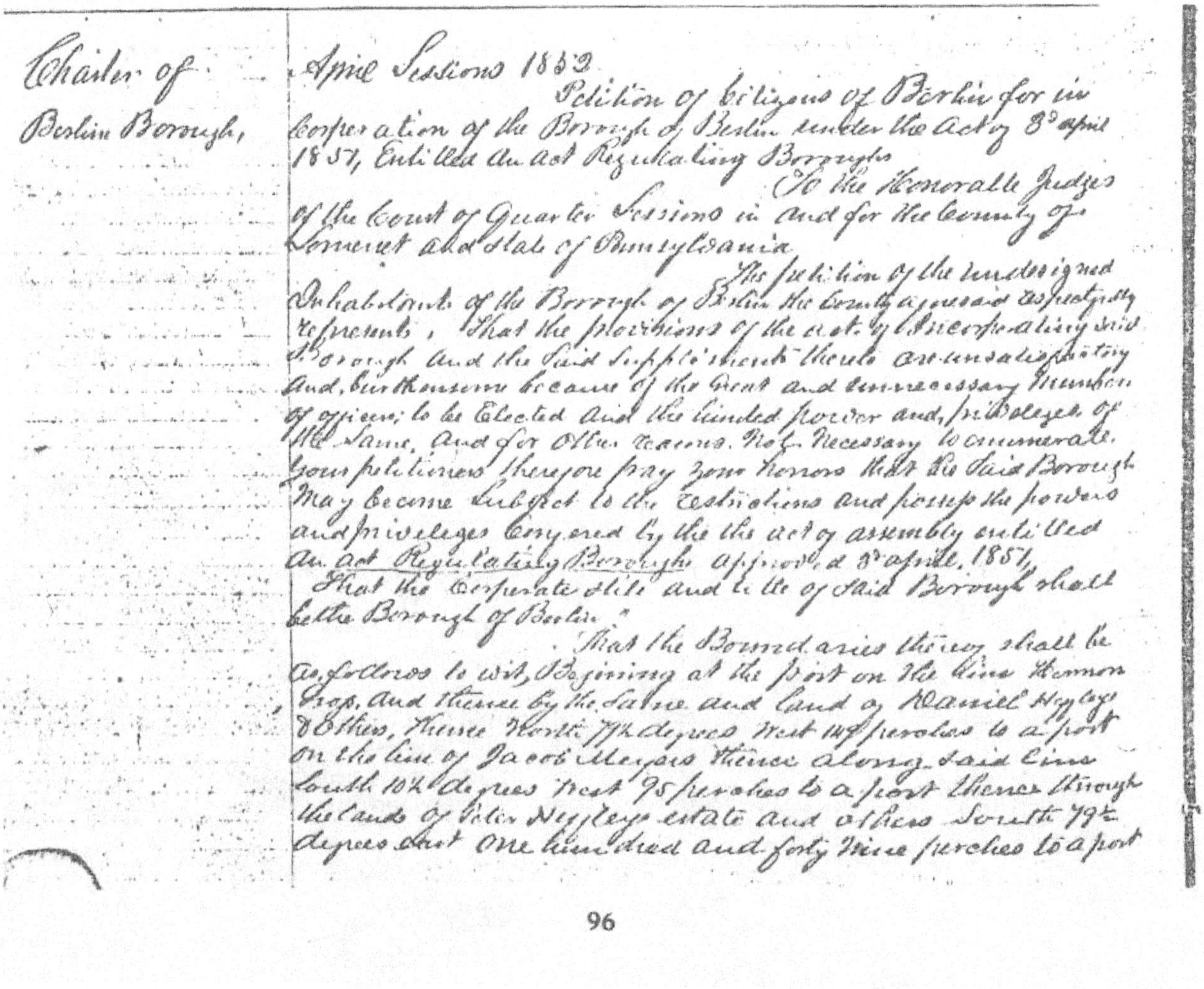

Charter of
Berlin Borough,

April Sessions 1852

Petition of Citizens of Berlin for in
corperation of the Borough of Berlin under the Act of 3d april
1851, Entitled An act Regulating Boroughs

To the Honorable Judges
of the Court of Quarter Sessions in and for the County of
Somerset and State of Pennsylvania

The petition of the undersigned
Inhabitants of the Borough of Berlin the County aforesaid respectfully
represents, That the provisions of the act of Incorporating said
Borough And the said supplement thereto are unsatisfactory
And burthensom because of the Great and unnecessary Number
of officers; to be Elected And the limited power and privileges of
the same, And for other reasons. Not. Necessary to enumerate.
Your petitioners therefore pray your honors that the said Borough
May become subject to the restrictions and posses the powers
and privileges Conveyed by the the act of assembly entitled
An act Regulating Boroughs Approved 3d april, 1851,
That the Corporate title and title of Said Borough shall
be the Borough of Berlin."

That the Boundaries thereof shall be
as follows to wit, Begining at the point on the line of common
Trap, And thence by the Same and land of Daniel Wigley
& Others, thence North 79½ degrees west 149 perches to a post
on the line of Jacob Meyers thence along said line
south 10½ degrees west 95 perches to a post thence through
the lands of Peter Negleys estate and others south 79½
degrees East One hundred and forty Nine perches to a post

96

thence a line along the east end of the old town north Fourth degrees
east 95 perches to the place of beginning That its corporate officers shall
be One Burgess and one Assistant Burgess Three Councilmen to
be designated the four Council One Street Commissioner and
Such Other officer as are now authorized and elected in the
several townships of Somerset County, aforesaid Provided that in
Case of a Vacancy of any officer by death or otherwise the corporate
officers Shall supply said vacancy until next Annual
Election That the Election of Borough and other officers shall
be held at the time and line and place now appointed by
law, for the Choice of Inspector of the General election election
And that the provisions of the former charter of the former Borough
May be annulled by the Court Sofar as they are in Conflict
With the provisions of said Act regulating Boroughs, and with
the amendments and alterations of the Charter asked for in
in this petition

Michael G Dively	Washington McGahan	A. Compton
Samuel Thilson	Frederick Geary	Wm Dively
Alexander Heyley	M A Brubaker	Jacob Barkey
Samuel J Allison	David McGahan	Solomon Glessner
Samuel H Geary	James C Shabbart	Wm Knepper
Jacob Saner	Henry Reitms	Wm P Carrol
Chaney Kantz	Philip Young	Peter Lane
Aly. Brubaker	John Heyley	Edward Zorn
Aly H Thilson	Jacob Kimmel	Ann Miller
John N Smith	Fred Gross	Wm Inshogg
Philip Shumber	Fred Gro	John G Hinchman
Jacob Emil	Jos H Leas	John Henderson
John Muser	Chas Kirsinger	Benjamin Sweiter
J C Shaw	David Brokaugh	Henry Willitony
Charles Stoner	Philip Gregnier	Joseph Weind
Charles Zorn	Henr Heiner	Theodor Kimmel
Jacob E Weiner	J P Wilson	John Bether
George Hoyle	Wm H Platt	Charles Heyley
J. Platt	Herman Grep	John Paton
J H Reidt	John Kupright	Henry Humter
Samuel E Dively	Peter Knepper	Henry F Swope
J. S. Fisher	John Heyley	Elmanuel Master
Geo B Armstrong		A J Horner

26th April 1853 Publication ordered, And, now, to wit 7th February
1853, Be it Ordered and Decreed that the Borough of Berlin be Subject
to the restrictions and possess the Power Privileges Conferred by
the act of Assembly entitled "An Act regulating Boroughs" approved 3rd
April 1851, and it is further Ordained and decreed that the provisions
of the former Charter of the Said Borough shall be and are hereby
annulled by this Decree So far as they are in Conflict With
the act of Assembly aforesaid   By the Court
                                              Jno J Schell
                                                  Clerk
Recorded 14th March 1853, In Minutes of Quarter Sessions

            Recorded 16th April 1863 E K Haines Recorder

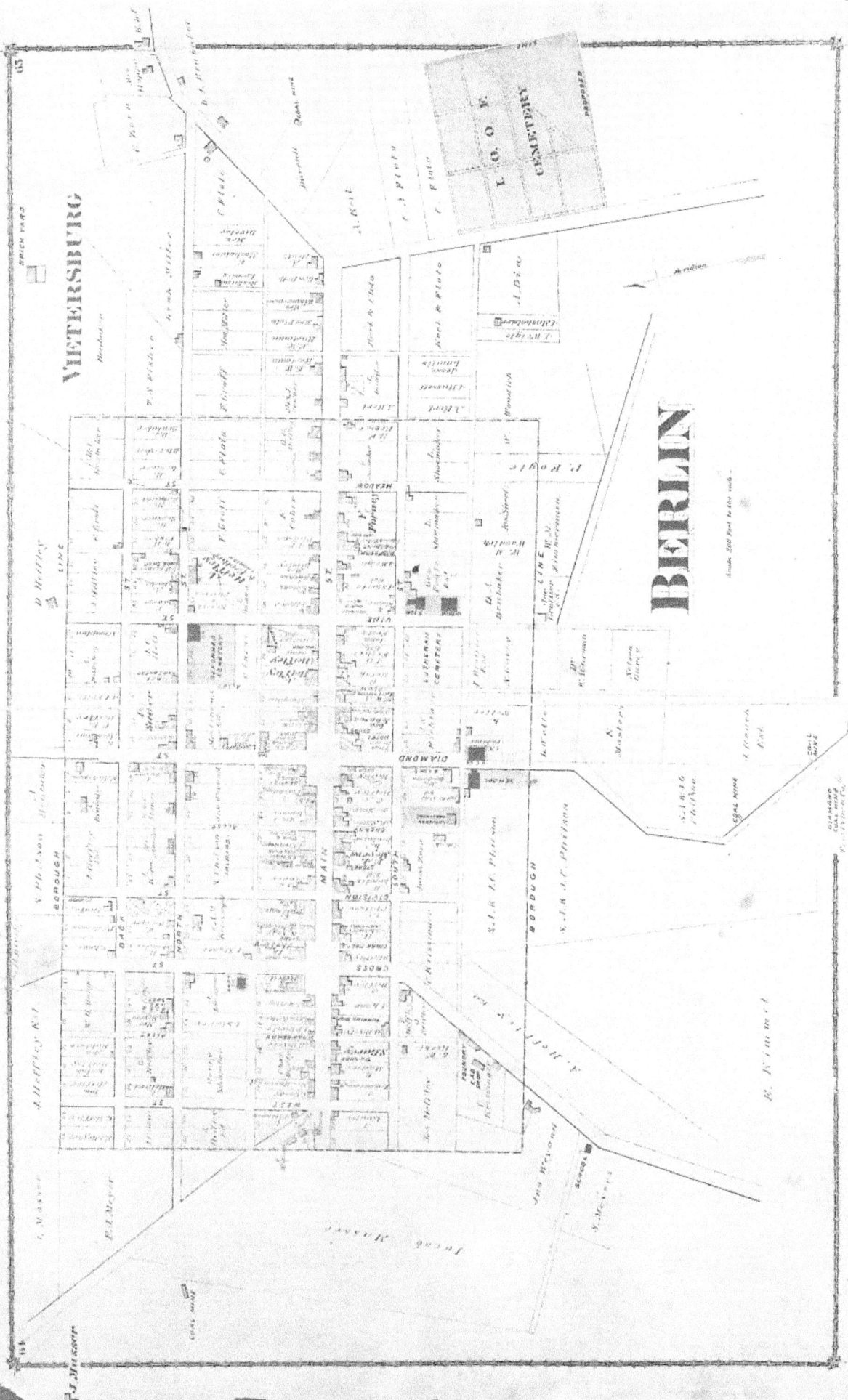

Walker map of Berlin borough (1860)

to construct and operate an Electric Street Railway in the Borough of Berlin, County of Somerset, and the State of Pennsylvania.

Ordained and enacted into a law this 9th day of March, 1907.

Z. T. Kimmel
President of Town Council

Attest: G. E. Fogle
Acting clerk of Council
Approved this 9th day of March, A.D. 1907
Ed. B. Walker
Burgess

Taken from minute book 1903 to 1914

Special Council meeting of July 15th, 1903 Berlin Borough Council voted to purchase an electric light plant for $8,800.00. July 20, 1903 Council voted to bond town for sum not to exceed $15,000.00 to buy and install plant. Special meeting of August 1903 Council fixed meter rate for electric light at 10 cents per thousand watts; $1.00 mimimum rate for under 10 lights; over 10 lights 10 cents each to be minimum. No meter connected for fewer than five lights, no meter rent to be paid.

On 23rd day of December Council approved an Ordinance to buy electric power from Pennsylvania Electric Company. Said Pennsylvania Electric Company not to deliver said power direct to Berlin consumer.

Berlin Water Co.

Name of corporation "Berlin Water Company, Inc., April 29, 1874. However, no lines were laid until 1901 or 1902. Its beginning was as follows:

We, the undersigned, being all the incorporators and stockholders of the Berlin Water Company, do hereby call a meeting of the corporators and stockholders of the said company, for the purpose of organization and other purposes, to be held at their office in the city of Pittsburgh, County of Allegheny, Pa., at three o'clock P.M. on the 20th day of December A.D. 1901. Capital stock $20,000, 200 shares, par value $100.

Name	Residence	No. shares
William H. Allen	Pittsburgh, Pa.	33
O. P. Shupe	Mt. Pleasant, Pa.	34
J. Wade Shupe	Mt. Pleasant, Pa.	34
T. N. Seaton	Mt. Pleasant, Pa.	33
Edw. H. Allen	Berlin, Pa.	33
W. A. Kalp	Mt. Pleasant, Pa.	33

Ordinance conferring privileges granted by Council July 27, 1902 to install lines, etc., and maintain water system. Borough to have right to purchase all Water Company property following a 60 day notice in writing on an agreed upon price. Around 1911 the principal stockholders buying into the Water Company were from Berlin.

The J. G. Gardill tract of 325 acres was bought at public sale October 17, 1922 for $2,175. The Joel Landis tract of 80 acres was leased for 99 years at $150 a year

rental. An agreement made with heirs to Mrs. Bessie W. Caton for purchase of the "Caton tract" of 150 acres for sum of $1,650.

At a special meeting of June 29, 1959, Berlin Borough Council adopted ordinance #154 approving the acquisition of all shares of Berlin Water Company capital stock by the Municipal Authority of the Borough of Berlin. This has since been a borough-operated corporation.

Adam Miller A Justice of the Peace

By D. C. White, Berlin, Pa.

Adam Miller born in Germany, May 14, 1750, landed in America in 1773, served as sergeant in Captain Clapsaddle's Company of Maryland Militia in Revolutionary War, thence to Brothersvalley, where he was commissioned justice of the peace at Berlin in 1791. His J. P. Docket was in care of his grandson, Francis Miller, then passed to his great-granddaughter, Mrs. Blain Hyde, of Bedford, Pennsylvania.

The following marriages were performed by Adam Miller, J. P., from 1791 to 1798.

Andrew Heck and Sarah Boone
Adam Kaufman and Cinnie Miller
Solomon Kimmel and Elizabeth Brubaker
John Stievler and Elizabeth Foust
Peter Smith and Elizabeth Shanafelt
John Blough and Nellie Barkey
Christian Wagaman and Margaret Keefer
Yost Leydig and Hanna Griesing
Casper Statler and Mary Lambert
Alexander Hay and Rebecca Bird
Jacob Schneider and Susanna Heiple
Frederick Fisher and Mary Foust
Conrad Suder and Katherine Suder
John Bemableblout and Eva Ward
Joseph Hostetler and Susanna Sever, 12 May 1794
Michael Ross and Susanna Good, 1 Jul. 1794
David Bennett and Katherine Sheets, 19 Aug. 1794
George Ankeny and Mary Putman, 1794
Adam Keffer and Julia Kitzmiller, 1794
James Sprague and Susan Rice, 25 Jan. 1795
Peter Foreman and Katherine Haines, 22 Mar. 1795
Michael Markfelt and Mary Boose, 5 May 1795
Matthias Beck and Eve Kaufman, 17 May 1795
Frederick Bittner and Katherine Eiler, 5 June 1795
Philip Shultz and Eva Shuck, 9 June 1795
Jacob Smith and Katherine Lebold, 9 June 1795
Michael Cable and Barbara Smith, 5 Jul. 1795
Joseph Riley and Mary Hebliglasner, 4 Jan. 1796
John Miller and Lillian Husband, 17 Jan. 1796
Daniel Bower and Elizabeth Stiffler, 19 Jan. 1796
David Zimmerman and Katherine Shultz, 23 Aug. 1796
John Bowser and Magdalena Bittner, 8 Nov. 1796
Daniel Baker and Sally Tressler, 25 Dec. 1796
Ludwig Baer and Catherine Shiler, 10 Jan. 1797
John Manges and Barbara Miller, 11 Apr. 1797
Adam Kaufman and Elizabeth Gardner, 11 Apr. 1797

Edward Stoy and Mary Neff, 14 Apr. 1797
Michael Keefer and Katherine Palm, 3 May 1797
George Friend and Mary Magdalena Knavel, 7 June 1797
Alexander McVicker and Jane Taylor, 28 Aug. 1797
Henry Bittner and Barbara Donner, 27 Mar. 1798
Jacob Sell and Katherine Cashman, 13 May 1798
John Draver and Barbara Barkinson, 13 June 1798
John Bittner and Rosanna Shaulis, 10 Jul. 1798
Andrew Rambo and Susan Kieffer, 7 Aug. 1798
Joseph Kaufman and Haley McGraw, 12 Oct. 1798
Jacob Hostetler and Mary Shultz, 16 Oct. 1798
Horonamus Bridigum and Susanna Bowman, 16 Feb. 1798

NOTE: Adam Miller resigned as J. P. in 1798 after his election as representative to the General Assembly. He was subsequently reelected to the Assembly in 1799, 1800, 1801, 1802. In 1808 the family moved from Berlin to Bedford County. Adam Miller died at Buffalo Mills Feb. 2, 1827 with interment at Berlin German Reformed churchyard. He and his wife, Rosanna Kirschner, 1765-1839, had eight children. Executors advertised in Somerset "Herald," January 1829, that they would sell the estate of Adam Miller, the White Horse Tavern, atop the Allegheny Mountain, 14 miles east from Somerset and six miles from Berlin, in Allegheny Township.

Ludwig Smith and Susanna Shenafelt
Jacob Glessner and Mary Foust
Jacob Kaufman and Mary Forsythe
Simon Brant and Mary Spriggs
John Dietz and Eva Sertan
Peter Walker and Charlotte Romesburg, 13 Nov. 1792
Peter Barnhart and Susanna Washabaugh, 24 Nov. 1792
Michael Ream and Catherine Glessner, 27 Nov. 1792
Casper Keller and Elizabeth Brandt, 18 Dec. 1792
Abraham Whipkey and Mary Lambert, 25 Dec. 1792
Philip Hager and Barbara Hull, 4 Jan. 1793
Christian Miller and Magdalena Blough, 25 Jan. 1792
George Lambert and Elizabeth Stahl, 23 Apr. 1793
Simon Slagal and Rosanna Klingaman, 13 May 1793
John Sutmeyer and Susan Bittner, 14 May 1793
Jacob Good and Susan Smith, 18 June 1793
James Watkins and Katherine Hen, 3 Jul. 1793
Martin Werner and Barbara Berkey, 16 Jul. 1793
David Livingston and Annia Mishler, 12 Jul. 1793
Jacob Faith and Elizabeth Hauger, 23 Jul. 1793
Ludwig Sherer and Barbara Springer, 17 Sept. 1793
Samuel Clark and Margaret Manges, 17 Sep. 1793
John Whipkey and Katherine Lenhart, 22 Oct. 1793
Henry Whipkey and Elizabeth Kieffer, 29 Oct. 1793

Alexander H. Philson, Justice of the Peace
1801-1873

The first native-born son of Berlin to gain prominence in his hometown was Alexander H. Philson. He was born in Berlin in 1801 and was justice of the peace in Berlin for over 30 years. Many of the oldest documents of the borough and many papers of business transactions in the early days of the borough bear his signature. He had the honor of being the first burgess of Berlin borough.

Alexander was the son of Robert Philson who emigrated from Ireland, and was the father of Samuel A. Philson, the grandfather of William F. Philson and the great grandfather of Bertha Philson Landis. He married Eleanor Crigler. Many others of his descendants are Berlin residents today.

A sample page from Alexander Philson's court proceedings.

First page from Alexander Philson's marriage book

101

Horace Bunn Philson

"Address of Welcome" Given by H. B. Philson at Berlin's Old Home Week Celebration in 1908

It is scarcely necessary for me to say in behalf of the people of Berlin and Brothersvalley Township, you are welcome to our town, our homes, and our hospitality.

The work we have done, the program we have prepared for your entertainment, speaks louder than words of our appreciation of your home coming and hope that your stay may be a pleasant one. This includes you all, whether born and raised here or located here in after life, makes no difference. We want you all to feel you are our boys and girls.

There is a cord that draws us to our old home and its hallowed associations—an indefinable longing that, no matter where we are called, what fame, wealth or success we have achieved in life, entwines its tendrils around our affections and will not let go.

This sentiment is beautifully expressed in the "Old Oaken Bucket." How dear to my heart it is. When you are entering the shadow and the sands of life are running low, your last thoughts will be of the old home and its associations—they will brighten your dimmed vision, put elasticity in your feeble steps and give your bent form a more erect carriage.

Berlin and vicinity has furnished more than its proportion of famous sons and daughters, who have achieved success in almost every walk of life.

In this connection we think a brief history of Brothersvalley and Berlin and also a forecast of the future of the town and township will be appropriate.

The first permanent settler in this vicinity was Phillip Wagerlein, who located on the John O. Stoner farm in 1768—this tract then included the three farms now occupied by John O. Stoner, Warren Mason, and Harvey Gindlesperger. Wagerlein, or Wegley as the family is now called, was followed shortly by George Countryman and Simon Hay. There is some dispute as to whether these settlers preceded Wagerlein or not but neither Countryman or Hay's names appear in the first assessment of Brothersvalley Twp. made in 1772 or 1773, but Wagerlein's does.

Harmon Husband, who first visited this section in 1771, wrote a full account of his first coming into what is now Brothersvalley Twp. He says on the 5th of June,

1771, he was coming down from the summit of the Allegheny Mountain through or along the valley of a small stream that flowed in a westerly direction, when his attention was arrested by a cloud of smoke that was ascending from behind a hill that ran down into the valley. This at once told him that he was approaching the clearing of a settler and the smoke arose from the burning of brush. As Harmon Husband came from Fort Cumberland and was on his way to find Isaac Cox, a hunter located somewhere north-east of where Somerset now stands. He probably crossed the mountain near the Shultz Distillery, and following the route of the Plank Road, crossed Buffalo Creek near the Hauger farm. Wagerlein's clearing was over the hill between Warren Mason's and Stoner's. His cabin was near where Stoner's farm buildings now stand.

Wagerlein addressed Husband in German but Husband did not understand that language. Wagerlein dropped his German and said in broken English, "Welcome, friend. Where you come?" Husband answered that he was from Hagerstown. "And where you will go in the bush? Come along, you be hungry, you be tired."

Husband even states that in the morning they had venison, boiled potatoes, and boiled rye for breakfast.

Husband was afterwards known as the "Quaker." He put this food on the market and called it Quaker Oats. This was the origin of the breakfast food habit.

At Husband's coming Wagerlein had already harvested two crops and was preparing the ground for for a third, which would make the date of his location of his claim in 1768. Welfley, in his history of Somerset County, says that Berlin was founded in 1784 but there were settlers in this locality as far back as 1769 and possibly a little earlier.

The town was laid out on a tract of land surveyed for Jacob Keffer in trust on a warrant dated July 27, 1784, and on which warrant and survey, the supreme execution Council of Pennsylvania on April 4, 1786, granted a patent to Jacob Keffer and his heirs in trust to the Lutheran and Calvinistic congregations of Brothersvalley Township.

The original article of agreement is on record in Bedford County and contains some curious and laughable provisions. For instance, Section 3 stipulates that each and every descendant of the undersigned owners of the city of Berlin (by the way, they always wrote the word City where it refers to Berlin with a capital C) as Lutheran and Reformed shall forever possess the right to church and school if he depart not from his religion, but should one or the other depart from his religion, so has he lost his right to church and school and it is forbidden to him to sell his right. If that wouldn't prevent backsliding among these frugal and thrifty Germans, we do not know what would.

Section 4 says that each and every possessor of a lot in the city of Berlin shall build a house, with a frontage of at least 22 feet, which shall have a stone chimney so that there may be no danger from fire . . . and be covered with shingles and each and every possessor or owner of a lot must pay to the owners one Spanish Milled dollar of seven shillings and six-pence ground rent. This ground rent is still being paid but not in Spanish Milled dollars.

Now listen to Section 6.

"It is agreed by the owners of the City of Berlin that no tannery shall be built at the spring other than Martin Diveley's tannery and no noxious trade shall be established." They made the original leather brush but in a few months the politicians will be telling us there were no brushes in those good old days.

Of the 17 signers to this agreement all but two wrote his own name, a remarkable fact when not over 50% of the population of the town could read and write, showing these pioneer Germans were of more than ordinary intelligence and education.

The first deed recorded in Somerset County is for lot 56 in the town of Berlin sold to Adam Miller for Fifteen shillings and on annual ground rent of one Spanish Milled dollar. This is the lot now owned by Mrs. Harmon Diveley. Miller represented Somerset County in the Assembly five consecutive terms. from the reminiscences of Henry J. Long, who died in Berlin about 1870, we glean the following:

Long ago he came to Somerset County in 1800, when 10 years old, he describes the first fair held in Somerset County in these words:

"In the year 1808 a fair was held in Berlin. Great crowds of people from all parts of the County were in attendance during its continuance of three days.

"There were no exhibits of any kind at this fair which was held on the Herman Brubaker farm. A race track a mile around was in front of where the present house now stands. Four hourses ran a race which was won by a horse from Ligonier called Ligonier pony. There was fiddling and dancing in all the taverns from morning till night and from night till morning. Among the fiddlers were John Lane, Peter Lane, and Benjamin Troutman from Southampton Township. Each of these fiddlers had his own place where he held forth.

"In short in those days horse racing and frolicking constituted a fair that is not a great deal different than a fair of today.

"This one wound up with a fast foot race for the whiskey between Ludwig Baer and Valentine Lout, who weighed 250 lbs. apiece and were over 70 years old. After a run of a couple of rods, Baer tripped Lout with his foot, both falling to the ground in a heap to the great amusement of the spectators."

Such were the amusements of our forefathers when they assembled for the purpose of having a good time. We are sorry we do not have time to read the whole of these reminiscences.

While the Germans settled, laid out, and named the town (they always called it a city), John Fletcher, an Irishman, was the first or second postmaster and his compensation for 1819 was the magnificent sum of $18.03. Even at that early day the Irish had a habit of sitting up and taking notice where there was a fat office to be given out.

It is no reflection on the other pioneers to say John

Fletcher was the foremost resident of the town in his day. He was a born leader of men and affairs.

He was one of the first three commissioners elected in Somerset County and received the highest vote on the ticket. He also represented the county in the Legislature. He was largely instrumental in organizing the first Sunday school in Berlin and at his death bequeathed a fund to the Lutheran and Reformed Sunday schools for the purchase of Bibles for the scholars as soon as they were able to read.

While active in civil and religious work it appears he had no taste for mustering, as they called it in those days, but most of the settlers took a keen delight in the militia.

We do not know the date the first company was organized but find that as early as 1800 Robert Philson was captain of a military company in Berlin. He succeeded Jacob Saylor as brigadier general of the militia in 1814. He was also in the Legislature and the first Congressman from this district.

He and Harmon Husband were arrested and taken to Philadelphia during the Whiskey Insurrection in 1794—for being leaders in that movement. Husband died in Philadelphia, but Philson was released without a trial.

Welfley in his history says: "It was deemed of sufficient importance to cause the arrest of Harmon Husband and General Robert Philson. The latter was one of the principal citizens of Berlin, at that time already a well established village. We do not entirely know the manner of his offending but among other things that traditions of that day lay at his door is that he erected a liberty pole in front of his house. Another is that he assisted in raising such a pole at Somerset, from which floated a flag bearing the legend 'Liberty and No Excise.' It is also alleged Husband had something to do with the raising of this pole. Philson's trouble may also have been that of a great man in a small community doing too much talking."

Brothersvalley Township, which at this time included the whole of Somerset County and part of Cambria County, had a military company as early as 1777: Henry Rhoads, Captain; Frederick Ambrose, First Lieutenant; Second Lieutenant, Jacob Glessner; Ensign, Philip Cable; Court Martial Men: Jacob Fisher and George Countryman. In the War of 1812 the Allegheny Blues, a Berlin company, tended its services to the government. This was a rifle company commanded by Casper Keller, First Lieutenant; John Brubaker; Second Lieutenant, John Crofford. This company volunteered to a man to go into service.

Peter Lane was also captain of an infantry company that went to the front at this time. His company all volunteered but three. We will not touch on the later military service of our people as you can, no doubt, get any information you desire from parties still living, but Berlin and vicinity were always to the front when there was a call for volunteers for military service. I will not enlarge upon her record in the Civil and Spanish-American War more than to say she is not ashamed of it.

One more incident and I am done with the history of the town—that is, the frost of June 4, 1859, which destroyed the crops and all vegetation in nearly every part of the county. All fruit was killed. The frost came on a Saturday night. By Monday morning the "Frosty Sons of Thunder" concluded they weren't going to starve just yet—even if the price of flour did go from $7.00 to $18.00 per barrel. After the frost Berlin was liberally sown in buckwheat and a crop of 550 bushels harvested. The county sowed a larger area in that grain and raised over 183,000 bushels, or more than 9 bushels for each man, woman, and child in the county.

We are proud of the men we have sent forth. We are proud of our Cabinet Ministers and Congressmen, our judges, our doctors (both medical and theological), our ministers, our professors; our businessmen, our financiers, our farmers, and our lawyers. You know, employing a lawyer is like carrying a revolver in Texas, sort of disreputable, but when you need them you need them mighty bad.

Solomon Coleman, an old Brothersvalley resident who has likely gone to his reward, in a conversation with my father about twenty years ago remarked, "Sam, they say we must send more farmers to the legislature and to Congress before things will improve. The only difference I can see in the farmers we did send is that they can be bought a little cheaper than the lawyers." Do not know whether this reflection is on the lawyers or the farmers. Yes, our lawyers are not the cheap kind, they are high priced and they are generally worth the money.

We have also produced presidential timber, but not being located in Ohio, we could not use it. Dory Kimmel probably had this in mind when he addressed the boys at a political meeting about 40 years ago. He said, "Boys, this is a great and free country. Some of you may be President someday," but, he added as an afterthought, "it's doubtful."

Even old mother Bedford has not been overlooked in the general distribution of good things. When she needed an upright and capable judge we sent that intellectual giant, Jeremiah Black. When she made the second requisition, we furnished a Kimmel, when she made the third request we gave a Baer, who defeated one of her ablest and best-known attorneys, the Hon. John Cessna.

When she needed a superintendent for her public schools we sent Prof. Harry Fischer, the impress of whose work is still felt in that county. When her daughters needed added sweetness we sent Sheetz, the candy man, and when their molars ached from overindulgence in Sheetz products, we loaned her Daniels, the dentist. To use a homely expression it looks a good deal like a case of the tail wagging the dog, but we are willing to keep on wagging.

We do not only furnish our own county with representatives for the Legislature but we have even heeded the call of our Macedonian brethren to come over and help them.

When Venango County needed a Moses to lead the Legislature out of the wilderness of corruption and extravagance, we furnished a Milliron. When an Aaron was needed to hold up its hands we sent Knepper and Floto, two Berlin boys. And if future assistance is needed we still have a Forney willing and capable to undertake the work.

When Fayette County needed a J. Pierpont Morgan, another Berlin boy, E. R. Floto was called. When the county needed a conservative commissioner to overlook affairs, Charles Zimmerman was selected.

When a county wished to devise ways and means to pay for a new courthouse Hiram Hay left his plow standing in the furrow to obey the call and for all I know it is standing there yet. We have no chronic office seekers but when the office begins to seek the man there are some of us with our ears at the phone waiting for the call.

But with all our rejoicing there is a note of sadness— all of our distinguished sons are not here. Some have already crossed the dark river and I wish to pay a special tribute to two of these. Many others are equally worthy, but I know from personal association, the sterling worth of these two young men.

When the western sun sinks into the Pacific its last rays light up a shaft marking the resting place of one of Berlin's brightest and brainiest sons—one who in a few short years of life made a name for himself in his chosen profession, second to none in his adopted state, and who offered himself a martyr to that profession. I refer to Dr. Charles Morrison Fischer. There is another who sleeps in yon silent city on the hill who gave his life for his country in the war with Spain. Morris Stanley Poorbaugh enlisted in the Fifth Regiment, Missouri Volunteers, and after six months' service was discharged with a record of faithful and efficient service. He immediately reenlisted in the U.S. Regular Army and served for three years in the Philippines. His superior officers say that he was one of the best soldiers that ever set foot on these islands. For aught we know, though absent in the body, they are present with us in spirit. Let us each resolve to visit our silent city of the dead at least once during this week of pleasure. Lest we forget. . . . Lest we forget. This is an old town, the oldest in the county, yet what we have accomplished has mostly been during the lifetime of one who is still with us, the venerable Levi Shoemaker, who has almost reached the century mark.

What will be done in the next 100 years? We speak of our timber and coal as valuable assets, but we had to dissipate our resources to realize their value.

Our water and climate are ten times more valuable than our coal and timber ever were. Our coal deposits are only a means to an end. God knew our abandoned coal working would make ideal storage reservoirs but He knew man would never make them without an inducement, hence the coal seams. Our hills and mountains will be clothed with the finest forests of pine, white and red oak, maple, locust, hickory, and chestnut. The forests will be under the joint supervision of federal and state authorities.

Water that is now running to waste will furnish light and heat, irrigate our valleys by an underground system of tile, which experiments have proven to be the ideal method. Impossible you say! I know of one farm in Brothersvalley Township of 160 acres which contains 50 acres . . . that can be irrigated by 3 small reservoirs fed by a never-failing spring, two of them located on the premises.

The whole of the Buffalo Valley can be irrigated by the streams from the mountain and ridge. The water that grows our crops will furnish power to market them, for three fourths of the water used in irrigation gradually seeps back into the stream again. By pressing an electric button in his library the land owner will turn the water from one field into another at his pleasure. He will not engage in general farming but grow fruit, potatoes, or perhaps poultry. His potatoes will be planted, worked, sprayed, dug, soaked, and marketed by electricity generated by his own water power. Eliminate bugs, blight, rot, and drought, and potatoes are so sure a crop that the farmer can estimate within 5 bu. per acre what his crop of merchantable potatoes will be. The bugs, blight, and rot can be overcome by spraying and the drought by irrigation. He will raise from 4 to 500 bushels to the acre and on account of superior quality will not be able to supply the demand.

At or near Ohio Pyle the water after being used over and over again by the Somerset County residents will be collected in an immense reservoir to supply the down river towns. It will be pure, for instead of allowing sewerage to pollute the streams, it will be made a source of revenue, as it now is in Paris, France. Do you say impossible!

New York city is not spending $160,000,000 on her water supply, condemning land for the purpose, including 23 towns, some of them larger than our own. There will be 1000 acres of cranberry bog between here and Shanksville, in the Stony Creek Valley.

That this land is adaptable to cranberry culture is shown by the fact that a Stony Creek farmer has marketed in Berlin as high as 20 bushels of berries in a single season. These grew wild on his farm and if they can be properly ripened are equal in flavor to the famous Cape Cod and Jersey cranberries. Cranberry land is so scarce in the United States that it is now bringing in Massachusettes and Wisconsin $500 per acre in the rough and $1000 after gotten in shape to grow cranberries. The net profits in an ordinary season are $300 per acre. This same land sold 20 years ago for $50 per acre. Someday we will awaken to our opportunities—there is no finer anywhere. God speed that day.

And now I will close with Walter Scott's tribute to our native land:

"Home, home, sweet home.
Be it ever so humble there is no place like home."
We welcome you all back home.

Typed for Dr. E. C. Saylor April 8, 1937.

Berlin Fife and Drum Corps

Rich with historical background, the Fife and Drum Corps continues to bring honor and praise to the community of Berlin. Nowhere in the state of Pennsylvania or in the entire United States has a fife and drum unit continued to exist for so many years. By June of 1982, the corps will prepare to celebrate its 200th anniversary.

In April of 1777, fife and drum music originated in Berlin through the efforts of George Johnson. Mr. Johnson died in Berlin in 1837, at the age of 72.

In 1782, the corps was officially organized. From the earliest years, many well-known residents carried the banners, the fifes, and drums. One of these men was Ralph G. Landis and as the unit continues today a number of succeeding family members are part of the famous unit.

At present and over recent years the unit has been directed by Alfred Queer.

Participation in the Bicentennial Parade in Philadelphia this summer was another of the corps highlights.

The Odd Fellows

The oldest secret society in Berlin is Berlin Lodge, No. 461, I.O.O.F. Its charter is dated November 18, 1851, and the lodge was instituted on January 9, 1852, with the following charter members: Samuel S. Platt, John Paten, L. J. Case, Daniel Heffley, Aaron Miller, Geo. B. Armstrong, Chas. Stoner, Wm. H. Platt, John S. Heffley, Washington Megahan, James C. Leabheart, Henry Shomber, Wm. P. Carroll, Henry F. Swope, Thos. Stewart, Henry Brubaker, Wm. P. Foust, Josiah Zimmerman, Walter Chalfant, John Roberts, Jonathan Statler.

The first officers were S. S. Platt, Noble Grand; John Paten, Vice Grand; Lemuel Case, Secretary; Aaron Miller, Assistant Secretary; Daniel Heffley, Treasurer.

Casper Esken was the first member initiated after the lodge was organized, having joined the lodge February 6, 1852.

The lodge is in flourishing condition with present membership 73. The lodge owns its own building as well as the I.O.O.F. cemetery, one of the finest and best-kept cemeteries in Western Pennsylvania.

Present officers in 1976 are: Thomas I. Maust, Noble Grand; Lewis E. Maust, Vice Grand; C. Edward LaBute, Secretary; Lester Kemerer, Treasurer.

Berlin Lodge, #461, I.O.O.F.

Chartered Nov. 18, 1851

Officers

Noble Grand–Samuel Platt	A. Secretary–Aaron Miller
Vice Grand–John Paten	Treasurer–Daniel Heffley
Secretary–Lemuel J. Case	

Charter Members

Samuel S. Platt	Henry Shomber
John Paten	William P. Carroll
L. J. Case	Henry F. Swope
Daniel Heffley	Thomas Stewart
Aaron Miller	Henry Brubaker
George B. Armstrong	William P. Foust
Charles Stoner	Josiah Zimmerman
William H. Platt	Walter Chalfant
John S. Heffley	John Roberts
Washington Megahan	Jonathan Statler
James C. Leabheart	

Present Membership–74

Cemetery Association

The Odd Fellows Cemetery, Inc., began August 29, 1910, and was dedicated September 17, 1910. Officers of the Association are Jacob J. Zorn, President; C. A. Floto, Secretary; John Groff, Treasurer; and J. W. Gardill, John Groff, F. E. Zorn, Trustees.

The first purchase was one acre from S. S. Platt. It was plotted and laid out by Washington Megahan, James Weigle, Clement Engle, and members of the lodge in May 1855.

There are now (1910) about seven acres in the cemetery plot. The cleaning of the ground was done by the lodge until January 1, 1873, when the Berlin Cemetery Association was organized, in order to care for and beautify the cemetery grounds. Each lot owner became a member.

The first officers were: Albert Heffley, President; John H. Knepper, Secretary; D. A. Brubaker, Jacob J. Zorn, August Kerl, Trustees.

April 1, 1873, a cemetery meeting was held and 21 members paid a membership fee of .68 as the beginning of a permanent fund.

The Cemetery Plot now (1976) contains about 20 acres with paved roadways, an office building (on the site of the old water fountain), and a large tool and machinery shed.

The present officers are:
Otis O. Bockes–President
Robert L. Miller–Trustee & Vice-President
Paul E. Pritts–Trustee and Secretary
Robert W. Fogle–Trustee & Treasurer
Walter A. Johnson–Trustee
Anthony Tallarelli–Trustee
Dale Leydig–Trustee

The superintendent of grounds is Jerry Charlton. Officers and trustees meet quarterly and the annual meeting is held the third Tuesday of every January.

History of Lady Berlin Rebekah Lodge, #277

Written by Rhelda Pritts, Noble Grand

Lady Berlin Rebekah Lodge #277 was instituted January 27, 1921. Mrs. Nathaniel Horner, District Deputy President, Stoystown, Pa., influenced the institution, assisted by Miss Mollie Muhlenberg—a member of the Stoystown Lodge at this time. Mrs. A. B. Cober of Berlin secured the names of 30 petitioners necessary to make the institution possible. At the afternoon session the institution was effected by Anna Kline, State President, assisted by State Marshall, Anna Dudly. There were two past Noble grands from Stoystown, Maude Gardner and Ida Horner, also six past Noble Grands from Sister Hood #256, Windber, Pa. At this meeting the following named persons were duly obligated—signed the Constitution—became members and received the Dispensation for Lady Berlin Rebekah Lodge #277:

Nellie Koontz Cober	Mathaldia Stahl
Nellie Zorn Miller	Daisy Rhoads
Mrs. Elizabeth Muhlenberg	Martha Stahl
Erma Lane	Elizabeth Zimmerman
Cora Miller	Lulu McLuckie
Ida Donner	Mary E. Dickey
Anna Menges	Marie Heffley
Besse Dively	Lulu Dively

Mary Heffley	Harriet P. Shaw
Maggie Fogle	Grover C. Dively
Mary Brubaker	Harry E. Menges
Bessie Fisher	Allan C. Miller
Minnie E. Dickey	Herman C. Heffley
Elsie Krissinger	Harry B. Krissiner
Rose Muhlenberg	Earl K. Brubaker

The President then declared the nomination and election of officers for the first period as follows:
Noble Grand - Elizabeth Muhlenberg
Vice Grand - Cora Miller
Secretary - Nellie Cober
Treasurer - Mary Brubaker
Warden - Besse Dively
Conductor - Minnie Dickey
Chaplain - Elizabeth Zimmerman
Right Supporter to N.G. - Anna Menges
Left Supporter to N.G. - Marie Heffley
Inside Guardian - Lulu McLuckie
Outside Guardian - Daisy Rhoads
Right Supporter to Vice Grand - Harriet Shaw
Left Supporter to Vice Grand - Rose Muhlenberg
Organist - Lulu Dively

At this date, January, 1976, the Order is fortunate to still have one of the first officers with them—Marie Beachley.

By special dispensation at the evening session it was possible to propose names of applicants, report, ballot upon, and initiate candidates. Fifteen more names were added to the membership roll this way:

Ada Baldwin	Pearle E. Hartman
Edward Baldwin	Harold (Hurty) Hartman
Emeline Heffley	Annie Miller
Mary Weimer	Nellie Countryman
Marie Ball	Jacob Countryman
Sadie Ball	Rose Lybarger
May O'Dwyer	Evelyn Smith
Christine Wetmiller	

The degree was conferred for these candidates by the Windber team with Emeline Heffley and Marie Ball traveling the degree.

January, 1976, the Order is fortunate to have five charter members:
Marie Beachley
Nellie Countryman
Marie Dively
Erma Lane
May Weimer

Mae T. Stuck held the office as Secretary of the Order for 34 years. October, 1965, Mae Stuck resigned from this office. Lost her by death December 22, 1968.

Belle Kreinbrook filled the office as Secretary since 1965—11 years.

Grace Altfather filled the office as Treasurer of the Order for 24 years. October, 1965, Grace Altfather resigned from this office.

The following filled the office as Musician for many years:
Myrtle Ball - 15 years
Elizabeth Muhlenberg - 17 years
Fern Maust - 15 years

The following filled the office as Noble Grand for two terms:
Besse Dively
Nellie Miller
Mary Weimer
Nellie Countryman
Mary Dickey
Florence Altfather
Belle Kreinbrook - 1 term at Mt. Pleasant
Naomi Ferner
Rhelda Pritts - present Grand serving second term 1976.

Past District Deputy Presidents:
Nellie Countryman - 3 terms
Geneva Leydig - 2 terms
Mildred Bear - 1 term
Beverly Mothersbaugh - present District Deputy President serving second term for Southern Somerset County

1956 - under direction of Noble Grand Dorothy Flick a 16-member drill team was formed. Since this time the drill has been drilled many times.

1957 - Under direction of Noble Grand Florence Carver the Degree was conferred and the team drilled for a District Meeting at Confluence, Pa.

1961 - Rhelda Pritts was awarded a "Certificate of Prefection" for giving the "Unwritten Work" of the Lodge at a District Meeting held at Somerset, Pa. To date this is the first and only certificate awarded a member of Lady Berlin Rebekah Lodge.

When the President of the Rebekah Assembly of Pennsylvania schedules a district meeting for Berlin the lodge hosts these meetings.

A delegate of the lodge attends the Rebekah Assembly I.O.O.F. of Pennsylvania, at the location assembly is held for 4 or 5 days.

If the family of a deceased member requests; services are conducted at the funeral home. Flowers are provided. The Lodge Charter is draped for all deceased members.

At Memorial Day Rebekah Flags are placed on all graves each year. Memorial services are conducted in June of each year for all deceased members.

The anniversary of the Order is celebrated each year in many different ways.

A Christmas party is held each year in form of a covered-dish dinner—entertainment and gift exchange.

Since May 1969, a Mother and Daughter Banquet is held each year in form of a covered-dish dinner. Members invite guests and entertainment is provided. Noble Grand Florence Engleka started the Mother and Daughter Banquet.

The members of the Order make many donations.

Two gavels and sounding blocks were presented to the Order. One was a memorial to the late Albert H. Musser by his family. A second one was a memorial to the late Dr. John Garman—a gift of his daughter, the late Mae O'Dwyer.

Gazelle Lodge #369 went defunct. The past several years several ladies from that lodge joined the Lady Berlin Lodge.

Various projects are used to raise money for the treasury.

Donations have been made by the lodge to:
T B Bond
Harvest Home
Aged and Infirm Odd Fellows Home
Rebekah Home of Western Pennsylvania
Rebekah Home Picnic
Mile of Pennies
Visual Research
Heritage Fund
Educational Foundation

Ill and shut-in members are remembered with greeting cards, planters and visits.

Special ceremonies and observances are conducted each year.

#1 - Jan. 15th - Anniversary of the birth of Thomas Wildey - founder of the Order

#2 - Mar. 23rd - Anniversary of the birth of Schugler Colfax - founder of the Rebekah degree.

All candidates receive the Rebekah Degree. The Rebekah Lodge is a secret order - is based on the Bible, Friendship, Love and Truth. Members are addressed as sister and brother.

The Order meets the 2nd and 4th Thursday of each month. At the conclusion of each meeting refreshment and social hour follows.

Present Officers

Rhelda Pritts - Noble Grand
Sally Miller—Vice Grand
Belle Kreinbrook - Secretary
Geneva Leydig - Treasurer
Carrie Elkins - Chaplain
Violet Ludy - Warden
Eleanor Maust - Conductor
Fern Maust - Naomi Ferner - Right and Left Supporters to the Noble Grand
Mildred Bare - Sylvia Miller - Right and Left Supporters to the Vice Grand
Delores Gordon - Inside Guardian
Aldine Long - Outside Guardian
Mary J. Chonko - American Flag Bearer
Emily Fritz - Rebekah Flag Bearer
Florence Carver - Elsie Wilson - Altar Bearers
Beverly Mothersbaugh - Pearl Scheller - Escorts to Chaplain
Frances Stuck - Musician
Virginia Platt - Past Noble Grand
Verna Countryman - Eunice Glessner - Nellie Countryman - Trustees
Florence Engleka - Mabel Thomas - Dorothy Brougher - Substitutes
Beverly Mothersbaugh - District Deputy President
1976 - Rhelda Pritts Noble Grand has for her motto - "Let's all take time to be good Rebekahs."
Emblem - "The Holy Bible"
Aim - "Friendship - Love - Peace and Harmony"
Colors - Pink and Green
Flower - Pink Rose
Present Membership - 92

PAST NOBLE GRANDS—6-month terms

Mrs. Elizabeth Muhlenberg	Sadie Baughman
Cora Miller	Mildred Deitz
Harriet Shaw	Nettie Hoffman
Marie Beachley	Florence Altfather
May O'Dwyer	Irene Maust
Elizabeth Zimmerman	Miss Elizabeth Muhlenberg
Rose Muhlenberg	Irene Cabel
Nellie Cober	Flora Rubright
Besse Dively	Matilda Stahl
Nellie Miller	Edna Handwerk
Mary Heffley	Nellie Ayers
Mary Brubaker	Anna Miller
Evelyn Smith	Anna Mays
Mary Weimer	Bertha Walker
Nellie Countryman	Belle Kreinbrook
Mary Dickey	Erma Lane
Leora Altfather	Gertrude Musser
Rebecca Johnson	Mary E. Smith
Lulu Dively	Carolyn Fogle
Mae T. Stuck	Margaret Logue
Marie Dively	Bertha Suder
Anna Menges	Florence Dively
Elsie Krissinger	Grace Deitz
Erma Walker	Minnie Menges
Margaret Coughenour	Geneva Leydig
Grace Altfather	Ruth Maust
Molly Muhlenberg	Nellie Johnson
Rae Hauger	Virginia Miller
Mae Glessner	Lena Tipton

1-year term began

Eunice Glessner	Olive Maust
Fern Maust	Mabel Thomas
Edna Boyer	Barby Webreck
Dorothy Flick	Mary Sheavly
Rhelda Pritts	Florence Engleka
Florence Carver	Beverly Mothersbaugh
Mary L. Zimmerman	Naomi Ferner
Eleanor Croner	Violet Ludy
Eleanor Maust	Lana J. Foor
Carrie Elkins	Virginia Platt
Anna Berkley	

Berlin Volunteer Fire Department

For 73 years the volunteer firemen have served the community of Berlin in protecting life and property and in 1903 organized fire fighting had its beginning.

Prior to 1903, the bucket brigade formed when the alarm of fire sounded and men, women, and children pumped water from wells on the premises at or about the scene of the fire to fill the buckets handled by the line of men who desperately tried to save the house or barn of the unfortunate owner.

In 1903 and following the construction of a water distribution system in the town, including fire hydrants, two separate fire companies were organized: the East End Company with H. F. Ball as captain and the West End Company with J. Henry Landis as captain. R. C. Heffley served for a number of years as fire chief of the companies. Each company was assigned a hose cart with five hundred feet of hose to be used as required by either or both companies. The ladies of Berlin financed the purchase of this equipment by holding box socials and chicken and waffle suppers.

These organizations functioned until 1921 when the two-company fire department reorganized at a meeting held in the Vine and Fletcher Street Borough Building. Both companies merged into the Berlin Volunteer Fire Department with W. H. Dively as President; Frank L. Thompson, Secretary; H. F. Ball, Treasurer; and John O. Ream, Fire Chief.

At a meeting of the department held on January 30, 1922, a resolution was passed directing the President to appoint a committee to look into the matter of acquiring a motor chassis with the necessary equipment for the purpose of being immediately ready for service upon the sounding of an alarm of fire. The President appointed a committee consisting of John O. Ream, H. F. Ball, and Norman Brant to consider equipment as directed in the resolution.

On May 12, 1922, the committee had a report at the special meeting called to consider the purchase of fire-fighting equipment. A resolution was passed providing for the purchase of a Type E fire engine from the American LaFrance Fire Engine Company of Elmira, New York, at a cost of $2,500. This piece of equipment was known as "The Old Ford," and carried a supply of hose and chemical fire-fighting equipment.

Since the "Old Ford" was not a pumper, fire-fighting activity was limited to supplying hose and the use of chemical fire extinguishers. Sentiment developed among the citizenry for more effective fire fighting and service to the rural areas, and at a meeting held on September 28, 1925, a committee consisting of H. F. Ball, Norman Brant, and H. F. Heffley was directed to go to the American LaFrance Plant at Elmira to get information on a pumper.

On March 12, 1928, a resolution was passed providing for the purchase of a modern fire engine, a reconditioned Type 75, American LaFrance Fire Truck with a 750 gpm. pump, at a cost of $8,000.

A second fire truck was purchased in 1937 from the American LaFrance Company equipped with a booster system. C. W. Altfather, H. F. Ball, and W. J. Walker served on the fire truck purchase committee. This was a custom-built, GMC chassis fire truck acquired at a cost of $3,600.

With the ever increasing demands for services of the Berlin Volunteer Fire Department and since the original American LaFrance fire truck was fast becoming an obsolete piece of equipment, the fire department, under Norman S. Handwerk as Fire Chief, promoted the need for high-pressure fire-fighting equipment and a larger booster tank for service in the rural areas around Berlin. Fire calls were now being answered in Allegheny and Northampton townships and New Baltimore borough.

In 1947, a third fire truck was ordered from the American LaFrance Company with delivery made in September 1948. Norman S. Handwerk, as chairman of the fire truck purchase committee, and Ernest S. Walker and Frank W. Pritts, assistant fire chiefs, were directed to go to the American LaFrance plant and place an order for a 750 gpm. pumper fire truck equipped with a twelve-cylinder aviation type engine with a booster tank capacity of 200 gallons at a cost of $16,000. This truck was equipped with an auxiliary pump outfit, a portable

Berlin Volunteer Fire Department

New Emergency truck

light plant, and ladders. With the installation of 1,500 feet of 2½-inch and 600 feet of 1½-inch hose, the cost figure totaled $18,000.

In 1953, with the advent of Civil Defense Aid and emergency rescue work, an emergency car was purchased as a custom-built vehicle from Brumbaugh Company, Altoona. This combination vehicle featured a 1½ Chevrolet truck chassis with squad car body and complete with a 200 gpm. pump, a 200-gallon booster tank, 800 feet of 1½ inch hose, a truck-powered winch, acetylene cutting torch, emergency light, and water pump outfits. Total cost of this vehicle was $13,000.

With the cooperation of the Berlin Council, the Fire Department purchased shortwave radio equipment consisting of a base unit, two mobile units, and two portable units with installation completed in November, 1955. Berlin, with call letters KGD 722, was the first fire company in Somerset County to join with the Somerset County Civil Defense and fire radio network.

Berlin Fire Department's dreams of adequate facilities for fire equipment, meeting rooms, and recreational accommodations were finally realized with the construction of the Berlin Borough-Berlin Volunteer Fire Department Community Building. After a period of three years of planning and construction, the fire department moved to their new quarters in April, 1965. The new community building also provided accommodations for the fireman's ladies' auxiliary meetings and serving banquet meals to the public. The dedication program for the Berlin Community Building was held on Sunday, October 24, 1965.

Since the trend of times decreed that funeral directors in Somerset County would discontinue ambulance services as of August 1, 1967, a Berlin Area Ambulance Association was organized with fireman J. Theodore Johnson elected as president. Berlin firemen agreed to operate the ambulance vehicles on a volunteer basis without charge to the association. Firemen available for this service completed the prescribed first-aid training course and now operate the assocation's two ambulances.

Again in 1970, President George S. Dively appointed a truck committee to prepare specifications for a new pumper to replace the 1948 pumper. The committee consisted of Ernest Walker, chairman; Clyde Miller, William Dively, Elmer Miller, and Terry Holland. The New American LaFrance equipped with automatic transmission, booster tank capacity of 850 gallons, 750 gpm. pump, 2000 feet of 2½-inch hose, and a 35-ft. aluminum ladder was delivered to Berlin in 1971, at a cost of $43, 700.

Several of the oldest living members of the department include Vernon Lyons, Earl Shultz, Harry Zimmerman, Albert Philson, Harry Driggs, and Walter Johnson. Ernest S. Walker passed away in January, 1973, after having served for 25 consecutive years as Fire Chief of the Berlin Fire Department. Robert Fogle is now in his 23rd year as fire department treasurer.

In 1972, the bylaws of the department were revised to allow 18-year-olds to join membership. Many young men have joined and are taking an active interest in tire-fighting procedures. In 1976, there are 232 members on the fire department roster. Fire calls average 22 men per call and the number usually doubles when the need arises.

In 1975, President Doyle E. Paul again appointed a new truck committee to prepare specifications for a new squad truck to replace the 1953 emergency car. The current committee consists of Elmer Miller, chairman; Clyde Miller, Carl Flamm, Terry Holland, and John Thomas. Hamerly Custom Productions from Hamburg, Pennsylvania, is designing the custom-built body on a Chevrolet C65 truck chassis. The new truck will feature a 300-gallon storage tank, 300 gpm. pump, emergency power plant, portable pump, and all the latest auxiliary tools and equipment needed in today's modern fire fighting. The department has eight self-contained breathing units. The new squad truck is expected to arrive in Berlin in September, 1976, ready for service, at a cost of $48,000.

In addition to protecting life and property, the department participates in the Somerset County Fire Training School each year, Battle of the Barrel performance events, and sponsors the annual block party, deer hunters breakfast, community canvass fund drive, dances, turkey raffle, and the hanging of the Christmas decorations.

Present officers of the department are President, Doyle E. Paul; Vice-President, Dale E. Leydig; Secretary, William A. Merrill, III; Treasurer, Robert W. Fogle; Fire Chief, Clyde E. Miller; First Assistant, Carl Flamm; Second Assistant, Terry Holland; Chaplains, John Baker and William Dively; Ambulance Captain, Warren Pugh; Fire Police, Frank Boburchock; and Truck Foremen, Nevin Keller and Donald Meyers.

Berlin Fire Auxiliary

The Ladies Auxiliary of the Berlin Fire Department was first organized in the year of 1927. At that time the Borough Building was behind the Berlin Brethren Church, and the first President of the Ladies Auxiliary was Mrs. Mary Heffley.

In April of 1965 the auxiliary moved into the new building. Mrs. Helen Spangler was President of the auxiliary at that time. A committee of four, Helen Spangler, Pearl Scheller, Mabel Thomas, and Libby Johnson, purchased the dishes, pots, pans, stove, tables, and chairs for the new community building. Later on, a dishwasher, new refrigerator, freezer, and ice maker were acquired. As of now the auxiliary has a modern and fully equipped kitchen.

At the present time Mrs. Lois Harris is President. The auxiliary serves many banquets, wedding receptions, anniversaries, and the Lions Club twice a month. It has sponsored a Little League baseball team for the past two years and a Little League Banquet is served to the teams. The auxiliary presents a Life Time Membership card to ladies of the auxiliary who have reached the age of 75 or over. As of now 21 members have received cards. At present we have 112 members of the auxiliary.

1976 Officers of the Auxiliary

President - Lois Harris
1st Vice-President - Pearl Scheller
2nd Vice-President - Violet Ludy
Secretary - Molly Trimpey
Treasurer - Belle Kreinbrook
Financial Secretary - Grace Sivits

Veterans' Organizations

American Legion

The local post was originally chartered in 1919. The original charter was lost and early records are not available.

Honoring a local veteran who died in the service of his country, the present Harry Fisher Post #445 was chartered on January 18, 1927.

As years passed, membership increased to the present 265 members. Included in this membership are 21 World War I members.

The Ladies Auxiliary of Harry Fisher Post #445 was organized on January 20, 1927. Mrs. P. D. Collins was the first president. The auxiliary also sponsors a Junior Auxiliary. Each year the Ladies Auxiliary sponsors outstanding programs for the community, for veterans, and for our school-age children.

Serving her second term as president is Mrs. Paul Ickes.

V.F.W. Post #7295

The Robert Walker Post #7295 was named for Robert Walker and was organized May 31, 1946.

The first commander was Robert Brick.

Present officers are: Dale Miller, Commander; Q.M., Wilmer Kreinbrook, and Adj., Al Queer.

This is a service organization. Total membership to date is 121 members.

V.F.W. Auxiliary

The Robert Walker Auxiliary #7295 was first organized November 15, 1946. The first president was Helen Brick. The first treasurer was Belle Kreinbrook. It is interesting to note that Belle Kreinbrook still remains the treasurer of this organization. The first secretary was Vivian Scheller.

Present officers are: President, Josephine Lyons; Secretary, Helen Smith; Treasurer, Belle Kreinbrook.

This is a service organization. The main object of this organization is to loan hospital equipment to anyone in need.

Total membership to date is 53 members.

Veterans Home Association

In 1949, the present Veterans' Home on Meadow Street was jointly purchased by the VFW and American Legion posts. Through the years, the building has served principally for meetings of the two posts and the Ladies Auxiliary meetings. Many social functions of the organizations are held here.

After many years of cramped space for various activities, it is notable that the veterans' groups, in this Bicentennial year, have completed a beautiful and large addition to the veterans' home—a fine tribute to the efforts of many members associated with the Veterans' Home Association, the American Legion, and Veterans of Foreign Wars.

Boy and Girl Scouts in Berlin, Pa.

Boy Scout Troop 135

The sponsoring institution for the Boy Scout Troop #135 is the Holy Trinity Evangelical Lutheran Church of Berlin, Pa.

The Troop Committee is made up of the following adults: Thomas A. Gerber, Institutional Representative; Alvin Lambert, Committee Chairman; James R. Flick, Committeeman; Richard P. Saylor, Committeeman; Paul E. Smith, Committeeman; Robert Swank, Committeeman; and Leroy Lehman, Committeeman.

Their scoutmaster is Lester L. Coslic. Assistant scoutmasters are: Thomas E. Sprowls, James W. Ferguson, John M. Heiple, Robert M. Mays, Jr.

Boys in the troop are:

Andrew Chonko, Jr.	Bradley L. Flick
Jonathan Croner	Robert Gerber
Daniel Coslic	Richard Hay
Matthew Deeter	Clifford E. Horner
Mark Engleka	Robert Landis
Jay Ferguson	Steven Landis

Douglas Lehman	Tommy Berkebile
Dean Lichty	Scott Scurfield
David Long	Michael Gross
Merle Ogline	Fred Deem
Jeffery Smith	Richard Scurfield
Thomas Sprowls	Craig Saylor
Stephen Sredy	Timothy Sprowls
Mark Swank	Martin Zerfoss
Michael Tataleba	Jaimie Zerfoss
Edward Wyant	Jeff Calvert
Christopher Walker	Clinton Clark
James Wyant	John Dunn
Robert Zerfoss	Keith Coughenour
John Baird	Jeffrey Brant

Earlier Boy Scout leaders were:
Major Philip Shaffer
Bertram S. Walker
George Dively
Wilfred Miller

Girl Scouts Troop 334 - Junior Troop

(grades 4-6) with Sally Yaple, troop leader:

Dianna Baird	Heather Merrill
Debbie Baughman	Wanda Mort
Sheri Berkebile	Deidre Paul
Dawn Cober	Gail Poorbaugh
Susan Coslic	Jacqueline Reffner
Nancy Clark	Tammy Smith
Caroline Gardill	Karen Tataleba
Amy Gardner	Christine Trent
Melodie Gumbert	Linda Trulick
Connie Jerkes	Karen Trulick
Sandy Jerkes	Kathy Wyant
Suzanne Madey	Jill Zerfoss

Girl Scout Troop 322 - Cadette Troop

(grades 7-9) with Sally Yaple, troop leader:

Jackie Bender	Michelle Coughenour
Ann Chonko	Tracy Coughenour

Judy Day	Michele Lindeman
Barb Deist	Dawn Miller
Barb Faul	Nancy Popovich
Tammy Hickman	Susan Sterner
Mary Keep	Sheri Walker

Girl Scout Senior Troop

(grades 10-12) with Joyce Twombly, leader:

Kathy Gumbert
Lori Gumbert
Tina Faul
Susan France

There is also a Brownie Troop and another Junior Troop with approximately 25 or more members.

In earlier years Girl Scout leaders were:
Mrs. J. B. Rinick
Mrs. Wilfred Miller
Mrs. Ralph Taylor

Brothersvalley FFA

The vocational agriculture curriculum was started in the Berlin Brothersvalley School District during the 1936-37 school year. In 1937 the Brothersvalley FFA received its charter with Mr. William Igoe as teacher and adviser. The first FFA President was William Rhodes. The 1976 President is Donald VanGilder. The adviser is Mr. Doyle E. Paul. The Brothersvalley FFA membership has steadily increased during the past 39 years to the present enrollment of 73 members.

The agriculture course includes both boys and girls in grades 9 through 12. Students may enroll in the program whether they live in the town or country. All students are required to have a supervised occupational experience program but need not take the traditional animal and crop projects.

The FFA includes many extracurricular activities carried out separately from the vocational agriculture course. The primary aim of the FFA is to develop agricultural leadership, cooperation, and citizenship. The purpose of all FFA activities is to provide an educational experience and to develop a strong competitive attitude.

Production and improvement projects, group projects, supervised occupational experience programs, crop and livestock production, farm management and agri-business, agricultural mechanics, the FFA activities and contest skills—all help the vocational agriculture student in preparing for a career.

Berlin Brothersvalley Community Fair Association

The first Berlin Brothersvalley Community Fair was held in September of 1937. Mr. William D. Igoe served as President during the first nine years. The first board of directors and officers consisted of 15 men and women elected from Berlin borough, Brothersvalley Township, Allegheny Township, Northampton Township, Fairhope Township, and New Baltimore borough. The same procedure for securing membership into this organization is still used today, except that the board has grown to 30 directors. Many people living in the Berlin Brothersvalley School District have served three-year terms on the Fair Board during the past 39 years.

The purpose of the Berlin Brothersvalley Community Fair Association is to encourage a spirit of cooperation among the people of the community, to create an interest in the improved methods of farming, to nurture a love for farm life and those things which pertain to agriculture and homemaking, and to present to the people of other communities a cross section of the activities carried on by the people who live here.

During the early years of fair activity, the crops, vegetables, fruits, and hobbies were all displayed in the classrooms. Articles were judged but no premiums were paid. Fifteen years later dime premiums were paid to the first-, second-, and third-place exhibitors. The Berlin Brothersvalley Community Fair has continued to grow over the years and in 1975 nearly $3,500 in prize money was paid to exhibitors.

The Berlin Brothersvalley Community Fair was incorporated on September 11, 1957, and today exhibitors from all parts of Somerset County bring entries to the fair. Most of the operating costs and premiums are subsidized by the Pennsylvania Department of Agriculture.

The 1976 fair officers are President, David Countryman; Vice-President, Doyle Paul; Secretary, Mrs. Dan Weighley; and Treasurer, Mrs. Jack Engle.

Berlin Lions Club

The club was organized and chartered on Wednesday, May 24, 1939, 6:15 p.m., at the New National Hotel.

Larry Slater, representing Lions International, presided. Serving as secretary was James O. Courtney of the Somerset Club, the sponsor.

Thirty-five charter members were in attendance.

Charter officers were as follows:

President - Norman Miller
1st Vice-President - H. Q. Rhodes
2nd Vice-President - C. R. Bauermaster
3rd Vice-President - H. B. Cober
Secretary & Treasurer - James P. McCabe
Tail Twister - Dr. I. C. Miller
Lion Tamer - Miles Lumbard

Director, 2 years - William G. Gill
Director, 2 years - Harry R. Forney
Director, 1 year - H. F. Ball
Director, 1 year - D. J. Musser

Since 1939 many major projects for community betterment have been initiated sponsored, and maintained by the Lions.

With due regard to many projects not listed, the following are some of the major contributions.

Community Playground - equipment and building
Annual School Athletic Banquet
Lions Eye and Vision Projects
Awards for Outstanding Scholars
Community Grove Facilities

The Pius Spring Women's Club of Berlin

The Pius Spring Women's Club was organized and federated in September 1952, with twenty-five charter members. The name for the club was suggested by Mrs. Jacob Schrock, a charter member, to honor the name of the first settlement of the town which was later to become Berlin. In 1962, the Pius Spring Women's club placed a granite marker on the wall directly above the Pius Spring which is located on the property of Mrs. Marie Beachley on Main Street. At the close of the club year, in May of 1976, the club had grown to include seventy-six members.

The Pius Spring Women's Club is a community service organization as well as a State and General Federated Club, and supports many state and national Women's Club projects. On the community level the club has provided a vitamin program in the Berlin-Brothersvalley schools, sponsored a Little League baseball team, sponsored the Senior Girl Scouts, and contributed to the Boy Scouts, as well as the high school library. The club has planted trees at the Berlin playground, the I.O.O.F. Cemetery, and throughout the town as a town-beautification project. Two senior high school girls, who have been chosen as Girls of the Semester, each year are honored and entertained by the club, and each year the Maple Princess is also honored by the club. Three English Awards are presented each year by the club to the grade and high schools and each spring the club has a tea for the senior high school girls and their mothers. Also, the Pius Spring Women's Club has contributed generously to the fund for new uniforms for the high school band, the new Berlin ambulance, the new fire truck, and also to the fund for buying new Christmas decorations for the town. Each year the club contributes to the Nurses' Scholarship Fund, which is a project of the County Women's Clubs.

Since their organization as a club, the Pius Spring Women's club has had several home tours and Christmas bazaars and also has an annual rummage sale in the fall of the year. The money made from these projects is used for State and General Federation projects, as well as to contribute to the community needs and projects.

History of the Berlin Area Ambulance Service

Early in 1967 the local funeral directors announced that as of August 1. 1967, they would discontinue ambulance service to the Berlin area. A meeting was held on February 23, 1967, with representatives of the borough council, surrounding township supervisors, civic clubs, and interested citizens to discuss the need for ambulance service in the Berlin area.

Temporary officers were elected at this meeting. Those elected were J. Theodore Johnson, President; Ernest Landis, Vice-President; Betty Pugh, Secretary; and James Sarver, Treasurer. Elected as directors were Rev. Randall Heckman, Rev. Ralph Mills, Glenn Kimmel, Homer Kreinbrook, and George Leecy.

President Johnson met with the Berlin Volunteer Fire Department to ask them to take over the ambulance service. After several meetings, during which at times tempers came to the boiling point, it was decided to set up an ambulance association and to have it incorporated as a nonprofit corporation. It was agreed that the ambulance association would be responsible for the purchase of necessary equipment and to conduct the membership drive. The fire company would be responsible to furnish and train the manpower to run the ambulances. Warren Pugh was named by the fire department to take charge of the personnel. He was then appointed to serve on the board of directors of the ambulance association. Letters were written to other ambulance services to get copies of their bylaws and methods of operation to be used as a guide. A set of bylaws were written and submitted to the Somerset County Court for approval and an application to be chartered as a nonprofit corporation to be known as the Berlin Area Ambulance Association, Inc. This was approved by the court.

The first business was to set up a fund-raising organization to raise money for equipment. The Berlin Lions Club took this task as a project. They made a house-to-house canvass of the area and were very successful in obtaining membership in the borough. Other volunteers covered the outlying areas to get prospective members. The first year we had around 1,200 members.

The next main task was to get the manpower trained. Mr. Lewis Weaver, instructor for the American Red Cross, started classes, with approximately 30 people completing the course by May 1967. Later a class of instruction was held in the Meyersdale Hospital by the Pennsylvania Dept. of Health. Eleven men completed this course in November, 1967. Various other courses of training were held in the following years including an Emergency Medical Technicians course held at the Somerset Vo-Tech School. This course was an 80-hour course and the graduates were certified by the Pennsylvania Dept. of Health. To date seven men have successfully completed this course.

Purchase of an ambulance and equipment was another important step to be taken. The first ambulance was a 1965 Cadillac, purchased in April 1967. A down payment on this piece of equipment was made with a balance of $7,500 to be paid. Mr. Gary Sterner of the Snyder's Potato Chip Factory presented us a check for this amount to pay the balance due. This relieved the financial burden on the Association and enabled them to purchase other necessary equipment to start operation. In August 1967 a 1959 Pontiac was purchased to be used as a back-up piece of equipment. In August 1970 the Shanksville Fire Company announced they were going to discontinue ambulance service. They contacted us to see if our Association would cover their area in with our ambulance service. We purchased their ambulance, a 1961 Dodge station wagon, to replace the Pontiac. Our equipment has been updated and we now have a 1972 Chevrolet van and a 1975 Pontiac coach.

A new Dodge van ambulance was purchased March 2, 1977, at the cost of $18,000.

The present officers are Clyde Miller, President; Gus Kern, Vice-President; Betty Pugh, Secretary; and Warren Pugh, Treasurer. In addition to the officers the present board of directors consists of James Engleka, Ernest Landis, Francis Maust, Florence Sarver, Carl Flamm, and Samuel Poorbaugh.

Berlin Area Senior Citizens

Berlin Area Senior Citizens group was formed in March, 1972. It is an independent group and any person over 55 years of age is eligible for membership. The dues amount to $2.00 a year.

The purpose of the organization is to promote and improve the welfare of all senior citizens, to enjoy social gatherings and entertainment, and to promote good fellowship.

Meetings are held the second and fourth Tuesdays of each month at 7:00 p.m. in the Community Building. At the present time there are 94 members in the organization. Mr. Wm. H. Lepley, R. D., Berlin, Pa., is the President.

Wheelers-N-Dealers Square Dance Club

"Do, Si, Do, and Right and Left Thru" are familiar words to the members of the "Wheeler-N-Dealer Square Dance Club" of Somerset County. The dancers enjoy dancing the first and third Tuesdays of each month at the Berlin Community Building. The club members have completed 75 basic steps in modern square dancing and earned a diploma and badge which enable them to do modern western square dancing anywhere they travel.

The club's first class graduated in June, 1971, in the armory at Somerset, Pa. Classes are open to the public in September of each year and lessons and club dancing is held at the Berlin Community Building in Berlin. Visitors are welcome at any time.

The club officers are:
President - Mr. and Mrs. Lloyd Shaffer
Secretary - Mr. and Mrs. Gary Speicher
Treasurer - Mr. and Mrs. James Stern
Hospitality - Mr. and Mrs. Larry VanSickle, Mr. and Mrs. Sheldon Pugh, Sr.
Club Sheriff - Roy Romesburg
Club Teacher - Mr. Alfred Knotts
Club Caller - Mr. Al Schwinabart, Elk Gardens, W. Va.

The club sponsors several activities each year, featuring special guest callers, national callers, and other entertainment for their Spring Festival, Fun Night Dances, Christmas Dinner Dances, New Year's Dance, and many others. Square dancing is fun!

Berlin Area Little League

The Berlin Area Little League, which includes the geographic boundary of the Berlin Brothersvalley and Shanksville-Stony Creek School District, was officially chartered by Little League Baseball, Incorporated, of Williamsport, Pennsylvania, January 1, 1975. Prior to the start of the initial season in June of 1975 much had to be done. In April of 1975, an official Little League playing field did not exist in Berlin, but through much hard work and generous gifts from the community, businesses, the school, and individuals, we were able to have a field ready for the beginning of the season.

The initial sponsors of participating teams were; Berlin Firemen's Auxiliary, Pius Spring Women's Club, and Western Auto. The first season consisted of a 25-game regular schedule and a best-of-3 playoffs. The first Berlin Area Little League champion was the Berlin Firemen's Auxiliary Team, followed by the Pius Spring Women's Club in second place. An All-Star Team was selected from the players of the Berlin Area Little League to represent the league in Intra-District play and other tournaments. The Berlin Area Little League All-Stars were successful in their first Intra-District game by defeating a team of All-Stars from Boswell, but were eliminated the next night by a strong team from Meyersdale. The Berlin Area Little League All-Star Team was eliminated from the Salisbury Tournament by dropping two games.

The first year of operation of the Berlin Area Little League was concluded with a banquet in the Berlin Community Building. The banquet was served by the Berlin Fireman's Auxiliary and we greatly appreciated the many fine things this group did for us. The main speaker at the banquet was Bill Mazeroski, former great of the Pittsburgh Pirates. Following the speech, trophies were presented to the league champion and runner-up. Awards were also presented to the All-Star Team and Most Valuable Players for each team.

The real joy of the first year was to see the tremendous cooperation of all facets of the community and to see 80 children participate in organized baseball.

The officers for the first year were:
John (Jack) Harding, President
Charles Dunn, Vice-President
Andrew Deeter, Secretary-Treasurer
Bob Coughenour, Safety Officer
Dale Smith, Player Agent
Mrs. Charles Maust, Chairperson, Women's Aux.
Jay Engleka, Umpire-in-Chief

During the fall, the Berlin Brothersvalley FFA sowed the Little League field with grass. The second year of the Berlin Area Little League started like the first with a lot to be done before the season started. Again great cooperation was evident, for in a few weeks we were able to construct two dugouts and a concession stand. The league officers and the team sponsors remained the same, but the schedule was reduced to 20 games and playoffs. The league champion in 1976 was Snyder's Potato Chip team, followed by Western Auto in second place. Another great season, for more children participated. An All-Star Team was again selected and we are at this time looking forward to their play in the Intra-District playoffs.

Early Berlin baseball team

Berlin baseball team of about 1912. Standing, left to right: Earl Brubaker, George Engle, Abbie Philson, Fred Groff (with tie), Cleave Earheart, Pat Fornwalt (with tie), Choate Landis. Front: Robert Brubaker, Ben Philson, Parley Baker, Lloyd Henderson, Sam Philson

Recreation and Sports

Berlin Area Playground

The plot of ground was deeded July 11, 1945, from Jacob B. Schrock to Berlin Borough School District.

Located on South Street and Meadow Street, the playground has been the center for children's activities for over 30 years. Original equipment was purchased through a $2,000 donation made by a Berlin woman. Maintenance and additional equipment has been provided by the Berlin Lions Club. Operational responsibility has been under the supervision of the Berlin Brothersvalley Area School Board.

The playground building was a welcome addition for various activities. In past years and at present it has been and is now used as a classroom by the local schools.

Attached to the building is a plate as follows: "This Building Erected in Honor of Dr. I. C. Miller, Friend of Little Children," 1955.

School Athletic Area

In 1950 many recreational- and sports-minded local residents saw the need for an outdoor recreational and sports area. Property was purchased adjacent to the school from Patrick Broderick. A nonprofit association was formed by a number of local residents to begin construction of playing fields.

In September of 1951, the football field was dedicated at the opening football game. The dedication was honored by the presence of Rosey Rowswell, the famed voice of the Pittsburgh Pirates for many years.

Within the school, the gymnasium was rebuilt and enlarged.

In 1975, the new Little League Baseball Field was dedicated. Located on school property behind the elementary school, this addition now adds to community sports activities.

The Community Grove

For many years the grove has been the center of many outdoor family and community affairs. The highlight is the annual community picnic held at the grove during the summer.

On January 6, 1944, a deed to the grove property was received by the School Districts of Berlin Borough and Brothersvalley Township from Jacob B. Schrock.

Maintenance and operation of the grove is principally provided by the Berlin Community Association and local organizations.

Left to right—seated: Joe Evel, Ben Philson, Pater Menges, (unknown), Don Kimmel—leader, (unknown), Howard Philson, Samuel Philson. Standing: Rudd Landis, Punch Nicholson, Worley Fogle, (unknown—Shanksville), Al Dudley, (unknown), Dabby Baldwin, Winn Fogle, Hen Menges, Harry Zimmerman, Frank Nicholson, Choate Landis.

Birth and Baptismal Certificate of 1839

(Geburt and Taufschein)

The following is a translation of the German text: "This wedded pair Johannes Bauman and his Wedded wife Elizabeth nee (born) Martininen is born to the world the 15th day of May in the year of our Lord 1839. This daughter is born in Brothersvallen Taunschip in Somerset County in the State of Penna. in North Amerika and was baptized and was named Lovine the 21st. day of July in the year of our Lord 1839 by Pastor Denius."

(Rev. Solomon K. Denius was in Berlin from 1835 to 1841. During his pastorate, he confirmed 130 persons and baptized more than 100 children. From Berlin, he moved west and served a number of other Reformed charges.)

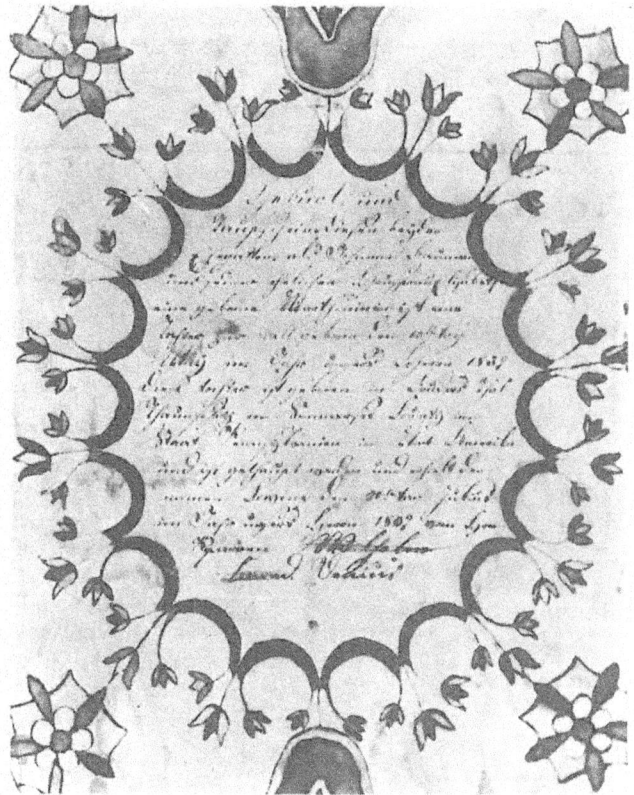

Berlin Post Offices

The post offices in Berlin had a number of different locations over the years. Sometimes they were in the homes of the postmaster.

Around **1785** Mr. John Fletcher was the first postmaster and his salary was $18.03 a year.

In **1893** Mr. F. B. Collins was the postmaster and the post office was on the lower diamond at 441 Main Street. His assistant was a Mr. Johnson.

1893—Captain Heffley was postmaster and his post office was farther down the street with his Justice of the Peace office. Miss Mary Johnson was his assistant.

1897—B. J. Bowman was postmaster in the Poorbaugh Room.

1897—Mr. Z. T. Kimmel, Don Kimmel's father, was postmaster.

1897—B. J. Bowman was again postmaster. He resigned soon afterwards and his wife, Mrs. Minnie Bowman, became postmistress.

1901—Mr. Bowman moved the post office to the Henrietta Brubaker property. He was reappointed in 1901 and his salary was now $1,000 a year and the post office became a third-class post office.

1905—It was moved two doors west to the building formerly used as a furniture store.

1907—W. V. Marshall was appointed in February. It was located near the location of present-day Painters Barber Shop on Main Street.

1907—Postmaster Marshall moved the post office to the Masters Building or where Kinetic Inn is today. Mr. Marshall was postmaster until 1916.

1916—Charles W. Krissinger was appointed postmaster in February and served two terms.

1917. In August the post office was moved from the Masters Building to the Philson National Bank Building on the lower diamond.

1924—C. Weller Saylor took charge of the local post office and his assistants were his son, James, and Miss Grace Miller.

1924—Due to ill health, Mr. Saylor resigned and Mr. George Wetmiller became postmaster.

1930's—Mr. Ed Walker was appointed postmaster. Mr. Ed Fogle was appointed acting postmaster after Mr. Walker died.

1942—Mr. Howard Philson was postmaster for six years.

1948—John O. Ream, Jr., was appointed postmaster until 1972. His assistant was Otis O. Bockes.

1972—Robert O. Hare was appointed postmaster and is presently the postmaster in 1977.

The Dively Store-1903

Harvey Dively began a variety and grocery store in 1903 in the building now occupied by the Gardner Barber shop at 629 Main Street. (Known as the Hillegas Building to old-timers.)

Harvey Dively's store in 1915

Interior of Dively's store in 1915

Farmers' Union Mutual Association and Fire Insurance Company of Somerset County

According to the Somerset County History published in 1901, the Farmers' Union Mutual Association and Fire Insurance Company of Somerset County was organized in 1867 at Pine Hill in Brothersvalley Township. It was founded by a group of farmers as a mutual company which would insure farm property only. As a mutual company it is owned by the policyholders who elect a board of directors to manage the company. Established as an assessable company, when losses occurred the policyholders could be assessed in order to pay off the claim if the assets of the company were insufficient. Today this is no longer true, as it has become a non-assessable company.

At its founding, the company insured only farm buildings against fire. With time, they added the line to cover contents also. In 1875, the Farmers' Union Mutual Association and Fire Insurance Company of Somerset County received a charter from the state of Pennsylvania to conduct the business of fire insurance among the farmers of Somerset County. The earliest printed policy in our possession was dated 1873 with Emmanuel Lichty as president, and Ezra Berckley as secretary and treasurer, both of whom resided in Berkley's Mills, Pa., which may account for that community's name being printed as the location of the company's office. Other directors listed on this policy include John G. Hay, William Horner who was later replaced by Peter

Membership Certificate of 1873

121

Berkley, Philip Hay, Jonas A. Miller, Samuel J. Miller, and John Rauch, who was replaced by E. J. Walker. The membership fee of one dollar was included on the policy, which was written as a six-year policy.

The company has continued to grow and develop under the present leadership of John Edw. Hay, executive vice-president and secretary. Officers and directors at present are Jay Hillegass, president; Homer Saylor, vice-president; John Edw. Hay, executive vice-president and secretary; Thomas Maust, treasurer and claims officer of the company; Warren K. Hay, past president; Clark Stahl, Harry Walker, Gerald Dumbauld, Lewis W.

Berkley, and William Glessner. Within the past five years the company has become a non-assessable company, added to its lines of coverage available, and expanded the area in which they write insurance to include all of Pennsylvania. They have changed the name to Highland Mutual Insurance Company of Berlin, Pa., which is the home of their new office. In 1975 they purchased the home of Clyde Dickey on Main Street, Berlin, and have completely remodeled it for their office headquarters. They moved into the new office in February of 1977 and have now hired an additional office secretary and a full-time claims officer, bringing the full-time staff to four.

Did You Know?

The two Berlin diamonds on Main Street were originally laid out so that travelers could camp on them.

Vietersburg was a part of Berlin which began on the east side of the Otis Bocke's property and extended to Cumberland Street.

From Cumberland Street to East End was East Liberty.

Chickentown was a part of Berlin beginning at the high school and extending to the Roxbury Road junction at East End.

Pennville was the area near the Dalphon Landis residence on the Beulah Road.

Goose Hill was so named because the residents kept ducks and geese and is the area near Ben Menges' house.

Peter Wingard bought a slave for one bushel of salt. He was given membership in the Trinity United Church of Christ, Berlin, Pa. Two elders in the church were then appointed to teach the slave the Lord's Prayer and the Apostles' Creed.

The first two-story house in Berlin was built on the north-east corner of the lower diamond. It was first a tavern and afterwards a store.

Most of Berlin, west of Seventh Ave., was developed by a Mr. Fletcher.

The Beulah Road, north of Berlin, was also known as Crab Alley.

Samuel Heffley, who made homemade vanilla ice cream and sold it for 5 cents a dish, put out a lighted lantern when it was for sale. He was the father of Denner Heffley. This was at 543 Main St.

An opera house, built by Albert Dively who was a plasterer by trade, was situated on the south side of Main

Street, west of High Street. It was erected about 1909, and was used for home talent shows, large public meetings, dancing, roller skating, and lyceum programs. Two huge round coal stoves on the floor heated the auditorium which also had a balcony in the rear. The High School Class of 1915 held their graduation program there and presented Tennyson's "The Princess." This class graduated William Werner, Marion Groff Maust, Salome Robley Coughenour, Emma Deeter Lowry and her husband, Jacob. C. Lowry, Walter A. Johnson, Ruth Deeter Heffley, Edna Ross, Jay Coughenour, Hazel Musser Hauger, Irene Deeter Smith, and Robert L. Miller.

The 1908 Old Home Week souvenir books sold for 25¢ each and netted the committee much needed cash for the week's activities.

Spring Avenue is now called Broadway.

In 1908 the oldest two-story house standing was the Brallier house, which was built in 1785. The next oldest was the Mays' house. Neither of these is still standing.

The post office was moved from the upper part of town to the Philson Bank Building in 1917.

Berlin in earlier days had kerosine street lamps which had to be lighted every night.

Main Street was bricked in 1918. The property owners paid around $1.70 a foot.

There are nine original log houses still standing in Berlin which have been remodeled and today are used as dwellings.

What is today the Central Hotel or Lishia's Hotel at one time was the residence of Mrs. Bell Krissinger and Mr. and Mrs. H. B. Philson. Then in 1904 it was purchased by Mr. A. B. Falknor, Mr. W. V. Marshall, and Mr. J. A. Berke and made into a hotel, operated by Mr. Andrew McQuade.

John and Frank Groff started a store on the lower diamond at 441 Main Street after their brother moved out of this building. They called it "The Leader" and later on moved down to 541 Main Street, where they operated a store for many years. Frank went to Somerset and John kept "The Leader."

Harry Groff was a Berlin electrician who lived at 615 Main Street and later moved to 401 Main Street.

Jake Musser bought the Berlin Opera House.

Norman Landis operated a bowling alley.

Harrison & Co., who built the road from Berlin to Garrett, owned a large garage on Fourth Street near the old Feed Store.

George Sheavley had a garage there in the summer of 1922. F. E. Steinley's Garage started on Fletcher Street.

In 1913 the Pastime Theater was located in the Old Mercantile Building. In 1923 it was sold to Poscoe, and in 1928 to Terrance McGary, Harold Miller, and Wilfred Miller. It was run for a short time by Clyde Donner and closed in 1931. Next it was the Blue Ridge Theater and was operated by Otis Bockes.

H. Frank Ball, born in 1873, was in the lumber business in the Berlin area for 62 years. At 75 years of age he continued to operate the only planing mill of its kind in the area. His first job was with E. Atcheson, original owner and operator of the mill, as an apprentice. Later he became associated with his father in a lumberyard in Berlin which operated under the name of S. J. Ball & Son. Twenty-six years later he purchased the business from his father and bought the planing mill from Jacob Schrock and Frank Suder. Through his more than 60 years association in the lumber trade he was acquainted with every machine to be found in a planing mill.

The *Berlin Dairy* was started around 1915 by Jay Musser who was the first to sell bottled milk in Berlin. Clyde Imhoff also worked there at that time, and a Bill Shockey helped to furnish the milk. This was located on Fletcher Street at the rear of the present-day home of James Wrebreck. Later it was moved to 506 South St. and around 1937 was sold to Schneiders. Around 1942 it was sold to William Scurfield and afterwards sold to Walkers Dairy of Somerset and finally to the Menzie Dairy Co. of Pittsburgh.

In 1931 William G. Gill and Joseph M. Chalk came to Berlin to start the Coca-Cola Bottling Company, which at that time was located directly behind the present Schellers Service Station on Broadway. It was not until 1940 that their new building was built (which now houses the service and parts division of Lafferty Chev. Co.).

Managers of the plant were W. G. Gill and J. M. Chalk, who came to Berlin from Baltimore, Md., in 1931 and started work in their plant. They installed quite a lot of new machinery after they came to Berlin. A fleet of large trucks delivered their products throughout the district daily. The bottling works was one of the largest industries in the community employing many young people in both the production and the distribution ends. The people employed in the new building were all from Berlin. The plant was managed by Russell S. Gill from 1954 until the business was sold in 1969.

The Berlin Area Business Association was organized in 1975. Paul Miller is president, Harold Bologna is vice-president, and Lois Harris is secretary-treasurer.

Officers of the Borough of Berlin—1977
    Paul Saylor—Mayor
    John Thomas—President
    James Suder—Vice-President
    Stuart Kreinbrook
    Stanley Smith
    Larry Schrock
    Andrew Deeter
    Blair Krause

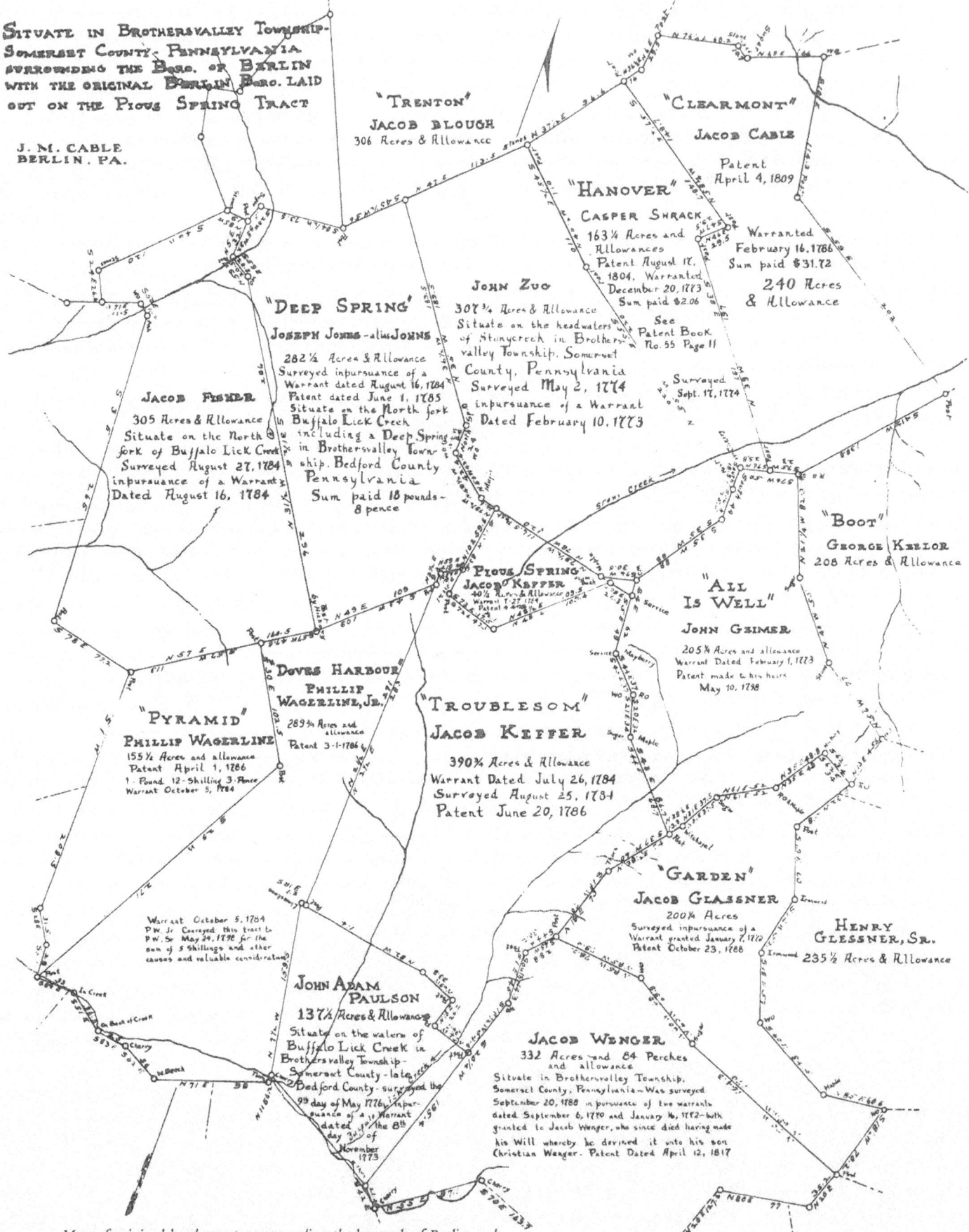

"Trenton"
Jacob Blough
306 Acres & Allowance

"Clearmont"
Jacob Cable
Patent
April 4, 1809
Warranted
February 16, 1786
Sum paid $31.72
240 Acres
& Allowance

"Hanover"
Casper Shrack
163¼ Acres and
Allowances
Patent August 17,
1804. Warranted
December 20, 1773
Sum paid $2.06
See
Patent Book
No. 55 Page 11

John Zug
307¾ Acres & Allowance
Situate on the headwaters
of Stonycreek in Brothersvalley Township. Somerset
County, Pennsylvania
Surveyed May 2, 1774
in pursuance of a Warrant
Dated February 10, 1773

Surveyed
Sept. 17, 1774

"Deep Spring"
Joseph Jones - alias Johns
282½ Acres & Allowance
Surveyed in pursuance of a
Warrant dated August 16, 1784
Patent dated June 1, 1785
Situate on the North fork
Buffalo Lick Creek
including a Deep Spring
in Brothersvalley Town-
ship. Bedford County
Pennsylvania
Sum paid 18 pounds -
8 pence

Jacob Fisher
305 Acres & Allowance
Situate on the North
fork of Buffalo Lick Creek
Surveyed August 27, 1784
in pursuance of a Warrant
Dated August 16, 1784

"Boot"
George Keelor
208 Acres & Allowance

Pious Spring
Jacob Keffer
40½ Acres & Allowance
Warrant 7-27-1784
Patent 4-23-1786

"All
Is Well"
John Grimer
205¾ Acres and allowance
Warrant Dated February 1, 1773
Patent made to his heirs
May 10, 1798

Doves Harbour
Phillip Wagerline, Jr.
289¾ Acres and
allowance
Patent 3-1-1786

"Pyramid"
Phillip Wagerline
155½ Acres and allowance
Patent April 1, 1786
1 - Pound 12 - Shilling 3 - Pence
Warrant October 5, 1784

"Troublesom"
Jacob Keffer
390¾ Acres & Allowance
Warrant Dated July 26, 1784
Surveyed August 25, 1784
Patent June 20, 1786

"Garden"
Jacob Glassner
200¼ Acres
Surveyed in pursuance of a
Warrant granted January 7, 1772
Patent October 23, 1788

Henry
Glessner, Sr.
235½ Acres & Allowance

Warrant October 5, 1784
P.W. Jr. Conveyed this tract to
P.W. Sr. May 24, 1798 for the
sum of 5 Shillings and other
causes and valuable considerations

John Adam
Paulson
137½ Acres & Allowance
Situate on the waters of
Buffalo Lick Creek in
Brothersvalley Township-
Somerset County - late
Bedford County - surveyed the
9th day of May 1776, in pur-
suance of a Warrant
dated the 8th
day 3rd of
November
1773

Jacob Wenger
332 Acres and 84 Perches
and allowance
Situate in Brothersvalley Township.
Somerset County, Pennsylvania - Was surveyed
September 20, 1788 in pursuance of two warrants
dated September 6, 1770 and January 16, 1772 - both
granted to Jacob Wenger, who since died having made
his Will whereby he devised it unto his son
Christian Wenger. Patent Dated April 12, 1817

*Map of original land grants surrounding the borough of Berlin and
a part of Brothersvalley Township*

Brothersvalley Township

Founded in the 1760's
Incorporated in 1771

Sugar Camp
Brothersvalley Twp.

Committee

Kathryn C. Bell
Mrs. R. E. Countryman
Helen S. Croner
S. Boyd Dickey
David R. Hay
Dorothy W. Killius
Thomas I. Maust II
Paul E. Pritts
Calvin M. Will

Other Contributors

Clyde E. Dickey
A. Gene Blubaugh
Owen Preston
Donald W. Hay
John Slifco
Bertha and Augusta Eckman
Maurice Brant
James L. Killius
William Lepley
Fr. Zackary Monet, O. Carm.
Doyle Paul
Anna M. and C. S. Glessner
Homer Poorbaugh Boger
Barbara M. Croner
Margaret Shober
Clara Hay
Harold Krause
Jubal E. Werner
Mrs. Asa S. Engle
Mary Krepelka
Harold W. Schmucker
Tommy R. Croner (Aerial Photos)
Wayne K. Darr (Pilot)
Fay Ohler, "The Meyersdale Republic"
Mary Boyd

Mr. and Mrs. D. Rayman
Mrs. Ward Kinsinger
Rev. L. N. Wilson
Mrs. Ray A. Glessner
Hazel R. Baker

Brothersvalley Township

Brothersvalley, the first township created west of the Allegheny Mountains in Pennsylvania, was formed in 1771 during the first session of the Bedford County courts.

Brothersvalley Township, when formed, was larger than any of Pennsylvania's present counties. It included all of the region lying between the crests of the Allegheny Mountain on the east and the Laurel Hill Mountain on the west, from the Mason and Dixon Line on the south to the divide between the waters of the Susquehanna and the Allegheny River on the north. This divide was known as the Old Purchase Line or the Old Huntington County Line.

Brueders Thal is German, meaning Brothers' Valley, given earlier to the area by the Indians, who called it the Valley of the Brothers.

Some of the first settlers of Brothersvalley were George Dibert (1739), Christian Blough, Frederick Cefar, Simon Hay, John Glassner, Valentine Lout, Henry Rhodes, Abraham Cable, Michael Cefar, Jacob Rhodes, Gabriel Rhodes, Philip Wagerline, George Countryman, and Frederick Altfather.

The Dibert Massacre—1739

George Dibert, his wife, and five children had settled on a small clearing on a tract, just a mile from present Berlin, Pennsylvania, now owned by John O. Stoner. Dibert was burning some stumps at the edge of his clearing. He had no gun with him and was at the mercy of the wilderness, for he did not believe in carrying a gun, except for obtaining meat for his family. He heard his wife screaming and the children crying. He heard a shot and his oldest son fell dead. Dibert, from the bushes, saw before him the most horrible sight of his life. Two Indians were dragging his wife out of the cabin by her hair. Amid the struggling and agony, he saw the scalping knife lift her beautiful hair from her still struggling body. An Indian brought the mercy blow with his tomahawk. With extreme horror, George Dibert saw all his family scalped before his very eyes. He would have rushed to their aid, except he reasoned that it would have been suicide to move from his hiding place. Two Indians were ransacking his cabin and he spied two others in the woods searching for him. He managed to elude them by running toward the pines in the hollow below the clearing.

For a terrible night and a day he occasionally caught glimpses of the braves on his trail. He hid by day in thick laurel masses of the mountain above Berlin. For three days and nights, Dibert traveled in a broad circle around his clearing and his massacred family. When he was entirely satisfied that he was safe from the Indians, he moved back toward his family and cabin. Late at night he returned to the field in front of the ashes of his cabin. In the darkness he knew he was safe from the Indians, for they would not venture near the dead after dark, for the spirits of the dead were nearby.

He crawled to where he remembered he last saw the body of his dear wife. He took his belt from his waist, a rawhide string that he had used for his possible bag and a combination belt. He tied it around the feet of the swollen and partly decayed body and dragged it to a deep ditch. One by one he dragged his children to the same ditch. By use of stones and sticks, he managed to cover hs family in a shallow grave. Almost exhausted from fatigue, sorrow, and lack of food, he sobbingly faced the White Horse Mountain and stumbled toward Carlisle, some 139 miles away. After a week of hiding and walking across almost trackless wastes, for he dared not travel by the rough Indian trail over what is now U.S. 30, he came, almost exhausted, into the fort and told his pitiable story. In 1768, George Dibert remarried and settled in Bedford Township.

Brothersvalley Township

Philip Wagerline arrived from Germany in 1768 and docked at Philadelphia. He made his way up the old route which is now U.S. 30. He cleared some land and built a log cabin for his family in the township of Brothersvalley in Bedford County. The original cabin was built on the farm that John O. Stoner lives on now.

In 1771, while riding along the countryside, Harmon Husband approached the plume of smoke that arose from the clearing near the headwaters of the Stony Creek River. Husband was hailed in broken English with, "Welcome, broder, where you come?" Husband replied, "From Hagerstown." Said the settler, "Come along, you be hungry, you be tired."

This was the welcome of Harmon Husband to the Stony Creek Glades by Philip Wagerline and his family in the late evening of June 5, 1771. After a night's rest under the Wagerline roof, Husband explained during a breakfast of venison, boiled rye, and boiled potatoes that he was looking for a man named Isaac Cox. In turn, Philip informed Husband that his nearest neighbors were five or six miles away.

The Wagerline farm came into being when Philip Wagerline, Sr., took a patent for land which was situated in Brothersvalley Township. This tract of land was called the "Pyramid" in the Buffalo Creek in the county of Bedford. This took place on October 5, 1789, and the land included 155½ acres. On the same date, Philip Wagerline, Jr., obtained a tract of land called "Doves Harbour" in the Buffalo Creek in Brothersvalley Township. This land contained 289¾ acres. These three sheepskin patents are now in the possession of the present owner, Paul E. Pritts, who received them from the original family of Philip, Fred, and John Wagerline.

John Wagerline built a cabin and barn in 1809. In 1824, a log spring house and a weaving mill were built for the purpose of making the Wagerline coverlets. This building now stands in fine condition.

The farm cemetery is located at the west end of the Paul E. Pritts farm along the township road. There are nine Wagerlines buried there, and the cemetery has been well maintained with sawed locust posts and 1½-inch galvanized pipes for a permanent fence. This farm has never been out of the relation, the present owner is the seventh generation.

In the 1830's and 1840's, Charles Stoner built a

Weigley Mill

foundry in Berlin. He made the first wood- and coal-burning stoves in this area. The coke that was used in the foundry was made on the Philip Wagerline, Jr., farm, now owned by John O. Stoner. It was called the Coke Oven Woods. This is where they opened a mine and hauled the coal out with a wheelbarrow that was made into coke. Mr. Chancey Long hauled the coke to Berlin by horse and wagon for the Stoner foundry. Miss Aldine and Miss Lillian Long are granddaughters of Chancey Long.

The Oldest Remaining House in Somerset County

"The Old Schweppy" was built by Frances Philipi, 1771. Elder John Groner (Croner) settled here the same year and used the building for a home and meetinghouse for church services, by 1773. It was later used as a home and doctor's office by Dr. John Groner, Jr. Thus it got its Pennsylvania German name above, for it was a place where the doctor practiced phlebotomy or "bloodletting," hence the strange name. Original shutters were made of strong oak boards with rifle loop holes. It was built over a strong spring. Note "pull-up" stairs for protection.

Today this is the oldest remaining house in Somerset County.

Dr. John Groner, Jr. (1779-1848)

"Old Schweppy"

The Glades Amish of Brothersvalley

A Bicentennial Study

by
Thomas Irvin Maust, II

August 3, 1976

Introduction

Like an intricate jigsaw puzzle, the piecing together of the evidence concerning the Glades Amish of Brothersvalley is a tedious process. The nearly complete absence of written Amish records necessitates reference to legal and governmental documents, traditions, family histories, immigration records, cemeteries, etc. And, considering the traditionally independent and anti-government stance of the Amish, along with the isolation of early Brothersvalley from governmental centers, even the official governmental records are sometimes questionable. Nevertheless, the pieces are now beginning to look like a whole, and the result is surprising—surprising because the Amish, who were so important to the early settlement of our area, have for decades vanished from Brothersvalley.

This study is an attempt to form this scattered evidence into a reasonable history of some of our earliest pioneers—The Glades Amish of Brothersvalley.

Acknowledgments

The works of Paul V. Hostetler and Dr. Hugh Gingerich, as well as the personal library of Catherine J. Miller, have been of invaluable aid in the preparation of this study.

The Glades Amish of Brothersvalley

A persistent failing of local histories by local historians has been the omission of the history of the Amish church and community in what is now Brothersvalley Township in Somerset County, Pennsylvania. Indeed, the very suggestion of such a history may come as a surprise to today's local residents. Nevertheless, it is possible to establish several facts about the Glades Amish and to add some well-grounded speculations.

First, the Amish, along with their German Brethren neighbors*, migrated from eastern Pennsylvania to become the earliest permanent settlers in Brothersvalley. As early as the mid-1720's trappers and hunters had been bringing buffalo and other hides to eastern Pennsylvania from the wilderness which was then the Brothersvalley glades.[1] And, no doubt, as word of the area's potential was rumored by these frontiersmen, and, as the population pressures of the large German families increased, there were those who joined their neighbors and moved from the overcrowded east to the open wilds beyond the Allegheny Mountain. Therefore, it is hardly surprising that most of the old Brothersvalley names can now be traced directly to neighboring homesteads in eastern counties of the state.

So it was that as early as the 1750's[2] and definitely by the 1760's, Amish neighbors down east had migrated through the dense mountain forests and resettled as neighbors again in an area beginning at what is now the town of Berlin and stretching north along two parallel branches which are the headwaters of the Stony Creek. Many of these early settlers were vanguards of civilization who preceded even the surveyors and tax collectors into the Brothersvalley wilderness and whose tomahawk claims defied the Proclamation Line of 1763.* At this early date, these pioneers' primary concern was survival rather than the legalities of an English-speaking government.

Among the early Amish settlers here were John Schrock (Schrack, Schrag, Schryack, Shrake) and Christian Blough (Blauch, Plough). A Schrock family sketch tells us that John, as a young boy, came with his half-brother to the vicinity of Berlin in or around 1765.[3] Although the sketch calls him a Mennonite, he was certainly Amish and later on married one of his Amish neighbors, a sister of Amish Bishop Jacob Miller (see below). Schrock grew to manhood here, purchased land from the Speichers (also below), died in 1813, and lies buried on the Lewis Maust farm. Christian Blough settled in 1767[14] on what is now the William Shultz farm, an area which, according to one Mennonite historian, became a sizable Amish settlement.[5] He died at the early age of thirty-three and was buried there in 1777. These graves remain today.

Apparently during the late 1760's, a heavy migration of Amish came to the glades, mostly from Berks County, Pennsylvania. Much of the land which is today im-

---

*H. Austin Cooper's *Two Centuries of Brothersvalley Church of the Brethren* deals with this history. However, although his overall history is generally accurate, Cooper erred greatly in listing many of the early Amish as Brethren and Lutheran. Appendix I of this study lists the Amish who were plotted on the first warrant map of Brothersvalley or who were listed in the first tax assessment for Brothersvalley.

*The proclamation officially prohibited settlement west of the Allegheny Mountain and remained in effect until 1768.

mediately north of Berlin was held at one time or another by these Amish. There is strong evidence that these Brothersvalley pioneers were actively supported by the Amish Church in eastern Pennsylvania. An old Amish Alms Book, containing financial records from 1768 onward for the Amish of the Reading-Berks County area, in a section kept by Deacon Hans Kurtz, lists a gift on November 15, 1768, of "XI pounds and six Pence"* to Christian Speicher,[6] who shortly thereafter came to Brothersvalley from Berks County and settled where Mr. and Mrs. Lewis Maust now live. Since that sum was nearly the whole amount contained in the treasury at that time, it would seem virtually certain to have been a major contribution from the eastern Amish Church to the pioneer Amish community struggling to survive in the Brothersvalley glades.

Certainly the most well-known Amishman to settle here in those early years was young Joseph Schantz (anglicized to Johns or Johnes) who came to America in 1769 at age twenty and settled soon thereafter with the Amish in Brothersvalley.[7] Part of his claim was in the heart of what is now Berlin, and it is difficult for us to imagine the dense, virgin wilderness he found there. Jacob Keffer's original indenture for the town of Berlin on Pius Spring lists "Joseph Johnes" as an owner of an adjoining tract. And, the first addition to Berlin, that part west from Division Street and including the upper diamond, was purchased by Jacob Keffer, John Fisher, and Francis Hay from Amishman Joseph Johnes. The agreement was made in 1787, but like so many early land transactions, was not deeded until 1796.[8] Joseph Johns finally sold all of his Brothersvalley property in 1793[9] and relocated at the confluence of the Conemaugh River where he founded a city which today bears his name—Johnstown, Pennsylvania.

Another notable Amish leader came to the Brothersvalley glades with the migration from eastern Pennsylvania. He was Jacob Miller, the first leader of the River Amish in Elk Lick (the church and community there remain active today).[10] Jacob was a son of Hannes Miller, Sr. (known as "Indian John"*) who was an early Amish settler on what is now the Tom Maust farm. Around 1782 at age twenty-eight Jacob and his young family moved to the glades where his father had settled a few years before.[11] While there he ministered to the Brothersvalley Amish before moving to Elk Lick sometime between 1785 and 1793 and finally moving again to Tuscarawas County, Ohio, where he became the first Amish-Mennonite leader before his death in 1835.[12] His mother, Magdalena, is buried on the home farm in Brothersvalley. The old cemetery is on an elevated ridge and looks west across the whole valley which was once the core of the Amish community. The hand-chiseled

stone reads "M1817M." One of Jacob's brothers, known as Glades Christian to distinguish him from nearly half a dozen local Christian Millers, remained on the home farm and became a prominent Brothersvalley farmer in the early 1800's.[13] The Miller sisters became Mrs. Joseph Speicher, Mrs. Christian Speicher, Mrs. Christian Mishler, Mrs. John Schrock, and Mrs. Jacob Kauffman. We can easily see from these family names that the Amish family of Hannes Miller, Sr., in keeping with Amish tradition, married members of other neighboring Amish families.[14]

Christian Zug (Zook), although not famous to our generation, must certainly have been famous to his generation in Brothersvalley, for not only did he settle where Mr. and Mrs. Jim Will now live sometime around or before 1770, but shortly thereafter six of his sons, sons-in-law, and stepsons-in-law settled on nearby farms.[15] Such family ties, as we have already seen, were common then as they are today among the Amish.

(A detailed list of the earliest Amish settlers in Brothersvalley will be found in Appendix I.)

Second, the Amish church in the Brothersvalley glades just north of Berlin was active for approximately the next 125 years.[16] Amish-Mennonite records tell us that Bishop Jacob Mast (Maust), born in 1738 and died in 1808, was a Berks County Amish leader of considerable ability who was charged with all of the Amish settlements in Pennsylvania, including three west of the Susquehanna River, one of which was the Glades.[17] More evidence of the Brothersvalley Amish comes from a conference of Somerset County Amish ministers held in 1837. At that meeting, these six men signed the final document as ministers to the Glades Church: Christian Yoder, Sr. (son of Schweitzer Yoder); Christian Yoder, Jr.;* Abraham Miller; Jacob Miller (not the same as above); Jacob Schwartzendruber; and David Yoder.[18] The text of the document, entitled **The Discipline of 1837**, is found in Appendix II.

A Mennonite historian suggests that by the early 1800's these Amish on the Stony Creek numbered up to 100 members in possibly three congregations.[19] On October 3, 1830, these churches hosted at least one of the church-wide Amish conferences.[20] Another sign of vigor during the first thirty-five years of the 1800's was the continuing migration of Amish from the mother country into the community. Among these later Amish immigrants were Daniel Brenneman and his wife, Mary Bender Brenneman, who brought their family from Germany in 1825[21] and lived temporarily in David Lehman's house near Berlin where their last daughter, Barbara, was born on April 5, 1827.[22] They farmed in Brothersvalley briefly as tenants before moving to the Elk Lick area.[23] Also, the aforementioned Jacob Schwartzendruber, one of the signers of **The Discipline of 1837**, was ordained as an Amish minister in Menger-

---

*The original German text reads: "mer in disen iahr aus geben von dem arm geld au Christ Schpicher XI fund und sechs benz." Miller's translation reads: "more paid out in this year of the alms money to Christ Speicher 11 pounds and six pence."

---

*The story of "Indian John" Miller is told on pages 33 and 953 of *Descendants of Jacob Hochstetler*.

---

*Dr. E. C. Saylor and J. B. Achrock in 1946 wrote a brief summary of the Yoder Cemeteries in Stonycreek Township. One of these ". . . contains the graves of four adults said to be Yoders whose descendants now live near Haven and Yoder, Kansas. Christian Yoder Senior and Junior both Amish ministers."

inghausen, Waldeck, Germany in 1826 before coming to America in 1833. He, too, settled first in Brothersvalley and ministered to the church there until 1840 when he joined in the movement south to Elk Lick.[24]

And yet, in spite of these signs of strength, by 1850 the local church had reached its zenith and mysteriously was nonexistent by the early years of the new century. The last bishop, Abner Yoder (grandson of Christian, Jr.), migrated west to Johnson County, Iowa, in 1866,[25] and, according to **The Mennonite Encyclopedia**, the last services were probably held during the 1870's. The same source reports that

Jacob B. Schrock, a jurist of Berlin, Pa., recalled in a personal interview in 1950, that as a boy he accompanied his parents on a visit to his grandparents, the Michael Schrocks, about 1879, and saw the old benches stacked on the back porch, left there after the last preaching service of the Amish in that community.[26]

The History of Bedford and Somerset Counties, published in 1906, mentions a sprinkling of Amish still living then in Brothersvalley and Stony Creek townships.[27] However, in 1910, the last local member on record died at the age of ninety-three.[28] He was Benedict Yoder.

And so we ask the obvious: What was the fate of this once prosperous Amish settlement? To answer we offer three reasons. First, migrations west to the lure of cheap and more fertile land, and north, like Joseph Johns, and south, like Jacob Swartzendruber, to the growing Amish settlements in Conemaugh and Elk Lick definitely was an early factor in weakening the Brothersvalley Amish. Indeed, common local Amish names of the 1760-1840 period, such as Schantz (Johns), Mishler, Dieffenbaugh, Troyer (Dreyer), Zug (Zook), Schwartzendruber, and Brenneman, completely vanished from the township in subsequent years as whole families migrated north, south, and west. One such exodus occurred in 1812 when the Jacob Zug family moved to Holmes County, Ohio.[29] Jacob was the son of the aforementioned Christian and several of that family are buried on Christian's home farm in Brothersvalley.

Second, internal dispute and division concerning moral behavior and adoption of modern lifestyles was a further factor in the decline of the Brothersvalley Amish. The contents of **The Discipline of 1837** (see Appendix II) are abundant evidence of both widespread immorality and adoption of wordly customs. Later, as the Civil War raged, Amish ministers condemned Amish youth for their immoral behavior while others were dying on the battlefields.[30] Part of the immorality problem was the bizarre custom of "bundling" in which the perspective Amish bride and groom slept in the same bed but fully clothed and separated by a plank.[31] Besides condemning this immorality, the signers of **The Discipline of 1837** came down hard against loud colors, high collars, silk neckerchiefs, and mirrors in the house. These controversies apparently became so widespread and so weakened the Glades Amish of Brothersvalley

that, in the words of their contemporaries, "The people became too ungodly and the church could not stand."[32]

Weakened internally, then, by migrations and by strife, we are logically led to a third fate of the Brothersvalley Amish. Since they and the Brethren had coexisted for generations as neighbors in the Berlin-Brotherton-Roxbury triangle of Brothersvalley Township (and nearby portions of what is now Stony Creek Township) our third possibility is that the strong and evangelistic Brethren simply absorbed many of the Amish. Brethren histories tell us of many intense evangelistic efforts sponsored by that denomination, especially during the so-called "Second Awakening" of 1785-1800.[33] Also, the practices of the Amish and Brethren were similar in an age when horses and buggies, lanterns, and homemade plain clothes were normal. Creek baptism, which was standard among the Brethren (hence the name Tunker or Dunkard), was not unusual among some Amish circles.[34] Indeed, what miner doctrinal differences did exist between the two groups were easily breached by the German language which was, of course, native to both. Combining these factors, then, with the probable internal weakness of the Amish, the case becomes even stronger. Many descendants of the early Amish pioneers later joined the Brethren, the United Brethren, or other denominations. Among these were the local descendants of Christian Blough (although those descendants who migrated north remained active for some time in Amish-Mennonite circles) and the John Schrock family (a son joined the Disciples of Christ).[35] Even today many local families bear names which are historically Amish.

In addition to the many local family names, traces of the Old Amish Lane, which ran through the heart of the early settlement, remain today as a vague legacy to the Amish of Brothersvalley. On the banks of the Stony Creek at the northern line of the Berlin Community Grove can be seen the approach embankments to an old bridge which carried the lane across the creek. Several decades ago the bridge was barricaded and soon after was washed away in a storm. The WPA Cemetery Survey for Brothersvalley Township describes the Lehman Cemetery on the Webreck farm as being located ". . . on the north side of an abandoned road, known as the Amish Lane. . . ." The cemetery and remains of the lane are still seen. Indeed, many older residents of the area recall crossing the valley between Berlin and Route 31 on east-west lanes in their younger days, but the name "Amish Lane" apparently originated generations before even the oldest living residents. Traces of an east-west lane are seen in the **1876 Atlas of Somerset County,**[36] but none on that map run the whole breadth of the area. Thus, more than a century ago, the Amish Lane meandered among Amish farms in a general east-west direction, connecting the forerunners of what we now know as the Webreck Road, the Beulah Road, and the Roxbury Road. Its traces today, scattered through the heartland and oral history of Brothersvalley, survive as one of the few reminders of Brothersvalley's enigmatic Amish community.

A Map of the Glades Amish of Brothersvalley
1767-1785

KEY

Amish homesteads (see App. I)

Amish Lane*

*Reconstructed here from Beer's *Atlas of Somerset County 1876*, the WPA Cemetery Survey, and local tradition.
The above map is taken from the *Somerset County Plat Book* 1972.

Footnotes

1. Sanford G. Shetler, *Two Centuries of Struggle and Growth* (Scottdale, Pa., 1963), p. 14.

2. *Ibid.*, p. 15.

3. William H. Welfley, *History of Bedford and Somerset Counties Pennsylvania* (New York, 1906), III, p. 62.

4. Elias Gnagey, *A Complete History of Christian Gnaegi* (Elkhart, Ind., 1897), p. 136.

5. Shetler, p. 51.

6. *Amish Alms Book*, translated by Catherine J. Miller (original copy from her library).

7. C. Z. Mast, *Annals of the Conestoga* (1942), p. 247.

8. Welfley, II, p. 589.

9. Mast, p. 247.

10. Shetler, p. 332.

11. Alsta Elizabeth Schrock and Olen L. Miller, *Joel B. Miller History* (Scottdale, Pa., 1960), p. 15.

12. Virgil Miller, *Descendants of Daniel B. Miller* (1970), p. 2.

13. Welfley, II, p. 585.

14. Rev. Harvey Hostetter, D.D., *Descendants of Jacob Hochstetler* (Elgin, Ill., 1912), p. 339.

15. Paul V. Hostetler, notes on the Amish in Lebanon and then Somerset Counties, December 22, 1973.

16. Shetler, p. 322.

17. *Ibid.*, p. 319.

18. Harold S. Bender, "Some Early American Amish Mennonite Disciplines," *The Mennonite Quarterly Review*, VIII (April 1934), 93-95.

19. Shetler, p. 324.

20. "Somerset County," *The Mennonite Encyclopedia*, 1959, IV, 574.

21. Albert H. Gerberich, *The Brenneman History* (Scottdale, Pa., 1938), p. 856.

22. Brenneman Family Bible, transcript by Catherine J. Miller.

23. Gerberich, p. 857.

24. "Somerset County," *The Mennonite Encyclopedia*, p. 574.

25. Shetler, p. 324.

26. "Somerset County," *The Mennonite Encyclopedia*, p. 574.

27. Welfley, II, p. 502.

28. Shetler, p. 324.

29. Paul V. Hostetler, unpublished letter, 18 November 1974.

30. Shetler, p. 324.

31. *Ibid.*, p. 45.

32. "Somerset County," *The Mennonite Encyclopedia*, p. 574.

33. H. Austin Cooper, *Two Centuries of Brothersvalley Church of the Brethren* (1962), p. 218.

34. Shetler, p. 329.

35. Welfley, III, p. 62.

36. F. W. Beers, *County Atlas of Somerset Pennsylvania* (New York, 1876), p. 61.

Appendix I

Early Amish Settlers in the Brothersvalley Glades

Earliest Brothersvalley Warrant Map: The following names plotted on the first Brothersvalley Warrant Map were Amish. Parenthetical information describes the approximate locations of these plots as found in the *1972 Somerset County Plat Book.*

Berkey, Jacob   warrant date unknown
  (Frank S. Carver tract adjoining Calvin M. Will. Berkey possibly was not Amish.)

Blough, Christian   1773 warrant
  (Southern parts of Sherman D. Glessner, Jr., and John W. and Vera Shultz tracts)

Diefenbach, Casper   1785 warrant
  (Deeter's Gap)

Johns, Joseph   1785 warrant
  (Frank Phennicie and upper diamond area of Berlin)

Leman (Lehman), Benedict   1773 warrant
  (Alvin S. Carver, southern part of Glenden A. Hillegass, eastern part of Clarence G. Carver, and Jason T. Charlton)

Leman (Lehman), John   1785 warrant
  (Karl and Anna Krepelka, Merl Vought, est. and western part of Bertha S. Vought)

Miller, Nicholas   1773 warrant
  (Norman E. Suder and Ray A. Glessner, et al)

Mishler, Joseph   warrant date unknown
  (Northern part of John W. and Vera Shultz, Earl L. Walker, and southern tip of Clyde L. and Ruth Platt)

Schrock, Casper   1773 warrant
  (Southeastern part of Calvin M. Will and Nellie Keefer)

Speicher, Christian   1809 warrant
  (Fern Glessner Maust)

Yoder, Christian   1773 warrant
  (Stony Creek Township)

Yoder, David   1777 warrant
  (Stony Creek Township)

Zug, Christian   1773 warrant
  (James I. Suder)

Zug, John   1773 warrant
  (Edwin P. Landis, Snyder's Potato Chips, Inc., Elwood Landis, part of Berlin Borough)

Other early Amish: The following names occur on either early Brothersvalley tax assessments, deeds, or warrants.

Blough (miscopied Benuch, Christopher) Christian 1773 tax

Johns, Joseph   1775 tax

Lehman, Peter   1779 tax

Miller, Hannes, Sr.   1785 warrant

Schrock, Jacob   1779 tax

Spiker, Christian   1773 tax

Troyer, John   1775 tax

Troyer, Michael   1775 tax

Yoder, John   1775 deed

Appendix II
The Discipline of 1837
River, Glade, Conemaugh Congregations
Pennsylvania, March 18, 1837

Concerning the Conference of the Ministry of the Three Congregations, River, Glade, and Conemaugh. Decisions as follows:

First: It is noted that decline has set in because the ordinance of God in the matter of the ban is greatly neglected. Decided that separation and shunning are to be practiced toward all disobedient ones without regard of person, whether man or woman.

Second: It is noted that there is awful pride in clothing, namely with respect to silken neck cloths (Halstuecher) worn around the neck, so that mothers tie silken neck-cloths on their children, and make high collars on their children's shirts and clothing; and the mothers permit their daughters to wear men's hats and go with them to church or other places, or that even the mothers have them themselves. Decided that such things shall not be among us.

Third: Decided that there shall be no display in houses, namely where houses are built or painted with various colors, or filled with showy furniture, namely with wooden, porcelain, or glass utensils (dishes), and having cupboards and mirrors hung on the wall and such things.

Fourth: Decided that worldly offices are not to be held, namely serving on juries, or holding elections to elect officials.

Fifth: Decided that excessive driving of sleighs or other vehicles is not to be, and also that vehicles are not to be painted with two colors, as has already occurred too much.

Sixth: Decided that those who marry outside are no longer to be received again so lightly into fellowship, unless they bring their marriage partners with them into Christian discipline, and are received after true repentance and change of heart has been shown.

Seventh: Decided that when two persons marry, both of whom are outside the church, and they desire to be received into fellowship, the ministers shall make plain to them the obligations of Christian marriage according to the ordinance of God, and when they are received they shall promise before God and the brotherhood to fulfil the obligations of Christian marriage according to Christian ordinance.

Eighth: Decided that the Sabbath is to be kept holy, that business is to be conducted on the six days of the week according to the ordinance, and Sunday is to be kept to the honor of God, except in case of emergency.

Ninth: With regard to the excesses practiced among the youth, namely that the youth take the liberty to sleep or lie together without any fear or shame, such things shall not be tolerated at all. And when it takes place with the knowledge of the parents and something bad happens on account of it, the parents shall not go unpunished.

Tenth: Decided that the tailors are not to make new or worldly styles of clothing for members of the church, but are to follow the old style and such as is indicated by the ministers and older people of the church.

Eleventh: Likewise, the cabinetmakers are not to make such proud kinds of furniture and not decorate them with such loud or gay ("scheckich") colors.

Twelfth: In conclusion, all the abovementioned articles are to be observed according to the Christian discipline and practice.

Signed by us, ministers of the three above-named congregations.

Conemaugh Congregation
  Jacob Oesch
  Christian Miller
  Christian Nissli
  Joseph Miller
  Jonas Yoder

Glade Congregation
  Christian Yoder, Senior
  Christian Yoder, Junior
  Abraham Miller
  Jacob Swartzendruber
  David Yoder

River Congregation
  Benedict Miller
  Jost Yoder
  Hannes Gingrich

Translated and edited by Harold S. Bender, "Some Early American Amish Mennonite Disciplines," *The Mennontie Quarterly Review*, April, 1934, Vol. 8, No. 2, pp. 93-95.

Bibliography

_____. *Amish Alms Book*. Translated from the German by Catherine J. Miller. Original copy from her library, Grantsville, Md., 1768.

Beers, F. W. *County Atlas of Somerset Pennsylvania*. New York: F. W. Beers and Co., 1876.

Bender, Harold S. "Some Early American Amish Mennonite Disciplines, "*The Mennonite Quarterly Review*. VIII (April 1934), 93-95.

_____. Brenneman Family Bible. Transcript from Catherine J. Miller. From her library, Grantsville, Md.

Cooper, H. Austin. *Two Centuries of Brothersvalley Church of the Brethren*. Historical Committee and the Planning Committee of the Brothersvalley Church of the Brethren, 1962.

Gerberich, Albert H. *The Brenneman History*. Scottdale, Pa.: Mennonite Publishing House, 1938.

Gnagey, Elias. *A Complete History of Christian Gnaegi*. Elkhart, Indiana: Mennonite Publishing Co., 1897.

Hostetler, Paul V. Unpublished letter. 11 November 1974.

Hostetler, Paul V. Unpublished notes on the Amish in Lebanon and then Somerset Counties. 22 December 1973.

Hostetter, Rev. Harvey. *Descendants of Jacob Hochstetler*. Elgin, Illinois: Brethren Publishing House, 1912.

Mast, C. Z. *Annals of the Conestoga*. 1942.

Miller, Virgil. *Descendants of Daniel B. Miller*. 1970.

Schrock, Alta Elizabeth, and Olen L. Miller. *Joel B. Miller History*. Scottdale, Pa.: Mennonite Publishing House, 1960.

Shetler, Sanford G. *Two Centuries of Struggle and Growth*. Scottdale, Pa.: Herald Press, 1963.

"Somerset County." *The Mennonite Encyclopedia*, 1959, IV, 572-575.

——————. *Somerset County, Pennsylvania Plat Book*. Rockford, Illinois: Rockford Map Publishers, Inc., 1972.

Welfley, William H. and E. Howard Blackburn. *History of Bedford and Somerset Counties*. Edited by Hon. William H. Koontz. 3 volumes. New York: The Lewis Publishing Company, 1906.

——————. *WPA Cemetery Survey*. Mary S. Biesecker Library, Somerset, Pa.

——————. Warrant Map of Brothersvalley Township, Bedford County, Pennsylvania. Recorder of Deeds Office, Courthouse; Somerset, Pennsylvania.

Frantz Distillery

The land was young. Virgin timber grew in the mountains, native trout swam in the pure streams of Somerset County, and adventurous men were carving their place in history.

Sometime before 1830, a man named Baer built a distillery five miles southeast of what is now known as Berlin. A house was soon added with hand-hewn rafters and joint corners. The site was chosen for its access to pure spring water which was brought down from the mountains in wood through aqueducts. Later pitch pine logs were bored through the center and a wooden pipeline was created for the purpose.

As the land grew, roads had to be built to accommodate the expansion of civilization. Lumber was cheap, selling for as little as one dollar a hundred feet, so it was decided in 1850 to build a plank road from Cumberland, Maryland, to West Newton, Pennsylvania. The planks were only eight or nine feet long and were placed close together on the ground where a level bed had been prepared for them. This wondrous "mud-free" road went by the distillery, and stagecoaches and wagons were soon stopping to stock up on liquid refreshments.

The next owner was named Shultz. In the mid-1800's he operated a business which saw three or four barrels of fine whiskey placed in his storehouse each day—hardly a thriving business—but one which kept the family gainfully employed into the 1900's. Then he sold to a man named Minor who in turn sold to Hawking. Despite the new ownerships, the name "Shultz Distillery" was associated with the building for many years.

Under the ownership of Hawking, the plant was remodeled. Pot stills were put in and the same process as in making moonshine was initiated. The mash was stirred until the boiling process began and then it was capped to complete the evaporation process necessary for distilling.

It was at this time the whiskey boom began. During the years 1908, 1909, 1910 the third track of the B & O Railroad was laid, the Western Maryland Railroad was under construction, and coal mines were scattered throughout the area. All of these industries produced hard-working, hard-drinking men.

Hawking began a delivery service. Placing jugs of the liquor on a dray wagon, he would make his rounds to the different camps. There were rules. The least amount you could buy was a gallon. After buying the prescribed amount you were then free to purchase any amount extra, such as a pint or half gallon. Perhaps he made his fortune by 1915 or he became aware of the growing discontent in the business. Whatever his reason, that year he sold to Leech.

The Leech Distillery never had a chance to establish itself. The quality of the brew was criticized and its production was halted by Prohibition.

The land lay fallow for many years after that. The buildings sank into disrepair as the United States remained "dry."

When the Twenty-first Amendment was passed in 1933, Frantz, from Pittsburgh, stepped onto the scene. The land was bought and the buildings overhauled. Operations began and some of the finest whiskey in the United States was reportedly made at this time.

Then, once again, the nation was plunged into war. Frantz Distillery was pressed into service. Whiskey was no longer distilled but rather alcohol was processed to be used in the making of methyl rubber. More structures were added to the existing ones and a 100-foot tower was erected for the storing of grain. The distillery began working 24 hours a day, seven days a week. They produced close to 2,500 gallons a day.

Water became a problem. The wooden pipeline had been replaced by the standard tubing, and a cooling system was now added to the plant in order to recycle the liquid.

Potato flour, yeast, syrup, and cattle feed were added to the production list. Trainloads of potatoes were brought in from across the county and parked at every railroad siding in the area. Getting rid of the refuse started a sideline business. The "slop" was used to fatten cattle and pigs.

Business was great and along with the prosperity

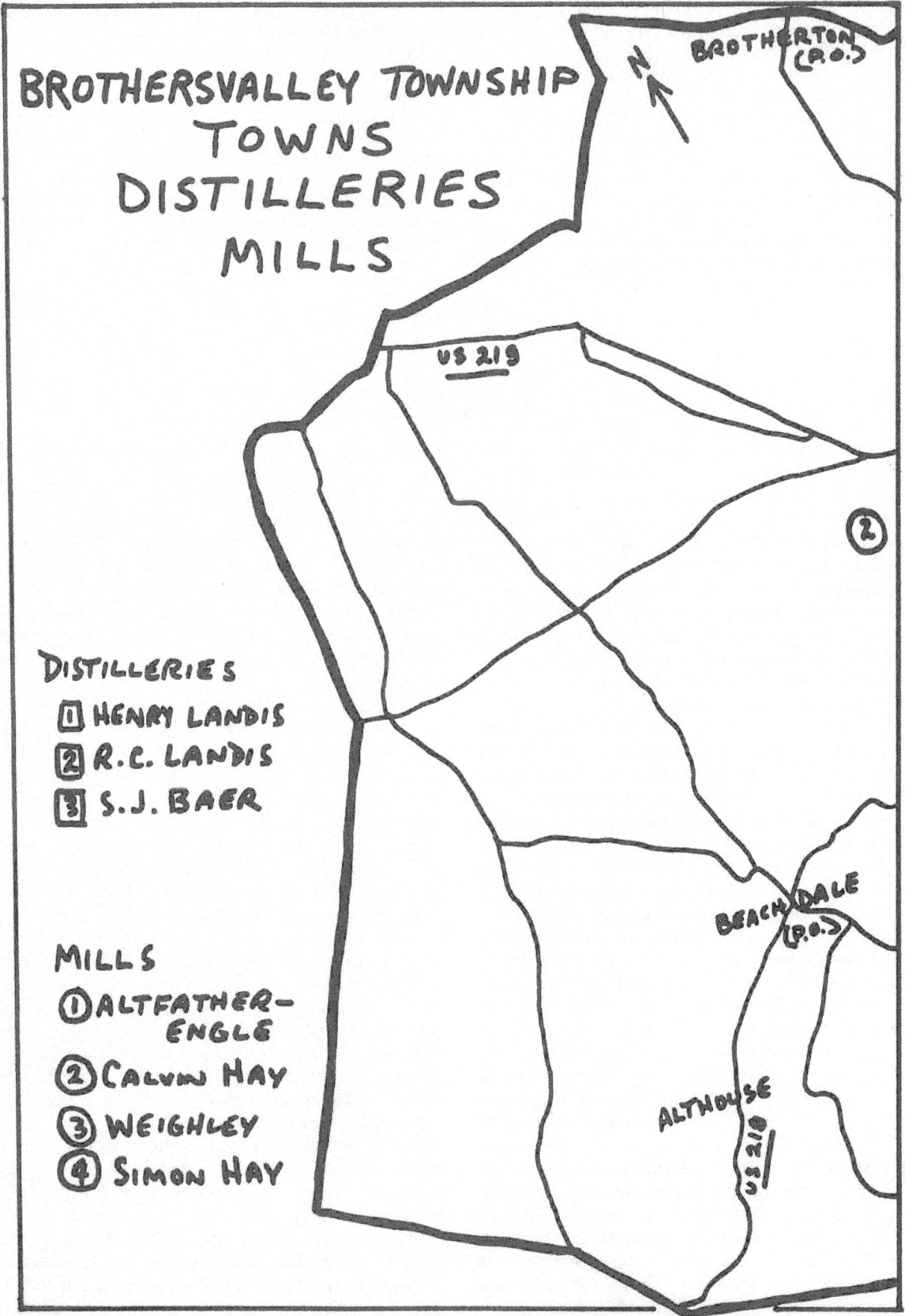

BROTHERSVALLEY TOWNSHIP
TOWNS
DISTILLERIES
MILLS

BROTHERTON (P.O.)

N

US 219

②

DISTILLERIES
1 HENRY LANDIS
2 R.C. LANDIS
3 S.J. BAER

MILLS
① ALTFATHER-ENGLE
② CALVIN HAY
③ WEIGHLEY
④ SIMON HAY

BEACHDALE (P.O.)

ALTHOUSE

US 219

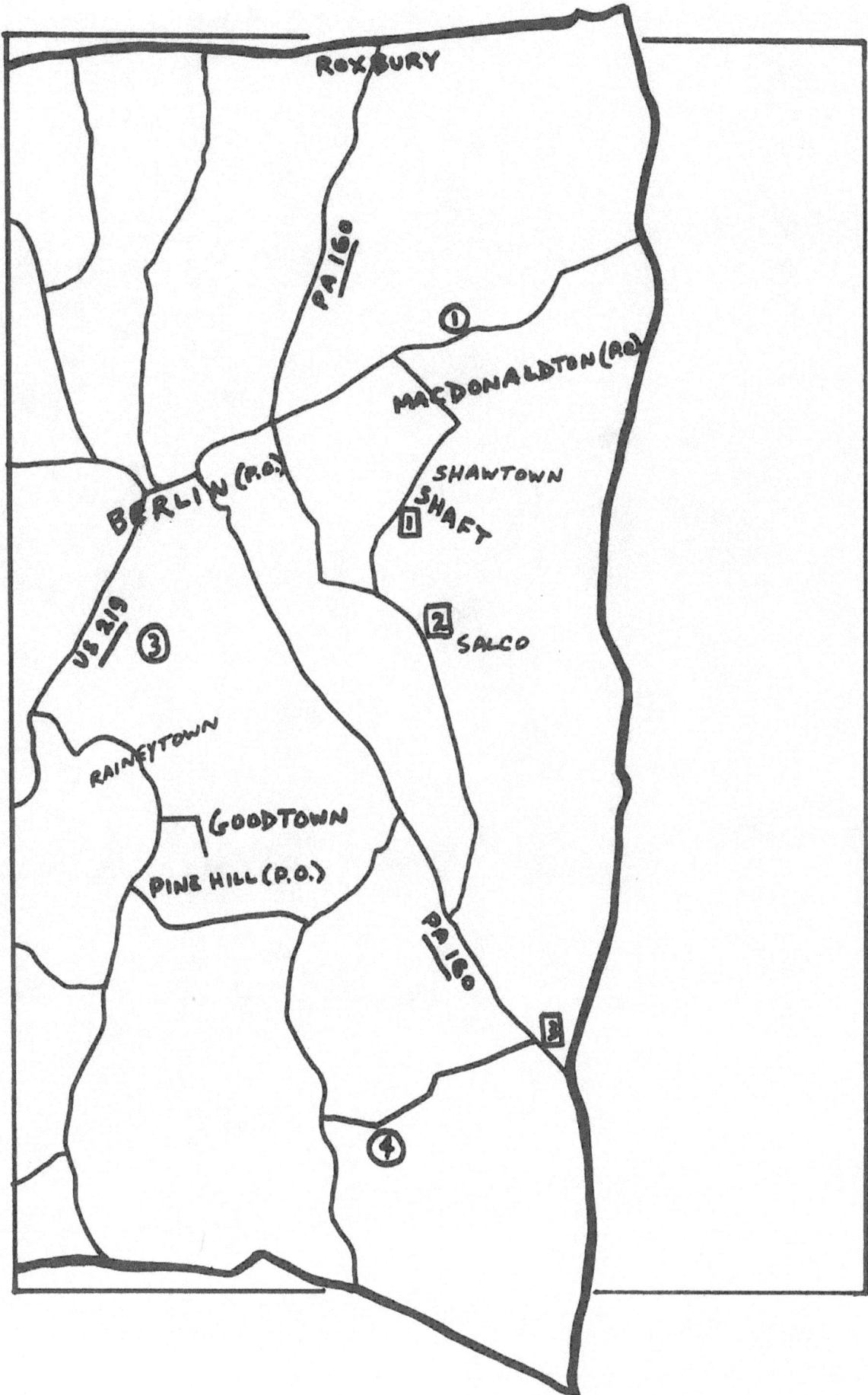

ROXBURY

PA 160

①

MACDONALDTON (P.O.)

BERLIN (P.O.)

SHAWTOWN

▢ SHAFT

▢2 SALCO

US 219

③

RAINEYTOWN

GOODTOWN

PINE HILL (P.O.)

PA 160

▢3

④

March 1944.

The Frantz Distillery, 1944

came the complaints of local citizens due to pollution of streams and the smell caused by the rotting potatoes.

The war ended but work continued. The potato flour was now sent to Germany—30,000 pounds a day!

In May of 1946 a fire destroyed the old drier house and its contents located at the rear of the main distillery building. The cost of the blaze was estimated at $30,000 and marked the end of the potato flour production. At this time the Frantz Distillery was listed as one of the largest industrial plants in Somerset County.

The other phases of the work went on as usual until the untimely death of Frantz in 1950. Within two years the employment dropped to five or ten men and then the distillery closed completely, although liquor was stored in the warehouse until 1956.

Now owned by the Najon Corporation in Somerset, the buildings are once again a source of puzzlement. Young voices ask, "What's that?" as they speed by on a smooth macadam road.

It is hard to explain that the crumbling buildings were once a part of history—the largest industrial plant in Somerset County. Smoke no longer rolls from the stacks of Frantz Distillery 24 hours a day. Instead quietness prevails as a local farmer uses the building to sell potatoes.

Special thanks to Jubal Werner, Glencoe, for information that could be found only in his memories.

Brotherton

How Brotherton Was Named

In 1760 Elder George Adam Martin, from Antrim Township, near present Waynesboro, led a group of German Baptists and Seventh-Day Baptists here and settled at the present site of Brotherton. Among the group of some sixty or seventy were three brothers also from Antrim Township, namely George, Henry, and James Brotherton, for whom Brotherton was named.

By 1770 Morgan Edwards called the place "Bruederstown," or Brotherton. James and Henry stayed until sometime after 1771 when they were ousted from their tomahawk claim when Lettus Hooper surveyed it and bought the land from the Penn Company. The present tract is that of the Robert M. Bauermaster farm entitled "Contention" in 1771.

From about 1760 to 1775 there came into this area sizable migrations of people of German extraction. There were two main reasons: first, they were Germans and wanted nothing to do with the impending war coming between the colonists and the lords of their homeland, England. Second, they were mainly Quakers, Mennonites, and Brethren, who did not believe in taking up arms. Then, too recently they were freed from the bonds of government and taxation and war in their homelands, England or Germany. They sought the quiet and freedom of the wilderness and the plentiful resources that God had planted there.

Brotherton

The Great Buffalo Kill

The last large herd of buffalo vanished from the area by 1809. Dr. E. C. Saylor, the Honorable Jacob B. Schrock, and Mr. Elmer Walker told this story. It was on a hot summer morning in August that someone in Berlin discovered that a large herd of buffalo had moved into the buffalo wallows, located in the flats below the present site of the old railroad station. These flats or wallows covered the glades over the Buffalo Lick Creek—that is how it got its name, from the sulphur springs in the glades where buffalo came to lick the salt deposits brought up by the spring water that came from down deep in the bowels of the earth. This accounts for the humid and foul odor. Even to this day one can detect the odor of salt and sulphur that has come to the surface as he goes through the glades in this area. The hot sun causes the gases to give off the sulphur odor.

On this particular hot August morning, the men and boys of Berlin fell upon the buffalo while they were still in the wallows and slew them by the dozens. They removed their hides, took the humps, the tongues, and the favorite cuts, and left the carcasses to waste in the hot sun. The stench was so terribly depressing in Berlin that people had to keep their doors and windows shut until the cold weather and snows covered up the remains of the beasts.

Beachdale

Beachdale was a railroad station on the Berlin branch road. It consisted of a store and a couple of dwellings, but there was a post office there as early as 1891.

At the present time there are approximately eleven families living in the village. There too one will find a very active church, the Beachdale Church of the Brethren.

Beachdale is also the location of the Valley Grange, which is a strong working group with a large membership.

Beechdale or Burkholder Bridge

The Beechdale Bridge (sometimes called the Burkholder Bridge) spans Buffalo Creek in Brothersvalley Township and serves as the entrance to the villages of Fogletown and Althouse. It was built in 1870 and was recently restored and repainted by the county. This 47-foot-long bridge is an example of the one-span Burr-Arch type, of which there are seven in Somerset County. The other three existing covered bridges are of the King-Truss type. Some years ago Eber Cockley listed 28 covered bridges in the county—only ten remain.

Burkholder Bridge

Althouse

All that remains in 1976 of the once lively, sometimes dangerous, mining town of Althouse, in southeastern Brothersvalley Township, is one lone vintage home, a remodeled version of the double, two-family dwelling it was during the great coal days of the village. It is the present residence of Mr. and Mrs. Charles Sicheri, Route 1, Garrett, who raised their family in the home, after mining operations in the Althouse area had closed down.

A large lawn surrounds the old dwelling, where many

of the original homes of the mining town were also built in the early 1900's. When the mines closed up, the company-owned dwellings and the land they stood on, reverted to J. Madison Shober, on whose farm the company town grew up. Other neighboring homes were built on the land of the Cornelius Judy farm. The mining company originally leased the coal on the Shober and Judy farms for a royalty of three cents per ton.

Althouse was an appropriate name for the small mining hamlet as it was started in 1898 by a firm of Philadelphia coal merchants, W. D. Althouse and Company. The hamlet was built around the Allegheny Mines in 1899 on a section of the J. M. Shober farm that had been leased by the Althouse Company.

On November 3, 1899, the first carload of coal was shipped from the Allegheny Mines in Althouse. The original goal of the company was to have a force of 250 men employed at the mines.

W. D. Althouse and Company had under lease at the Allegheny Mines and vicinity from 1,200 to 1,500 acres of land and had expended between $40,000 and $50,000 to get ready for mining operations.

By the fall of 1899 the company had already built a dozen houses above the mine, along the old road between Beachdale and Garrett. A new schoolhouse was erected and Harry Hay of Berlin was the first teacher. Eight grades were taught in the school with approximately 75 pupils on the roll. Later teachers included Alda Buechley Walker, Etta Shober Landefeld, Mellie Fox, Naomi Smith, Hazel Smith, a Mr. Blough, Alverda Long Brant, and others. The Althouse school finally closed when township schools were being consolidated. The schoolhouse was eventually sold to John Cook of Route 1, Garrett, who tore it down, using much of the lumber in building himself a home near the present Valley Grange hall.

W. D. Althouse and Company were also operators of the Ponfeigh Mines in the same area and also had several other mines in Pennsylvania, Maryland, and West Virginia, handling a half million tons of coal per year in 1899. They exported most of their coal to Cuba, South America, and Central America.

Early officials of the Allegheny Mines included: superintendent, H. S. Walter; mine boss, John A. Carroll; engineer, J. M. Ray; and blacksmith, John J. Hauger. McKelvey C. Foor and Ed McQuade were also early employees of the mines.

During its peak years, the mining town of Althouse had 12 three-room bungalows, three double dwellings where six families in each could reside, a bosses house, as well as three large wooden block houses in which six families each resided.

John Friend was the company storekeeper for a number of years. When John Sechler (father of Mrs. Pearle Weyant) learned of plans for building Althouse, he hurriedly built a store building out of green lumber in hopes he could sell merchandise to the miners. Much to his dismay, the miners were forced to patronize the company store. The Sechler store relied upon business from other neighbors to keep open for many years.

Althouse

Near Althouse was a large hotel-like dwelling, originally owned by Cornelius Judy. From this building, Samuel Brant cut and sold meat for many years. Mr. Brant was a familiar figure on the streets of Althouse, selling fresh meat from his spring wagon to the mine families.

Another large home on the outskirts of the mining hamlet was owned by Mr. and Mrs. Charles Hoover. They kept boarders in their home and Mrs. Hoover specialized in baking pies and cakes for miners who seldom got the delicacies at their own homes.

Fred Brant was once a mule driver in the large stable in Althouse. Francis Christner of Garrett delivered the mail in his horse and buggy to residents of Althouse as a post office never opened in the town. Residents have always been serviced by Route 1, Garrett, Pennsylvania.

Many of the Althouse miners were brought from European countries to work in the mines. Many couldn't speak English when they arrived but gradually learned enough to be understood by others. There were Negroes, as well as many vicious-tempered miners living in Althouse. Althouse was often a dangerous place as knife fights were frequent when the mines were going strong. At least one murder has been recorded in the mining town: John Johnson, a Southern Negro employed in the Althouse mines, was murdered by a fellow Negro workman November 24, 1917, after a vicious quarrel that had started earlier the same day while the two men were at work in the mines. Davy Jackson was charged with the murder.

In later years the Consolidation Coal Company took over the operations of the Allegheny Mines at Althouse.

When the coal was all gone, Althouse died. Today, scrub brush has grown over the once heavily trampled acres that once was the lively town. Only an occasional car or truck passing over the dirt roadway breaks the long silence that has reigned since the "black gold" disappeared.

Fogletown

Tucked away in a secluded glen of southeastern Brothersvalley Township is the quiet settlement of nearly 20 homes known as Fogletown. Access to the village is made by crossing the red Burkholder Bridge and following a winding road that leads off to the left, about two miles south of Beachdale. The old Route 219 passed through the village and continued on approximately two miles to nearby Garrett.

The settlement is named for Herman and Ellen (Judy) Fogle, former owners of the farm on which the town is built. About 1900 Herman Fogle build five houses on his farm for his family to live in. His family consisted of four sons and two daughters, Miss Hilda, Annie Fogle Gnagey, Charles F., Edward, Samuel N., and Robert C. Fogle, all longtime residents of the settlement.

Mr. Fogle also built a number of other rent houses on the farm, which in later years were sold to individuals after the mines closed down and many of the miners left the area.

Many of Herman Fogle's grandchildren have stayed on in the settlement, building many of the new homes that grace the lone street that runs between the two rows of houses.

Names long associated with the Fogletown area include those of Sechler, Burkholder, Commotes, Estnick, Woullard, and of course, the many Fogle families. The mining town of Althouse was located about one mile north of Fogletown.

Fogletown

Raineytown

Raineytown was a mining village that grew up about 1898 on the sloping hillsides of the James S. Hauger farm, two miles south of Berlin and about a half mile north of the present-day village of Goodtown. The Hauger farm in 1976 is owned by the John Popovich, Sr., family of Berlin, Route 4.

The village was located at what was also known as the Pine Hill Station along the railroad that operated between Berlin and Garrett.

It was named for William T. Rainey, a well-known coal operator in the Berlin area, who owned the deep mine on the Hauger farm. Mr. Rainey built sixteen or more company bungalows to house the employees of the mines.

Raineytown was the scene of the Number 3 mine of the Coronet Coal Company of Pine Hill Station, as well as the Will Mines, Nos. 1, 2, and 3. After the mines were opened by W. T. Rainey about 1818, John Will, a coal broker of Philadelphia, began operating the mines under royalty.

Raineytown, in its earliest days, was also sometimes referred to as "Red Raineytown," since most of the mining houses had been painted a bright red color. As the years ensued, the color faded and the town became better known as Raineytown.

Raineytown was also the scene of the large company store known as the Penn-Marva Coal Company store at Pine Hill Station, which in 1903 was managed by Henry Brant. The three-story framed store building burned to the ground on December 4, 1903. During the same fire, the nearby home of Frank Coleman, superintendent of the Raineytown mine, was also destroyed by fire.

Some years later a large concrete dwelling was built on the site of the store, in the 1950's being the residence of the John Sass family.

Raineytown had its own train station and some of the area farmers brought their milk regularly to the station where it was loaded on the train and hauled to town.

In the late 1920's the mine became depleted and the bungalows were sold for taxes. During that era, John O. Ream, Sr., of Berlin purchased the land.

In the summer of 1921, Raineytown was the scene of a still and moonshine raid in the basement of one of the residences.

Goodtown

Fewer than three dozen persons reside in this small valley where, when coal was king, nearly a thousand persons crowded to live and work the mines. Less than a dozen of those residing in the area in 1976 can recall events as eyewitnesses. None that this writer talked with were living in Goodtown at the beginning of the town's existence.

Named for Isaiah Good, the mining town had its beginning in 1900. Property was purchased from Norman D. Hay and Solomon Coleman by Isaiah Good, Norman Knepper, and Daniel B. Zimmerman. Buildings from the Coleman and Hay estates still overlook the settlement. The large, colonial-type house which sets on the Hay farm is unoccupied, but both houses on the original Solomon Coleman farm are still being used and in remarkably good condition, as are all three barns on the farms.

Shortly after 1900 the coal seams were opened to mining and cleaning tipples and chutes were constructed. Several residences were constructed and the town was born. As mining progressed the settlement grew. The first immigrants began arriving in 1905 from Poland, Romania, Czechoslovakia, Northern and Southern Russia, Holland, Germany, Austria, Hungary, Italy, and Sweden. Nearly all of them stayed, got jobs, married, and became good citizens of this melting pot we call the United States of America. If a census would have been taken of Goodtown in 1913, the count of residences would have shown "more than 70 houses" and only eight of them were single units. This indicated approximately 150 families living in Goodtown and Upper Goodtown. In addition to at least one family, each unit also housed eight to ten boarders.

This kept the women of the house busy washing clothes, baking bread, cooking for many hungry mouths, packing lunches for the miners, and continually cleaning the mud and dirt from the unpaved streets and the tippling and cleaning operations of the mines.

To serve the area, in addition to the public roads which are still maintained by Brothersvalley Township, right-of-way was purchased from Soloman Coleman by the Buffalo Valley Railroad Company. A spur line was laid from Raineytown through Goodtown, Gold Brick, and Upper Goodtown. These were sidings to shunt the railroad coal hoppers so that as each car was filled the brakes were released and gravity moved the filled car below the loading chute. At the same time, gravity placed the next car under the chute to be filled. The Buffalo Valley Railroad Company was later absorbed by the Baltimore and Ohio Railroad, also known as the Pittsburgh-Connellsville Railroad Co. This railroad, founded by a local group of farsighted businessmen, served the settlements in Brothersvalley Township from its beginnings in 1886. Although most of the tracks have been removed, portions of it still serve to haul some coal from Goodtown today.

The railroad also served as transportation to and from the trading area of Berlin and was a convenient way to travel for the residents. Most of the immigrants to the area arrived at Raineytown via the railroad train and walked the short distance to find relatives and friends in Goodtown. In addition to the clothes they wore, most of them proudly displayed a clean handkerchief.

To supply the townspeople with food, clothing, necessities, and a few extras, the coal company erected a building and opened a company-owned store. Nearly all residents patronized this store for convenience, credit,

Goodtown

special purchases, and advice. The store was a popular meeting place. It also housed the post office—Pine Hill Station. A separate building, also owned by the coal company, housed the butcher shop.

It was the responsibility of the "store boss" to keep records, as most transactions were made on a credit basis. On payday the miners were paid—less their store bill.

Since few of the residents could understand or write and read English, the store boss kept personal records for some. In a case related to me, he computed each fair share of household expenses for fifteen male boarders and a young married couple who resided in one house. The boss saw that each one of the boarders paid the young housewife their $2.00 monthly board bill and their fair share of the food and other household expenses.

A fire razed the store building on January 24, 1913, and for a time trading was done at nearby stores in Pine Hill, Raineytown, and Berlin. The store was promptly rebuilt and remained open until the Depression of the late 1920's when operation of the mines ceased.

Coal production in the Goodtown area grew from 1900. Consolidation Coal Company shipped about 80 railroad cars (approximately 4,000 tons) of coal daily. Due to a lack of siding space, engines came from Garrett several times daily to shift the cars and place empty coal cars for loading.

June 4, 1902, emerges as the day of creation of a school for the immediate area. On that date, Messrs. Good, Knepper, and Zimmerman transferred property to the Brothersvalley School District. Known as the Glen Norris school. It served until 1922 when a new four-room building was erected near Pine Hill to serve a larger area. Each of the four rooms housed two grades.

As the community grew, leaders recognized the majority of them were without a place of worship. In 1917 property was transferred from the coal company to build a church. The people, largely of Eastern European origin, raised $4,500 themselves and Sts. Peter and Paul

Goodtown

Greek Orthodox Church became a reality. A Berlin contractor erected the church building in 1917. The church building stands in excellent condidtion in 1976. It is cleaned by the very few members who still reside in the area. Services are held once each month by a visiting priest, a tribute to the faithfulness of those few surviving members. Sts. Peter and Paul are honored each July 12 with special services.

Several attempts were made to organize the mine workers and affiliate them with the United Mine Workers of America. No strikes or violence of any consequence were reported until 1922, when "en masse" the workers left their jobs. Evicted from the company houses they, along with their families, camped in tents and such shelter as they could muster. They existed in this way for most of that year in the surrounding fields and sugar woods. Regular daily patrols by the Pennsylvania State Police (Militia) maintained order. A small dole from the union treasury kept the workers from starvation.

This attempt failed to organize the miners into a union. With the approach of winter, workers sought work and new shelters for their families.

The unionization of the miners was finally accomplished in 1933 and United Mine Workers of America, Local Union #6216, was chartered. The local unit remained active until post World War II when the charter was united with other local units and the meeting place moved to Garrett.

To aid the morale and well-being of the population, a recreational program was developed early in Goodtown's history. The recreational building, remembered by some as the band hall and by others as the pool-room, was erected on coal company grounds. Instruments, music, and uniforms were supplied for the small band. This "Miners' Concert Band" performed at community affairs and picnics. The band traveled to local parades and competitions to present concerts regularly.

As in most mining towns, baseball was the number-one sport or "all-American pastime." The playing field for the Goodtown team was near Pine Hill on a farm owned by the coal company. This same farm was used to raise grain, hay, and for the housing of the mine mules and ponies. Dairy cattle were also sustained on the same farm.

Offers were made to good baseball players by opposing companies. Easier and better jobs were often promised if men would change employers and play baseball for a new employer. Often families were moved to different towns for better working conditions, depending upon a miners' ability to play baseball. Team spirit was high and a member of a winning team was held in high esteem by his peers. To most youngsters this was the big league of baseball.

Although none of the houses in Goodtown were wired for electricity until post World War I, the coal company operated its own power plant to power the trolley-type motors which were used to tow the mine cars from the mines to the tipple. Generating 230 volts DC, this unit operated on steam produced by three coal-fired boilers. This was dismantled during the Depression of the 1920s.

The Depression left a lasting impression on the attitude and appearance of Goodtown. The need for coal in great quantity diminished. Mine after mine operation shut down or changed hands as companies tried to minimize their losses. Houses were sold, some to the occupants, but most to those outside the town. Many of them were torn down and the lumber reused to build farm buildings and other dwellings.

From 1930 to 1940 the population dwindled to just over a hundred persons. Though mining experienced a slight comeback, the workers chose to travel by automobile to work rather than settle in the once established and bustling town.

Underground mining became more expensive and operators looked to open pit or strip mining as a less costly way to mine coal. Presently there are no deep mines operating in the Goodtown area. There is one open surface (strip) mine and a cleaning and loading plant in the area.

Very few railroad cars have been loaded at Goodtown sidings in this Bicentennial year. Large multi-wheeled trucks now haul coal to the stockyard near what remains of the town. The coal is blended with coal of other grades and reloaded, often on the same trucks. Then it is hauled to steel mills, huge utility power plants, and wherever a customer for "king coal" can be found.

Coal production in the area as printed in the February 25, 1927, edition of the Berlin Record, lists the following:

Consolidation Coal Co.	1,271,889 tons
Pine Hill Fuel Co.	107,116 tons
Pine Hill Smokeless Coal Co.	21,498 tons

Consolidation Coal Company operated two mines at Goodtown, as well as mines in other areas. Pine Hill Fuel Company operated one mine at Gold Brick. Pine Hill Smokeless Coal Company operated one mine at

Goodtown. Other companies which were or are presently involved with coal production at Goodtown include the founders, who formed a partnership called the Somerset Coal Company in 1902. Consolidation Coal Company operated the mine and town for them and is credited with the development. Succeeding the Consolidation Coal Company was T. Boone Brown and the Caruse Brothers of Meyersdale. The Pine Hill Fuel Company mine at Gold Brick was later reopened by William O'Dwyer of Berlin. The Pine Hill Smokeless Coal Company mine was reopened by Ponfeigh Coal Company of Garrett. This became their No. 6 mine. They also reopened and redeveloped the Goodtown No. 2 mine (Consolidation Mine No. 113). Several surface mining operators have been active. Among them being Croner, Inc., and Ponfeigh Coal Company, now owned by Penn Pocahontas Coal Company.

There is recorded a transfer of land in or near Pine Hill from John Gambert to "Pine Hill Dairy Co.," which is not part of this report.

Gold Brick

Gold Brick was the name given to the tiny settlement of eight or nine houses that built up around the two mine openings of the Pine Hill Fuel Company. While two of the houses set alone along the hillside, the others were built in a row.

Gold Brick was slightly south and across the railroad tracks from Upper Goodtown, and also a short distance north of the village of Pine Hill.

Gold Brick began operations in August, 1916. William H. Statler of Meyersdale and Wilson J. Gumbert of Pine Hill were two of the men instrumental in opening the mines. One opening was known as the upper Gold Brick mine and the other as the lower Gold Brick mine. Coal from one vein was especially good for steam-making purposes, while coal from the other vein was excellent for domestic use.

Land for the settlement came from the John Gambert farm and eventually reverted to the same farm after the mines closed down and the houses were sold and torn down.

In 1918 the officers of the Pine Hill Fuel Company at Gold Brick were: president, R. H. Philson, Meyersdale; vice-president, Jacob B. Schrock, Berlin; secretary and superintendent, William H. Statler, Meyersdale; treasurer, Clarence Moore of Meyersdale. These men, with Wilson J. Gumbert of Pine Hill, formed the board of directors.

The mine foremen of the fuel company in 1918 were Frank S. Pride and Thomas Turnbull. Ralph W. E. Salkeld also served as a later mine foreman for a brief period of time.

In 1918 the company was shipping an average of six carloads of coal per day.

Pine Hill

The village of Pine Hill is one of the oldest communities west of the Allegheny Mountains. Situated on the fertile brow of a large hill, four miles southwest of Berlin, it has never grown larger than eight or ten homes, although early historians considered it a good business location.

Older residents say it got its name because of a beautiful old pine tree that stood out prominently above all the others on the hillside plot where the town built up.

It was a strange fate in 1783 that the project of laying out of town at the location of Pine Hill was abandoned. The race story and accident in which Revolutionary War veteran Jacob Wacker (Walker) was critically wounded and later died appears elsewhere in this publication under the title of "The Walker Tragedies."

The accident was looked upon as a bad omen and the project of laying out that section for a town was abandoned. One year later the town of Berlin was laid out in lots four miles away. Pine Hill grew up on a small scale after the accident, a schoolhouse having already been in operation before the formation of the town.

Turner's Store was the earliest name of the village. About 1850 Lewis A. Turner constructed the first store in the village and in 1857 a post office was established in the store under the name of Turner's Store. In 1874 the name of the village was changed to Pine Hill. The Honorable Lewis A. Turner was the first postmaster. He was active in politics and in 1871 was elected Associate Judge of Somerset County for a term of five years and served on the bench during the same time as Judge Josiah Mowry.

The mercantile business proved very successful under Lewis Turner and in 1863 he engaged in manufacturing and purchasing barrel staves, commonly called shook, which at the time was one of the principal industries of southern Brothersvalley Township. He gave employment to a large number of workmen, but finally met with financial reverses, owing to the unpaid moneys from commission merchants to whom he consigned the product of his shop. It is recorded that he lost $8,000 on a single consignment of barrel staves shipped to Havana, Cuba.

Staves from the factory were hauled via horse and wagon to Cumberland, where they were assembled. Groceries were brought back to his Pine Hill store on the return trip.

His son-in-law John R. Boose served as proprietor for a time in the store until a Smith family of Cumberland purchased it. Eventually, Henry Gumbert purchased the store and post office from the Smith family.

The store building was a large two-story dwelling, still standing in the village in 1976, although it deteriorated greatly over the years. Later Henry's son and daughter, Wilson and Miss Sadie Gumbert, operated the store as did Henry's son-in-law and daughter, Russell and Elizabeth (Gumbert) West. Many roomers were kept in the large dwelling over the years when the store was in operation.

Josiah L. Burkholder completed a new cooper shop in Pine Hill in the fall of 1884. One portion of it was spaced off for a grocery store. After his death, his widow, Sarah

Pine Hill

(Coleman) Burkholder, remarried John Buckalew and continued to operate the general store until her death in 1900. In 1836, Josiah Fritz, a farmer, was mail carrier. In 1840, Jacob Gumbert had a shoemaker shop.

Like all small towns, a blacksmith shop helped form Pine Hill's nucleus. It was set up by Samuel Stahl. His son George Stahl had a carpenter's shop next to the blacksmith shop.

In 1920 George Stahl and his son-in-law Alvin Turney operated a store in the village. On April 25, 1922, fire completely destroyed their store and charred several other nearby buildings.

The little village also had a candy factory, as well as a creamery for a while. The Candy Kitchen was opened in 1922 by George Stahl and was in the small store building which is now on the Leo Ohler property. It lasted eight years.

Neighboring farmers organized and established a creamery and hauled their milk there for its processing. John M. Gambert, a nearby farmer, headed the operations, while Oscar F. Walker managed it for some years.

Butter found a ready sale on the McKeesport Markets. Gambert also operated a large stock business on an adjoining farm: buying, feeding, and selling cattle and sheep, and also dealing in horses. He assisted in the formation of the First National Bank in Berlin and served as a director for many years.

In December 1902 public auction was held at the Pine Hill Creamery and J. Allen Hay purchased it for $950. It later became a residence and in 1976 is owned by the John Drabish family of Ohio, who use it as a summer home.

Much of John Gambert's farmland touched the border of Pine Hill, including a wooded picnic grove east of the village which was used many years for the annual Pine Hill picnics.

In 1899, the Pine Hill Coal Company started shipping coal from their railroad siding nearby. The nearby mining towns of Goodtown and Raineytown grew up around the mining operations.

In the 1903 Somerset County Directory are listed the names of John Speicher and Samuel Stahl as blacksmiths, Simon and Josiah C. Werner as carpenters, and Henry and Wilson Gumbert as merchants.

In 1775 Lutheran and Reformed families were meeting in their log cabins for religious services in the Pine Hill area. In 1790 Nicholas Coleman deeded one acre of ground to the Lutherans for the building of a church house for worship service. Three church buildings have added to the complicated history of the St. Michael's Lutheran Church, a separate story which also appears in this same publication.

Miss Virgie Pritz at 85 years of age is the oldest resident of Pine Hill, she being the only present resident of the village that was born and raised there. She was a daughter of Jonathan and Magdalene (Baker) Pritz, longtime residents of the village.

Other residents of the village in 1976 include the families of Jay A. Miller, Leo Ohler, as well as Roger Deeter. At least half of the town's homes stand empty or are used as summer homes.

At the western edges of the village is the old Pine Hill Lutheran Cemetery. A short distance away is the cemetery of the S.S. Peter and Paul Russian Greek Orthodox Church of nearby Goodtown, a three-acre plot of ground donated in 1917 by the Consolidation Coal Company. The coal company also donated the lot in Goodtown on which the church was built and dedicated in 1918. Many of the tombstones in the cemetery are written in "old-fashioned hard Russian," according to one of the old miners, who remembers many of those buried there immigrated from Europe to work in the Goodtown area mines.

Two or three schoolhouses have served the Pine Hill area over the years. On January 21, 1824, when temperatures hovered below zero, the schoolhouse north of the cemetery and village burned to the ground, the origin of which was due to an overheated flue.

During the mining operations, many of the homes lost their water source and for many years the residents relied on cisterns to store rainwater for use in the homes.

1910 Storm Strikes Pine Hill

June 18, 1910. . . . The mere mention of that date still sends shivers and chills up the backs of those who remember the severity of the storm that struck many areas of Somerset County late that afternoon. Brothersvalley Township was hit hard by the storm and the most miraculous thing about it was that no one was killed in its wake.

Mrs. Edna Florence (Werner) Mognet of Somerset remembers vividly the details of the storm as it struck the Pine Hill picnic grove. She has recorded in her diaries many details of the storm, and like most others who lived through it, she readily admits she thought it was the end of the world.

The Pine Hill neighborhood gathered that day in the picnic grove in a woods belonging to the John Gambert farm, slightly east of the village, to celebrate the purchasing of new white uniforms for the Miners' Concert Band of Goodtown. The band consisted of approximately 25 men who played under the direction of Charles Hoffa. The Concert Band members wore their new uniforms and were scheduled to play during the afternoon program.

Miners Concert Band of Pine Hill and Goodtown about 1914 or 1915. Front row, left to right: Norman Werner, Jeremiah Smith, Frank Blubaugh, William Salkeld, John Gumbert, Albert Watkins, Josiah C. Werner, James Hoffa, Boyd Salkeld, Andrew Eckman, and Ralph Waldo Emerson Salkeld. Second row: Austin F. Blubaugh, Simon Werner, William L. Werner, Charles Blubaugh, Charles Hoffa, director, Howard Hoffa, Fred Watkins, Allen Smith, and Joseph Stahl.

This was a special picnic and was not the annual Pine Hill picnic that was such an important event in the area in those days. The Pine Hill picnics met in the same grove with the St. Michael's Lutheran Church in Pine Hill and the nearby Mt. Zion (Hay's) Evangelical and Reformed Church alternating in planning the picnics. People attended from a wide area and many say some of the happiest times of their lives were spent at those picnics.

It had been a rainy week and the ground was saturated. When the rains left up in the morning, the residents of the neighborhood began gathering about noon for the special picnic. Among the many families in attendance were those of Edna Mognet's parents, Josiah and Lydia (Stahl) Werner, who resided on a small farm near the Hay's Church. Joe Werner was one of the members of the Miners' Concert Band and his family was in charge of operating the small candy store on the grounds that day.

Edna Werner Mognet walked to the grove about 3:00 p.m. Shortly afterwards the sky turned a scary dark color and by 4:00 p.m. it was completely dark. Most of the neighbors had already started for home, but those who were left at the grounds witnessed a storm that they never forgot. The Werner family stayed in the candy shop to insure that the merchandise would be protected from the rain.

It rained, hailed, thundered, and lightninged more than anyone had ever experienced. The storm continued for approximately two hours and when it was over, the Pine Hill grove was ruined. Joe Werner counted at least 24 trees falling down as he walked out of his candy shop to see which way they should head for safety.

Rain leaked through the flimsy roof of the candy shop. The Werner family dumped a large washtub of lemonade away and held the tub over their heads inside the building to keep dry.

Joseph Walker was pulling out of the grove with his horse and carriage when a large tree fell in front of him. As he was backing his rig, another large tree fell closely behind him and he was unable to go home. Large oak trees were uprooted and lay across the pathways to the nearby road that led to Pine Hill.

Since the storm seemed to come from the east, the Werners decided they would head west to Pine Hill to the homes of various relatives living there.

In the darkness and excitement, Mrs. Lydia Werner started walking towards Pine Hill. She thought she was following her husband but later learned she was following another member of the band, Bob Grove, who was about the same size as her husband. As they walked towards Pine Hill the water gushed onto the road and forced them into the nearby field. As Bob Grove held the fence for Lydia to crawl under, lightning struck the fence and stunned Mrs. Werner. She laid on the ground and pleaded with Bob Grove to leave her lie there and proceed on his way. Bob Grove was aware of the seriousness of leaving her there, and nearly dragged her to Pine Hill to save her life. He put his band hat on her head to protect her. Several days afterwards he was still able to see the marks on his head from where the hail struck him.

Mrs. Werner was confined to her bed for several weeks after the storm but eventually recovered, although she was terrified of thunderstorms the rest of her life.

Meanwhile back at the grove, Edna, her sister Ida (later Mrs. John M. Suder), and her dad, had decided to walk to Pine Hill. They had only gone a short distance when Edna stepped out of her rubber and lost it in a large mudhole. She kept going and when her father went back to retrieve it, she shouted, "I won't need it anymore!" Like so many others, Edna was sure the end of the world was coming! Edna Mognet spoke of her dad as "the master of every situation." The storm was the only time in her entire life when it was evident to her that even her dad was scared.

When the storm finally subsided after 6:00 p.m., it was a miracle that no one had been killed. Bridges were washed out, trees uprooted, and windowpanes broken. People talked about the storm for many months and believed that Haley's Comet had something to do with it. Everyone had a different tale to tell about the storm and even to this day, those who lived through it, remember vividly the fears they felt. The storm seemed to hit only certain areas but the areas it hit were damaged severely. Sixty-five years have done little to erase the memories of that traumatic experience.

The Walker Tragedies

Hundreds of those living in Brothersvalley Township and the Berlin area in 1976 can trace their family lineage to pioneer Jacob Walker and his grandson, George P. H. Walker, both of whom met tragic deaths in the Fritz Church corner of Brothersvalley Township many years ago. To get more of the facts of both tragedies, David R. Hay talked with two descendants of the Walker men, Mrs. Jacob (Nettie Walker) Suder and Mrs. Guy N. (Edna Walker) Hartman, both well-known genealogists and well versed in early history of southern Brothersvalley Township.

The Race

The pioneer Jacob Walker was mortally wounded in the spring of 1783 while engaged in riding a horse in a race, to determine the location of a town which was to be later named Berlin. The accident occurred in what we refer to as the Fritz Church area, near Pine Hill, on the farm owned in later years by Elias Cober. This same farm is owned in 1976 by Paul Cober of Gettysburg. Harold E. Hay resides there and operates the farm for the Cober family.

The one who got to the site first was to have the choice lot. A tree stood in what was merely a bridle path in those days, the path leading on both sides of the tree. Jacob, thinking that his horse was going to pass on one side of the tree, leaned that direction, but suddenly his horse swerved to pass on the other side. Jacob was dashed against the tree and mortally wounded. Many accounts of the race say he was killed instantly, but this had been proven incorrect in the past ten years when his will was uncovered in the probate records of Bedford County. The will was dated March 16, 1783, and was probated April 19, 1783, which proves that Jacob Walker could have lived as long as one month after the race. The exact date of his death is unknown.

This tragic event delayed the laying out of the town, and a year later (1784) the present site of Berlin was chosen for the town.

Jacob Walker is buried in a small farm cemetery where he resided, owned in 1976 by John Saylor, but still often referred to as the Newton Saylor farm, near the Meyersdale Municipal Airport. The 1782 tax records of Bedford County show Jacob Walker owning 300 acres of land. His farm later became the Jerome Countryman farm, and later still was divided into the Newton Saylor and William Ebaugh farms.

In 1953 a wall was built around the small cemetery under the planning of two of his descendants, Dr. Ezra C. Saylor of Berlin and Hiram Walker of Summit Township. Each year a flag is placed upon the grave of Jacob Walker in recognition of his Revolutionary War service.

Jacob Walker, son of Francis Walker who sailed to America and landed at Baltimore in 1732, was a second lieutenant in Captain Henry Rhoades' company of Bedford County in the Revolutionary War.

Jacob Walker was married and the father of seven children. The oldest, Philip, was 17 years of age, and the youngest, Frederick Walker, was three years old at the time of the race when their father was critically wounded.

Jacob Walker's grandson, George P. H. Walker, met a gruesome death in the meadow of his farm in 1827, the account of which follows:

The Scythe Murder

George P. H. Walker, second son and third child of Phillip and Elizabeth (Coleman) Walker, and grandson of the pioneer Jacob Walker, was the victim of a tragic murder July 11, 1827. An Irishman, a stranger named Burns, had come into the community and was assisting in hand-mowing the grass on the farm meadow of George P. H. Walker.

This farm has continued to belong to members of the Walker family ever since. In 1976 it is owned by his great-grandson, Walter T. Walker, and is located about one mile south of the village of Pine Hill on the road that leads to the Fritz Cemetery.

When George Walker reprimanded Burns for bad mowing, Burns became very angry. Mr. Walker had a bad toothache at the time and Burns knew it. Burns said that he could cure the toothache, at which instant he slashed his sharp scythe across the body of George Walker, completely disemboweling him. During the excitement which followed this tragedy, Burns disappeared and was never apprehended. Someone told Burns' wife about the tragedy and she remarked, "Did he do something again like that!" Some time later,

Burns' wife also disappeared. Supposition was that Burns was hiding somewhere and came one night and got his wife and both fled from the area.

George P. H. Walker was buried in the Pine Hill Lutheran Cemetery and the following inscription was placed on his tombstone: "In memory of George Walker, son of Phillip Walker, died 11th of July 1827, aged 30 years, 6 months and two days." A German inscription on the gravestone also tells that the murderer did not expiate his crime in this life, but that he would be called upon to do so in the "Great Hereafter."

George Walker left a widow and six children, the oldest being ten-year-old Josiah Walker (grandfather of Walter T. Walker). The youngest, Rosannah Walker, was a mere five months old.

Tragedies have followed the Walker family. Many other descendants and the stories of how they died could be easily added to these two tragedies.

Shawtown

Shawtown, a small village in Brothersvalley Township near the mining area known as the Shaft, was named in honor of Dr. William P. Shaw, a Berlin area physician. Dr. Shaw and James P. McCabe were owners of the nine-acre, V-shaped tract of land, below the J. Calvin Altfather farm, where the small grouping of homes built up.

The exact location was approximately a mile south of present-day Macdonaldton, along the Shaft road that connects Macdonaldton with the Salco road.

Long before Shawtown came into being, one Landis Distillery was already in operation there, along the headwaters of Buffalo Creek. About 1894 this distillery was owned by C. Walters and Company and Joseph Speicher was the distiller. The distillery eventually was made into four apartments and rented until it was torn down in the 1940's.

Shawtown consisted of about eight houses, the distillery building, and the bond house. A large tipple stands at the location of the bond house in 1976. Six apartments were made in the bond house and it was also rented during its last years.

Three or four of the houses were built by Dr. W. P. Shaw and James P. McCabe and sold to area miners. Several of the other houses were erected by others and were very primitive, having up-and-down siding with narrow lap boards over the joints. Most of the buildings were erected in the early 1900s.

Shawtown was the location of the Number 5 mines of the Brothersvalley Coal Company and the land was originally a portion of the large Frederick Altfather estate, on which Macdonaldton was also built.

Mike Lucas was a miner and cattle dealer in Shawtown for many years.

The children from this area attended East End #2 School, located along the B & O Railroad near Macdonaldton.

Nothing remains of Shawtown in 1976. Several children of Lewis F. Altfather, Somerset, have cottages in the area. One son, Lewis Clay Altfather, moved home from Michigan in 1976 to live in a mobile home directly above where the old distillery once stood. Remains of the old mill race are still discernible on the Altfather land.

An old Landis distillery near Shawtown. Picture taken about 1894 when owned by C. Walters and Co. Left to right are: John Altfather, John Davey Foust, Joseph Speicher, the distiller; Gertrude Speicher Shockey, and Mrs. Joseph (Bessie) Speicher.

The Shaft

Pen-Mar Shaft No. 2 was the official name of the W. K. Niver and Co. Shaft that was sunk in Brothersvalley Township in 1901 on land of the C. W. Landis farm, south of the present village of Macdonaldton.

The mine operation consisted of two shafts 385 feet deep. One shaft was used to haul the miners to the coal seam below. The other shaft was used to lower the empty car to the bottom and also to bring the loaded car to the surface. Steam power was used to operate this equipment and also to operate the pumps that kept the mine shaft from filling up with water.

The mining village grew up nearby with ap-

Pen-Mar Shaft No. 2

proximately 35 houses, most of which were double homes. The children attended a one-room school (Sugar Grove) which at times had an attendance of from 55 to 58 pupils.

In the early 1900's the combined population of The Shaft and Shawtown was greater than that of Berlin.

M. J. Murphy of Windber had the contract for putting down the shaft.

Over three hundred citizens of the Berlin area attended the ceremonial of christening of The Shaft, June 25, 1901. S. P. Brubaker, who was one of the men chiefly instrumental in bringing the area coal to the notice of capitalists, acted as master of ceremonies.

Miss Helen Collins, the 19-year-old daughter of Mr. and Mrs. F. B. Collins, turned over the first shovelful of earth and performed the act of christening The Shaft with its title, breaking a bottle of champagne across a small boulder lying within the area upon which the shaft was to be sunk.

The W. K. Niver and Co. Pen-Mar Mine No. 1 was located at Niverton, Pa.

Salco

Construction of four houses in Salco. Last house in row is the farmhouse where Walter Lane lived prior to the building of the mining town.

Trestle where Salco Mines loaded coal onto railroad cars. Near Henry Fritz farm buildings.

One ramshackle old dwelling stands as a lone sentinel in the middle of a productive farm field in 1976, the sole reminder of the existence of the mining town of Salco. The same fields a half century ago contained more than 30 homes that were part of a short-lived mining town that grew up about 1918 and lasted less than ten years.

The lone two-story frame house was the most elaborately built home in Salco and was used as the mine foreman's house. It was built by Henry Herman with beautiful hardwood used throughout the interior of the house. The style of the dwelling was patterned after the house approximately two miles away where Mrs. Sherman B. Berkley resides in 1976.

The house is located approximately 3,000 feet off the hard-surfaced "Salco Road," three miles southeast of Berlin, along the foothills of the Allegheny Mountains.

The old house and the land the town was built upon was owned in recent years by the Lloyd B. and Paul L. Bird families. The Bird family has used the old house as a storage for fertilizer and other supplies handled in the family's explosives business.

The Salco Mines of the Berlin Coal Company was the big disappointment of several Johnstown area men's golden dream.

The original owners' last names were Salisbury and Cook and the name "Salco" was a combination of the two names. They succeeded in purchasing the coal rights under many of the neighboring farms. The company houses built up in several rows, clustered around the farmhouse and barn on the former Walter Lane farm. The homes were built by William Dickey, Henry Herman, Frank P. Flamm, and John M. Suder, all residents of southern Brothersvalley Township.

There were numerous one- and two-story single and double houses in rows. There were three large dwellings in which four families resided. One row of one-story houses with slanted roofs stood on land bordering the Ralph H. Hay farm. Some of the houses were painted red, some were painted white, and there were a number of homes that were never painted. Most of them had no basements and some of them stood on posts.

Although there are no known records of the Salco Mines of the Berlin Coal Company in existence, it is a well-known fact that many local residents secured employment in the mines. In later years, many European immigrants also made their livelihoods in the mines there.

The first mine opening, as well as the blacksmith shop and the dinky barn, were at the northeastern edges of the village. James Burd was a blacksmith in 1924.

There was a large building there that served as a meeting hall, as well as a storeroom. Harry Mankamier was a storekeeper for a number of years.

Edward Conn was the engineer of the dinky engine and Lloyd Bird was a brakeman and foreman of the dinky. Stuart Pritz was the first superintendent of the Salco Mines and was responsible for the first ten-foot test holes that were drilled at Salco to learn how deep the coal was embedded. P. P. (Parley) Baker was a later superintendent.

A long dinky track ran down the sloping hillsides and eventually crossed the present highway near the Sugar Grove School, slightly west of the present Henry Fritz home. There was located a trussel on which the coal cars ran onto the tipple. Coal was dumped onto train cars of the Berlin Branch of the B & O Railroad. The same branch of the railroad continued east into the areas of The Shaft operations of the Brothersvalley Coal Company. On the west the tracks led to the Niver Junction of the Berlin Branch.

As one entered the dirt roadway into Salco, there were two flagpoles, one on each side of the road. Nearby was the ball field where neighborhood youngsters gathered frequently on Sunday afternoons to play ball with the youngsters of Salco.

There was a union hall near the present location of Paul L. Bird's modern storage building, across from the barn on what was the William Dickey farm in Salco's day.

Salco Supply Company was a general merchandise store (no connections with the mining company) operated about a mile away by Clarence Fisher and Ed Johnson of Pittsburgh. David Wyant is the present owner of the store property.

In 1920 the coal business was booming at the Salco Mines and the men were drawing big paychecks. In 1921 the great miners' strike hit the Salco Mines of the Berlin Coal Company, as well as the neighboring Brothersvalley Coal Company's operations.

In April 1921 the Brothersvalley Coal Company closed all of its operations and worked only a few men to look after the powerhouse that supplied lights for Macdonaldton and two or three pumpers.

The Salco Mines closed up with only the mine foreman and one pumper remaining on the job. A few of the men of these mines found employment with the Harrison Company, building the Berlin-Garrett State Highway, and a few with the paving of Broadway Street in Berlin. Neither of these construction projects aided greatly in the great financial problems that faced the families.

During various periods, financial problems plagued the Salco Mines and at one time strangers were brought in from Cambria County to do the payroll.

By the summer of 1921 the Salco miners and the union they were a part of were forced to move out of the company-owned houses in the village. A group of them rented a wooded area near a large sand spring about a half mile away on the J. Nevin Hay farm. Here they erected tents and other cheap shelters that were their homes for several months. They brought their cows and chickens along with them. The cows often grazed along the edges of the woods. Boards were nailed between several trees for chickens to roost upon.

Many of the miners helped neighboring farmers pick potatoes or do other fall harvest work to exist during those tough times. Gradually the miners found other houses or places to work and by early winter the last families were moving out of the temporary quarters on the Hay farm.

Edward Conn served as caretaker for the Salco homes during the strike period to insure that none of them were disturbed. The state police rode by frequently on their horses to insure that law and order were maintained.

Salco eventually went bankrupt and many of the farmers eventually were able to buy back the coal rights to their farms.

A white frame one-room schoolhouse was built by Henry Herman along the present-day highway where students from Salco, as well as from the neighborhood, attended. The following is a record of teachers at Salco School; the date listed being the fall the term began:

1918 - Laura Bauman
1919 - Mary J. Dickey
1920 - Mary Hay
1921 - Mary Dickey
1922 - Caryl Storey
1923 - Lenore A. Will
1924 - Mary J. Dickey
1925 - Edna Judy
1926 - Louise Stuck
1927 - Closed
1928 - Mellie Fox
1929 - Closed

Scores of names have been associated with Salco's history. Many miners left Brothersvalley Township to work in the mines in many other locations.

Today Salco is nothing more than a few memories and a name on a few road signs!

Macdonaldton

The largest mining town in Brothersvalley Township is Macdonaldton. It was laid out by the Williams K. Niver Coal Company in 1902. There were 484 lots on the plot of the town as it was recorded.

An early 1919 map of mine operations in Brothersvalley Township lists the Brothersvalley Coal Company in Macdonaldton.

In 1917 Macdonaldton was a booming coal town with at least 300 men employed in the mine. Mr. Howard Reed was president and foreman of the mine. Wages were about sixty dollars every two weeks. The price of coal was three dollars a ton.

The Mill School, a one-room school, closed and a two-building four-room school was used.

There were two churches to serve the people of Macdonaldton. St. Gregory's Catholic Church, with 75 members, met every other Sunday. Father Miller from West Salisbury was the assigned priest. An interdenominational Protestant church was served by visiting ministers.

Housing was owned by Brothersvalley Company. Each unit had three rooms downstairs and two rooms upstairs. Rent was five dollars a month with no electricity or water. The upstairs rooms were rented to boarders at fifty dollars a month. The gristmill water was an excellent supply for the town until 1920 when it was diverted to the mine. Then the water came from Sand Spring.

Food was purchased from the company store called Pen-Mar Supply Company. One had to buy from Pen-

Macdonaldton, Pa.

Macdonaldton surveyors

Daniel Altfather mill. Later, Soloman and John S. Engle gristmill near Macdonaldton.

The Macdonaldton one-room school and students

The mine tipple at Macdonaldton, Pa.

Fire at hotel on Good Friday, 1925.

Mar or lose one's job. Brothersvalley Coal Company issued bogus script that was to be used for groceries and meat until the miners received their next paychecks. Then the company deducted the script amount from the pay.

Macdonaldton had an inn called the Henderson Hotel. The hotel burned in the spring of 1925. The post office was operated by Rachel Wilson. Dr. George B. Masters was the only physician.

The **Strike** started in 1920. It was to last for three years and though it ended with the breakup of the union, Macdonaldton was never the same. Many people moved away in search of other jobs.

In 1943 E. H. Scurfield took over the mining operation.

About forty families live in Madonaldton today.

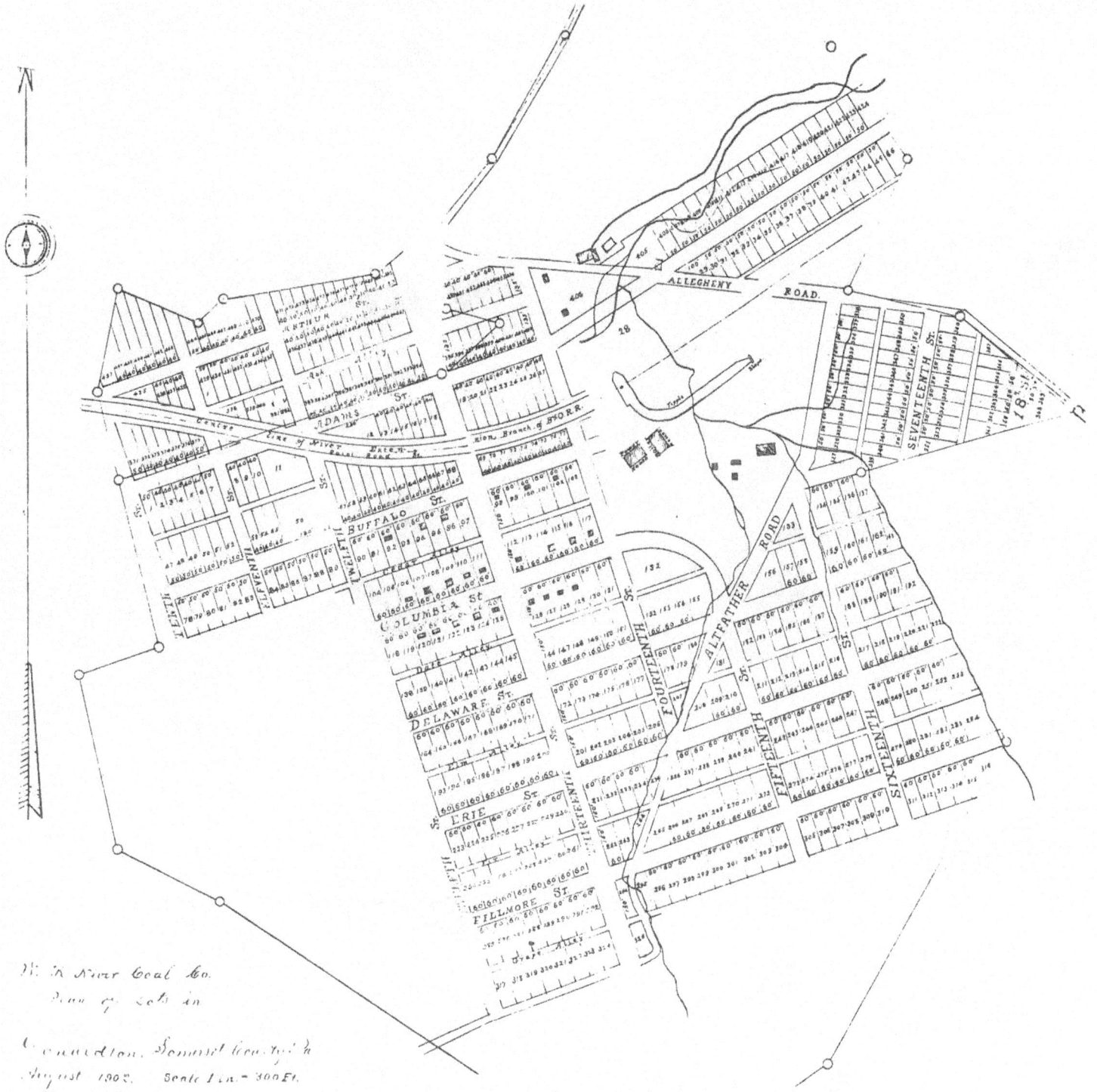

W. K. Niver Coal Co. plan of lots in Macdonaldton, Pa.

The Company Store

During the two years that Harold Schmucker worked in the Pen-Mar Supply Company under George Lane he delivered meat to houses in a covered wagon. The wagon was pulled by an old white horse named "Charlie." Mr. Schmucker had to carry a supply of bones to ward off vicious dogs. Many of the homes were tidy, but there were some homes where the chickens had to be chased from the table to make room for a pan of meat. Employees of the store were: George Wetmiller, Harry Dickey, John Lane, Roy Miller, Myrtle Baldwin, Ruth Wilson, and Robert Pryor.

Building of the Macdonaldton dam near Berlin in 1911. Many farmers, including Guy H. Walker of Brothersvalley Twp., came with their teams to build the dam. It was built for the people to get ice in the wintertime to put in their icehouses so they could get ice in the warmer months. Niver owned the coal mines in nearby Macdonaldton.

Macdonaldton

The Macdonaldton dam today

Macdonaldton Dam

William W. Engleka who lives on a farm near Macdonaldton worked on the construction of the dam. From an old time book he kept on hours he worked the following record was taken.

Construction of dam started June 7, 1911. The dam was excavated and breastwork completed August 5, 1911. On a Sunday night believed to have been August 13, 1911, a hard rain completed filling of dam and breast did not hold. After repairing the break an earth breast was built in front to support the masonry and this work was completed December 15, 1911. The dam has held since with no breaks.

Hay's Mill

Picturesquely situated on the banks of the Blue Lick Creek in the southwestern corner of Brothersvalley Township is the scattered village of Hay's Mill.

The village consists of less than ten homes in 1976 and has never grown larger than it was during the 1800's and early 1900's when the collection of houses built up around two mills in operation in the neighborhood.

The village was named in honor of Simon Hay, one of the pioneers of that well-known family in the township, who immigrated to America with two brothers in 1767. While working as a miller near Hagerstown, Maryland, Simon Hay became acquainted with George Jacob Gunderman (Countryman), who brought his grain down out of the mountains of Somerset to this mill. Countryman persuaded Simon Hay of the wonderful opportunities of Brueders Thal (Brothers Valley) and in

Hay's Mill

Hay's Mill

Baker home. Left to right outside fence: Conrad Baker, Hiram Baker, Peter Baker, Rebecca Baker; inside fence: Mrs. Coon Baker, William Baker, Lewis Baker, Mahlon Reich, Catherine Baker, and Margaret Boger.

1768 Simon came to what is now known as the Hay's Mill neighborhood, where he began the huge task of clearing portions of his squatter's claim.

In the early 1790's he constructed his first gristmill. This mill didn't prove profitable because the fall of the water was not adequate to operate the mill. It eventually was used as a carding mill by Simon Hay when he built the second mill in 1806. The second mill was a three-story log structure which continued in operation for at least 110 years, ceasing operations about 1916. A dam was built for extra water supply to operate the 2½-story-high waterwheel that powered the second mill.

Thomas Short, an Irish stonemason, built the beautiful stonework of the foundation, a portion of which still stands in 1976.

Hay's Mill was on the old Cumberland Road, over which there always was much travel in the early days. The gristmill was the stopping point of neighbors near and far who brought their grain to be ground into flour or feed. It was operated for various periods of time by Simon Hay, Valentine Hay, William Hay, David Hay, and George Hay, until approximately 1854 when it was sold, along with nine acres of land, to John Graf, a native of Milford Township, for $2,300.

John Graf operated the mill briefly and eventually ran into financial difficulties. In 1854 he committed suicide by cutting his throat in his Hay's Mill home. He was buried in an unmarked grave in a corner of his mountain field, which in later years was plowed over.

Jacob P. Becker purchased the mill from the Graf estate for $2,100. After some years of operation, he also met with financial troubles and the mill was sold at sheriff's sale for $101 to his son, George Becker, who was the last miller.

About 1915 he sold the mill and his small acreage to Ephraim E. Boger, owner of the adjacent farm, from which the land for the mill had originally come from after pioneer Simon Hay's lifetime. E. E. Boger's sons, Baden and Homer P., operated the mill on a small scale for their own use, as well as for several close neighbors.

The mill gradually deteriorated and needed a new roof. The cost of a new roof was estimated at $1,000 and E. E. Boger decided it was not feasible to repair the building. In 1928 Homer P. Boger bought the farm and the land with the mill on it. He tore much of the lumber away, using some of it in other buildings on the farm. The wooden cog wheels, which turned all the machinery, can be seen at the Mountain Playhouse, Jennerstown.

For many years a store and post office operated on the

Gristmill at Hay's Mill—operated until 1918. Left to right: Alda Boger, Essie Boger, Melissa Boger, E. E. Boger, Russell Boger,
Ephriam Bowman, Ephriam Hay on horse, Boden Boger in front of Mrs. Boger. Miller, Jake Becker.

second floor of the mill. Neighbors picked up their mail at the post office. Eventually, Alphonso Boger became the first mail carrier and delivered mail to homes within a radius of several miles of the village. Gradually the Hay's Mill Post Office was closed and the Meyersdale Post Office absorbed the territory for one of its rural routes.

The box section of the old Hay's Mill Post Office, with its 60 partitions, has been restored and is displayed in the home of Homer S. Boger, Meyersdale, a son of Homer P. Boger of Hay's Mill.

The second mill, the famous log mill built in 1806, was listed as an outstanding example of log construction in America in the book **Early Architecture of Western Pennsylvania**, written by C. M. Stotz for the Buhl Foundation of Pittsburgh. In the Museum of Philadelphia is an old loom of Simon Hay's with the date of 1774.

In the 1850's John Wasmuth and John Holzhoer were the village weavers and Herbert Hibner was the tailor. A blacksmith shop also existed in the village. M. Durant operated a fulling and carding mill.

The Hay's Mill Forest Fire Tower was erected in 1923 by the Pennsylvania Department of Forests and Waters. At the point where the tower was placed, the Allegheny

Mountain rises to an elevation of 2,900 feet.

Hay's Mill Schools

Three schoolhouses have existed in the Hay's Mill area. The original was a log structure on top of Cherry Hill, near the old Cumberland Road. The second structure was already in use in 1876 on the same foundation where the third building was constructed in 1890, on the edge of the village. The third schoolhouse continues to stand in 1976, although it is in dire need of repairs and has been used in recent years as a machine shed by Homer P. Boger.

Some of the earliest known teachers in Hay's Mill include: Samuel A. Philson of Berlin who was teaching in 1852; "Bootsie" Brubaker, in 1877 or 1878; Warren Mason in 1886; Harvey G. Hay, 1890; William R. Stahl, 1891;William Cober, 1894; Stella McLuckie, 1898 or 1899. Since 1900, the following persons have taught at the Hay's Mill School (the year is the fall the term began):

1900 - Lizzie Miller
1901 - Lizzie Miller
1902 - Emma Cober and Fred Miller
1903 - Cyrus Glessner
1904 - Calvin Lohr

1905 - Orpha Dickey
1906 - Susan Walker
1907 - Susan Walker
1908 - Margaret Miller
1909 - Ralph H. Hay
1910 - Harry F. Werner
1911 - Florence Walker
1912 - Minnie Dickey
1913 - Ruth Naomi Dickey
1914 - Ellis Werner
1915 - Etta Shober

1916 - Susan Meyers
1917 - Verna Dickey and Harry Saylor
1918 - Harry Saylor
1919 - Homer P. Boger
1920 - Vella Leech
1921 - Vella Leech and David Baker
1922 - Mabel Beal
1923 - Grace Swearman
1924 - Marian E. Dively
1925 - Mae Martin
1926 - Mae Martin

1927 - Helen Catherine Hay
1928 - Maggie Miller
1929 - Maggie Miller
1930 - Margaret E. Lee Baer
1931 - Bertha Eckman
1932 - Ruth Dickey Broeseker
1933 - Harry Carver
1934 - Harry Carver
1935 - Closed

Brothersvalley Township Cemeteries

1. **Hay Farm**—Owned by Harry Hay. About 50 rods southwest of the buildings in the second field below the barn near a ravine. 14 graves - oldest 1825.
2. **Carver**—On the farm owned by Frank Carver about 300 yards south of the barn near the edge of the woods. 10 graves - oldest 1826.
3. **Foust**—On Carl Foust farm on the right side of a private road leading from the buildings up the hill to some fields north of buildings above orchard. 28 graves - oldest 1852.
4. **Kimmel**—On farm owned by U. S. Reitmeyer, formerly Floyd Hoffman. Located about 51 rods northwest of the buildings at the upper edge of the orchard. Also known as the Ed Bauermaster farm. 10 graves - oldest 1836.
5. **Black**—On the Leon Knepper farm. West of buildings along the Old Glade Pike at top of hill near the Brotherton Cemetery enclosed by a stone wall. 6 graves - oldest 1803.
6. **Lewis E. Maust Farm**—In sugar grove, south of buildings and west of the sugar camp. About halfway up the grove and near the north fence. 8 graves - oldest 1811.
7. **Countryman**—On old Countryman farm, later known as the John H. Hartman farm. A few rods east of the house. 17 graves - oldest 1778.
8. **Brenison**—Leon Knepper farm. Northeast of buildings about 10 rods at upper edge of the orchard, under two wild cherry trees. 2 graves - oldest 1846.
9. **Landis**—On farm owned by Henry Fritz about 40 rods on a hill northwest of the buildings, and about the same distance south of the shaft opening of the Brothersvalley Coal Co. 22 graves - oldest 1817.
10. **Good-Gover**—On line between Edwin Landis farm and Calvin M. Will farm. 30 graves - oldest 1820.
11. **Altfather**—Farm owned by Frank Glessner. In the field above the orchard at the edge of the woods and about 25 rods from the house. 21 graves - oldest 1816.
12. **Croner**—Farm owned by Tom Croner. Northwest of the farm buildings on a hill in the field next to the barn (about 300 yards). 57 graves - oldest 1813.
13. **Knepper**—On old Knepper farm owned by Harold Croner. In a field south of the buildings (about 15

rods) and near the edge of the sugar grove. 15 graves - oldest 1839.
14. **#3 Musser**—Frank Phennicie farm. About 50 rods southwest of buildings. 27 graves - oldest 1825.
15. **Beachley**—Earl Croner farm near Beachdale north of the buildings about 30 rods along an old abandoned road. 79 graves - oldest 1845.
16. **Berkley Farm**—Owned by Earl Walker in field above barn. 29 graves - oldest 1855.
17. **Altfather**—William Engleka farm. At the right side of the road leading from East End of Berlin to White Horse. On the brow of the hill opposite the home of William Engleka, and only a few rods from the site of the old Altfather Mill, near the slope mine at Mac-Donaldton. 7 graves - oldest 1862.
18. **Braucher**—On farm owned by Robert Hay. Along the line fence between the farm and the property owned by Frederick Stuck. About 50 rods above the Stuck buildings. 1 grave - 1846.
19. **Queer**—About 2½ miles west of Berlin near the old Mud Pike. On farm owned by George Cook. About 20 rods northwest of the buildings. In the field above the house. 17 graves - oldest 1855.
20. **Elias Cober Farm**—On farm owned by Paul H. Cober near Beachdale. Formerly, the old Michael Beachley farm. 31 graves - oldest 1812.
21. **Weigley**—Paul E. Pritts farm west of the buildings about an eighth of a mile along the old road leading to Raineytown. 6 graves - oldest 1824. Philip Wegerline, first permanent settler in Berlin region.
22. **Lehman**—Farm owned by Richard Webreck. On north side of old abandoned road known as Amish Lane. In the field south of the buildings and adjoining the orchard. 12 graves - oldest 1838.
23. **Cable**—On Calvin Will farm at a turn in a private road opposite a hay shed on Calvin Will farm. 5 graves - oldest 1809.
24. **Penroad**—Calvin Will farm. In a field south of the buildings and near a limestone quarry. Also a few rods north of another cemetery on the same farm, near Knepper hay shed. 4 graves - oldest 1850.
25. **Brubaker**—On Jacob. J. Glessner farm. In field west of the house (about 10 rods). 4 graves - oldest 1815.
26. **Kimmel**—Farm owned by James Will. In the or-

chard a few rods above the barn. 10 graves - oldest 1866.

27. **Blough**—Owen Stellingwerf farm. Known as the Upper Gardill farm. 6 graves - oldest 1777.

28. **Blough Farm**—On William Schultz farm, west of buildings. 36 graves - oldest 1777.

29. **Cober**—On farm owned by John O. Ream. Formerly known as the Cornelius Cober farm. Peter Cober died in the year 1804. The burial ground is at the edge of a forest about an eighth of a mile south of the house. The spring identified the location of the home. The place of burial is unkept. It is partly enclosed by a wall of stones loosely thrown together. 15 graves, quite a number of graves not inscribed. One colored man buried outside the cemetery enclosure. The cemetery was rededicated to the original owner who was buried in 1804. The inscription on the bronze tablet is as follows: "Peter Cober original owner of this homestead died in 1804."

30. **Cober**—On Alfonso Simone, formerly Robert J. Maust farm. A short distance west of the buildings at the edge of the woods. 45 graves - oldest 1851.

31. **Pine Hill**—In village of Pine Hill. 254 graves - oldest 1787.

32. **Ridge Reformed Church**—115 graves - 13 uninscribed - oldest 1856.

33. **Fritz Lutheran**—321 graves - oldest 1847.

34. **George Cook Farm**—Formerly Daniel Landis farm. Samuel Smith a former Civil War veteran. 18 graves directly west of the barn ¼ mile.

35. **Walker Cemetery**—John Saylor, present owner of the farm. 3 miles from Pine Hill. Jacob Walker, Revolutionary War soldier.

36. **Flickinger Cemetery**—Located on the Croner Inc. Farms along township road leading southeast from D. J. Beachley farm. Anthony Flickinger - Civil War veteran. 20 graves.

37. **Hays Reformed Church Cemetery**—

38. **Young Cemetery**—On Abraham Sivits farm. 4 graves.

39. **Lape Cemetery**—On the Paul Countryman farm. Destroyed.

40. **John Croner Cemetery**—Formerly Aaron Cober farm. Near the old buildings. John Mosholder, a Revolutionary War veteran.

41. **Schrock and Cable Cemetery**—On the Edwin Landis farm.

42. **Hans Miller, Sr., Cemetery**—About 200 yards east of the buildings on the Thomas I. Maust farm. 12 graves, possibly more.

43. **Foy Cemetery**—Walter Foy farm. 11 graves.

44. **Casebeer Cemetery**—On the Verna Countryman land. 3 graves.

45. **Ray Glessner Farm**—Possibly Lehman burials in field below the house.

46. **Charles E. Maust farm**—300 feet at edge of farm. 3 graves.

These records were compiled by Dr. E. C. Saylor, 1929-1933, and Paul E. Pritts, 1976.

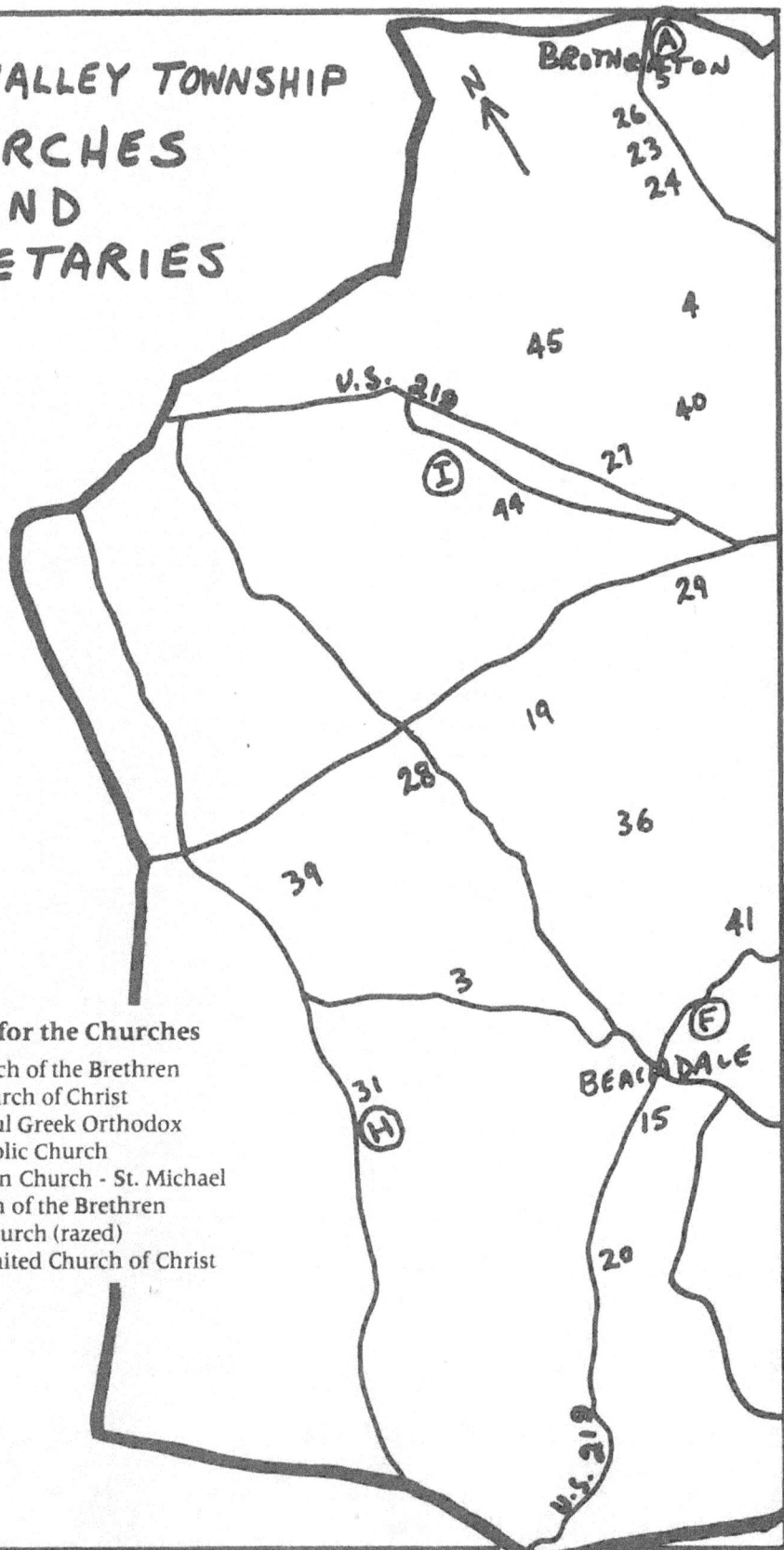

BROTHERSVALLEY TOWNSHIP
CHURCHES
AND
CEMETARIES

Key for the Churches

A   Brotherton Church of the Brethren
B   Hay's United Church of Christ
C   Sts. Peter and Paul Greek Orthodox
D   St. Gregory Catholic Church
E   Pine Hill Lutheran Church - St. Michael
F   Beachdale Church of the Brethren
G   Fritz Lutheran church (razed)
H   Ridge St. Paul United Church of Christ
I   Salem Brethren

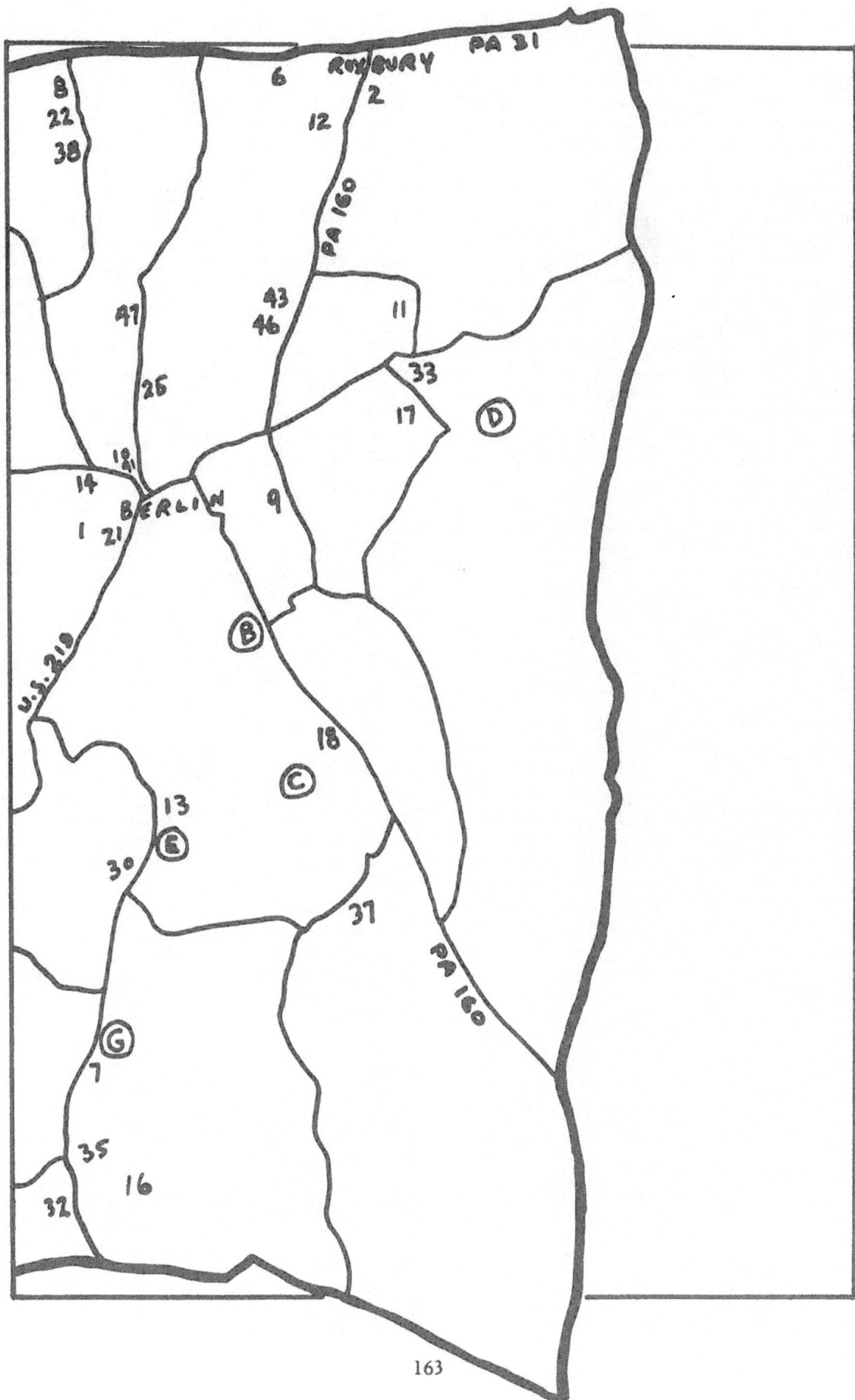

Brotherton Church of the Brethren

Taken from the "History of the Church of the Brethren of the Western District of Pennsylvania," by Elder Jerome E. Blough. Published by the Brethren Publishing House, Elgin, Ill. Copyright 1916 by Elder Jerome E. Blough.

The beginning of settlements by the Brethren in "The Glades," now Somerset County, is discussed in Chapter III, "Early Settlements of Brethren in Western Pennsylvania" (The Glades). Here is a quotation (page 39) from Dr. Brumbaugh: "The first movement of the Brethren across the Allegheny Mountains in Pennsylvania was to Bruederall, Brothersvalley, in what is now Somerset County, Pennsylvania. In 1762 this congregation began under George Adam Martin. He was, at this time, a Seventh-Day Baptist, and the congregation at the beginning held to the same doctrine. They soon, however, returned to the practice and faith of the Brethren Church. The number of members in 1770 was seventeen: Elder George Adam Martin and wife; Henry Roth, Sr., wife and daughter; Henry Roth, Jr., and wife; George Newcomer; Philip Aswald, wife and daughter; Abraham Gebel and wife; Philip Kimmel and wife . . . Wildebarger and wife.

"In 1762 George Adam Martin moved to Stony Creek. He married one of the Knippers (Mary Knepper) and was the father of many children."

Next I will quote from Elder H. R. Holsinger's "History of the Tunkers and the Brethren Church": "In the spring of 1783 a young Tunker Deacon, by the name of John Keagy, emigrated from York County Pennsylvania, to the backwoods of Somerset County (then Bedford), into the valley lying between Allegheny and Negro Mountains, and located at a point about 13 miles south of the village of Berlin. At the time of his arrival there were living in the vicinity a few scattered members of the same denomination. One of these was John Burger, who lived on the farm now known as the Buechley Estate. In the fall of the same year some ministering brethren from the east visited Brother Keagy, hunted up other members in the valley, and held a love feast at the home of John Burger, and organized the little band into a church."

Much of the history of this congregation is given in the history of the Brothersvalley congregation, by Elder W. G. Schrock. When, in 1849, the county was subdivided into four large congregations, that division of which Berlin was the central point and chief town naturally took the name "Berlin." Though this section was also known by the name of "Glades" and "Brothersvalley," its correct name was "Berlin" and this is the name used in the minutes of the district meetings until the further division in 1880. Berlin congregation at that time was bounded by the Elk Lick, Middle Creek, Quemahoning, Shade Creek, and Dunnings Creek (the latter in Bedford County) congregations, and embraced Brothersvalley, Stony Creek, and parts of Somerset and other townships.

So far as can be ascertained the following elders presided over the Berlin congregation: Michael Meyers, Peter Cober, John Forney, Sr., Jacob Meyers, and Jacob Blough. Other active elders and ministers were John P. Cober, Solomon Knepper, Daniel P. Walker, Ephriam Cober, George Schrock, William Sevits, Peter Musser, Henry R. Holsinger, Joseph W. Beer, Solomon J. Baer, and Michael Weyandt.

Here I take the liberty to quote from Elder H. R. Holsinger's "History of the Tunkers": "The church increased in numbers from time to time, until, in 1880, it had a membership of over four hundred. Then it was deemed proper to subdivide the territory. This was accomplished at a council meeting appointed for the purpose on October 9, 1880. Committees were appointed to name the boundaries and report to the next council meeting, on the 23rd of the same month.

"The meeting of the 23rd was presided over by Elder P. J. Brown, of Ohio. The committees on boundaries reported the lines of four separate congregations, and the report was unanimously adopted, with a few amendments.

"The names adopted by the several branches were: 1. Berlin church, embracing the town of Berlin, the meetinghouse known as Peter Beeghly's (Schmaltz Thal), and the appointment at Custer's. The officers were: ministers, Dr. John P. Cober, and H. R. Holsinger; deacons, John J. Bittner, Jacob Musser, Joseph G. Coleman, and Peter Beeghly, with a membership of one hundred and fifty. . . . 4. Brothers Valley. This congregation is bounded by the other three congregations, and the Quemahoning on the north. Its officers were Elder Jacob Blough, George Schrock, William Sevits, and Daniel P. Walker, ministers; and Lewis J. Knepper, William G. Schrock, John S. Meyers, and Samuel F. Reiman, deacons. It had a membership of about one hundred, and two houses of worship."

The first Beachdale (Schmaltz Thal) meetinghouse was built many years ago. At different times two additions were built to it and in 1881 it was suitably arranged for love-feast purposes. In 1911 a fine new church, costing about $4,000, was erected to take the place of the old one. It was dedicated by J. H. Cassady, September 24, 1911.

Brothersvalley
By Elder W. G. Schrock

The history of the Brothersvalley congregation dates from the latter part of the eighteenth century. At this time some members of the Church of the Brethren settled west of the Allegheny Mountains in what was then known as the Stony Creek and Brothersvalley "Glades." They named their new home "Brueders Thal"— Brothersvalley. This name may have originated with the Indians, who called them the "White Brothers of the Valley." Later on, when new townships were created, the principal part of the "Glades" was taken up and named Stony Creek and Brothersvalley. Stony Creek, the principal stream, draining nearly all of this vast territory, has its source in Pius Spring, in Berlin. This may account for the name of the new township, taken from Brothersvalley in 1792, being called Stony Creek. This accounts for the different names: "Glades," "Berlin," and "Brothersvalley," the last one the most endearing of all.

From 1763 to 1770 a general Indian outbreak caused much trouble among the first settlers on this side of the mountain. It is surmised that the colony was scattered and driven out for the time being. However, it is probable that some very familiar names, somewhat modernized in spelling and pronunciation, such as the Rhoads, Cables, Kimmels, Kneppers, and others, have come down to us from these pioneers. All these names are found in our church records, and their descendants are living in our congregation at the present time.

From 1770 to 1825 this church has no written record, and all we know is by tradition. Many of the church fathers, who were earnest workers for the Master during this period, left us no data for writing up a church history of Brothersvalley. There is a wide gap between the time when Elder Martin passed away and 1825, of which very little is known to the present generation, however important or interesting it might be to coming generations. During this period the church increased in membership, both by immigration and conversions. In less than 75 years, from the time the first Brethren crossed the mountains, they were found in many parts of Somerset County and even beyond. If we can at least rely on tradition, the church's activity centered around Berlin later. That probably accounts for the first meetinghouse being built in that vicinity, and the congregation being called Berlin. Up to 1825 this large territory was without system and unorganized.

Brotherton Church of the Brethren

There is a question in the mind of the writer who succeeded Elder Martin in the eldership. From the best information obtainable, Michael Meyers, a resident minister near Berlin, was ordained about the year 1800, and had the oversight of the church for a quarter of a century, or longer. It would seem that the next in order of time to be ordained was Peter Cober and John Forney, Sr., in 1837. This brings us up to 1849, when Somerset County was divided into four local congregations. In the early day of the history of the church, itinerant preaching was largely in vogue in most of the churches. Members were regularly visited by preachers, and all the services were held in private houses, barns, or schoolhouses, and nearly all were conducted in the German language. To solve this problem the Brethren built a large meetinghouse, in 1845, in sight of Berlin, and called it the Grove house, since they were no longer able to accommmodate the people by other means. In this house regular services were held for sixty-two years. The Grove house was torn down in 1907. Berlin congregation contains Garrett, Beachdale, and Berlin, and was bounded on the south by Elk Lick, on the north by Shade, on the west by Middle Creek; and on the east by the Bedford County line, with Berlin as the center of activity.

From 1849 to 1880 the following elders presided over the Berlin church: Peter Cober, Jacob Meyers and Jacob Blough. Elder Blough was elected to the ministry in 1851, and ordained in 1868. Samuel Meyers and Jacob Good may have been deacons prior to 1849, and served in said office up to their death. The following ministers assisted in the work of the church during this period: John Cober, Ephraim Cober, Solomon Knepper, George Schrock, William Sevits, Michael Weyandt, Solomon Baer, Peter Musser, Daniel P. Walker, Henry R. Holsinger, and Joseph W. Baer. Deacons elected prior to 1880: Lewis J. Knepper, Jacob Meyers, Joseph G. Coleman, John J. Bittner, Dr. John Beachley, Valentine Blough, Jacob Lichty, Jacob Musser, John S. Meyers, Peter Beeghley, Josiah Kimmel, William N. Trent and Philip F. Cupp. Most of the ministers named first served in the office of deacon.

1880 to 1915

In 1880 the old Berlin congregation was divided, as is noted in the history of that congregation. The same year an election was held for church officers. George Schrock and William Sevits were ordained to the eldership; W. G. Schrock and Samuel F. Reiman were elected to the ministry, and John J. Blauch and Daniel H. Walker, deacons. The organization now was: Elders, Jacob Blough, George Schrock, and William Sevits; ministers, Michael Weyandt, Daniel P. Walker, W. G. Schrock, and Samuel F. Reiman; deacons, John J. Blauch, D. H. Walker, and the above-named brethren still living who had served prior to 1880.

Elections for church officials have been as follows: for ministers—1886, D. H. Walker and Philip F. Cupp; 1897, Perry U. Miller, Samuel U. Shober, and Ira D. S. Walker; 19—, George Reitz (was not installed); 1906, Galen K.

Walker and John H. Fike (latter not installed); 1912, Lewis S. Knepper and Ralph W. Reiman. Dr. Peter Musser, a minister had moved into the congregation from Virginia during the seventies, but moved back again before the division. Ephraim Cober, an able minister, who was reared here and called to the ministry, moved to Sabetha, Kansas, many years ago. Elder Joseph J. Shaffer moved into the congregation from the Shade Creek congregation in 1909, and Annias Beeghly also moved here from southern Illinois in 1909. Brother Beeghly was for a number of years an active deacon in the Quemahoning congregation, but moved to Illinois and was called to the ministry, and then returned to his native county.

Deacons were elected as follows: in 1883, Cyrus H. Walker and Perry U. Miller; 1886, Jacob O. Kimmel, George J. Schrock, Christian Reitz, John F. Reiman; and Jeremiah J. Reiman; 1896, George Reitz, and Mahlon S. Reiman; 1897, Uriah F. Reiman, Jacob F. Knepper, Emanuel M. Knepper, and Sherman Peck; 1904, Clinton K. Shober, Jacob C. Reiman, Allen F. Mostoller, and George S. Reiman; 1912, William W. Cupp, Alvin Knepper, Edward S. Schrock, and H. N. Mostoller.

Ordinations: 1886, Michael Weyandt; 1895, W. G. Schrock and S. F. Reiman; 1899, D. H. Walker; 1908, P. U. Miller and S. U. Shober.

In 1903 a large brick love-feast house was erected at Brotherton, to take the place of the old Pike meetinghouse, which had been in use for, perhaps, nearly half a century, and by the side of which the Brethren have buried their dead for many years. This new church, centrally located, also takes the place of the old Grove meetinghouse for love feasts and other large gatherings. In the spring of 1907 the old Grove house was razed to the ground, and a neat brick church now occupies the place. In addition to the Grove and Brotherton houses, the congregation has the Salem house on the Ridge, and the Rayman house, near Friedens, and a share of the Summit house at Geiger Station, on the line between the Brothersvalley and Middle Creek congregations.

The first Sunday school in the congregation was organized in the Pike church, in 1865 or 1866, and the superintendents were W. G. Schrock and Lewis J. Knepper.

Inasmuch as the church kept no records until 1880, it was impossible to give a clear and systematic outline of data and facts in regular order. Any errors or omissions in the above are due to oversight or want of better information.

In 1916 the records show that the following were officers of the Brothersvalley Church of the Brethren: elders, W. G. Schrock, D. H. Walker, S. U. Shober, P. U. Miller, and J. J. Shaffer; ministers: A. J. Beeghley, Lewis S. Knepper, and Ralph Reiman; deacons: John S. Meyers, John F. Reiman, Jeremiah J. Reiman, George Reitz, M. S. Reiman, J. M. Knepper, E. L. Knepper, Sherman Peck, J. C. Reiman, A. F. Mostoller, George S. Reiman, C. K. Shober, W. W. Cupp, A. R. Knepper, E. S. Schrock, H. N. Mostoller, and B. B. Dickey.

Those also who have served or are serving as deacons are the following: C. R. Bauermaster, G. S. Platt, C. E. Reiman, P. H. Glessner, Meyers Knepper, B. J. Donner, John L. Knepper, Calvin M. Will, Charles Custer, Clyde L. Platt, Calvert Rhodes, Emerson L. Knepper, Kenneth Ross, William Cochran, Robert W. Bauermaster, C. R. Bauermaster, Jr., Clair M. Reiman, and Harry J. Emerick.

Those ministers who have served as pastors since the full-time pastorate began in 1919 are as follows:

November 24, 1919 to May 14, 1922	Lewis S. Knepper
1922 to 1924	Ralph E. Shober
1924 to 1942	H. Q. Rhodes
1942 to 1947	Roy S. Forney
Summer 1947	Quentin Evans
1947 to 1955	H. Austin Cooper
1955 to 1967	Herald V. Seese
1967 to 1974	Kenneth Blough
1974 to date	Owen Preston

MT. ZION (Hay's) Reformed Church

(Now United Church of Christ)

The Mt. Zion congregation can trace its origin to 1818, when a patent for land, in that section of Brothersvalley Township known as Pine Hill, was granted by the state legislature to the German Lutheran and Reformed people. The Lutheran representative was George Hay. On this plot of ground, which contained twenty-three acres, was erected, in 1819, a union church, and a part of the ground set aside for burial purposes. However, the Reformed people had as yet no regular organization. The members belonged to the Reformed church in Berlin, whose pastor held services occasionally in the same union church for the convenience of members living rather far from the church at Berlin.

In 1847 a petition was presented to the state legislature by the German Lutheran and Reformed people of Pine Hill, asking permission to dispose of about twenty acres of the plot and use the proceeds in the erection of a new union church at Pine Hill. This was granted, and the land was sold in 1848. A two-story brick building was erected at an approximate cost of $1200, the bricks for which were burned on the church property. The name of the congregation was "The Union Church at Pine Hill." After this was built the Reformed people felt that they should now become a regularly organized congregation. Accordingly, a congregational meeting was held in the Union meetinghouse at Pine Hill, in charge of Rev. William Conrad, pastor at Berlin. A congregation was organized; thirty-six members, mostly from the

Berlin Church, entered the organization. After the organization, an election of officers followed which resulted in the selection of Jacob Hauger and Daniel Bauman as elders, to serve for a period of four years. Jacob Bowman, Jonathan Knepper, and David Hay were elected deacons to serve for two years. Benjamin Hay was elected trustee to serve for four years and David Hay to serve for two years. After the installation of the officers, Rev. Conrad preached a sermon in the German language from Acts 2:42. The first communion was held May 27, 1849, the service being in charge of Rev. H. Knepper of the Reformed Church and Rev. C. Young of the Lutheran Church. For a number of years these two congregations were worshiping in one house of prayer and held what was known as "Union Communion."

This arrangement continued until 1857 when the Reformed people felt that the time had come for them to have a building of their own. A congregational meeting was called in December and funds solicited, which justified them to appoint a committee to erect the church. Benjamin Hay donated ground for the new church house located about two miles east of Pine Hill, on the road leading from Berlin to Meyersdale. Simon Hay and Daniel Boger were appointed the building committee. The instructions to this committee were simple, namely the size of the building 40 x 60, and to have the building ready for dedication the following autumn. In October 1858 the church was dedicated. The pastor, William Conrad, was assisted by Revs. F. K. Levan of Somerset and George Fickes of Grantsville, Md. The sermon was preached by Rev. F. K. Levan of the Somerset charge in the German language while the pastor performed the service of dedication, and gave the church the name of Mt. Zion Reformed Church. The first communion service was held in Mt. Zion, October 24, 1858. The pastor preached two sermons, one in the German language from the text St. John 21:17, the other in the English language from St. John 7:14. At this service forty-five persons presented themselves at the Lord's table.

During the pastorate of Rev. J. S. Wagner, 1884-1887, Mt. Zion church building was renovated and a pulpit recess added, improving the appearance of the building. The church was rededicated on Wednesday, November 10, 1886.

While the Reformed people had never disposed of their share of the Union Church at Pine Hill, it was necessary, in order to retain their property rights, to hold at least one service annually in this building. This was done for many years. Not only the pastor of Zion's charge, but any pastor in the Classis could hold this service. The late Rev. Dr. Shick, pastor of Amity church, Meyersdale, held one of these services. These services were very well attended. The main auditorium, as well as the gallery, were filled with anxious and curious worshipers. The building at this time was the property of the Missouri Lutheran congregations. In 1899 when St. Luke's and Trinity, Roxbury, were detached from the Zion's charge, it became necessary to satisfy their interest in the parsonage property in Berlin. Accordingly an effort was made to dispose of the Reformed share in the

Union Church at Pine Hill which was finally consummated after a number of meetings with the other side of the house. The proceeds of the sale of the union church were applied on the parsonage of the St. Luke's and Roxbury congregations. The union church building was sold a few years later to George Gumbert, who used the material in the erection of a modern house near Pine Hill.

In June 1897, during the pastorate of Rev. E. P. Skyles, a congregational meeting was held for the purpose of discussing the erection of a new house of worship. On motion it was decided to build a new church the following spring and summer, said church to be of brick. The following were appointed the building committee: Philip Hay, Benjamin G. Hay, Hiram Hay, Lewis Berkley, Austin Bauman, R. S. Walker, and Simon Hay. The new church was dedicated in the fall of 1898. Rev. J. C. Bowman, professor in the seminary at Lancaster, and Rev. J. C. Musser, editor of the Reformed Church "Messenger," preached at these services. The church was dedicated free of debt. In 1908 the cornerstone of this church was broken open by thieves and relieved of the coin contained therein. The literature remained undisturbed.

In 1905, during the pastorate of Rev. H. W. Wiant, a Moller two-manual pipe organ, costing $1,200, was in-

Hay's Reformed Church

stalled. Half of this amount was donated by Mr. Andrew Carnegie.

During the pastorate of the Rev. J. E. Scheetz, repairs were made to the interior of the church, such as lathing, plastering, and frescoing. The floor of the auditorium was carpeted with a fine Brussels carpet, and a baby grand piano placed in the main auditorium of the church. The Sunday school was more thoroughly organized, and the main school moved into the auditorium of the church.

Rev. S. C. Stover served the charge for a very brief period, arriving in the charge on June 1, 1924, and being called to his eternal reward December 25, 1925, on his way home from a Christmas service at St. Paul's Church.

During the pastorate of Rev. F. D. Witmer, which began in June 1926 and extended to June 1951, several important events happened at Mt. Zion Church. Mt. Zion Church, cooperating with the Hill Crest Grange, and various neighbors of the church, had an electric line built and the church wired and lighted. At this time, also, an electric blower was installed in the pipe organ.

Mt. Zion and St. Paul's also cooperated in the purchase of a new parsonage. Grace Church, not seeing fit to join in the program, paid a yearly rent as their share of the charge expenses.

In preparation for the centennial celebration in 1949, the building was extensively repaired—the brick repointed, a new roof, and interior painting.

After the termination of the pastorate of Rev. F. D. Witmer, the church found the modern-day minister was not interested in accepting a call to a rural three-church charge. Except for a brief pastorate of Rev. Eli Fabian and of Rev. (Mrs.) Mary Wenck, who traded pulpits with her husband, Rev. Edwin Wenck, pastor of Trinity, Berlin, the church has relied on supply seminarians from Lancaster Theological Seminary and on supply ministers ordained by other denominations.

Convinced that it would not again have need of a parsonage, a belief concurred in by St. Paul's Church, the parsonage was sold and the proceeds invested as an endowment for the support of the church.

Beginning in 1971 and continuing through 1976, major repairs and decorating were done on the building. The interior was painted and new wall-to-wall carpet was installed, also a new heating system, a public-address system, and a new roof. The bell tower was repaired and a new mounting for the bell was installed.

At this writing services are conducted weekly at 9:00 a.m., Sunday, and although the membership is declining, attendance at worship services is good and the church is providing a needed service to the community by a dedicated service to God.

Greek Orthodox Church at Goodtown

Early in the 20th century, immigrants from Europe came to the United States seeking a better lifestyle. Many of these settlers wanted to improve their lives, so they came to the mining towns of Pennsylvania, since it promised more opportunities. Many of the people who settled in the Goodtown and MacDonaldton areas came from the same localities in Europe, namely Austria.

After they arrived in this country and adequately settled down, they found that they were in need of a place to perpetuate Orthodox Christianity. A committee was formed to establish a place to worship. Some of the people who worked with this committee were: the first priest, the Very Reverend Father John Komar; president at the time, Frank Mohilchock; vice-president, Nicholas Rizak; secretary, Lishko Linko; and treasurer, John Basara. After much prayer and planning S.S. Peter and Paul's Greek Catholic Orthodox Church was built in 1917 in the booming mining town of Goodtown, Pa.

Some of the early members included: Semko (Samuel) Kutz-meda, Steve and Harry Bruce, Vasily (Charles) Hummel, Vasily Nider, Mike Russian, Charles Chipelock, Nicholas Biconich, Mike and Wasco Drabish, Frank Druzitsky, Mike Swet, and his son John.

Nicholas Rizak, Charles Tataleba, Lena Swet, Mary Chipelock, John Matieszyn, John Popovich, Mrs. Ferrence, and Mary Kutzmeda are some of the founding members that are still living.

Throughout the sixty years of its existence in Goodtown, the Orthodox Church has been served by a number of priests. These include the Very Reverend Fathers Komar, Luzak, Hanchak, Pianovich, Kurhaesky, Lazar, Kirichenkoff, Barna, Okaly, Barany, Staphanko,

Goodtown Greek Orthodox Church

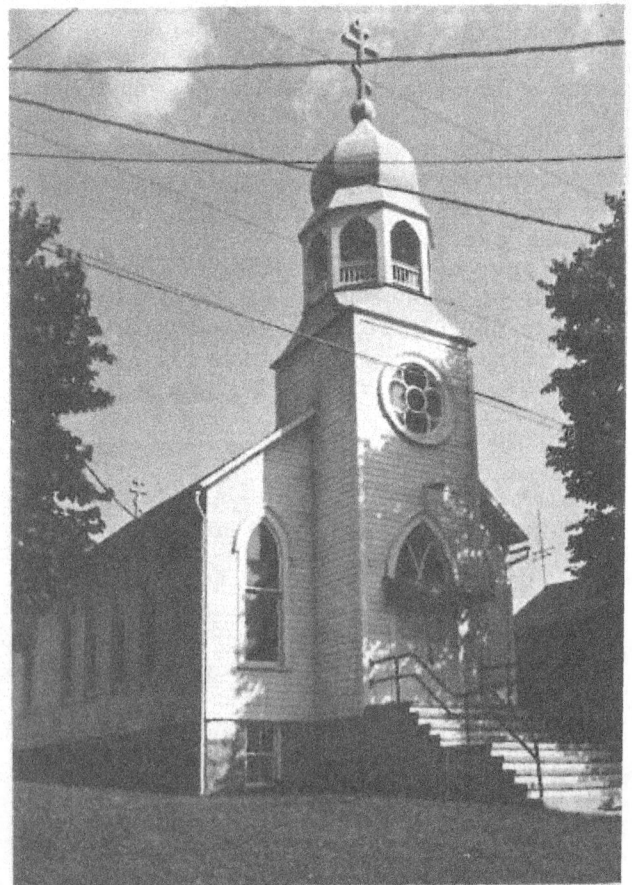

Yankovich, and presently Father John Gourusik.

The first couple to be married in this church were John Swet and Lena Yonish in the year 1919. Lena Yonish Swet is still living.

Present officers are: John Slifco, president; John Popovich, vice-president; Frank Popovich, secretary-treasurer; Mrs. Anna Hummel Lohr leads in the liturgical singing.

St. Gregory Catholic Church of Macdonaldton

St. Gregory established in 1911, lies two miles east of Berlin in the town of MacDonaldton, now Berlin, R.D. #3.

It is estimated that in 1910 there were upwards of 5,000 inhabitants in MacDonaldton, mostly immigrants of Slavic, Greek, and Italian background and largely Roman and Greek Catholics. The Donald Coal Company gave several lots in the town to both the Roman and Greek Catholics on the condition that a church be built within ten years or the land would revert to the coal company.

History becomes clouded at this point, but it seems that the Roman Catholics built the present church, which was used by both the Roman Catholics and the Greek Catholics for a time. In recent years St. Gregory is composed entirely of Roman Catholics.

The parish records state, "MacDonaldton baptisms not found recorded here may be found in the books at Meyersdale and Windber." The first recorded baptism at St. Gregory was November 4, 1911 (Francis Ausfeld).

The number of souls baptized over the years averaged 30, the peak year being 1915 at 47. By 1928 there were 12 baptisms, and since 1928, the average has been five to six per year.

Marriages average five to six per year through 1975. The first recorded was June 8, 1912 (between George Humering and Sue Coutras.)

The parish has been administered under the diocese of Altoona-Johnstown, with the assistance of the Capucian Fathers of Frostburg, Maryland, and the Carmelite Fathers of New Baltimore, Pa. Since 1968 St. Gregory has been administered by the Carmelite Fathers.

St. Gregory Catholic Church of Macdonaldton

St. Michael's Lutheran Church

The history of St. Michael's Lutheran Church in Pine Hill dates back to 1787 when the congregation was meeting for worship in the schoolhouse. The first baptisms recorded were performed August 26, 1787.

On July 10, 1789, Nickolas Coleman and his wife, Frederika, granted one acre of ground from their land, secured by patent of June 19, 1797 from the Commonwealth, to Michael Keffer and Michael Miller, in trust, for twenty shillings for the use of the Lutheran congregation at Pine Hill. The first house of worship was placed in what is now the church cemetery, and was likely erected the summer of 1798.

As the first pastor's name was Rev. Michael Steck, and he had been ordained in St. Michael's Church, Philadelphia, and as that was also the name of the first two trustees, it likely came natural to name the church "St. Michael's."

In 1818, the Penn heirs granted to George Walker and George Hay, trustees for the German Lutheran and German Reformed congregations, respectively, at Pine Hill, 23 acres of land which had been left vacant by the settlers for school and church purposes.

In 1842, members of the congregation living towards the Casselman River considered it convenient and advisable, for the sake of the scattered membership, to erect a church nearer them. The St. Paul's (Fritz) Lutheran Church thus originated, and a number of members withdrew from the Pine Hill congregation to join the Fritz Church.

In 1847, an act of the legislature was passed which allowed the selling of 20 acres of the 23 secured in 1818. Accordingly, there was built in 1848, with the money, the Union brick church owned jointly by the Lutherans and the Reformed people; the latter had worshiped previously in Berlin. It was 40 by 26 feet, had a gallery on three sides, a high pulpit, and was built at a cost of $1,000.

The two congregations got along harmoniously until the pastorate of Rev. Eli Fare, 1851-1854. He estranged some of his members by lack of judgment and tact and was finally threatened with a gun if he didn't leave.

The result was that a petition was sent to Allegheny Synod in 1854, signed by 27 members of the congregation, asking permission to withdraw from the Berlin charge. A paper signed by 23 members of the Berlin congregation was also presented, asking Synod to refuse. Synod refused the request, but gave the Pine Hill congregation the privilege for the time being to ask any pastor of the Allegheny Synod to supply them. Feeling, no doubt, that the Synod had not treated them properly, Rev. Franz Julius Bilz, a member of the Missouri Synod, of Cumberland, Maryland, was invited to visit them. Sometime after his visit, a majority of the congregation voted to leave the General Synod and to become a member of the Missouri Synod, with Rev. Bilz as pastor.

The Reformed congregation now withdrew and built the Hay's Mt. Zion Church in 1856. Rev. Bilz served from 1856 to 1860.

The departure of this pastor from the charge seemed the occasion for the reorganization of a new General Synod Church, having for a nucleus some of the original congregation who declined to go to the Missouri Synod. Accordingly, the General Synod pastor at Berlin, Rev. Philip Sheeder, secured the following officers, August 17, 1860: Daniel Fritz, Samuel Boger, and William G. Coleman, trustees. On September 22, a constitution was adopted, a charter asked for, and by October 20, 1860, a congregation was organized by the election of Daniel Fritz and John G. Walker, elders; William N. Coleman and Nickolas Dickey, deacons. A charter was secured on the petition of Daniel Fritz, John G. Walker, Nickolas Dickey, Samuel Boger, William G. Coleman, Jonathan Walker, William N. Coleman, Samuel Stahl, and Solomon Coleman, on April 22, 1861. A legal suit in the Somerset County Court for the right of possession of the brick church resulted in a verdict for the General Synod. The Supreme Court, however, overruled this and decided that each synod had a right to it. The General Synod supporters then secured a lot of one fourth acre for $20, deed dated November 10, 1860, from William N. Coleman and Matilda Coleman, his wife, and erected thereon a second St. Michael's Evangelical Lutheran Church. It was dedicated in 1861 and was a frame building, 35 by 50 feet, with a gallery at the rear, as well as a tower. On October 13, 1861, the following 17 persons were enrolled as charter members: John G. Walker, Nickolas Dickey, William N. Coleman, Daniel Fritz, Samuel Boger, Samuel Stahl, Solomon Coleman, Susannah Hay, Catharine Dickey, Dinah Boger, William G. Coleman, Phoebe Cover, Maria Turner, Emeline Hay, Mary A. Coleman, Ludwig and Catharine Kobe.

In 1865, Rev. Winecoff reported 30 members of the congregation. For the first ten years, progress continued slowly. The use of the German language was discarded,

under the pastorship of Rev. Poffenberger.

The efficient Pastor Gruver began to reap increased membership and to see events point to a time when the General Synod would again come into possession of its own. Repairs to the building and gains to the church were made under the devoted care of Dr. M. L. Young, of whose pastorate St. Michael's became a part in 1893.

By 1903 the congregation felt itself able to erect a new church. It extended an invitation to the seven surviving members of the Missouri Synod congregation to unite with it in the enterprise, as the Union brick was also too old to be profitably repaired. This was agreed to by them. The St. Michael's congregation then paid to the Mt. Zion (Hay's) German Reformed congregation the sum of $150 for whatever right, title, or interest they had in the remaining three acres of the original 23 acres of the 1818 grant. In 1904, Peter Gumbert, surviving trustee, conveyed to the St. Michael's congregation a portion (1½ acres) of the tract and the present brick structure was erected during the summer.

The cornerstone was laid July 10, 1904; the sermon being preached by Rev. R. L. Patterson. On December 4, 1904, the beautiful edifice was dedicated free of debt. The brick building is 50 by 30 feet, with many beautiful art windows. The annexed Sunday school room is 30 by 22 feet. The total cost of the structure was $8,000.

In 1905, the frame church was deeded to Simon P. Fritz, who remodeled it and used it for his home. In 1910, the Union church was sold to George Gumbert, who removed the building and built a house.

In 1911, Peter Gumbert, surviving trustee of the Missouri congregation, was received into the fellowship, and in like manner in 1912, Henry Gumbert and Peter Baker, the remaining resident members, were received. With them came also the residue, about $700, of a legacy of $1,000 given to "the Lutheran Church at Pine Hill for the support of the preaching of the gospel," by George Fritz. They also conveyed the remaining portion of the tract of 1818, about 1¾ acres, which was then resold to Henry Gumbert for $250, the interest of which sum was

St. Michael's Lutheran Church

170

to go to the upkeeping of the Pine Hill Cemetery.

And, thus, after two generations of divided homes and estranged friends, there was again none but a General Synod Lutheran Church at Pine Hill, as there was prior to 1846.

The first Luther League in Somerset County was organized in St. Michael's Church, December 22, 1894, under the pastorship of the Rev. M. L. Young.

Rev. Ephraim Dickey and Rev. William R. Stahl were the congregation's gift to the ministry.

Pastors have been: (1) Rev. Michael John Steck (Steg), (2) Rev. Frederick William Lange, (3) Rev. Ernest H. Tiedeman, (4) Rev. Jacob Crigler, (5) Rev. George Leiter, (6) Rev. Charles Reese, (7) Rev. Louis Gustiniani, (8) Rev. Jesse Winecoff, (9) Rev. Charles Young, (10) Rev. Elias Fare, (11) Rev. Franz J. Bilz, (12) Rev. Philip Sheeder, (13) Rev. A. M. Strauss, (14) Rev. J. W. Poffenberger, (15) Rev. C. B. Gruver, (16) Rev. M. L. Young, (17) Rev. A. H. Burke (supply), (18) Rev. W. E. Brown, (19) Rev. W. H. B. Carney, (20) Rev. W. Blair Claney, (21) Rev. Frederick L. Will, (22) Rev. Samuel F. B. Tholan, (23) Rev. Charles I. Rowe, (24) Rev. Ellwood I. Stahl, (25) Rev. John Hoenstine, (26) Rev. Howard Bock, (27) Rev. Glen Keidel, (28) Rev. Frederick C. H. Scholz, (29) Rev. Andrew P. Kazar; and (30) Rev. Gene J. Abel, present pastor.

Beachdale Church of the Brethren

The Church of the Brethren was first organized in 1708 by Alexander Mack in Schwarzzenau, Germany. The first group of Brethren migrants to America settled at Germantown, Pa., in 1719.

Elder Peter Becker organized the church on December 25, 1723, and it was known until 1830 as the German Baptist Brethren.

The first movement of Brethren across the Allegheny Mountains in Pennsylvania was to Brueders Thal (Brothersvalley) in the Stony Creek and Glades area.

The first Church of the Brethren in Somerset County was organized by Elder George Adam Martin. There were seventeen adult members. This was in 1762.

In 1785 the third meetinghouse in the district was established. This was known as the Michael Buechley meetinghouse. It was located on the property now owned by Rupple and Gladys Brant. This became the Love Feast House and Mother Church of the Beachdale and Garrett congregations. The building was a large dwelling house with removable partitions to make room available for the love feast services. There were two an-

Beachdale Church of the Brethren

nual conference meetings held at this location.

By 1880 the church membership had increased and the territory was subdivided, the boundary being the Grove meetinghouse about one mile north of Berlin on the property now owned by Wayne Darr. The Berlin congregation included Berlin—the community known as Beachdale and Garrett. In the division the Progressive Brethren took about half the membership, while the conservatives held the meetinghouse known as Peter Beachley's (Schmaltz Thal).

The first church known as Beachdale was built in 1860 on the ground where the present house is now located. At different times, two additions were built. The present brick building was erected in 1911 at a cost of about $4,000. It was dedicated by C. C. Cassady on September 24, 1911, under the pastorate of Galen Walker.

In 1953 the basement was made suitable for classrooms. A new heating system and plumbing were also installed at this time. Dedication service for these additions was held in November 1953 with Dr. Guy Hartman, Rev. Austin Cooper, and Rev. Walter Berkebile as speakers.

In 1956 a parsonage was built next to the church. In 1963 the name was officially changed from the Berlin congregation to the Beachdale Church of the Brethren.

With the membership of the church steadily growing, the church decided to build an addition to the church. A 30 x 48 foot basement was finished. This included a baptistry, more classrooms, and a kitchen. These improvements were dedicated May 31, 1968, by Brother Dean Shetler and Brother William Hay.

In June 1972 Ronald Beachley was ordained to the ministry, after graduating from Bethany Theological Seminary. Ronald is the son of Mrs. Elsie Beachley and the late DeVon Beachley and is married to the former Linda Brougher. They have three children. He is currently serving a pastorate in Virginia.

The church membership continues to grow and an addition to the sanctuary is being constructed at the present time.

The following is a list of pastors who have served the

congregation over the past years: Jacob Buechley, J. P. Cober, R. L. Pollard, W. W. Blough, G. K. Walker, J. J. Shaffer, D. H. Walker, B. F. Waltz, D. W. Long, D. K. Clapper, A. J. Beeghley, George L. Detwiler, Guy Wampler, John D. Long, A. Jay Replogle, R. K. Showalter, Fred Seese, Dean Shetler, and William N. Hay. Raymond Mankamyer ordained at Hostetler Brethren Church.

These are the deacons who served over the years: John J. Bittner, Jacob Musser, Joseph Coleman, Peter Beachley, Francis Brant, N. A. Beachley, William Cossel, H. H. Brant, H. H. Yoder, F. O. Brant, Joseph Long, Russel E. Brant, John H. Hentz, Charles Fogle, Robert W. Hay, Maurice S. Brant, Galen Miller, Charles Thomas, Sr., John Long, Frank Phennicie, Charles Thomas, Jr., William Fogle, Donald Mankamyer, Richard Cunningham, and Gary Phennicie.

St. Paul's Lutheran or Fritz Church

Fritz Church has a history that dates back to May 4, 1842, when a number of people, members of the Pine Hill congregation, decided that there should be a separate church to care for the people living between Pine Hill and the Casselman River.

The land was donated by Mr. and Mrs. William Fritz. The first church was a one-story frame building which was built by Simon Knepper and was dedicated around 1844 under the pastorate of Rev. Jess Winecoff. The building committee consisted of Jacob P. Walker, Frederick P. Walker, and John Fritz.

In 1845 the church became part of the Allegheny Synod. Preaching service was held once a month and mostly in the German language. The second preacher, Rev. Charles Young, preached every two weeks. By 1865 there were 75 members.

In 1874, during the pastorate of Rev. A. M. Strauss, it was decided to build a new church. The building committee included Peter P. H. Walker, William Fritz, William H. Fritz, Hiram P. Walker, Silas Walker, Herman N. Walker, A. J. Boose, and H. C. Wahl.

The cornerstone was laid by the pastor August 4, 1874, on which occasion Rev. A. M. Whetstone preached a German sermon and Rev. D. Earhart an English one. At this event 600 dinners were served free in the grove of the church and $5,000 was secured in cash and pledges at this service. The church was completed in July 1875 and dedicated the next month. Dr. James A. Brown, at that time president of Gettysburg Seminary, preached the sermon and Rev. S. W. Poffenberger, pastor, read the dedicatory service. The total cost of the church was $8,000 and it was dedicated free of debt July 1879.

Rev. Poffenberger, last of the Berlin pastors, was the first to use the English language exclusively. He resigned in 1879 and his church joined with the Meyersdale Church to form a new charge with Rev. J. Milton Snyder as pastor. Garrett and Center churches were added in 1889 and the Pine Hill Church was included in 1893.

The Luther League was organized in June 1949, which was the first league for about forty years.

The 100th anniversary of the church was celebrated in 1942. The church was dismantled in 1966 and a memorial erected in 1968.

Ministers who have served are as follows: Charles Reese, Jesse Winecoff, Charles Young, Elias Fair, Philip Sheeder, A. M. Strauss, J. W. Poffenberger, J. Milton Snyder, M. L. Young, William E. Brown (supply), A. H. Burk (supply), W. H. Bruce Carney, W. B. Claney. F. L. Will, S. F. Tholen, Charles I. Rowe, Elwood I. Stahl, John S. Hoenstein, Howard W. Bock and Glen B. Keidel.

St. Paul's Lutheran (Fritz) Church

St. Paul Church of Christ-Ridge

The St. Paul's (Ridge) Reformed Church stands on a plot of ground that was given for that purpose by Jesse Brant and is located in Brothersvalley Township, about four miles west of Berlin.

The original church was built in 1859 by people who were living in the community but were attending services in the Pine Hill and Berlin Reformed churches.

There were 29 original members (namely): Brants, Haugers, Kneppers, Smiths, and Mosholders. The first elders were Jacob Hauger and Nicholas Smith; the deacons were Frederick Knepper and William Hauger.

One of the main features of this early church was a

singing school conducted by Elder Jacob Brant for many years and was very popular in the Berlin area.

The original building, a 30 x 40 foot wood frame structure, built at a cost of $410, plus some gratis labor, was used for 48 years. In 1907 the membership had grown to 112, of which about one third were Brants. It was decided to build a larger house of worship. The cornerstone for the new church (which is a brick-cased structure) was laid July 7, 1907. The new church was dedicated debt-free May 3, 1908.

Before the dedication some of the members reported that the new church would have some new oak pews. However, while the congregation knelt in prayer, a blind member from a neighboring church discovered that the seats were not oak, only the backs and ends were oak. An eyewitness to this test told the writer that the blind man used his tongue and fingers to make his examination, and he was right.

The fortunes of the church remained about constant until around the turn of the Second World War. Since then many of the members have moved away from the community. Some have died, and the people who have replaced them belong to other churches so that the present membership is around forty.

Services are held weekly by lay minister Harvey Stauffer from Cumberland, Md. The present officers are Elders Samuel Maust, William Lepley, and Merle Romesberg. Deacons are Galen Shaffer, Herbert Hoover, Ray

Laughery, and Ronald Walker.

The plot of ground that Jesse Brant donated to the church was large enough to accommodate the church house, a sizable area for horses and carriages, as well as a cemetery. When the original cemetery lots were all sold, Henry Brant, Jesse's son, who owned the surrounding land, donated additional ground for lots. By the time these lots were all sold, Henry's daughter, Marian, and his son-in-law, Adam Lepley, owned the farm, and they donated more ground to bring it to its present size.

Ridge Reformed Church

Salem Church of the Brethren

Little historical data is available about the colorful, little Salem Church of the Brethren along Plank Road in Brothersvalley Township.

Older members of the church recall, however, that the frame edifice was constructed about 1896. Among the leaders in the construction plans was Rev. Perry U. Miller, who had been deacon, elder, and superintendent of the church and Sunday school. He was responsible for keeping the congregation going for many years.

First pastor of the church was Rev. S. U. Shober. He was followed by Elders D. H. Walker, W. G. Schrock, J. J. Shaffer, and Rev. Miller, a resident elder. More recent pastors of the church have been Revs. Lewis Knepper, H. Q. Rhoads, Roy L. Forney, Quentin Evans, and Austin Cooper.

History of the charge dates back to the latter part of the 18th century when members of the church settled west of the Allegheny Mountains in what was then known as Stony Creek Township and Brothersvalley—"Glades." They called their new home "Brueders Thal." No written records of the churches are available from 1770 to 1885, but the lists of pastors and church leaders are fairly complete since 1885.

The Salem Church, according to veteran members of the congregation, had a well-attended Sunday school during its early history. The first superintendent was Mr.

Miller. He was followed in line by Elmer H. Hoffman, Mrs. C. W. Knepper, Mrs. Minnie Hoffman Emerick, Frank Albright, John Saylor, Mrs. Ralph Watkins, and Philip H. Glessner. At this time the church has a membership of fifty-four.

Salem Church of the Brethren

BROTHERSVALLEY TOWNSHIP
SCHOOLS
AND
TOLL GATES

BROTHERTON

N

U.S 3/9

BROTHERTON

8

1

A

4

SCHOOLS
1 BUFFALO VALLEY
2 FACTORY
3 FAIRVIEW
4 FLICKINGER
5 LONG
6 MACDONALDTON
7 PLANK ROAD
8 SANDY HOLLOW
9 SUGAR GROVE
10 SUMMIT
11 PINE HILL
12 CROSSROADS
13 EAST END NO.1
14 GLENNORIS
15 HAY'S MILL
16 SALCO
17 PIKE
18 WALKER
19 PLEASANT VALLEY
20 EAST END NO.2
21 MILL
22 SANNER

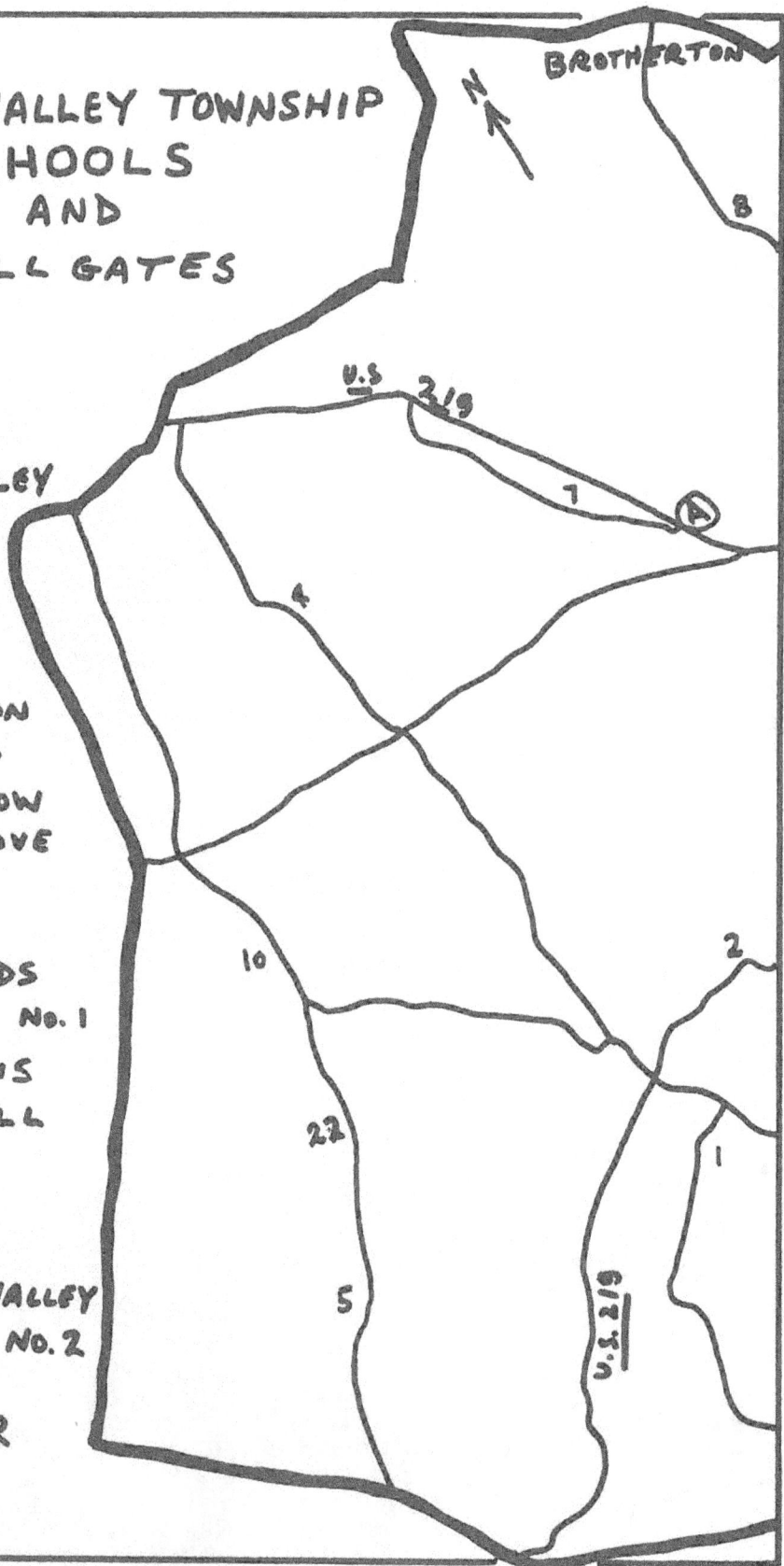

10

2

22

1

5

U.S. 2/9

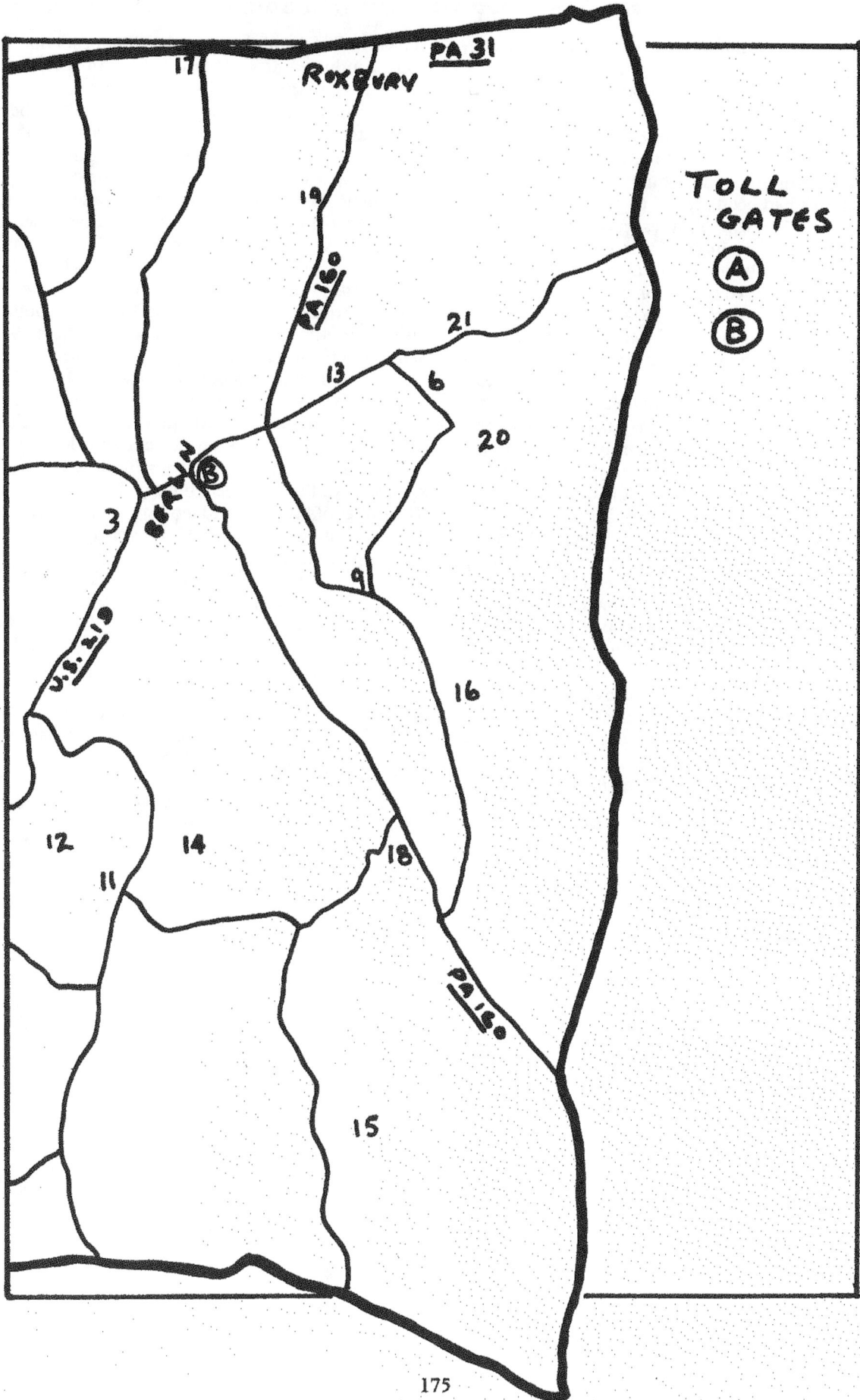

TOLL GATES
Ⓐ
Ⓑ

PA 31
ROXBURY

17
19
PA160
21
13
6
20
3 BERLIN
Ⓑ
9
U.S. 219
16
12
14
18
11
PA160
15

175

Brothersvalley Township Schools

The history of the development of the Brothersvalley schools has as its beginning the settlement of the area which is now Berlin dating from about the year 1750. The town of Berlin was laid out by Jacob Keffer, Jacob Fisher, and Frantz Hay on June 2, 1784. The lots were donated alternately to the Lutheran and Calvinistic (Reformed) churches for church-school purposes. Church-schools had been erected by both congregations as early as 1777. The schoolhouses were constructed in a rather rudimentary fashion of rough logs and were furnished with slab benches and tables of rough-hewn boards. Though each congregation had its own school, enrollment was not on a strictly sectarian basis.

The first schoolhouse, located near the corner of the present Mulberry Street and Fifth Avenue, was used by both Lutheran and Reformed congregations for school and church purposes. This building was later taken over solely by the Reformed church. The Lutheran congregation subsequently built its own combined school and church building on the corner of the present Vine and Fletcher Streets, the location of what is now the Old Lutheran Cemetery.

In 1825 the Reformed congregation erected a stone building in place of the former "union house." At approximately the same time the Lutheran congregation erected a frame school building, known as the **"Red Schoolhouse,"** on the site on which the high school building was to be built in 1914 (now Cedar Heights Apartments).

In 1834 the Pennsylvania legislature enacted the **Pennsylvania Free School Law.** A majority of citizens in Brothersvalley Township were opposed to this action and as a consequence the people of Berlin withdrew from the township and in 1836 formed an independent school district.

It is not possible to accurately determine where schools were first held in Brothersvalley Township. In the early history of the township it appears that schools were conducted at various locations in private homes. These first efforts at local schools were the result of the concern of a few men who felt education to be in the best interest of their own families and of the community. The curriculum of these early schools consisted of "branches" in German, reading, writing, and arithmetic. The residents of Brothersvalley were slow in accepting common schools, fearing that a school tax would be unduly burdensome. Finally, in 1849, after having lost some $3,000 of appropriations from the commonwealth, Brothersvalley accepted the common school system. Prior to this, few houses had been built exclusively for school purposes.* In 1850 there were six schools in the township.

Education moved along steadily and by 1887 there were twelve thriving schools in the township. A list of these schools, together with their respective teachers and the teachers' monthly salaries, appears below.

The teachers in the country school performed many duties in addition to teaching for their monthly salary. The duties of building and tending the fire, sweeping the room, filling the water coolers, washing blackboards, winding the clock, cutting grass, and cleaning the building in general were all part of the day's work. Quite often the teacher engaged the service (for a fee) of an older student to be the janitor, including fire building. The teacher taught all subjects in all eight grades, plus being mother, nurse, confidant, disciplinarian, and playground supervisor.

Older students were often assigned duties of caring and helping younger students when their class was not in session. Also, they shared in helping younger children to dress for recess and for returning home.

This was truly an open classroom and progressive education in its fullest context.

The **"Eighth Grade Promotion Examination"** was

School	Teacher	Opening Date	Closing	
Pleasant Valley	Mahlon Reiman	Sept. 19	Mar. 13	$25.00
Sandy Hollow	Ruhamaha Knepper	Sept. 19	Mar. 14	28.00
Coleman	P.U. Miller	Sept. 19	Mar. 15	28.00
Flickinger	Jesse W. Ball	Sept. 12	Mar. 6	25.00
Hoover	A.W. Hoover	Sept. 12	Mar. 7	22.00
Factory	Flora B. Turner	Sept. 12	Mar. 8	22.00
Cross Roads	William H. Fritz	Sept. 12	Mar. 8	22.00
Pine Hill	B.J. Bowman	Sept. 12	Mar. 8	22.00
Hay's Mill	Irv Baer	Sept. 12	Mar. 8	22.00
Walker	E.L. Knepper	Sept. 12	Mar. 6	28.00
East Liberty	C.M. Blough	Sept. 19	Mar. 13	22.00
Fairview	J.C. Gnagey	Sept. 19	Mar. 16	25.00

*The *Koontz History of Bedford and Somerset Counties,* however, reports that a combined church/school building had been constructed in Pine Hill before 1778 (Vol. II, pp. 59-60).

Pike School

Fairview School

Sugar Grove School

Walker School

Sandy Hollow School

Hay's Mill School

Plank Road School

a traumatic experience, as illustrated by the following quotation from the 1930 Annual School Report: "Eighth grade examinations for promotion to high school are given each year under the direction of the County Superintendent in all the districts, except the larger boroughs having Supervising Principals who make promotions to high school without the Superintendent's Examination.

"Uniform questions for all other districts are prepared in the County Superintendents Office. The Examinations are conducted by committees of teachers appointed by the Superintendent. The president and secretary of the school board in the district in which the examination is held are also members of the examining committee.

"The pupils' manuscripts are all forwarded to the office of the County Superintendent and are corrected under his supervision.

"All pupils who are qualified, in the judgment of the teachers, to take the examination must be recommended on individual cards provided for that purpose. No pupils are recommended for high school unless they have previously been recommended by their teacher, with a statement that they have been a full year in the seventh grade and also a year in the eighth grade.

"Unfortunately a few teachers, contrary to instruction, and acting very unwisely, recommended some seventh grade pupils again this year. This was not discovered in several cases before the results of the examinations were published. This, of course, causes some confusion when pupils are notified that their manuscript cannot be considered for the reason that they have not completed all of the seventh and the eighth years work.

"We take this occasion again to request teachers not to recommend any pupils who have not been enrolled for two years in the A class, that is, one year in the seventh grade and one year in the eighth grade.

"A number of pupils in some of the districts, last spring, made a zero in music. All they wrote on their papers was 'Our teacher did not teach music.'

"We also wish to advise teachers and directors now that since music is a legal requirement in our elementary schools that hereafter the grade made in music will be considered in determining the qualifications of the pupil for high school entrance. It is the duty of School Boards to see that music is taught in every school room, and it is the duty of a teacher to qualify for teaching music when employed in districts in which no special music teacher is employed.

"Promotions from grades one to eight are determined by teachers and principals. In schools having no supervision the important matter of promoting a pupil rests entirely with the judgment of the teacher. The following instructions are sent out from the County Superintendent's Office to each teacher, sometime before the close of the school term.

"'In determining merits for promotion take into consideration the pupil's class work, the average of the grades made during the monthly examinations, and the final examination. The average of these three will give the grade in each subject and will be the mark upon which promotion shall be based and the one to be inserted in your School Attendance Register under Scholarship Record of Term.

"'Pupils whose term record is 75 Percent or over should be promoted. There are some instances in which lower grades should be accepted for promotion. The teacher must use her best judgment on the important matter of promotion, keeping in mind continually this proposition:

"'Will it be better for the child to repeat the grade or to take up the work of the next higher grade? Nothing but the individual welfare of the child must be considered in making promotions.'"

Results of the examinations were mailed to the student with % grade received in each subject and decision as to whether they would be accepted to high school.

A summary follows for Brothersvalley Township as taken from the 1924 Annual School Report:

Length of Term	8 Months
Number of Teachers	23
Number of Pupils	733
Average Attendance	617
Pupils Taking Eighth-Grade Exam	37
Number of Pupils Passing	15

The records show that in the year of 1912 there were only seven students from the township attending the high school, which was located where the Fogle Cigar Factory, later the Art Glass Factory, now stands. After building the Berlin High School in 1914, where the Cedar Heights Apartments are located today, the enrollment from Brothersvalley Township increased rapidly. By 1936 the Berlin High School drew about 50 percent of its pupils and financial support from Brothersvalley.

In the spring of 1937 the consolidation of Berlin Brothersvalley Schools was a reality and preparations were made for the opening of the new school in the fall of 1937.

Following is a list of the schools, the teachers and the year that the school was closed in preparation for this era of education for the Brothersvalley students:

Brothersvalley Township—No. 8

Buffalo Valley	— Wayne Suder	1937
Factory	— Annie Schlosnagle	1937
Fairview	— Elinor Glessner	1937
Flickinger	— Fern Hentz	1937
Long	— Helen Hay	1937
MacDonaldton	— Earl Croner, Prin., 7-8 Grades	1937
MacDonaldton	— Mary Elizabeth Fogle, 5-6 Grades	1937
MacDonaldton	— Mildred Scurfield, 3-4 Grades	1937
MacDonaldton	— Margaret Stahl, 1-2 Grades	1937
Plank Road	— Ward Lehman	1937
Sandy Hollow	— Mary Dickey	1937
Sugar Grove	— Geneva Altfather	1937
Summit	— Raymond Martin	1937

Pine Hill	—	George Dively, Prin., 7-8 Grades	1937
Pine Hill	—	Anna C. Rhoads, 5-6 Grades	1937
Pine Hill	—	Anna C. Frazier, 3-4 Grades	1937
Pine Hill	—	Margaret Engle, 1-2 Grades	1937
Cross Roads	—	Closed	1936
East End No. 1	—	Closed	1926
Glennorris	—	Closed	1923
Hay's Mill	—	Closed	1935
Salco	—	Closed	1927
Pike	—	Closed	1935
Pine Hill	—	Closed	1923
Walker	—	Closed	1935
Pleasant Valley	—	Closed	1926
East End No. 2	—	Closed	1935
Mill	—	Closed	1914

The following persons were the members of the Brothersvalley Township School Board at the time of consolidation and construction of the present high school: S. B. Berkley, James E. Walker, A. Bruce Brant, R. E. Countryman, Joseph W. Croner. A further school history will be found in the section on Berlin Schools as there is one history after consolidation of the Berlin and Brothersvalley schools.

Justices of the Peace in Brothersvalley Township

1771 Abraham Cable
1778 Henry Rhoades
1779 Abraham Cable
1786 Abraham Cable
1799 Jonathan Kurtz and George Johnston
1805 Pleasant Valley District # 3, Henry Lore and Philip Walker
1809 Pleasant Valley District # 3, Henry Lore and Philip Walker
1819 George Walker
1822 Christian Moyer, Jacob Kimmel, Jacob G. Miller
1831 Alex H. Philson
1835 Solomon Baer
1836 Wm. Fletcher Dively
1840 Geo. Walker, John N. Coleman
1845 Samuel Kuhns, David Dickey

1848 Jonathan Knepper
1850 David Dickey
1852 Henry Landis
1855 George P. Hay
1857 John Rauch
1860 Lewis Glessner
1862 David Dickey
1865 Lewis Glessner
1867 David Dickey
1870 Jacob J. Coleman
1871 Joseph H. Pritts
1874 Daniel J. Brubaker
1875 John R. Boose
1875 D. J. Brubaker
1886 D. J. Brubaker and Francis J. Countryman

County Commissioner

1795 John Fletcher

Assessor

1795 John Groner

Assistant Assessors

1795 Jacob Matthews and Jacob Keefer

179

Brothersvalley Places of Business—THEN

Ira Beachley (general store), Beechdale
George Horning (general store), Beechdale
Jake Sharrah, Brotherton
Tips Inn (gasoline and general store), Berlin, R.D. #4
J. R. Boose (general store), Pine Hill
Burkholder (general store), Pine Hill

Orange Moon (grocery store and picnic grove), Brotherton
Company Store, Goodtown
Dale Walker (grocery), R. D. #3, Berlin
Pen Mar Store, Macdonaldton
Henderson Hotel, Macdonaldton
John Thomas, Salco Supply, Salco

Brothersvalley Places of Business—NOW

Maust Brothers Trucking
Don's Service Station—Donald Engleka
Surge Sales and Service—Walter Athey
Lewis Ankeny Car Wash
Darr Electric
Phennicie's Soft Freeze
Naugle Feed and Supply, Inc.
Garlitz Metal Works & Welding
Carol Custer Beauty Shop
Llewellyn Antiques
Red Barn Antiques
Krause True Value Home Center
G. I. Walker Trucking
Blubaugh Auto Parts—Gene Blubaugh
Baker and Landis Beauty Shop
Llewellyn's Greenhouse
House on Wheels—Robert Chonko
Lasure General Store

Bernard Sperry Well Drilling
Bittner Contracting and Painting
Paul Bird Explosives
Scurfield Coal Co.
Brotherton Garage—Clark Miller
Ankeny—New England Log Houses
Homelite—Bernard Keim
Simon Swift Contractor
Croner, Inc.
Leo Ohler—Coal
Woodmen of America—Steve Jano
Penn Pocahontas Coal Co.
Veterinarians—David C. Welch and George Schlagnhaufer
Berlin Motors—Joe Petro
Body Repair—Paul Petro
Robert Suder—Builder and Contractor
Herbert Smith Trucking

Brothersvalley Chapter of the Future Farmers of America

American Farmers (8)
Harry S. Hillegass (1947)
James K. Will (1968)
Larry J. Hay (1970)
Daniel J. Will (1971)
Dennis G. Hay (1974)
John C. Will (1974)
Roger L. Platt (1975)
Gary M. Hillegass (1976)

State Farmers
Claude W. Smith, Jr.
Dorlin Hay
Harry Hillegass
Edwin Landis
Francis Maust
Earl Hillegass
Robert Coleman
Nevin Mitchell
Paul Beal
Vernon Weidner
Carl Flamm

Edison Paul
Harold Hay
Ted Lehman
Frank Shipley
James Mowry
Philip Lehman
Donald Shipley
Dale Leydig
Richard Poorbaugh
Carl Hay, Jr.
Dalton Paul
Doyle Paul
Leon Paul
James Walker
David Malas
Mark Speicher
Charles Miller
David Countryman
Robert Flick
William Landis
Charles McCurdy
William Thomas

John Landis
Allan Platt
James Will
Robert Foor
Larry Hay
Daniel Will
Wayne Miller
David Shaffer
Stanley Norris
Barry Bittner
Richard Shaffer
David Platt
Paul Menhorn
Dennis Brant
John Will
Joseph Mitchell
Dennis Hay
Roger Platt
William Shaffer
John Hartman
Gary Hillegass
Robert Tataleba

Leo Suhrie
John Hoffman
Gregory Coleman
Andy Hummel, Jr.
Bryan Bittner
Neil Maust
Garland Hillegass
Timothy Bruck
Tammie Horner

Honorary Chapter Farmers (23)
Edison Hay (Deceased)
John Knepper (Deceased)
Claude Smith, Sr. (Deceased)
James M. Cassel
Paul E. Hay
Sherman Berkley (Deceased)
Charles Merrill, Sr. (Deceased)
Clarence E. Paul
John Edward Hay
John H. Hartman
Samuel J. Poorbaugh

Anthony J. Cugini	Karl H. Hay	Clyde L. Platt	Doyle E. Paul
Paul H. Cober	Lewis W. Berkley	William J. Glessner	Paul W. Menhorn
Calvin M. Will	Everett E. Nicklow	M. Geneva Altfather	Harold M. Bush

4-H Clubs and Leaders

Brotherton
Mrs. Carl Cotter
Miss Karen Kinsinger
Mrs. Richard Ferguson
Mrs. Robert Duppstadt
Mrs. Cindy Walker
Mrs. James Brant
Mrs. Edward Haselbarth
Mrs. Byron Glessner
Mrs. Wayne Kiehl

Potato Chips
Tommy Croner
Dennis Zimmerman
Douglas Hillegas

Milksquirts
Jane Smiley
Dale Leydig
Wayne Schrock
Harold Hay

Glencoe
Jean Ogburn
Darlene Poorbaugh

Valley
Goldie Thomas
Mary Nicklow
Judy Brown
Anna Coleman
Charles Thomas, Jr.

Casselman Valley Livestock
Ferne Bittner
Merle Coughenour
Debbie Spangler

Brothersvalley
Mrs. Warren Pugh
Mrs. Donald Trent

Agriculture in Brothersvalley Township

The past two hundred years have seen what is now Brothersvalley Township transformed from a vast wilderness into one of the most progressive agricultural areas of Somerset County.

When the first settlers arrived here, they began clearing land with crude hand tools. They burned and girdled trees to permit the sunlight to reach the soil.

Trees were used to build cabins for families; and oats, rye, and wheat were sown among the stumps. Potatoes, grown in hills along with corn, also provided food for the early tables.

The first farm implements, of which there is record, were dragged across the land by oxen. A harrow was made from a large bush pulled over the ground with a sweeping motion. This harrow was soon replaced by a peg-toothed version which consisted of a triangular wooden frame with hand-whittled wooden pegs for teeth.

Wooden plows were used to break ground, and in 1797, Thomas Jefferson designed a plow that was manufactured in America. Before that time, most of the plows were made by the farmers, as were other tools such as rakes, forks, and shovels.

Harvesting was accomplished with the sickle, scythe, and cradle. One of the most important inventions for the early farmer was the reaper, which made it possible to grow more grain with less labor.

Flailing and trampling by horses were the first threshing methods. Because of the difficulties of transportation, a large portion of the grain was distilled into whiskey on the farm.

Before the whiskey rebellion in 1794, there were about 21 stills in Brothersvalley Township. The still house was an important farm building, and some farms had as many as three stills.

After 1840, more and better farm machinery became available, and more of the forest land was cleared.

Until the early twenties, most of Brothersvalley

Fodder on the shock

Frank and Paul Pritts hauling corn fodder.

Baling on Jacob Countryman farm. Harry Moore with the Norman Kinsinger outfit.

Threshing at the Broderick farm. Norman Kinsinger outfit (Norman standing at tractor).

farmers had small herds of milk cows. A cream separator was used to divide the skim milk and the cream right on the farm. The skim milk was fed to pigs and calves, and the cream was churned into butter. This chore usually fell to the farmer's wife.

Butter was marketed in large rolls or pound prints and sold both locally and as a shipped item. It was taken to eastern cities in wooden "firkins" or kegs with the producers name branded into the wood.

Locally, butter was a main barter item at the general store, and provided weekly cash for those who sold it to itinerant hucksters who traveled to the farms buying farm products.

The dairy industry took a sharp upturn when a group of prominent farmers formed a co-op, "The Dairymen's Cooperative Sales Association," in the early 1920's.

The Meadow Gold receiving station was built near the B & O Railroad depot, and raw milk was trucked there in five- and ten-gallon milk cans. From that time on, the dairy industry grew rapidly, and is today the largest source of agricultural income in Brothersvalley Township.

Farmers became interested in herd improvement, and a Cow Testers Association was formed. This organization is known today as the DHIA, Dairy Herd Improvement Association.

From a copy of a 1927 "Berlin Record," the association reports 25 herds tested in Brothersvalley Township. The highest rated cow, a grade Shorthorn, produced 1,098 pounds of milk and 52.7 pounds of butterfat for the one-month testing period.

The DHIA is now a county-wide association, and in 1975, the average for the year on all herds tested was 13,280 pounds of milk and 517 pounds of butterfat. The honors of having the highest-producing butterfat cow and highest milk production cow were won by two Brothersvalley farmers in 1975.

The leading breeds of cattle are now Holstein, Ayrshire, and Brown Swiss.

Beef cattle herds have declined in recent years, but with high labor costs, some farmers are switching from dairying to beef raising. Herfords, Black Angus, and more recently Santa Gertrudis are the common beef breeds in Brothersvalley.

In the early days of farming, the poultry flocks were given the run of the premises. The hens laid their eggs where they found a suitable place. The flocks were replenished each year by chicks hatched and brooded by hens.

Many times these flocks were the "Joseph's Coat" variety, or a mixture of breeds. After hatcheries began operating and chicks could be shipped by parcel post, the quality of the flocks improved.

Better housing, management, and feed soon developed the poultry industry into a profitable venture. One of the greatest advances in feeding was the addition of Vitamin D, which eliminated eggless months when flocks were confined indoors.

The small farm flock had all but disappeared, but is again gaining popularity. Several sizable operations are located in the township.

Turkey raising was once a profitable operation, but has now declined to a few birds being raised for family use on some of the farms.

Hogs had an important place on the early township farms, and were found in large numbers until the whole milk market opened up. The skim milk was fed to hogs and calves when butter was the main dairy product. The strict sanitation rules made keeping hogs and poultry in the barn where dairy cows were milked impossible. Some farmers still raise hogs for market, but this is not a leading business in modern Brothersvalley.

Several sizable flocks of sheep are kept in Brothersvalley, and they have figured prominently at the county fair and farm show. The early settlers used homegrown wool for spinning and weaving into clothing and coverlets.

The soil and climate of Brothersvalley has made it a good place for potato growers. This crop was first grown here by early settlers who planted potatoes in hills. After the soil became more tillable, the crop was planted during the same operation as plowing. A furrow was opened and the seed pieces dropped into it. The next furrow covered the seed.

Each family grew its own winter supply from the seed saved the previous fall. As potato machinery was invented to take some of the hand labor from planting and harvesting, the acreage of the crop increased.

The two leading varieties of potato grown locally were the Rural Russet and Mason.

In a story printed in the "Berlin Record," written by county agent C. C. McDowell, the history of the Mason potato is traced.

In 1903, a Mr. Berkebile, Warren Mason's father-in-law, was helping to unload a carload of Western potatoes at Uniontown. He picked out three fine-looking potatoes and brought them along back to Brothersvalley for the Masons. Two of the potatoes met the fate of the boiling pot, but Mason saved one to plant in the spring.

From this one tuber, seed was saved and eventually over several years, Mason managed to harvest a crop of his special potatoes. He gave some to his neighbors, and by the 1920's, this was the preferred variety in Somerset County.

Since those days, many more varieties have been introduced to meet the needs of the potato chip industry and local markets. It was through a cooperative effort of a group of farmers and businessmen that the Snyder's Potato Chip Plant was built in Berlin. This business furnishes an outlet for homegrown potatoes and employs many local people.

In pioneer days, almost every farm had a sugar camp. The early ones were crude, but because of the price and difficulty of obtaining cane sugar, maple sugar, and syrup were needed at home.

In the past decade, many of the choice maple groves in the township have been sold for timber, and the rough boards of the sugaring buildings have disappeared. There are a few admirable souls left in the township that boil sugar, but most of the people who own trees sell the sap in the raw state to central evaporating plants.

Farmers in Brothersvalley Township have done well over the years. There are several people who should be remembered as forerunners of early agricultural progress.

Jacob M. Musser was the first president of the Somerset County Agricultural Extension Service, and a prominent Brothersvalley farmer.

Mrs. C. W. Knepper was an early member of the executive committee of Extension Association.

4-H Clubs were organized soon after the coming of C. C. McDowell, who although he was not a native of the township or county, should be credited with starting an agricultural education program for the township youth. One of the first 4-H clubs was the Brotherton Club, later changed to Brothersvalley. This was for many years the oldest continuously organized 4-H Club in Somerset County. Many of the original members are still residents of the area and now have grandchildren who are members of the various local 4-H Clubs and the more recent FFA (Future Farmers of America) and FHA (Future Homemakers of America).

Brothersvalley Farm Names and Owners

Farm Name	Owner	Farm Name	Owner
North View	Calvin and Mary Will	Meadows	Edward and Etta Landis
Goodwill	James and Mary Will	Sandy Hollow	Clyde and Ruth Platt
Twin Pines	Wilson and Harriet Marts	Clovernook	Boyd and Francine Dickey
Grandview	Richard and Rose Webreck	Trenton Place	J. William and Vera Shultz
Ed-Lon	Leon and Elmira Knepper	South Sun	Harry and Garnet Hay
Crossroads	Nevin and Delores Mitchell	Grandview	Dwight and Marjorie Maust
Fairview	Lewis and Ferne Maust	Buffalo Valley	Don and Betty Cober
Shady Nook	Donald and Barbara Poorbaugh	Hareve Acres	Harry and Evelyn Hillegass
Sugarbottom	Charles and Colleen Maust	Sugar Grove	Henry and Emily Fritz
Valley View	Jay P. and Victoria Walker	Grandview	Clara and Ralph Hay
Sugar Level	Richard and Helen Croner	Belfast	Earl and Elizabeth Dickey
Golden Rod	Clyde Walker	Oak Acres	Harry and Evelyn Hillegass
Pleasant Valley	Jay and Norma Hauger	Crystal Springs	Lewis and Barbara Berkley
Maple Row	Tom and Sara Maust	Highmanor	John Edward and Dorothy Hay
Hickory Meadow	Alvin and Jess Carver	Mountain Brook	Dr. Wilbert and Phyllis King
Pleasant Valley	Ray and Jane Glessner	Meadow Brook	John Edward and Dorothy Hay
Roselawn	Owen and Dichie Stellinswerf	Hilltop	Ferd and Hilda Krause
Big Red	Earl and Mary Boyer	Leyhill	Dale and Carol Leydig
Hillside	Floyd and Edith Hoffman	Blue Lick	Robert and Grace Hay
Stephen's Green	Robert and InaLee Hittie	Elder Meadow	Robert and Zona Coleman
May Hill	Harry and Virginia Rhodes	Clearfield	Frank and Jean James
Shober	Jack and Margaret Shober	Fairview	Edison and Anna Hay
Hillside	Alton and Mabel Coleman	Sandy Glen	Wayne and Nancy Schrock
Ferndale	Don and Cheryl Glessner	Swamp Creek	John and Joan Sayler
Landsdown	Paul and Marie Countryman	Clover Hill	Walter T. and Mary Walker

Farm Name	Owner	Farm Name	Owner
Harvern Acres	Harold and Betty Hay	Skyview	Frank and Donna Percosky
Elizabeth Delight	Rupple and Gladys Brant	Stormy Acres	Guy and Katie Clites
Philson	John and Minnie Hay	Mill Town	John and Betty Croner
Pyramid	Paul and Emma Pritts	Spring Water	Merle and Jean Lehman
Dove's Harbor	John O. and Pearl Stoner	Stoney Ridge	George and Eda Hittie
Sulphur Springs	Joseph and Elmira Mason	Fairfield	Harold and Catherine Croner
Meadow Farm	John and Betty Croner	Labastein Choice	The Merrill Family
Willow Grove	Robert and June Burchell	Green Meadows	J. M. and Ada Shober
Mt. Vernon	John and Evelyn Hartman	Rising Sun	Earl and Barbara Croner
Poverty Ridge	William and Peggy Menhorn	Deep Spring	Frank and Edna Phennicie
Do-Van	Don and Catherine VanGilder	Ponfeigh	The Merrill Family
Wencrest	Galen and Jean Shaffer	Hillside	Urban and Jeanne Reitmeyer
Dying Fawn	Carl and Thelma Foust	Markland Edge	Gary Sterner
Le Dor Acres	Leo and Dorothy Bittner	Spring Meadow	David and Sara Meyers

Maple Sugaring

Folklore tells us the Indians discovered that the sap of the sugar maple tree was sweet. By cutting a groove in the trunk of a tree with a tomahawk and placing a stem or stick in the cut, the Indians could collect the sweet water. Then by dropping red-hot stones in the liquid it could be boiled down to syrup. This was their only "sweet."

The pioneers, using a hand auger, bored holes in each tree, inserted pipe stems or spiles and collected the water in wooden buckets or keelers. The water collected was boiled in iron kettles. Boiling was necessary to reduce the water to syrup. The syrup was then transferred to a trough made by splitting a five-foot tree in half and hollowing out a deep groove. The hot syrup was stirred to eventually produce cake or crumb sugar. When syrup was desired, water was added to a cake and boiled.

Around 1850 large groves of sugar trees were tapped by many landowners. Crumb sugar was sold far and near. When sugarcane was grown, granulated sugar was marketed and the maple sugar producers were put out of business. About 1900 the tin syrup can was used and less and less sugar was made.

Today, fine syrup is made by a special pan called an evaporator which keeps the sweetest water moving ahead of the other water which has to be boiled out. Keeping the water cool helps to make light-colored syrup.

Water was first collected in wooden keelers made by

Maple sugaring

people called coopers. The wooden keelers had to be scalded in boiling water and cleaned with a handmade hickory broom. Steel spiles came into use. Then, easy-to-clean galvanized tin keelers were used. The later use of plastic tubing solved many labor problems.

This account of sugaring was presented by Homer Poorbaugh Boger, who was Maple Sugar King three times and says, "Large operations have taken over and gone is the glamor of the sugar season at small camps, making spotza, having taffy pulls, eating it, and enjoying yourself."

Coal Mining in Brothersvalley

The first discovery of coal in Brothersvalley Township is supposed to have been on the Countryman farm; the time is not known. As late as 1810 blacksmiths at Somerset procured their coal from this mine, hauling it a dozen or more miles.

In the Berlin coal field, the first mine from which coal was shipped, so far as can be ascertained, was opened by Thomas Price in 1875. Samuel Adams opened a mine on

the Berlin branch in 1876. These mines were not operated very extensively. More extensive were the Althouse mines, opened in 1899, and the mines of the Pine Hill Coal Company, also opened in 1899. This company had 2,200 acres of coal land in Brothersvalley that had been purchased or optioned by Isaiah Good, Norman E. Knepper, and Daniel B. Zimmerman, of Somerset, and who were the principal stockholders of the company.

Left to right: John Hoffman, James McQuade, Chauncey Wechtenheiser, back, Ed Tremel, Chas. Hoffman, Wm. Rubright—driver, Ben Rayman, Sam Dively, George Knee, C. J. Baker, Levi Hoyle, Herman Floto—driver. Taken about 1891.

There are two mines, known as Lottie Nos. 1 and 2, named after a daughter of Mr. Good. The village that grew up around these mines is known as Goodtown. At the time they were sold to the Somerset Coal Company their daily output was between five and six hundred tons.

In 1902 the Somerset Coal Company, a corporation with a capital of $4,000,000, absorbed many smaller companies, including the Pine Hill Coal Company and the W. D. Althouse Co. in Brothersvalley Township. The holdings of the W. K. Niver Company were mostly in Brothersvalley Township, where they acquired 15,000 acres of coal land in 1901. This body of mineral lands lies between Berlin and Stony Creek post office, on the Bedford pike, and was optioned in 1900 by Z. T. Kimmell, S. P. Brubaker, F. B. Collins, A. C. Floto, G. P. Brubaker, and J. J. Hoblitzell of Meyersdale. Development of the lands was at once commenced and several openings were made. A part of the coal here can be mined by slope, but a part must be taken out by shaft. At Pen Mar No. 2, near McDonaldton, a shaft 360 feet deep was completed in 1903. Fifteen months after its commencement this mine had a capacity of 2,000 tons per day.

In 1874 the Berlin Branch of the Buffalo Valley Rail Road was built. It was an undertaking by the citizens of Berlin and Brothersvalley Township and connects with the Pittsburgh division of the Baltimore and Ohio Railroad at Garrett. It was then 8¼ miles long and contrac-tors Yutzy and Scott completed its grading within eighty days.

The completion of the Buffalo Valley Rail Road marked the starting of the coal industry on a large scale in Brothersvalley Township. This branch line which eventually when completed transversed the township from south to north starting at Garrett, Pa., where it was connected to the main line of the B & O Railroad, following the Buffalo Creek in a northerly direction to Berlin and eventually through Macdonaldton to Shippleytown, located on Route 31, which is the northern boundary of the township.

A number of mines with large tonnages along this branch line starting above Garrett were owned by Enterprise Coal Mining Company and Hocking Coal Company located at Fogletown. Somerset Coal Company had their Allegheny Mine at Althouse and two other mines at Goodtown and Raineytown. John Ream and John Stoner had large mines at Berlin. Brothersvalley Coal Company opened mines at Salco and Macdonaldton. Another large mine was located at Shippleytown. Many small towns sprang up around these mines which have virtually disappeared today.

A lot of these mines changed owners over the years. A good example is Somerset Coal Company, which was later Consolidated Coal Company. This was then merged with Pittsburgh Coal Company and was called Pittsburgh Consolidated Coal Company and now has been

Ponfeigh coal tipple

sold to Continental Oil Company.

The Merrill family who ran Enterprise Coal Mining Company, Ponfeigh Smokeless Coal Company, and Pine Hill Smokeless Coal Company were one of the largest mine operators from 1875 to 1971, when they sold all their holdings to Penn Pocahontas Coal Company.

A branch line of the Western Maryland Railroad was built in Brothersvalley Township around 1926 to the Blue Lick Mine and this was called the Blue Lick Branch.

In 1809 coal was being mined on the Countryman farm near Berlin in Brothersvalley Township. This coal

was taken to Somerset for blacksmith purposes for Fred Huff, who later served as a captain in the War of 1812. Many small house coal mines were scattered all around the township from the first around 1809 to 1960 when federal and state regulations became so strict. The start of the First World War in 1914 was one of the big reasons for the rapid expansion of the coal business in this area.

The year 1927 was the greatest year for the coal business, tonnage-wise, with a high of 10,761,486 tons produced. With the panic of 1929 and the stock market crash, the tonnage sharply declined with many companies going bankrupt and many of the large deep mines being abandoned for all times.

In the late 1930's coal stripping began on a small scale in Brothersvalley Township and was greatly expanded during the Second World War in 1941.

At the present time there are no deep mines in the township. All the coal is removed by the strip mine method. However, Brothersvalley Township still has many millions of tons of deep coal to be mined and in the future there will again probably be a number of deep mines opened.

Coal was used for blast furnaces, to burn limestone, and for heating long before the railroads were here. An early 1903 map of mine operations in Brothersvalley Township lists the following active mines:

Smokeless Coal Company
John O. Stoner

186

W. T. Rainey - 2 miles
Somerset Coal Co. - Pine Hill No. 1
Somerset Coal Co. - Pine Hill No. 2
Berlin Coal Co.—Salco Mine
Somerset Coal Co. - Allegheny
Somerset Coal Co. - Ponfeigh

An early 1919 map of mine operations in Brothersvalley Township lists the following active mines:

Brothersvalley Coal Company No. 3
Brothersvalley Coal Company No. 4
Brothersvalley Coal Company No. 5
Brothersvalley Coal Company No. 6
Brothersvalley Coal Company No. 2
J. O. Ream
Stoner Coal Company No. 1
Stoner Coal Company No. 2

John Wills No. 3
John Wills No. 2
John Wills No. 1
Merrill & Brown
Pine Hill Fuel Company
Consolidation Coal Company No. 113
Consolidation Coal Company No. 112
Pollard & Brant, Inc.
Consolidation Coal Company No. 111
Fogle Coal Company
Garrett Smokeless Coal Company
Riverside Coal Company
Tri State Coal Company
McAllen Coal Company
W. A. Merrill & Son - Ponfeigh Mine
Home Fire Fuel Company

Surface Coal Mining

Surface coal mining had its beginning as an industry in the Berlin area during World War II. With the development of large, heavy-duty, earth-moving equipment, it became more economical to mine coal by the open pit method than by the deep mine method. Local as well as outside companies moved into the area and began to mine coal by this method. By 1976, several hundred thousand tons of coal a year were being removed by open pit mining in Brothersvalley Township alone.

There is a 100 percent recovery of all coal uncovered when the open pit method is used. Thus, it is not uncommon today to remove one hundred feet of surface or overburden to recover two or three feet of coal. This is a ratio of 20 or 30 to 1. To anyone unfamiliar with the industry, this does not seem to be feasible. It would also appear to be a very destructive method of mining coal, both to the land and to the underground water table. This is not the result when the coal company backfills the land, replaces the topsoil, and returns the land to the farmer on which to plant crops. Sometimes the land is unsuited for cultivation, so the company plants trees on it.

Open pit mining has been completed on areas surrounding the town of Berlin as well as in the borough itself. A visitor to the town cannot see any evidence of this today. The photograph in this article will attest to that fact.

Coal mining in the Berlin area is vital to the economic life of the people. Each job in a heavy industry, such as mining, is said to support at least four jobs in related services and businesses. It is, therefore, to the advantage of the inhabitants of our area to keep the coal industry productive and growing.

Farmland after strip mining

The Whiskey Rebellion

For the early settlers, the distilling of whiskey was an economic necessity. Grain could be raised in abundance, but the early settler could load only four bushels of rye on his horse to take to the distant market. However, if it were distilled into whiskey, he could carry the product of 24 bushels.

Alexander Hamilton's 1791 excise tax on all distilled spirits was not received well in western Pennsylvania. This area felt unfairly discriminated against and rallied with the slogan "Liberty and No Excise."

An event which happened in Brothersvalley Township involved the New Jersey militia as it approached Berlin to pick up Robert Philson and Harmon Husband as prisoners. During the approach, the soldiers, so drunk they leaned on each other to keep from falling, were alarmed by a rumbling noise along the mountainside beyond Buffalo Creek. It was thought that the noise was hoofbeats of rebels and the colonel in charge urged the soldiers onward. He became enraged at a teamster who stopped to water his horses.

The colonel struck at the teamster with his sword, missed, and struck his own horse which bolted and threw the colonel into Buffalo Creek. The teamster fled into the woods, where he found that the rumbling noise was made by stones rolling down the hillside. One man, Adam Menges, quarrying millstones, had frightened a whole regiment.

The Society of Farm Women

The Society of Farm Women of Pennsylvania was founded October 14, 1914, in the home of Mrs. Frank B. Black on the Holland Farm near Meyersdale, Pennsylvania.

A group of women from nearby farms met with Mrs. Black to discuss the possibilities of organizing a society. There was a strong appeal to foster the love of farm and rural life and to raise the standards of rural living.

Twenty women were enrolled in that first society and they named their society "Die Hausfrauen." At a later date the name was changed to the Society of Farm Women. The motto was "For Happiness," the official flower was the hollyhock, and the the official song was "Brighten the Corner Where You Are."

Mrs. Flora Snyder Black was elected president at the first state convention held at the Holland Farm. She represented her society as well as all rural people as she served on state and national committees. She always spoke with enthusiasm about the farm and rural living and encouraged elected officials to enact legislation to upgrade the lives of country people.

The Preamble and Purpose of the Constitution of the Society of Farm Women reflect Mrs. Black's ideals as well as the ideals of all members of the organization. The Preamble is as follows:

"Believing it to be necessary and advisable to perpetuate that which was good in the pioneer homes of our grandmothers; and to preserve their spirit of patriotism and sacrifice; to foster a love for the farm and rural life of today; to uphold the dignity of farming; to teach the responsibility that lies in working the soil; to enhance the charm of a real country home; therefore, to create and maintain organized groups to accomplish these ends, we, the Society of Farm Women of Pennsylvania, do associate ourselves together and adopt this Constitution."

"It shall be the purpose of the organization in all its activities, to contribute to the power and influence of farm women; to increase the influence of the farmhome; to contribute to the community activity of farm women; to develop leadership and to promote better living and working conditions in the farm homes of Pennsylvania."

The Society of Farm Women is the oldest organized group of women in Somerset County and now has ten societies. The organization has spread to seventeen counties with over four thousand members. Annual county conventions are held and a state convention is held each January in conjunction with the Pennsylvania Farm Show in Harrisburg. Prizewinning animals, poultry, and fruits and vegetables raised by members are on display. 4-H leaders come from among the members, as well as active Extension leaders and workers. These are reminders of the early days of the society when contests, demonstrations, and classes were held to promote interest in a better way of life.

In this year of 1976, we still honor two of the members of the first society: Mrs. Clara Hay—the only living charter member, and Mrs. Ruth Broesecker—past state treasurer during Mrs. Black's term of office.

The Second Society of Farm Women was organized May, 1916, at the home of Mrs. Frank Glessner. Officers: President - Mrs. Mary Gnagey; Vice-President - Mrs. Charles Knepper; Secretary - Mrs. Silas Hauger; and Treasurer - Mrs. Harry Glessner.

In 1976 the officers are: President - Mrs. Claude Smith, Jr.; Vice-President - Mrs. Jack Shober; Secretary - Mrs. Harry Meyers; and Treasurer - Mrs. Mabel Whitacre. There is an active membership of 32 members who reside mainly in the Berlin-Brothersvalley area.

Recent state presidents from Somerset County were Mrs. Edward F. Boyd, 1961-1964, and Mrs. Virgil Duppstadt, 1970-1973.

The History of Hillcrest Grange

The year 1976 will go down as a big one in the record books of Hillcrest Grange of Brothersvalley Township as it was the 60th anniversary year of the farm and family fraternity. None of the 57 charter members of the organization had the slightest dream the organization would survive more than a half century of service, especially after the Depression years hit and the membership rolls dwindled to only a few members. A faithful few kept the fires kindled and today the Grange has approximately 80 members.

The story of Hillcrest's beginning goes back to 1915. Dorsey R. and Nettie (Walker) Hoffman of the Pine Hill neighborhood felt there was a need for a Grange in their section of the township, even though Valley Grange was meeting less than two miles away. Dorsey's father, Henry Hoffman of Husband, was a staunch believer in the Grange, and volunteered his help to stir up interest in the community for the chartering of a new Grange. Henry Hoffman and the well-known State Grange Deputy Master, J. B. W. Stufft, of Ralphton, came by train, and went with the Hoffmans to visit various farm families in the neighborhood. A day or two of visiting provided a list of many names of persons who were willing to give Grange a try in their neighborhood.

Permission was granted by Mr. and Mrs. S. Sylvester Hay and their son and daughter-in-law, Mr. and Mrs. Edison M. Hay, for the group to use the small summerhouse on their "Fairview Farm" for the first meetings of the organization. Miss Lulu Knepper (later Mrs. Dalton Walker) was living with the Hay family and recalls scrubbing the summerhouse and moving benches into it, so it was ready for the charter meeting, March 16, 1916.

That evening all the benches and chairs were filled and some persons had to stand, as the summerhouse was small. The interest was so great that the new Grange came into being and some 57 persons are credited as being charter members. Since the summerhouse was not big enough to accommodate the crowds, early meetings were held in both the Pine Hill and Walker schools. Several months later, charter members Harvey J. and Sarah Walker donated one/fourth of an acre of land, in a corner of the woods of the farm they operated jointly with his parents, Amos and Louise Walker, to the Grange for the purpose of building a hall for future meetings.

The name Hillcrest was chosen for the name of the Grange because of the location of the plot of ground on the crest on a hill overlooking a fertile farming neighborhood. Also, about the same era, Rev. Ellis S. Hay family was living on the adjoining farm and had nicknamed their farm "Hillcrest."

Volunteer work was used in clearing the wooded area to build the new hall. Farmers brought their horses, scoops, and other equipment to make ready for the erection of a two-story hall. The building committee consisted of B. Frank Suder, George A. Stahl, and B. Frank Dively. Herman Baker did most of the mason work. By November 22, 1916, the Grangers were able to conduct their first meeting in the hall. A day-long dedication service was held January 16, 1917, in the hall with many prominent speakers on the program. A quintet of Ralph H. Hay, William Werner, Edna Werner, Ruth Dickey, and May Walker sang "Mortgaging the Farm." The cost of the building was approximately $1,290, which was for building supplies. Labor was donated freely by the members.

A modern kitchen, electric lights, inside plumbing, and many other improvements have been made during the following 60 years. Approximately 31 different persons have served the office of Grange master and have played a great importance in the continuing progress that has transpired.

From the beginning, the Grange took advantage of cooperative buying from the Keystone Grange Exchange, and purchased quantities of needed farm and home commodities. This continued until other cooperatives made their appearance and the Grange was no longer able to compete with them. Ephraim Walker and B. Frank Dively are two storekeepers that helped Hillcrest realize substantial savings for the members.

Through its years, Hillcrest has had a number of outstanding degree teams which were able to give the secret work to hundreds of neighbors of the community. Hillcrest has initiated over 400 applicants over the years and its membership reached its highest peak in 1927, with 186 members. Television and the many other activities in the community have dealt a severe blow to attendance in recent years. However, Hillcrest continues to be an extremely active Grange.

Hillcrest has contributed money towards the building of a dormitory at State College, and was known far and wide for its fine orchestra and chorus in past years. The Hillcrest chorus won first place in the state Grange in 1936 at Altoona, and again in 1937 won first in the state at Harrisburg. Members of the chorus were: Paul Critchfield, Rev. Robert E. Dickey, William Rhoads, James P. McCabe, William A. McLuckie, Joseph Stahl, Director Don M. Kimmel, Mrs. Emma Rowe, Mrs. Anna Catherine Rhoads Flick, Mrs. Ralph H. Hay, Mrs. R. Earl Dickey, Mrs. Edward Broeseker, Mrs. Don Kimmel, Elizabeth Glessner Snyder, Miss Lydia Glessner, Mrs. Daisy Rhoads, Mrs. Nettie Hoffman, and Minerva Hoffman Bennis.

Eber K. Cockley of Meyersdale has served as State Grange Deputy Master and through his work the Grange gained many new members in the 1950's. He served as community service chairman many years, during one of which Hillcrest won a third prize in the entire state.

In 1966 Hillcrest observed its 50th anniversary with special festivities, including the publication of a historical booklet on its own history written by David R. Hay. David R. Hay was chosen by both the state and national Grange in 1966 as the recipient of the youth travel scholarship.

Miss Mary J. Dickey, a 60-year-member, served 37 years as secretary of the Grange and has been assisted by three other secretaries in keeping a complete record of all meetings held by Hillcrest since its beginning.

Mrs. Elizabeth Dickey won third place in the National Grange Photography Contest in 1971.

Two of the charter members of Hillcrest have remained active members throughout the entire 60 years. They are Mrs. Edward (Ruth Dickey) Broeseker and Mrs. Dalton G. (Lulu Knepper) Walker—both were single when the Grange began. Mrs. Broeseker's sister, Miss Mary J. Dickey, was a member of the first class of Grange initiates 60 years ago. All three of them received 60-year pins June 9, 1976, from State Grange Master J. Luther Snyder of Harrisburg.

Other members of Hillcrest with 50 or more years of service are: Walter T. Walker, 58 years; Harry F. Habel,

57 years; Mrs. Sherman Berkley, 56 years; Harvey Boose Walker, 55 years; Lloyd P. Long, 54 years; Miss Laura Bauman, 53 years; and Mrs. Guy N. Hartman, 52 years.

Deceased 50-year members are: Guy H. Walker, Mrs. Laura Broeseker, Mrs. Emma Fritz, Mrs. Lucinda Habel, Mrs. Elizabeth Dickey, Sherman B. Berkley, Mrs. Mae Lynch, John H. Rhoads, Dalton G. Walker, Edison M. Hay, and Eber K. Cockley.

Hillcrest Junior Grange was inaugurated in August, 1963. Original leaders were Mrs. Patricia Sperry, Mrs. Marie Miller, and Mrs. Emma Gene Engle. After several years of dormancy, it was revived in 1975 by Mrs. Nila (Shaffer) Cogan, and the youth group meets in the basement during the subordinate meetings.

In the early 1970's three new community service projects were added, giving recognition to persons in the community who have been outstanding. The program awards are: "Green Thumb" for outstanding gardeners, "Good Neighbor" for exemplary qualities as a good neighbor, and "Man of the Soil" for those long associated with making their living from the soil.

These persons have received recognition thus far in annual ceremonies: Green Thumb Gardeners: Mrs. Edith Raupach (1970), Mr. and Mrs. Charles Bittner (1971), Mr. and Mrs. William J. Glessner (1972), Mr. and Mrs. Jubel Werner (1973), Mr. and Mrs. Mahlon J. Schrock (1974), and Mr. and Mrs. Jack A. Engle (1975).

Good Neighbor Awards: Mrs. Ruth Broeseker (1971), Mrs. Nora Ackerman (1972), Mrs. Pauline Bauman (1973), Mr. and Mrs. S. J. Poorbaugh (1974), Mr. and Mrs. Walter T. Walker (1975), and Mr. and Mrs. Doyle E. Paul (1976).

Man of the Soil awards have been given to: Jay M. Hauger (1972), Walter T. Walker (1973), Mahlon J. Schrock (1974), and Jay H. Walker (1975).

In 1971 Hillcrest assisted in hosting the State Grange Convention in Somerset. Mrs. James M. Cassel organized a kitchen band in the 1950's and planned the celebration for the 40th anniversary program of the Grange.

In 1976 Mrs. Betsy Bauman of Berlin, sponsored by her mother-in-law, Mrs. Pauline Bauman, was named State Grange (first place) winner for a rust-colored suit she made for her husband, Daniel Bauman. The suit went on to national judging.

Jay H. Walker of R. 2, Friedens, serves as the 1976 Grange master, while David R. Hay serves as program chairman. Mrs. Emma Gene Engle has served as secretary for the past 14 years. In the Grange hall are displayed numerous ribbons won by the Grange at the county fair, in state and county Grange contests, as well as many awards for community service projects. Larry Cogan of Hillcrest Grange served as State FFA President in 1974.

Hillcrest Grange takes great pride in serving the Hay's Church neighborhood and is proud of its rich heritage. New members are always welcome.

Valley Grange

Valley Grange #878 was organized on April 1, 1889. The first meetings were held in a little log house belonging to Wesley Hauger. There were eighteen charter members, namely, Mr. and Mrs. A. J. Cober, Mr. and Mrs. Alex Coleman, Mr. and Mrs. J. M. Shober, Mr. and Mrs. Peter Beeghley, Mr. and Mrs. Wesley Hauger, Lincoln Brant, John H. Brant, Sam Shober, A. A. Bittner, E. E. Brant, Francis Brant, William Hauger and O. M. Knepper. J. Madison Shober was the first Master; Francis Brant, Treasurer; and A. A. Bittner, Secretary.

Within a year plans were made to build a Grange Hall and one-half acre of ground was purchased from Simon Hauger at what is now the junction of Route 219 and the road through Beachdale. The hall was built by the members themselves. Some of the chairs and all of the stands bought then are still in use at Valley. The Grange property abuts B & O Railroad and for years space was rented to lumber dealers to stack lumber, bark, and ties for loading in railroad cars.

Cooperative buying was also engaged in. Such things as groceries, furniture, dinner bells, twine, harnesses, barrels of kerosine, spring wagons, and stoves were bought. Later fertilizer was added to the list.

A real community spirit prevailed and when a member was incapacitated the others grouped together and harvested his crops, etc.

The use of tobacco became an issue, the more delicate sensibilities of some being offended by its use during meetings. Finally, a fine of fifty cents was set up for anyone using (chewing) tobacco during a Grange session.

The small frame building built that first year is still in existence, having been moved to the property of Mrs. Harvey F. Kendall a mile below Beachdale, where Mr. Kendall used it as an automobile repair shop for some years before his death.

By 1920 the old hall was no longer big enough to accommodate all the members, so a new building was erected on the same plot of ground. It consists of a basement with two floors above. The second floor has a sizable stage and the first floor used for years for recreation and banquets, etc. In recent years the first floor and basement have been rented to George Horning for a grocery and feed business. Attorney P. G. Cober, a member of Valley grange, gave the main address at the dedication of this building June 10, 1920. The Shober Orchestra, composed of the children of J. M. Shober, furnished the music. Free lunch and supper were served to all. During the years before Mr. Horning rented the first floor it was used by the neighboring churches as well as the Grange for socials and suppers. Square dances were often held also. The County Wool Growers were banqueted here a number of times.

There was a time when the Valley Degree Team was widely known among Granges over the county.

In 1939 the Golden Jubilee was observed. Hon. John H. Light, then State Secretary of Agriculture, was principal speaker and Valley Grangers presented a pageant, "With Golden Gleam."

Now this Grange is proud of its record of holding meetings continuously for sixty-one years, a boast which cannot be made by any other Grange in the county. In many ways it is a monument to J. Madison Shober, the first Master. His children carry on the tradition in the persons of Mrs. Etta Kendall, Mrs. Etha Landefeld, and Jack Shober. Miss Lucy Shober is a Golden Sheaf member, having been a member more than fifty years. Charles Cook of Somerset is also a fifty-year member. Another active member who is a descendant of charter members is Mrs. Pearl Brant.

J. Madison Shober and Oliver F. Brant were guiding spirits when the new building was erected and obligated themselves financially. Oliver's son, Maurice S. Brant, and daughter, Mrs. Galen Shober, are still members.

Other members who contributed much of themselves to the building and success of the Grange are Mr. and Mrs. Oscar Walker, the late Mr. and Mrs. Homer Fritz, Mr. and Mrs. A. M. Cober, Mr. and Mrs. Adam Lepley, and Mrs. Mae Lynch.

Present Officers Are:

Master - Mr. Richard E. Deaner
Overseer - Mrs. Ella Hittie
Lecturer - Mrs. Richard Deaner
Steward - Mr. Norman Menhorn
Assistant Steward - Mrs. Mary Sweitzer
Chaplain - Mrs. Elmira Mason
Treasurer - Mrs. Galen Shaffer
Secretary - Mr. William Menhorn
Gate Keeper - Mr. Joe E. Mason
Ceres - Miss Karen Fitzmaurce
Pomona - Mrs. Bernadine Sarver
Flora - Mrs. Margaret Shober
Finance Chairmen - Adam Lepley, Galen Shaffer and Joe Mason

Recreation Areas

Landis Grove
Community Grove
E. L. Knepper Grove
Tip's Inn
Bone Yard Woods
Edison Hay Grove
Owl Hollow
Beechdale Grove
Pine Hill Grove
Hollywood

Hollywood Inn

In a shady nook, north of Beechdale, Mrs. Robert B. Walker opened Hollywood in 1922-23. It started as a summer dance hall where Bill Fritz taught dancing classes.

During the late 1920's, a top floor was built on Hollywood using lumber from houses bought in Althouse. It was now a year-round resort for thirty to thirty-five boarders, many from Pittsburgh.

From 1932, Hollywood was used for school parties, dinners, and dancing. It was also used for neighborhood square dances. Johnny Kochever fiddled for three dollars a night.

In 1934, a group of season ticket purchasers, called the Alumni, held monthly dances. Music was provided by Nat Friedline and a group of seven others for fifteen dollars a night. Alumni tickets cost $1.75 for four dances.

Early in the 1950's, activities at Hollywood stopped.

Mrs. Robert Walker died in February 1963.

The property that was Hollywood is now owned by North American Protective Services, Inc.

Hollywood Inn

The Huckleberry Railroad

Long before the advent of modern highways, trucks, and automobiles, the Berlin area's main link with the rest of the world was the old Huckleberry railroad. Construction of the initial phase of the Huckleberry, officially known as the Berlin Branch of the B & O, was completed in 1871. It extended from the main line of the B & O at Garrett through the Buffalo Valley to Berlin. Construction of this track was pressed for and presided over by Samuel Philson. Eventually the line was extended to what is now MacDonaldton.

How the Huckleberry railroad received its nickname is an unusual history in itself. For the farmers in those days who lived on the mountains and ridges of Brothersvalley, Allegheny, and Northampton townships, one of the main cash crops was huckleberries. In the late summer months huckleberries were picked and shipped by the wagonloads to Berlin. One of the main collecting points, especially for those who lived on the eastern side of the Allegheny Mountain, was Albert Miller's store in Dividing Ridge. After the local farmers brought their berries to the store, Miller hauled them on wagons over the mountain to the railroad. The huckleberries were packed in ten- or twelve-quart pails and loaded from the wagons into boxcars, flat cars, or anywhere else, and shipped to markets in the eastern cities. Truly the Berlin Branch of the B & O was a Huckleberry railroad!

Nor were huckleberries the only unusual product shipped from the area aboard the Huckleberry Railroad. Like the berries, chestnuts, too, were plentiful and much in demand and were gathered and marketed by the farmers until the disastrous blight came and eliminated the chestnut trees entirely. Other unusual cargoes were maple sugar, swamp grass, ice, and whiskey.

Maple camps, which were found on nearly every area

The Huckleberry engine

farm in the late 1800's and early 1900's, provided tons and tons of maple sugar and maple cake for shipment on the Huckleberry. Charles Cook, one of the maple sugar buyers, shipped carload after carload. In later years, maple syrup became popular and was marketed by Fred Groff. Groff sent local maple syrup as far as Australia, but, near or far, the journey always began aboard the Huckleberry.

Swamp grass was another unusual but vital product from local farms in those years. Late in the season the farmers in the glades of Stony Creek and Brothersvalley townships would mow the swamp grass, store it in the barn, and ship it to Berlin in the winter where it was sold to be used to pack fragile items such as china, glass, crockery, tile, and furniture. Since the demand for this packing material was very great, the carloads of swamp

192

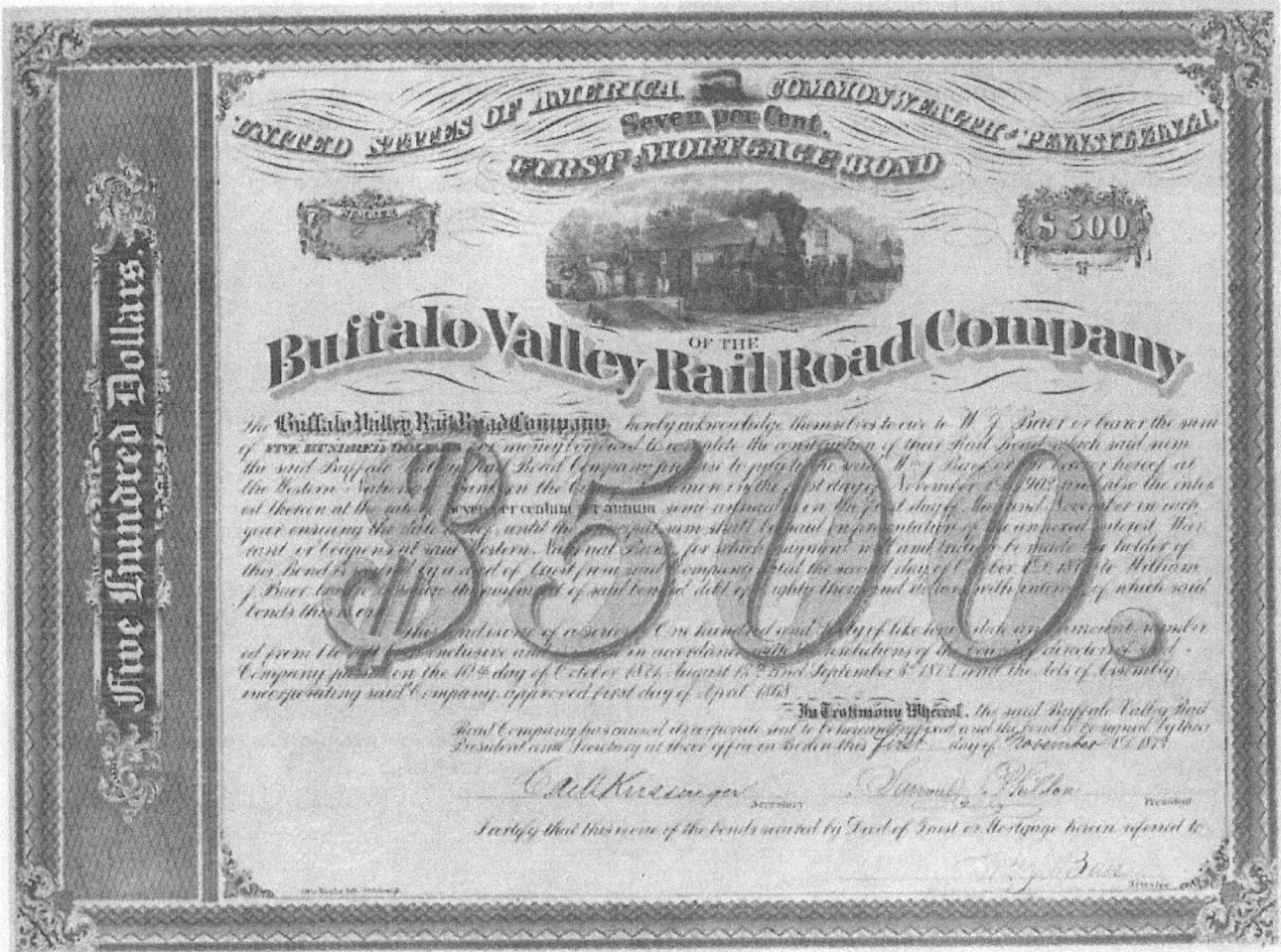

Five Hundred Dollars

UNITED STATES OF AMERICA COMMONWEALTH OF PENNSYLVANIA
Seven per Cent.
FIRST MORTGAGE BOND
$500

Buffalo Valley of the Rail Road Company

$500.

grass hay shipped on the Huckleberry were more valuable to the farmers than even clover or timothy hay.

In our age of electric refrigeration, we may be surprised to know that another important product shipped from the Berlin area was ice. The need for large chunks of ice for city iceboxes was incessant, and the cold Allegheny Mountain winters were ideal for meeting that need. A large dam in the area of the Burkholder Bridge was used for ice with a very large ice house nearby for summer storage. In later years Adam Edward Groft had a dam in MacDonaldton where he cut ice for shipment and for the meat markets in Berlin (this business was continued and "modernized" when Simon W. Groft and Ralph E. Groft began using a one-cylinder gasoline engine to cut the ice during the winter months). And so, depending on the severity of a winters cold, the Huckleberry hauled varying amounts of ice to the markets of the East. Speed was vital since each delay saw lost profit in the melting ice.

When the Franz distillers were in business, hundreds of cars full of rye and barley could be found on the Huckleberry's sidings waiting to be converted to whiskey and shipped out again in that form. Later, when the distillers began making alcohol for the government, potatoes were used.

However, in spite of the unusual products just mentioned, two products from the beginning remained fairly stable cargo aboard the Huckleberry—lumber and coal. Lumber, of course, was taken from the dense, virgin timberland on the Allegheny Mountain and other areas, and, although virtually all of the virgin timber is gone, lumbering remains one of the area's vital industries.

The real coal boom began in the late 1890's and lasted into the early decades of the 1900's. Suddenly in those years the Huckleberry found is tracks lined with new boom towns with such names as Althouse, Goodtown, and MacDonaldton. As the boom grew the Huckleberry began using two crews daily and sometimes three for round-the-clock operations. During the war years of 1914-1919 the coal boom reached its great peak. In these years the Huckleberry hauled not only coal out of the region but also hauled Eastern European immigrants into the area to work the mines.

During these boom years the Huckleberry hauled its two most dangerous cargoes—dynamite and money. The dynamite was vital to the mines and many carloads were shipped to I. A. Engleka's East End Powderhouse. Another dangerous cargo was the hundreds of thousands of dollars sent in strong boxes to the coal companies and banks. These dollars financed the mines, paid the miners, and stimulated the area economy.

Perhaps it was inevitable that following several

193

decades of such intense activity, the Huckleberry would fall into neglect and disuse. The coal boom ended, modern roads and trucking prevailed, and the Huckleberry railroad passed into history and legend. Now only a few of our oldest residents can reminisce about riding the Huckleberry, can tell about the derailment when a man lost his spectacles in a huge pile of spilled huckleberries, can remember the troops who rode the Huckleberry to war but never rode it home, and can see in their mind's eye the little railroad stops at such places as Ponfeigh, Mineral Springs, Pine Hill Station, Althouse, Beachdale, Burkholder, and Salco. Without the Huckleberry our community is diminished; with memories of the Huckleberry our heritage is enriched.

Interesting Facts About the Berlin Branch of the Baltimore and Ohio Railroad

Berlin Branch of the B & O Railroad stations from Berlin to Garrett: Berlin, Niver Junction, Raineytown, Bittner Road, Mineral Springs, Beachdale, Shober, Althouse, Burkholder, Seeley's, and Ponfeigh.

The water tank was at Beachdale. Seeley's stop was discontinued after the Seeley's Dam was gone.

The train carried a combined baggage car, a smoker, and a day coach.

Some of the conductors were: Mr. Seese (called Daddy Seese), Clint Christner, Harry Swarner, and Zean Leslie (Zenas).

Engineer and fireman: Peter Zimmerman and Platt Zimmerman.

Brakemen: Ellis Hoover, William Long, and George Perena.

Freight and express men: William Swearman, Harry Cassel, and Robert McQuade.

Night crew for the coal train: Harvey Tipton, engineer; Jake Grew, fireman. These two men were from Meyersdale. Harry Zimmerman, fireman; Sam Bockes, conductor; Frank Beachley and Wilson Boyer were the brakemen. Simon Nickelson was the boss of the repair crew. Edward Imhoff, the hostler. Otis Cook and Ira Nickelson were Berlin station agents.

The fare to Berlin from Mineral Springs was ten cents. Fare from Mineral Springs to Garrett was fifteen cents.

This interesting information was provided by Mrs. Asa S. Engle of Berlin.

Transportation

The Cumberland-Pittsburgh public road existed for many years before it became known as the Cumberland-West Newton Road. In the earlier period that portion between Hay's Mill in Brothersvalley Township, Somerset County, and Cumberland was more commonly referred to as the Simon Hay's Road. This is on record at Somerset. To the westward of Hay's Mill the course of the road was several miles south of Berlin and Bakersville. Traveling south from Hay's Mill road, it crossed Allegheny Mountain at what is still known as Baughman's Corner. It is reported that in later years Baughman's Corner was a tollgate on the old Plank Road and is now on today's Route 160.

Brothersvalley Township supervisors today report that seven tenths of Simon Hay's Road is in use and runs from Hay's Mill to the Nevin Schrock farm. All the rest is abandoned for regular use, but it reportedly can be driven over with a four-wheel drive vehicle.

Taken from the Annals of Southwestern Pennsylvania. By Lewis Clark Walkinshaw, A. M., Historian, Pennsylvania Society, Sons of the American Revolution, Volume III:

The organization of the Wellersburg and West Newton Plank Road Company came about 1850. These plank roads in several counties were built because the timber was plentiful, and it was a quick way to get a smooth road. The planks wore out in time, and through the failure of the companies to keep up the road by renewing it, the roads fell back to township management.

Here and there were "clay pikes," so called, because little work was done on them, and they afforded diagonally cross routes to and from eastern markets. They were the favorite of drovers in bringing their herds through, because of the softer roadway on the feet of the stock. Sometimes great flocks of turkeys were driven through, and at nightfall they would roost in a nearby woods until the break of day, and then the journey would be renewed. One of the last portions of these old pikes to be abandoned was the portion of the Robbstown and Mt. Pleasant Turnpike, it being first a part of the old Glade Road and then a connecting link of the old Wellersburg and West Newton Plank Road Company.

Incorporated in 1818, and taken over by decree of the court as a township road on December 20, 1897, it had a continuous existence for a period of about eighty years. In the earlier years Henry Null was its President, and at the time of dissolution, Henry H. Null, Sr., was eighty three years of age, was its President, on account of which it became known as the "Null Pike." The younger Null had been a teamster on the old plank road as far as

Cherry Hill. Left to right: Frank Dively, Milton Baer, Mahlon Hay, Herman Baker, Irvin Stahl, Sylvester Hay, Robert Stahl, Frank Stahl, Harry Bittner, Edward Hay, Ephriam Boger, William Bittner, William Baker, Herbert Boger, Alfonso Boger, *Henry Boger, Frank Bowman. On horses: Edison Hay, Ephriam Hay, Samuel Brant, Peter Hay. On bank: Samuel Fogle and Conrad Baker.*

Wellersburg and Cumberland, and married Eleanor Dom of Berlin. Of historical interest are the rates of toll of the date of December 15, 1870, as shown by the following notice posted along the road.:

Rates of Toll

of the
Robbstown and Mt. Pleasant Turnpike Road Company

For each Horse or Mule, rode or led, 1 cent per mile, or fraction of a mile.

Sulky or Chaise, 2 wheels, for each Horse or Mule, 1 ½ cents per mile, or fraction of a mile.

Carriage or Buggy, 4 wheels, each Horse or Mule, 1 ½ cents per mile, or fraction of a mile.

Wagon, for each Horse or Mule, 1 ½ cents per mile, or fraction of a mile.

Sled or Sleigh, for each Horse or Mule, 1 ½ cents per mile, or fraction of a mile.

For each Yoke of Oxen, 1 ½ cents per mile, or fraction of a mile.

For each Score of Cattle, 4 cents per mile, or fraction of a mile.

For each Score of Hogs, 3 cents per mile, or fraction of a mile.

For each Score of Sheep, 2 cents per mile, or fraction of a mile.

For each loaded team going over this road, and not returning over the same Road, double the above rates.

Penalties

For Violating the Laws Regulating Turnpike
Road Companies

First—Any person misrepresenting the distance traveled, or refusing to pay Toll, a fine of Five Dollars.

Second—Any person taking a Horse or a Mule out of a wagon, for the purpose of passing through any bars, or gates, to avoid paying Toll, a fine not exceeding Ten Dollars.

Third—For leaving a Wagon standing on the artificial part of the Road over night, a fine of Five Dollars.

Fourth—For any person putting on any fences, or letting water upon the artificial part of the road, or any other obstructions, subject to a fine of Five Dollars.

Fifth—Any person driving their Wagons or Vehicles in Water Tables, unless in case of necessity, or who shall tie fast a wheel, unless the road is covered with ice, or dragging logs over the road, when the road is bare, for each offence, shall forfeit and pay a fine of Five Dollars.

By order of the Board of Managers,

H. H. Null, President
John B. Tarr, Secretary
December 15, 1870

Brothersvalley Township, created in 1771, shown in volume #2, page 584, "Early History of Somerset County."

Robbstown and Mt. Pleasant Turnpike Road Company is a part of its early history.

The Old Plank Road

Finances for construction for this road were procured through the sale of 4,000 shares of stock at $25 a share. A small share of the money to be collected at the tollgates, which were to be placed at intervals along the road, was to be paid to the stockholders as a dividend on their investment.

Early in 1851, construction began. First, a roadbed of rocks, gravel, slate, or other hard material was laid. Next, along the sides of the roadway, long wooden string pieces were embedded in the underlayer. Then the planks were placed crosswise on the road and pinned to the string by wooden spikes. Owing to the varying length of the planks used, the road was wider in some sections than in others, usually ranging from 10 to 18 feet.

The New roadway became an object of great local interest—the source of legends about robberies, adventures, escapades, and an abundance of actual historical facts.

For nearly 20 years the **Road** enjoyed, or suffered from, heavy traffic. In addition to regular stagecoaches and heavy lumbering freight wagons, great flocks of turkeys and herds of cattle and sheep were driven over the plank highway.

As a financial venture, the Plank Road was never a success. The tollgates yielded an average monthly income of sixty dollars each. After the gatekeeper had received his salary of five dollars, the rest was collected by Samuel Philson of Berlin, who was treasurer of the company. Most of these funds were used to keep the road in some kind of repair.

Did You Know?

Glenn Norris was the original name of the settlement now known as Goodtown. Respect for the general manager, Isaiah Good, led to the place being nicknamed "Goodtown."

The Josiah C. Werner family owned one of the first phonographs in the Hay's Church-Pine Hill district.

Brothersvalley Township had at least four persons whom have lived to observe their 100th birthdays: Mrs. Emma Rayman, Ella Countryman, Mrs. Elizabeth Meyers, and Solomon Albright.

The MacDonald Land Co. was laid off in lots southwest of the present-day St. Gregory's Catholic Church in MacDonaldton. The lots were northwest of The Shaft, between the railroad and the J. Calvin Altfather farm. The project never materialized and no buildings were ever constructed at the site.

Solomon Coleman built the large two-story brick home near the entrance to Goodtown in 1849. In 1976 it is the residence of John Popovich, Sr. The farm was operated for many years by James S. Hauger, son-in-law of Solomon Coleman. Raineytown was built on a hillside of this farm.

Miss Tillie Stahl, Mrs. Joseph Stahl, Mrs. George Stahl, and Mrs. Lillian Dellbrook, all of Pine Hill, made cottage cheese and buttermilk each week and sold it to the mine families in nearby Goodtown.

In 1901 miners walked from Berlin to work 12 hours in the mines at The Shaft and were paid $1.25 per day for their labor.

In 1911 the Dull Mercantile Company of Goodtown purchased the entire stock of goods of the defunct Black Diamond Supply Company at Pine Hill Station (also Goodtown).

In 1913 the large store of the Dull Mercantile Company at the Pine Hill mines of the Consolidation Coal Company, Goodtown, was totally destroyed by fire. The loss was estimated between $8,000 and $10,000. Jeremiah G. Smith was the manager of the store.

In the Berlin IOOF Cemetery is a handsome and massive headstone marking the last resting place of heroic Grace Garman, the lady telegraph operator who sent out the historic message during the 1889 Johnstown Flood: "Help, too late, the dam is broke, good-bye, good-bye." She was 22 years old and was the daughter of Dr. W. A. Garman of Berlin.

Brothersvalley Township has had two farmers honored with the distinction of being Pennsylvania Master Farmers. Edison M. Hay received the honor in 1928, and Richard Croner was so honored in 1965.

In 1976 Brothersvalley Township's oldest retired farmers included William F. Butler, Charles W. Musser, and Ralph C. Engle, all over the 92-year mark.

Harvey Gindlesperger was the owner of the first two-row corn planter (40 inches between rows) in the township.

Mrs. Cordie (Stuck) Dickey was the last surviving widow of a Civil War veteran.

Cecil Clare McDowell retired from official duties as County Farm Agent, July 1, 1955.

Somerset County Grassland Field Day was held June 12, 1956, on Richard Croner and Ray Glessner farms.

The Ag. Progress Field days were held August 1972 on the Calvin Will and Richard Croner farms.

Salem Church of the Brethren was named for Salem Ball, builder of the church.

Something of Interest

This is an interesting article taken from a newspaper dated 1875, given by Mrs. Asa S. Engle. The story is about the wedding of her parents.

The Berlin Branch passenger train had a great part in the event.

Henry Harrison Smith and Margaret Elizabeth Humbert were married by Rev. A. E. Truxal, pastor of the Reformed Church of Somerset, April 22, 1875, at the home of the bride's grandmother, Mrs. Ludwig Sanner, of near Rockwood, with whom she lived. The bride's father was Henry Humbert of Black Township (then Milford), a lieutenant of the Civil War, who died of typhoid fever while home on a furlough near the end of the war. Her mother was Delilah Sanner of Black Township. The groom was the son of William Smith and Elizabeth Coleman Smith of Brothersvalley Township. Belle and Bill Spangler were bridesmaid and best man at the ceremony.

The wedding trip lay between the bride's home in then Milford Township and the groom's home in Brothersvalley Township. The party went by train from Rockwood to Meyersdale, where there was an overnight stop at a hotel, then on still by train and up the Berlin Branch to Beachdale, where the wedding party was entertained in the home of Simon and Rosie Hauger, father and mother of the bridesmaid. The next day the trip was resumed about a mile and a half up the Mill Stream to the "in fare" dinner at the groom's home.

It was on this honeymoon trip that the young bride and her bridesmaid and their young men were much discomfited. The then new Berlin Branch train was wrecked—who knows how—a carload of corn dashed down the embankment at the side of the track, but the coach was held in place presumably by a carload of rock behind it. Not much seems to be said of how the bride and groom took the shakeup, but in spite of all Bill could do, Belle jumped out (or off) the coach.

Brothersvalley's Oldest Resident

L. Nevin Wilson was born in Fulton County, Ill., June 11, 1879. He was the oldest son of McComron C. and Sarah E. Wilson. At an early age he moved with his parents to Kansas, where he received his elementary training in the public schools and prepared for college at Hiawatha Academy. In 1899 he entered Franklin and Marshall College, graduating in 1903. At college he took an active interest in literary work and for four years was a member of a dramatic organization called the Green Room Club. He entered the Theological Seminary where he studied for two years, when he obtained leave of absence to teach in Interior Academy, an institution of the reformed Church located at Dakota, Ill. The next year he became principal of the school. For two years he was instructor in Hiawatha Academy and for one year he was principal of Marysville (Kan.) High School.

In 1910 he resumed his studies in the Theological Seminary, completing the course the following year. While in the seminary he won the prize in sacred history. In 1912 Franklin and Marshall conferred upon him the degree of Master of Arts for postgraduate work in biology and history. He is the author of several publications, among which are "Into the Deep," "Beggar and Monk," "A Manual of Religious Instruction for Children," and "The Wilhelms and the Wilhelm Charge." For eighteen years he was editor of the **Somerset Classis Visitor**, a monthly publication of the Classis.

He served the following charges: Harrisville, at Tom's

Brook, Va.; Brunswick, Md., Wilhelm Charge, 1915-20; Stoystown Charge, 1920-22; Glade Charge, 1923-24; St. Luke's (Mountain), 1933-36. He has been president of Somerset Classis and treasurer of Pittsburgh Synod. In 1905 he was married to Anna Mae Weaver of Lancaster, Pa., who died in February of 1961. They are the parents of one son, Paul Nevin.

As a boy, L. N. Wilson learned the printing trade. During his ministry he devoted himself to printing as a hobby. While serving the Glade charge he acquired controlling interest in the "Berlin Record," a weekly paper which he edited for eight years, when this paper was sold to Somerset interests (now "Daily American"). The first year of operation under L. N. Wilson resulted in a profit of $600. The "Berlin Record" purchased the first cylinder printing press used in Somerset County. The original location of the "Berlin Record," and later the Berlin Publishing Company, was on the upper diamond, where the William Scurfields now live. In 1929 the printing shop was moved to its present location on Division Street at Fletcher. At the present time he and his son Paul are active in the daily management of the printing enterprise.

Photography has been an interesting and profitable hobby for L. N. Wilson for many years. It served to provide supplemental income during his college years, and was an absorbing pastime later on during his adult life. Not only was he an accomplished "technician" in photography, including developing and printing his own film, but he also made a camera with a revolving lens which permitted panoramic photography.

Allegheny Township

Miller's Store
Dividing Ridge
Allegheny Twp.

Book Committee—Allegheny Township

Lorene Hoppert
Thelma Boyer

Great appreciation for much of the information about the early history of Allegheny Township is extended to the following people as well as any others who may have contributed.

Emma Robb
Pearl Glessner
Hazel O'Brien
John and Florence Restley
Richard and Emma Deaner
Richard and Rheta Hillegas
Custer Brothers
Richard Poorbaugh
Lillie Frazier
Jane Hay
Leroy Coughenour
Winmer Coughenour
Harold and Gladys Deeter
John Fochtman
Henry Hankinson
Nora Felton
Bruce Brown
Edna Woida
David Hay
Dorothy Will
Leon McQuade
Karl Brick
Mildred Buchanan
Fred Hoppert

References

History of Somerset, Bedford, and Fulton Counties 1876
History of Bedford and Somerset Counties 1906
Pastors and People of Somerset Classis,
   The Reformed Church in the United states,
   Copyright 1940 by L. Nevin Wilson
Two Centuries of Brothersvalley,
   1762 Church of the Brethren 1962,
   H. Austin Cooper
Church records
Records of E. C. Saylor

Allegheny Township

Allegheny Township was formed from a portion of Southampton in 1805. It takes its name from the Allegheny Mountain, which forms its western border, and is a portion of that part of Londonderry Township, Bedford County, that was annexed to Somerset County in 1800. The township is traversed by both the Forbes and Glades roads and their successors. The part north of the Glade Road was annexed to Stony Creek Township in 1801, remaining a part of that township up to 1805. Lying between the Savage and Allegheny mountains the country is wild and broken, and mostly covered by the Catskill sandstone and Chemung shales. Such being the case, the land in it is not the best for farming purposes, and there is much unimproved land. No coal is found in the township, and except that there may be some beds of fire clay in its southern part, it has no mineral wealth.

Settlements were made slowly in this portion of the county, and it was many years before this township outgrew its primitive qualities. After other portions of the county had become comparatively well populated, much of Allegheny remained unimproved and afforded a favorite resort for hunters. As will be seen from the following tax list, the population of the township was small in 1814.

The following were the taxable inhabitants of Allegheny Township in 1814, according to a duplicate list made by Wm. C. Dorsey, Esq., assessor, and Henry Imhoff and John Fleming, assistant assessors: John Black, Jac. Burkhart (weaver), Jac. Burkhart, Dan Burkhart, Sam Burkhart, John Burkhart, Jona Boyer, Henry Boyer (sawmill), Adam Boling (innkeeper), Geo. Brant, Henry Black, Dr. John Cook (innkeeper), Jos. Cohenour, Cornelius Devore, Wm. C. Dorsey (justice), John Fleming, Christian Grove, Peter Gardner, Christian Gensler, Jas. Galiher (distiller), Val. Hoon (innkeeper), Dav. Husband, Henry Imhoff (innkeeper and sawmill), Jac. Kellar, Caspar Kellar, Christian Kinglesparger, Thos. Kennedy, John Lush (shoemaker), Terrance Morrison (weaver), Elizabeth Mull (widow), Mich. Mull, John Mull, Dav. Mull, Jac. Menges, Abram Miliron, Henry Menges, John D. Peterson (minister), Ph. Purbaugh, Henry Purbaugh, Adam Ross (joiner), Caspar Statler, Andrew Server, John Shaffer, John Shaffer, Jr., Geo. Shaffer, Wm. Tipton, John Teeter, Henry Ware, John Wiley, John Teeter (sawmill), Teeter & Mull, Jac. Weyand, Jac. Yoner. Single freeman: Isaac B. Falkerton, John Knough, Fred. Peterson, Henry Purbaugh, Eli Runman (blacksmith), Abram Shaffer (stage driver), Peter Shaffer, Jonathan & Thomas Tipton (shoemakers), Aquilla Wiley.

The following was taken from the "History of Somerset, Bedford, and Fulton Counties—1886."

Matthias Suhre was born in Germany, in 1803; came to America in 1834, and settled at Fossilville, Bedford County. In 1851 he purchased four hundred and forty-six acres of land in Allegheny Township, where he still resides. Mr. Suhre is a miller by trade. He is now eighty years of age, and his wife, Mary Louisa, is seventy-eight years old. Francis Suhre, son of Matthias, was born in Summit Township. In 1863 he settled on a farm of one hundred and forty-six acres, purchased of his father, in Allegheny Township. Mr. Suhre has held various township offices.

Henry Felton, a mason by trade, was born in Germany, and came to America in 1856. After residing two years in Baltimore and four in Cumberland, Maryland, he removed to Allegheny Township, and purchased a farm of two hundred acres, upon which he now resides. Mr. Felton has held the office of school director for eight years.

Charles F. Smith, a native of Germany, born in 1823, came to America at the age of sixteen, and commenced work in Bedford County, near Mann's Choice. He afterward purchased of his father-in-law, Lewis Wambaugh, the farm in Allegheny Township on which he now resides. Mr. Smith has the best orchards in Somerset County; indeed they will compare favorably with any in this section of the state. He raises all kinds of fruit in great quantities, and ships to local markets as well as to Altoona and other points. Twenty-two years ago, his farm of one hundred and fifty acres, of which eighty are cleared, was a dense forest. Mr. Smith, by industry and careful management, has today one of the finest and most productive farms in this section.

Philip Walker was born in Somerset County. By his own industry and hard labor he became the owner of several farms situated in Summit and Brothersvalley townships. He died about 1834. He married Elizabeth Bettner, and was the father of George, John, Frederick, Peter, Elizabeth (Hay), and Susanna (Boos). George was born in Brothersvalley Township, and lived on a farm given to him by his father. He met his death on July 11, 1828, at the hands of an Irish laborer named Patrick Burns. Burns got into a dispute with Mr. Walker, and taking up his scythe, cut him across the abdomen so that he died almost instantly. The murderer escaped. George Walker married Elizabeth Miller, and was the father of George G., Josiah, Abraham (deceased), William, Samuel, Rosanna (Barron), and Catharine (Horner). Hon. George G. Walker was born on the old homestead in Brothersvalley. In 1861 he settled in Allegheny Township, where he owns a large and valuable farm. Mr. Walker has held various local offices, including that of justice. In 1859-60 he served as a member of the state legislature.

John Ware was an early settler of Allegheny Township. Among his children were: John, George, Henry, Joseph, and Susanna. John was born in this township in 1807, and died in 1874. About 1846 he purchased the farm of three hundred and sixty-three acres on which his son William now resides. William has held several township offices. He served a short time in the late war.

John C. Reitz, who was born in Stony Creek Township, settled in Allegheny in 1868, on a farm of four hundred and fifteen acres, purchased of Jacob B. Hillegass. In 1877 he erected a planing mill, and in 1882 rebuilt it. He also has a sawmill and a sash and door factory. All are run by steam power. Mr. Reitz manufactures all kinds of building lumber.

In 1859 Jacob B. Hillegass, now of New Buena Vista, Bedford County, purchased of John Keff's heirs a tract of fifteen hundred acres of land in Allegheny Township.

He has since disposed of about one thousand acres. His son, William H., owns nearly seven hundred acres of the tract mentioned, having purchased it in 1881. He is principally engaged in farming and stock-raising.

John Geiger, a native of Berks County, came to this township in 1834, settling upon an unimproved farm, of which he has since cleared about seventy-five acres.

White Horse Mountain and Tavern

White Horse Mountain is one of the beautiful sights to behold in Allegheny Township. In the autumn it is clad in all the hues of vermilion, green, and gold. The snow and ice of winter is a beauty to behold. Then comes the spring and summer with all the blossoms and deep green foliage.

At the top of Allegheny Mountain at the intersection of the old Burd Road leading from Bedford to Berlin, there stood a stone house which was a stopping place and tollhouse along the highway. This was known as "The White Horse Inn" which was located at this spot on the old Wells map of 1812. This building was relocated higher up in the mountain and was a really beautiful stone structure.

Why is this area of the Allegheny Mountain called "White Horse Mountain"? Early settlers have told interesting legends about naming the old inn and hence the mountain. One version is there was an Indian raid made on a number of travelers who were crossing the mountain seeking a site for a home in the wilderness. That was many years before the present road was build.

In 1777, the whole frontier was aflame with Indian raids by the Shawnee tribes. It was about that time that the raid was perpetrated. A group of settlers had stopped their Conestoga wagons at the spring (which is still running) on the west side of the Allegheny Mountain. The spring was called "Deeter's Spring" on a level clearing at the bend of the road. There the Indians attacked! The people were scalped, their wagons were burned, and the contents plundered. The rims of the wagon wheels were taken for the iron to be used for knives, tomahawks, tools, and lance heads.

The raid took place during a hard snowstorm. All the horses were taken except one white mare that escaped and ran off into the mountain, where it lived among the wild beasts of the forest and field.

Later it was said the white mare was seen at times by travelers on the mountain road. Some thought the white mare was a ghost of the animal which was hunting the area in which the raid had occurred. There were those who said the principal reason why the white mare escaped from the Indians was that there was such a blizzard at the time of the raid that they could not see the white beast against the snow.

It was related as a part of the story than an Allegheny Mountain man by the name of McGraw, and a group of his neighbors caught the mare and rebroke her into the

White Horse Tavern

harness as a workhorse. Thus, the mountain became known as "White Horse Mountain."

The Deeter spring was named for the man who built the White Horse Inn. It is not known what year the inn was built. History tells of George Keller's "Big Log Inn" being on the site about 1790. Some say Keller was there soon after the Revolutionary War ended, about 1783, or even by 1781, after the fighting was practically over.

George Keller's unpublished manuscript tells how his sons once foiled the Robber Lewis gang. Lewis did not start his operations until the War of 1812. He joined the U.S. Army and then deserted. Seems that he was paid for joining and that he joined and deserted at least three times. When he found that he could rob the government without being caught, he became bolder and bolder until he launched his mad career of robbing on the Philadelphia-Pittsburgh Turnpike.

If that is true, then the Kellers and their "Big Log Inn" must have been there 40 or 50 years, and they might have sold out to Mr. Deeter. Then Deeter tore the log building down.

Two prominent pioneers of this area were Tobias Musser and Mr. Henry Black. They had been appointed by the governor of Pennsylvania to build a road to run through this section, extending westward from Philadelphia to the Ohio River. This road took much work, but after it was completed and used for some time, it was found to be one of the best roads in the country and became one of the most frequently traveled highways.

As travel increased, there arose the need for inns and

taverns along the way. This was a desirable location for a tavern. In addition to being famous for its beautiful view, it was also a suitable stopping place for horses, wearied by their long pull up the mountain. Tobias Musser, a stonemason and farmer, was notified to bid on the contract and the construction was begun.

The building was constructed at the top of the Allegheny Mountain along the pike previously built by Mr. Musser and Mr. Black. It was built largely of dressed stone with some framework. The tavern, which seemed very large to the people who lived in the community, contained eighteen rooms.

But alas! When the building was finished, it was found that the bid agreed upon by Mr. Musser did not cover the cost of construction. What could he do? He would have to find some way to pay his helpers, even if he himself did work for nothing. When the accounts were settled, he was able to pay all his helpers but one.

What about this one? At last Mr. Musser hit upon a plan.

He consulted his helper, who agreed to accept a fine white horse as pay for his work. Mr. Musser did not wish to part with the fine steed, but he was obliged to do so. Soon it became known all over the country that the white horse had been required to meet the obligations of the contract. The travelers who stopped at the tavern received a hearty welcome and warm hospitality. Sometime during their stay someone was sure to mention the story of the white horse. When the time came for the proprietor to hang up a sign bearing the name of the tavern, he decided to use the picture of the white horse on it. After that, the tavern became known far and wide as the "White Horse Tavern." Some of the innkeepers succeeding Mr. Deeter were Joseph Fleming, Samuel Jordan, and A. M. Glessner.

In the palmy days of the old road and the pike this old

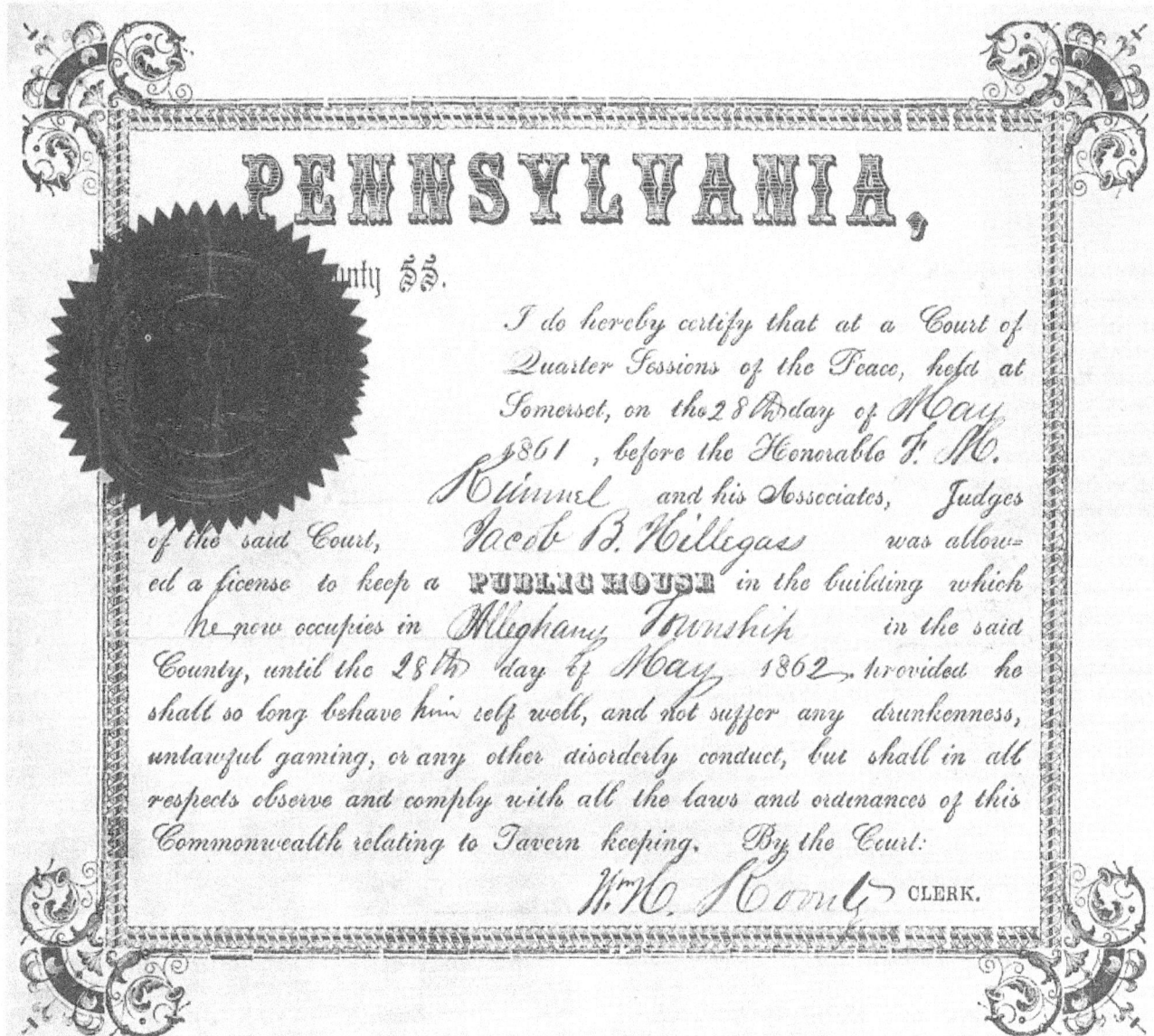

PENNSYLVANIA,

...nty ss.

I do hereby certify that at a Court of Quarter Sessions of the Peace, held at Somerset, on the 28th day of May 1861, before the Honorable F. M. Kimmel and his Associates, Judges of the said Court, Jacob B. Hillegas was allowed a license to keep a PUBLIC HOUSE in the building which he now occupies in Alleghany Township in the said County, until the 28th day of May 1862, provided he shall so long behave himself well, and not suffer any drunkenness, unlawful gaming, or any other disorderly conduct, but shall in all respects observe and comply with all the laws and ordinances of this Commonwealth relating to Tavern keeping. By the Court: Wm H. Koontz CLERK.

tavern did a thriving business, and there were but few days in the year that the house was not filled with guests, the stables with horses and the pastures with cattle. All the stagecoaches stopped here and the passengers dined.

With the building of railroads and the invention of automobiles, taverns were no longer needed. When the old road was rebuilt, the tavern became an obstruction in the plans of the engineer. Half of the unoccupied half endured the summer's sun and winter's snow for many seasons. Finally it began to crumble until at last only one corner remained standing to prove the superior workmanship of the mason who built it, stone upon stone.

At the foot of the Allegheny Mountain there was a tavern that in more recent years was known as the "Hillegas Place." It was also known as Black Horse Tavern. Here a Mr. Boose, the ancestor of a family still well known in Somerset County, kept a tavern before 1800. When the turnpike was in its glory this was a noted drove and wagon stand. This was afterward known as the Henry Imhoff tavern, later kept by John Duncan, and last by Jacob B. Hillegass.

Job's Tavern was where Albert Hillegass lived. Hugh Sproat for many years kept a tavern on the George G. Walker farm.

At Mt. Zion, Samuel Walker started the construction of a tavern. He died in 1888 before it was completed. His widow lived there until her death. It was then owned by Mr. and Mrs. James Tipton, Mrs. Tipton being his daughter. It is now the residence of Mr. and Mrs. Lee Hoppert. Mrs. Hoppert is the great-granddaughter of Samuel Walker.

These taverns were all situated along the "Old Pike" on the present Route 31.

Samuel Walker started to build a Tavern here. He did not complete it.

Johannes Detrich (John Deeter), 1760-1828

John Deeter and Catharine Springer, his wife, settled in Deeter's Gap in 1784 in what was then Brothersvalley and Quemahoning townships, Bedford County, Pennsylvania. This is now Allegheny Township, Somerset County. The old homesite is 1½ miles north of Pa. Route 31 on the New Baltimore Pike, located between White Horse and Allegheny mountains.

John Deeter served his country in the Revolutionary War in the Cumberland County Militia, Eighth Class. He was paid with worthless paper money for participating in the war. With this money he purchased the original 269½ acres of land with a warrant in 1783 from the state of Pennsylvania. The patent (which meant he had a clear title and would pay taxes on it) was granted in 1794. He lived his entire married life on this farm which eventually totaled more than 1,600 acres of ground. The farm buildings were located where the cleared land at Deeter's Gap is at present.

The wooded area where the cemetery in which John, his wife, Catharine, his eldest son, John, 2 unnamed children, and a child named Henry are buried was once a meadow. A millstone was placed at the gravesite and a pine tree grows on John's grave. Legend has it that a colored man is also buried here but no proof has actually been found.

Legend also has it that John was in this part of the country serving with the militia when he met his wife, Catharine.

According to John's own records he hired a man named Brown in 1789 to build a dam and a mill. His

The millstone marking the grave of John Deeter

sawmill and gristmill were among the first along the Allegheny Mountain. From that time on he sold lumber and started making and selling millstones which sold for as much as $36 a pair. He sold meat, hides, salt, rum, butter, grain, and garden vegetables. He traded one pair of millstones for a barrel of brandy and then sold the brandy.

John Deeter was a religious man. According to his own records between 1812 and 1816 he did a lot of business with a Lutheran minister named John Deeter Peterson. The minister bought lumber from Deeter and used this lumber to build a church. No records have been found showing these two men to be any relation even though their names are similar.

The last Will and Testament of John Deeter follows:

Will of John Deeter
written May 31, 1823

In the name of God amen, I John Deeter of Alegany Township Somerset County and State of Pennsylvania being unwell but of sound disposing mind Memory and understanding thanks be given unto God calling into mind the mortality of my Body and Knowing that it is appointed for all men once to die do make and ordain this my Last Will and Testament that is to say in Principally and first of all I Give and Recommend my Soul into the hands of Almighty God that Gave it, and my Body I Recommend to the earth to be Buried in decent Christian Burial at the discretion of my Executor hereafter mentioned, and as Touching Such worldly Estate wherewith it hath Pleased God to bless me with in this Life, I give devise and dispose of the Same in the Following manner and form. It is my will that my Just and Lawfull debts and funeral and other Expenses Shall be first paid off as soon as conveniently may be after my Decease.

It is my will and do order and direct that my Son Samuel Deeter Shall Give unto my beloved wife Catharina the use of the two Back rooms where she now lives at present and part of the Seller the stove is to stand in said room where it stands at present for her use and part of the gartin and must keep two cows for her and Shall feed the said two cows as he feeds his own cows and to be in the same pasture with his own cows, and is to give her fifteen Bushels of wheat a year and he is to get said wheat ground into flower and to deliver the flower and brann into her house, and must give her one hundred weight of pork, and fifty weight of beef, one bushel of Salt Eight bushels of potatoes, and cabich coffee tea and sugar as much as she shall want for her own use, and apples and cider as much as she Shall want, one bed and bedstead one chest and spinning wheel and the loom with the geers one cubert one pot one tea kettle, and the third part of the rest of my household Furniture Shall be for my wife Catharina during her Life and my Son Samuel Shall give her every year during her Life Six pounds of heckled flax Six pounds of tow and Six pounds of good wool She Shall keep six chickens for her use or more, and her fire wood Shall be hauled to the house and cut Small for the Stove and Shall have her Share of the Kitchen fire, and the two remaining parts of my household Furniture Shall be Equally divided among my six children Except the Stove and the Blacksmith tools and all the Stock of cattle which I bequeath to my Son Samuel Deeter and the Stove after the death of his mother. It is my will and I do order and direct unto my Son Samuel Deeter the Plantation where I now Live on with all the buildings and thereto belonging situate in Allegany Township Somerset County and State aforesaid for the Sum of Four Hundred and Seventy five dollars, Said Land Laying and being on the turnpike road Containing two hundred and Sixty nine acres and is to pay as follows, To my Daughter Magdalena Deeter now Magdalena Grove two hundred dollars Lawful money of the United States one year after the Death of my Wife Catherina, The third year he Shall pay unto my Daughter Elizabeth Deeter now Elizabeth Brant Fifty dollars Lawful money of the United States, and the fourth year he Shall pay unto my Son Jacob Deeter the Sum of Seventy five dollars Lawful money of the United States, and the Fifth year he Shall pay unto my daughter Catherina Deeter now Catherina Miller one hundred dollars Lawful money of the United States and the Sixth Year he Shall pay unto my Daughter Mary Fifty dollars Lawful money of the United states and Shall Give her the said Mary two cows and two sheep Two pigs and one bed and bedstead one Chest and Spinning wheel and She Shall Stay with her Mother till of age, and When my Wife Catherina Shall be Ill or Sick my Son Samuel Shall attend her During her life, further I give and bequeath unto my Daughter Magdalena Deeter now Magdalena Grove one hundred and five and one fourth acres of Land where they now Live on Lying and being in Allegany Township Somerset County and State aforesaid, with the Patent, I Give and bequeath unto my Daughter Elizabeth Deeter now Elizabeth Brant three hundred and ninety acres of Land with the Warrant thereof being the land What She now Live on Lying and being in Allegany township Somerset County and state aforesaid, I Give and bequeath unto my Son Jacob Deeter the Land Where he is now Liveing on Situate in Allegany Township Somerset County and State Aforesaid

I give and bequeath unto my Daughter Catherina Deeter now Catherina Miller Seventy Eight acres of Land where they are now Liveing on Lying and being in Allegany Township Somerset County and State aforesaid with the Patent thereof I Give and bequeath unto my daughter Mary three hundred and two acres of Land Lying and Being in Allegany Township Somerset County and state aforesaid with the Patent thereof, and Lastly I do nominate and appoint Samuel Deeter Sole Executor of this my Last Will and Testament and do hereby utterly disanull Revoke and disallow all and every other former Testament Will Legcies bequests and Executors by me in any wise before named willed or bequeathed Ratifying and confirming this and no other to be my Last Will and Testament, In Testimony Whereof I have hereunto Set my hand and Seal this thirty first day of May in the year of our Lord one thousand Eight hundred and twenty three

Signed Sealed Published Pronounced
and declared by the said John
Deeter as his Last will and Testament
in the Presents of us who In his
Presence have hereunto Subscribed
our Names
Tobias Musser
M Hugus
George Shaver

(Signed in German by John Deeter)

N.B. I hereby bequeath to my Daughter Polly all My Kitchen knives, a loom with all the cutters, and thirty six dollars owed me by my son Samuel. Signed and Sealed by my own hand the 25th of November 1825.

John Deeter

Witness:

    Samuel Deeter

Somerset County SS: Personally appeared Tobias Musser and George Shaver before me register for the probate of Wills and Granting Letters of Administration in and for said County who on their oaths duly administered saith they were present and saw and heard John Deeter the Testator, sign, seal, publish, pronounce, and declare the foregoing Instrument of writing as and for his Last Will and Testament, and that at the time of so doing he was of perfect sound mind memory and understanding to the best of their knowledge and belief and that the witness Michael Hugus the other subscribing witness to said Will is in the Proper hand writing of the said Michael who is since deceased. They further state that the name John Deeter signed to the within Nota Bene or codicil they believe to be the hand writing of the said Testator.

Affirmed Sworn and Subscribed
Me 5 Sept. 1828
A. Ogle Jun. Reg.

Tobias Musser
George Shaver

Facts and Figures

In 1810 Allegheny Township had 31 cabins and 15 houses. The following data has been gathered from the census in Allegheny Township.

Year	1820	1830	1840
Population	372	506	633
Taxables	83	104	138
Acres cleared land	1,546	1,992	3,287
Houses	15	40	58
Cabins	34	40	52
Horses	69	81	125
Cattle	82	153	167
Gristmills	2		3
Sawmills	3		5
Stills	2		1
Taverns	5		5

In 1850 there were 502 males, 446 females with a total population of 948.

In 1860 the number of inhabitants was 988.

In 1870 Allegheny Township had 982 native born, 151 foreign born, with a total of 1,133.

In 1880 the number of inhabitants was 1,201.

In 1900 there was a total of 970 inhabitants.

Foundation of Distillery

Pictured is the remaining foundation of the barrel house of a distillery in Allegheny Township at the headwaters of the Raystown branch of the Juniata River on the property of Richard and Emma Deaner. The 1820 census recorded two stills in the township. This is believed to be one in operation at this time. Five Indian arrowheads have been found on this site. Many other arrowheads and Indian stones for making corn meal have been found on the farm.

Bond House

The South Pennsylvania Railroad

It now remains to tell the history of a great railroad enterprise that never came to a finish, and on which millions of dollars were wasted.

The first survey for a railroad over the general line on which the South Pennsylvania Railroad was afterwards located was probably made as early as 1837, under the direction of Hother Hage. This was from Chambersburg to Pittsburgh. Under Mr. Hage there served as division engineer Colonel James Worrall, who, recognizing the advantages of following the crest lines, made them the study of his life. John A. Roebling, who afterwards constructed the Cincinnati and Niagara suspension bridges, and who also designed the famous Brooklyn Bridge, served a part of his apprenticeship in this same engineering corps.

In 1844 J. L. Schlatter examined a line from Harrisburg to Pittsburgh. This was done under the direction of the state. But this project for a short line through the southern counties of Pennsylvania appears to have remained dormant until 1854, when the Pennsylvania legislature chartered the Duncannon, Landisburg & Broad Top Railroad Company. In 1855 the name was changed to that of the Sherman's Valley & Broad Top Railroad Company. In 1859 the name was again changed by legislative enactment; this time it was the rather high-sounding one of the Pennsylvania Pacific Railroad that was bestowed on the bantling. This name it bore until 1863, when its name was once more changed to that of the South Pennsylvania, or South Penn Railroad, as it is called by popular usage. The several extensions of time for the building of the road and additional rights obtained are largely to be credited to the watchfulness and personal efforts of Colonel Worrall, who became president of the company in 1864, and to whom the hope of seeing this road built had almost become a hobby.

Beyond keeping the charter alive, but little was done until 1881. About that time the franchises and rights of the company passed into the hands of what in the railroad world are known as the Vanderbilt interests. New life and vigor were instilled into the enterprise, and surveys were again commenced under the direction of Oliver W. Barnes as chief engineer, and William F. Shunk as assistant chief engineer. The spring of 1882 found a large force of engineers in the field; it is said that their number was upwards of three hunded men. One of the most exhaustive and complete surveys that the annals of railroads can produce was made. It is said that ten-foot contour maps covering over one thousand square miles of territory were made. In the fall of 1883 a definite line was adopted, and contracts for the masonry of the bridge across the Susquehanna River, near Harrisburg, and the construction of the seven largest tunnels on the line, were let.

The road entered Somerset County near the village of New Baltimore, passing from there to the eastern foot of the Allegheny Mountain. Here a tunnel almost six thousand feet long was required to carry the road through to the western side of the mountain. Stony Creek Township was next traversed; from there it came into Somerset Township in a westerly direction until to within a few hundred yards of the County Home, where it turned to the northwest. The line of the road crossed the Johnstown Pike at a point about four miles north of Somerset. Continuing on through Somerset Township, it entered Jefferson Township and found its way to the foot of Laurel Hill, through which a great tunnel must be pierced.

In securing its rights-of-way the company obtained them by purchasing the necessary amount of land from the owners through whose land the line of the road passed, thus acquiring title in fee simple instead of condemnation. As projected, the road was to be built with a double track. Through the winter of 1883-84 the work was prosecuted. It was even announced that the road would be completed by July 1, 1886.

But toward the fall of 1885 ominous rumors were afloat. There was a slacking up in the amount of work being done, and presently it was announced that the South Penn Road had been sold to the Pennsylvania Railroad Company. Work ceased at once, contractors with their plants and forces of men left the road, the engineering corps was dismissed on November 1, and the South Penn Road was dead. What engineers of sound judgment had pronounced as being the best line of railroad between the Atlantic Seaboard and the Ohio River that ever had been or that can be projected, built or operated, was smothered, after a sum exceeding four millions of dollars had been expended on its construction.

What real purposes of the Vanderbilt interests were in taking up the construction of this road and then abandoning it can only be a matter of surmise. Possibly it may never have been their intention to complete the road. There had been a deep rivalry between them and

Reminders of the South Penn Railroad

the Pennsylvania Railroad, and their interests frequently clashed, and their taking up of the South Penn Road may have been only to use it as a weapon with which to force their rival to yield in some other matter in which they were interested. The road certainly was a menace to the interests of the Pennsylvania Railroad, as it paralleled their line through the state of Pennsylvania, and they purchased it to rid themselves of what would have become a dangerous rival.

The total length of the South Penn Railroad as projected was a trifle over 208 miles. On its line were nine tunnels, having a total length of 37,389 feet. Of these the following were in Somerset County:

Somerset County:	Length	Total Amount. of Exca- vation Done
Allegheny Mountain	5,919 ft.	3,946 ft.
Negro Mountain	1,100 ft.	734 ft.
Quemahoning	700 ft.	412 ft.
Laurel Hill	5,389 ft.	1,285 ft.

Of the nine tunnels on the line, taken as a whole, it may be said that two thirds of the work on them had been completed at the time of the suspension.

Great hopes had been founded on the building of the South Penn Road among the people of all the counties through which its line passed. On the strength of it miniature towns sprang up, investments were made in property, improvements were projected and started, and the prospects for the era of prosperity looked rosy enough.

But all who had placed their faith on this new road were doomed to disappointment, and in many cases to losses.

It has been already said that the right-of-way had been acquired in fee simple by purchase of the land. After the collapse of the enterprise these rights of way in Somerset County were assessed and returned to the county commissioners' office for the purpose of taxation. The taxes not being paid, the lands covered by these rights-of-way were sold as unseated lands. In some cases they were bought in by the original owners; in others, they were bought for purposes of speculation. Whether they will or will not develop into a crop of lawsuits at some future time remains to be seen.

Such is the history of the South Pennsylvania Railroad. In the beginning it presented a healthful appearance, but we now know that it was rotten to the core.

However, the South Penn Railroad was the forerunner of the present Pennsylvania turnpike which follows much of the same route as the "Old South Penn."

The Great Frost, or Buckwheat Year

The year of 1859 was a memorable one in the annals of Somerset County. On the night of June 4 there was a heavy frost, which destroyed the crops and all vegetation in nearly every part of the county. All fruit was killed. The rye was then in blossom. It, along with the wheat crop, was almost entirely blasted and destroyed. So it was with corn. Even the hay crop suffered. Sugar and maple trees shed their leaves just as the approach of winter. The farmers were panic-stricken. They were the first to realize the amount of damage that had been done. No one could tell or knew how wide an area of country it had extended. It might have been and was supposed to be general. Visions of famine loomed up before the eyes of many.

There was no surplus of grain from the preceding year. The frost came on a Saturday night. On the following Monday morning numbers of farmers living in the southern townships went to Frostburg and Cumberland, Maryland, which were the nearest points at which flour could be purchased, and had their wagons loaded with flour. The stock on hand was speedily exhausted. The price, also, in a few days rose from about seven to eighteen dollars a barrel, with eager takers at almost any price.

In the course of a week the farmers began to take a more hopeful view of the situation. It is true the then-growing crops were practically destroyed, but there was still one crop that yet remained to be sown. This was the buckwheat crop, of which at least a patch was sown every year on almost every farm. Why not sow enough of it to tide over until another year? The ground was rapidly prepared, and a large area was sown in that grain. A phenomenally large crop was raised, and the year 1859 is still spoken of as the great buckwheat year. Under the instructions of the county commisioners, the township assessors made a return of the number of bushels raised that year. Allegheny Township raised a total of 6,000 bushels of buckwheat. The figures for Jefferson and Larimer townships cannot be found, but as published in the newspapers of that day the entire crop in the county exceeded 183,000 bushels.

Dividing Ridge

The following are a few dates, a few facts, and a general outlook as to how life was lived in Allegheny Township around the turn of the century in and around a country store.

Albert W. Miller was born in Allegheny Township on the seventh day of December, 1869, a son of Joseph H. and Loretta (Garman) Miller), Loretta having been born in Germany. Near the end of the nineteenth century, probably either in the year of 1897 or 1898, "Ab," as he was known to his many friends, opened a general store in the hamlet of Dividing Ridge.

Dividing Ridge was located along Route 31, the main traffic route between Somerset and Bedford, at the bottom of the White Horse Mountain. There are several stories as to why this hamlet was named Dividing Ridge with the most likely being that the waters south of Dividing Ridge flow into the Potomac River, and the waters north of Dividing Ridge flow into the Susquehanna River. Also, the waters west of the White Horse Mountain flow into the Monongahela and on to the Ohio River.

The original store was located in a building owned by William Hillegas. Shortly after he opened the store, Ab purchased about one half acre of ground from the Hillegas family for the purpose of erecting a building which would serve as his home and a general store. Ab, at this time, was not married. The new building was probably completed during the year of 1900. After he was firmly established in his new home and store, Ab married Missouri E. (Sue) Weightman on June 26, 1901. Their marriage yielded two daughters, Jessie and Mary, and one son, Barron, who died early in life. Ab later added another one half acre to his plot of ground, again a purchase from the Hillegas family. This acreage was to play a prominent role in his life as a merchant.

For many years Dividing Ridge could be found on many of the road maps published by the major oil companies. The reason for this identification being that in the year of 1899 Ab was appointed postmaster of Dividing Ridge, and areas having post offices were listed on the routes of travel. Ab held this post until the Rural Free Delivery Service started delivering mail to each family. Ab made provisions for this public service as a room was included in his new building that was used exclusively as a post office.

The store was the center of activity for the immediate area and retained that distinction until it was closed in the early 1960's. This store handled almost any item that a family of that era would need to purchase, from vinegar to sugar, from medicines of that era to gasoline, from spades to plows, and from Long-Johns to lace, and if the store did not have the item in stock, it would most certainly be ordered for the buyer.

Money was not a plentiful item in that era and the barter system was often used. Mrs. Miller would often relate how the room at the rear of the store would often be filled with various items of farm produce and with the products of nature such as buckets of huckleberries, blackberries, walnuts, hickory nuts, and almost anything edible. Mr. Miller would load these items on his

Ab. Miller's Store at Dividing Ridge, Allegheny Township

horse-drawn wagon and would go over the mountain to Berlin, by the way of MacDonaldton, peddling the items around the mines of MacDonaldton. Ab, with his wagonload of produce, was always a welcome sight, and he would arrive in Berlin with an empty wagon. There the wagon was reloaded with items that had arrived at the freight station along with any other products that he purchased to be resold in his store. Of course, with the coming of the automobile, the wagon was retired. When "Bird," the faithful horse that made so many trips over the mountain, died, she was buried with dignity and ceremony at the "Huckleberry Gate."

Mr. Miller made use of his land and he supplemented his income by raising vegetables to be sold in the store and to be hauled over the mountain. His ideas of planting a garden passed to the next generation. Every potato had to have the eye turned just right, the seed or seeds had to be planted at just the exact depth and the correct distance apart regardless of the aches one found in his back. The many varieties of trees bearing cherries, apples, pears, plums, and prunes attested to the fact that these were also items to be found in the store.

Of course there was the "ice room" located in the barn. Mr. Miller would cut blocks of ice on the MacDonaldton Dam during the winter and would haul them home to be stored in sawdust. When the warm weather arrived, they would be uncovered and used in the household, the store, and of course some were sold.

Mr. Miller died when he was sixty years of age, and the store passed to his daughter Mary and her husband, Freeman W. (Tom) Poorbaugh. The store was operated much in the same manner that Mr. Miller had operated it except that the barter system gave way to the increase in currency, for now times had improved.

The store remained the community center. A building known as the Election House was rented to the citizens and twice a year voters gathered at Dividing Ridge to elect their favorite candidate. Politics was an important matter in that area, and the final tabulations were met with great jubilation or much sorrow. On election day it was not uncommon to have a nip from a bottle of homemade spirits which seemed to appear from nowhere, and after warming the recipient, vanished until needed again.

Young people gathered in numbers around the store for a game of ball in the Hillegas Meadow, and of course, many spectators leaned on the fence to watch the progress of the games. In the winter groups enjoyed the sport of sled-riding down the numerous hills around the

store. Of course, many of the old games of Hide and Seek, Run-Sheep-Run, Wolf in the Ring, and so on passed away the twilight hours. Sometime in the forties, the upstairs of the barn was converted into a basketball court of sorts and many a hotly contested game was played there, even during the winter when the boys of the neighborhood played with hands so cold and numb that it was difficult to hold onto the ball.

During the heavy snowstorms, when the roads were blocked with tons of snow, the men of the community would walk to the store for the staples that were needed at home to tide the family until the roads were cleared and vehicles could move once again to the store. More often than not, the men would arrive before lunchtime and would first warm themselves and then refresh themselves with hunks of cheese and crackers washed down with bottles of pop. During the afternoon many games of "500" would erupt and would continue until evening when the men would load their groceries into burlap sacks, throw them over their shoulders, and begin the journey home. It is not known if the men engaged in card games during the early years, but we do know that they gathered around the pot-bellied stoves found in the store and many stories were told and much tobacco was chewed. At one period when Mrs. Miller had a choice of adding a convenience to the home, she chose central heating, hoping to eliminate the tobacco juice that would miss the stove and the coal buckets and would consequently add to the cleaning chores.

The store played its part well during the war. Many tires that were incapable of holding a breath of air were gathered into the barn along with many, many tin cans that were flattened with a heavy shoe and of course the bushels of elderberries that were to be made into jellies for the men in service. Yes, War Bonds were also sold during that important time. A stranger looking for information or for a certain family was always directed to the store at the bottom of the mountain and there he received the final information that he needed.

Tom Poorbaugh died in the early forties and Mary in 1963. The store was sold in 1964 and today it stands empty with only memories of the olden days filling the shelves and waiting for someone to browse and perhaps carry the best of them away. Perhaps somewhere in the future with the increase in population and the decrease in our natural energies, there will once again be a need for the country store and then another Ab Miller will once again fulfill that need.

Glen Savage

Glen Savage is located about two miles south of the crossroads of Route 31 at Mt. Zion. The general store in Glen Savage, now owned by Mr. and Mrs. Leonard Miller, has been in existence since 1890. It was built by Ann Coughenour, sister of Charles, Alex, and Prof. Samuel Coughenour. She and her brother Alex had a

store together for a while in his home, but she bought land from Conrad "Coonie" Schiller and had the store built where it still stands.

Ann married Wesley Frazier in 1889 and they had the store and post office in what is now the living room of the house. Mail was carried from Glencoe to Glen Savage by horseback until 1906 when the post office was moved to Fairhope. Ann died in 1899, but Wes continued in the store. Ann's brother Charles built a new store on his property on the opposite corner from the Frazier store. So, for a few years there were two stores in Glen Savage. Charles later had his moved to Fairhope.

In 1914 Wes sold the store in his brother, Andrew J. Frazier, and went west. He returned a few years later with a new wife, the former Effie Stone of Kansas.

The A. J. Fraziers moved into the store from their farm in Bedford County. They built an addition and did some remodeling. They lived there until it was sold to their son, Earl, in 1927.

Earl and his wife, the former Lillie Deeter, moved into the store that autumn. It was the E. E. Frazier store until his death in May 1959. Mrs. Frazier continued in the store alone until December of that year. The building was vacant from then until August of 1970 when it was bought by the present owner.

Oliver Meyers was an 1898 Spanish-American War veteran. When he returned, he started his undertaking establishment at what is now the Charles Robb farm. Later he bought the home of Charles Dorn in Glen Savage and moved his undertaking business there. He apparently made caskets and followed the undertaking business until at least the early 1920's. He also did some

Village of Glen Savage

blacksmith work. In approximately 1925 the house was sold to be used as a parsonage for the German Lutheran Church at Glen Savage. In the late 1930's the undertaking building was sold to Mr. DeVore, torn down, and rebuilt as a home on Route 96 north of Hyndman.

Left to right: Hattie Coughenour (Miller), Mary Coughenour (Kennel), Dessie Coughenour (Glessner), Ellen Frazier (Bond), and Wess Frazier

211

Sawmill owned and operated by Frank and John Scheller, 1905

Lumbering

Forests covered most of the land the pioneers settled. Therefore, lumbering became a leading industry. The first sawmills were very crude compared to the modern mills.

The farm of Oliver Deeter was located two miles from Dividing Ridge. In 1900 he owned and operated an up-and-down sawmill. The pictured steam-operated, wood-fired sawmill was located on the Oliver Deeter farm in 1905. This mill was owned and run by Frank and John Scheller. The land is now owned by Harold Deeter, Jr.

A tram road or wooden railroad ran from this mill to the farm of Edward Coughenour now owned by John Deeter. Sections of the tram road are still visible. The horse-drawn tram car hauled the logs to the mill to be sawed. Lumber was then loaded on wagons and taken to the railroad at Fairhope.

Some of the workmen pictured are George Core on the ladder, Sam Deeter on the pony, Jackson Ware, Will Ware, Ed. Coughenour, Oliver Deeter, Frank Barkley, and John Scheller.

The B. & O. Railroad built a tram road of wooden rails and ties at Fairhope. It is known to have existed at least one hundred years ago, as it is pictured in the Beers Atlas of 1876. At one time it is believed to have been from seven to ten miles long. It eventually ran to sawmills located in Fairhope, one on the Joseph and later Henry Miller farm, now owned by Regis Wolff; the Oliver Deeter farm, now owned by Harold Deeter, Jr.; the John McQuade farm, now owned by Gilbert McQuade. A sawmill was also located on the Fred Kern farm, now owned by Julius Kern.

A water-powered sawmill was operated by Joseph Miller on his farm along Hillegass Run. In 1923 his son, Henry Miller, owned and operated a sawmill powered by a steam engine at the same location. This mill was then converted to gasoline and used until 1945 or 1946, when it was sold to Ed. Grimm and George Zimmerman.

Henry Miller also had a shingle mill on his farm where he sawed and packed shingles. This mill was moved from place to place as shingles were needed for barns and other buildings. This shingle mill is now in a museum at Lancaster, Pa.

Doc and Sam, the two horses pictured, were owned by George and Charles Scheller. A sawmill owned by the Schellers was located down Bruck Hollow on the John Bower farm in 1908. They also had a mill operation at the Henry Hoppert farm.

212

The Scheller Brothers' lumber wagon

The loaded wagon was on its way to the railroad at Fairhope. Irvin Robb, Millard Coughenour, and Elmer Glessner are the workmen.

Breastwork Run, a favorite resort of fishermen on account of the large number of brook trout which it contains, derives its name from breastworks thrown up at its source during the Revolutionary War. "Breastworks" is defined as a low, defensive wall of earth or stone, often temporary. The head of the stream is on the farm owned by Henry Wolfhope, a mile north of the Pittsburgh Turnpike.

The pictured cannonball was found by John Restly along Breastwork Run several miles below Forbes Road. Supposedly, it was used during the war.

The Babcock Lumber Company built a standard gauge railroad which extended from Babcock Mill at Ashtola through Breastwork to New Baltimore in 1907. Logs were taken off the mountain with horses or were slid down the mountain and loaded onto the railroad. Several camps were provided for the lumbermen who were mainly Austrians.

Diminishing timber resources forecast the closing of the mills after 1910. The logging railroad was working along Breastwork Run in Allegheny Township and over the summit of the Allegheny Mountain.

As cutting continued the quality lessened, and this factor, along with increasing transportation costs, forced the company to discontinue cutting. The present Breastwork road follows much of the same route as the logging railroad from New Baltimore to Route 30.

About 1920 McNeal Lumber Company bought the Pugh tract of land located along Route 30 in Allegheny

Cannonball

213

Lumbering operation along Breastwork Run near New Baltimore in 1908

Township. A large lumbering operation was established. Logs were hauled by truck from various areas into this mill. A village, mainly employees of McNeal Lumber Company, was soon in evidence. As was to be expected this was known as "McNeal Town." A one-room school was built for the education of the children. This little town flourished only as long as the timbering flourished. Today there is very little remaining of this "lumbering town."

Over the years other sawmills in Allegheny Township were the Cooper Lumber Company, Lawrence Housel, and many other locally owned mills.

Topper Gristmill

The Topper gristmill was built by John Topper. It was located just west of New Baltimore along the road leading into the Breastwork Road. Farmers from the surrounding community brought their grain with horses and wagons to the mill to be ground into meal.

At one time near this mill there was also a "fulling mill." Fulling was a process for shrinking and cleaning woolen and worsted fabric, matting the fibers, and producing a firm, compact cloth. Hot soapy water was used, followed by pressing through rollers.

Topper gristmill

Custer Blacksmith Shop

Harvey Custer operated his first blacksmith shop on the farm of his father, Samuel Custer. The house on the Harvey Custer farm was built in 1905. The blacksmith shop, which is still in use, was built several years earlier. Woodworking and furniture making were also done at the shop. An addition was put onto the original shop in 1951. A pot-bellied stove still stands in the corner. Each of the five Custer sons inherited the skills of their father.

Many horses were shod at the Custer shop, the cost being fifteen cents per shoe. During World War II horseshoes were purchased by the keg from Shipley Hardware in Meyersdale. The blacksmith would then weld on toes and bend the heels which was commonly called dressing the shoes. During this period of time the dressed horseshoes were sold in Roxbury, New Baltimore, Manns Choice, and Berlin at Homer Croner's Store.

Wagons were made from scratch. The only piece of the wagon they needed to buy was the skein, which went into the hub of the wheel. The last wagon built by Harvey was sold to Irvin Robb. The cost of the wagon, excluding the box, was $70.

Bobsleds were also a product of the Custer shop. It was necessary to purchase the soles for the sled runners at the foundry in Boynton. In order to obtain these they would have to travel to Berlin and then go by train to Meyersdale. There they would board the streetcar to Boynton. The cost of a complete bobsled was from $25 to $30.

Other items the Custers became well known for making are all kinds of wagon wheels (including the spokes), buggy wheels, fingers for grain cradles, wooden washtubs, meat barrels, butter tubs, hand rakes, dry sinks, corner cupboards, kitchen cabinets, extension tables, handles for axes and hammers and most other hand tools, refinishing sugar keelers, and sharpening tools.

Work has slowed down at the Custer shop since the illness and death of Merle. However, Bill continues to work as he is able. Brother Charles, who lives in Berlin, still makes some furniture, although he is limited by his health.

Pictured are customers at the Custer shop. They are Zac Brant, John Tipton, Jake Miller, W. A. (Ab) Miller, and Harvey Custer, blacksmith.

Custer Blacksmith Shop

Education

Until the bodily needs of our pioneer ancestors were satisfied, they could not bestow much thought upon education. The population was scattered and sparse. The country was covered by forests with few roads and bridges. Therefore illiteracy prevailed.

Little is known of early teachers or their qualifications. Some were men living in the communities in which they taught school and were of good character. There were also some who were strolling vagabonds, addicted to drunkenness and profanity.

As late as 1819 Jacob Weyand of Allegheny Township, by advertisement in the "Somerset Whig," offered a reward of ten dollars for a runaway schoolmaster calling himself John Rodgers, sometimes John Norton and John Fleming, saying that he had taken away with him a number of books from the schoolhouse and burned others.

The early schools of Allegheny Township, like almost everywhere else in the county, were taught in private houses. A school was taught at Shaffer's Church in 1810 by a teacher named Appleman. In 1835 free schools were adopted by the township.

The first state appropriation that we know of is that of 1855. It allotted to Somerset County $934.56. The amount received for Allegheny Township was $29.94, the smallest amount allotted to any township or borough.

School year ending June 5, 1882

Allegheny Township - No. of schools - 9 ½
    Average number months taught - 5
    No. of male teachers - 6
    No. of female teachers - 3
    No. of pupils attending - 205
    Total expenditures - $1815.09
    Wages of male teachers - $28.92 per month
    Wages of female teachers - $23.75 per month
    Population in 1880 - 1,201
In 1882 - Taxables - 280
    Value of real estate - $140,585
    Horses and mules - 215
    Cattle - 351
    Value of taxable property - $149,705
(6 mills on dollar) County tax-assessed - $898.23

As the township became more densely populated there was a need for more schools, located to best accommodate each area. At one time there were eleven one-room schools. When Allegheny Township became part of the Berlin-Brothersvalley Area Schools in 1942, the eight remaining were all closed and sold. Three still remain on their original location, the Mountain, Felton, and Suhrie.

Schools (Key)

1 - McNeal School
2 - Felton School
3 - Suhrie School
4 - Imgrund school
5 - Hillegass School
6 - Werner School
7 - Mt. Zion School
8 - Glen Savage School
9 - Pine School
10 - Mountain School
11 - Harmon School

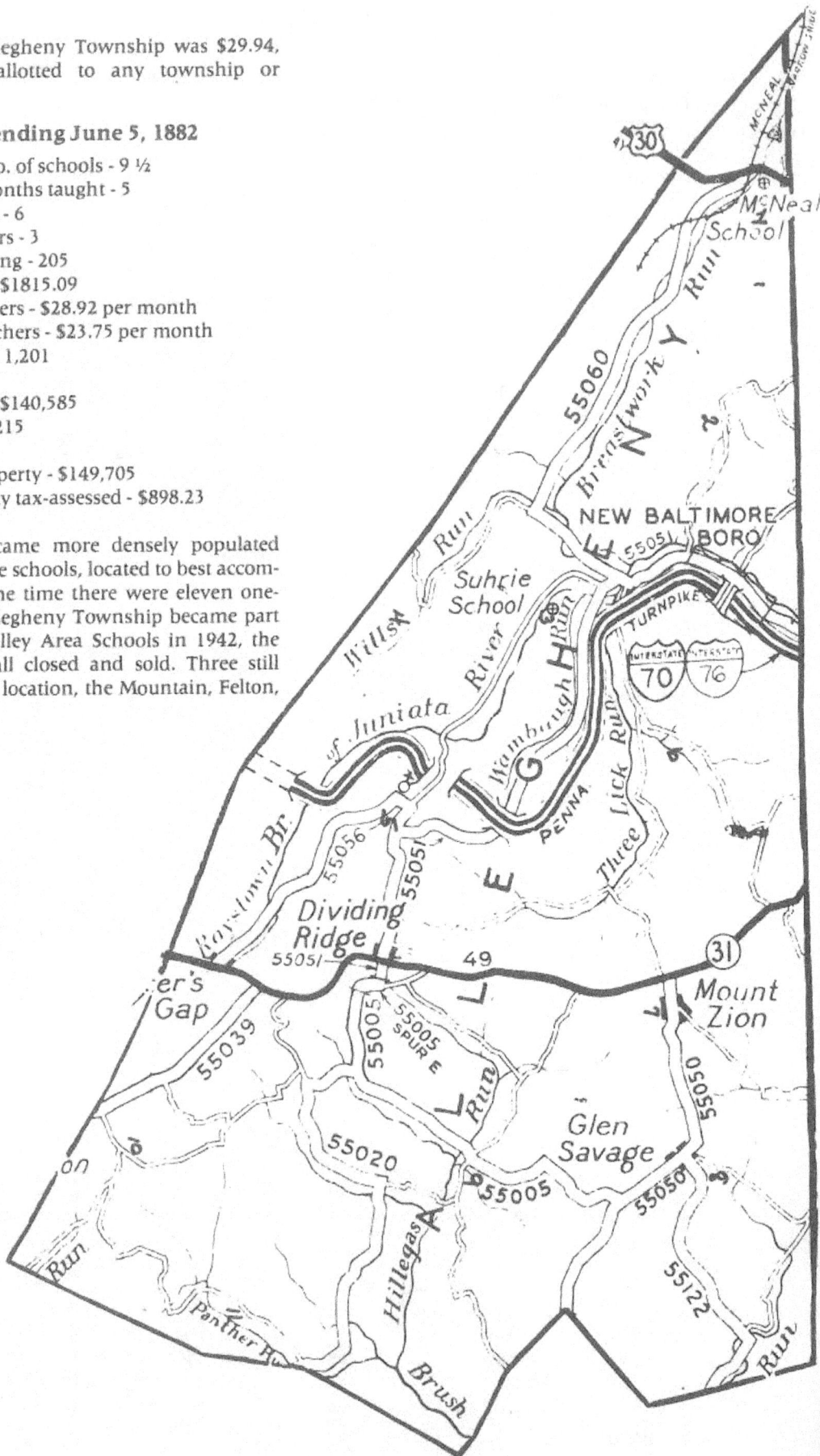

Roxbury Normal School

Allegheny, Northampton, and Fairhope
1914

Row 1 - Clara Felton, Nellie Manges, Tom Hillegass, Grace Caton, Bessie Hall
Row 2 - Annie Hall, Celia Caton, Florence Will, Gertrude Shaffer, Minnie Baer, Edith Clites
Row 3 -Stella Emerick, Billy Broadwater, Naomi Emerick

Felton School

The Felton School was located approximately two miles north of New Baltimore and one mile south of Mountain Meadow Farms. It was closed in 1942, but the building still remains at the same location.

Felton School

Glen Savage School

The Glen Savage School was located near Glen Savage. In 1900 the school building burned down. School was then held in an old building on the corner where Charles Coughenour later built his store. Then it was held in Alex Coughenour's summer house until the new school was built. The teacher was Sam Coughenour. There were about forty or fifty students in grades one to five.

This picture was taken approximately 1908. The pupils are:

Row 1–Matt Browning, Clara Hartge, Merle Hillegass, Nanny Browning, George Mowry, Lizzie Meyers, Bertha Browning, Edith Coughenour, Lizzie Hartge, Bill Browning

Row 2–Alverta Hartge, John Browning, Frank Coughenour, Wilson Meyers, Sarah Coughenour, Mae Coughenour, Kate Coughenour, Blanch Browning, Ira Mowry

Row 3–Sam Coughenour, Teacher, Irvin Tressler, Leroy Coughenour, Fred Hoppert, Ollie Poorbaugh

Row 4–Stephen Mowry, George Coughenour, Pearl Hoppert, Erdie Mowry, Edward Hartge

Harmon School

The Harmon School was located on the farm now owned by Harry O. Smith near Brushcreek. It was closed in 1928.

Hillegass School–1914

The Hillegass School, a one-room building, was located approximately two miles north of the crossroads on Route 31 at Dividing Ridge. In 1942 Allegheny Township became part of the Berlin-Brothersvalley School District, therefore this school was closed.

The picture was taken in 1914. The pupils are as follows:

Row 1–Quentin Boyer, Carrie Ross, Mary Ellenberger, Clarence Glessner, Alfred Caton, Mary Miller, Catherine Reese, Charles Ross, Alma Shroyer, Mable Shroyer, Marie Hillegass

Row 2–Leon Shroyer, Blaine Cameron, Harry Caton,

Mabel Sarver, Gladys McVicker, Leora Glessner, Nellie Manges, teacher

Row 3–Katie Boyer, Marybelle Cameron, Vince Hillegass, Jess Miller

Row 4–Rae Harmon, Hazel McVicker, Burma Ellenberger, Webster Reese, Nellie McVicker

Row 5–Pearl Caton, Daisy Ellenberger, Blanch Caton, Velma Hall

Imgrund School

The Imgrund School was located on the Imgrund farm approximately four miles northwest of New Baltimore. Because of the decrease in the population the school was closed in 1914. Florence (Will) Restly was the last teacher.

Mountain School

The Mountain School was located one fourth mile south of the road leading from MacDonaldton to Route 31. It was bought by Ralph Groft in 1942 and remains at the same location. The following pupils attended in 1903.

Row 1–Harry Landis–teacher, Grace Diveley, Lottie Diveley, Robert Hostetler, Edna Engleka, Hilda Landis, Minnie Baer, Ephriam Brant, Linda Frahlich, Dewey Caton, Carrie Keefer, Elmer Diveley

Row 2–Millard Brick, William Landis, Albert Brick, Ralph Groft, William Engleka, Ida Groft, Mary Keefer, Grace Bear, Elsie Landis, Martha Frahlich

Row 3–Harry Gindlesperger, Clyde Bear, Anna Groft, Bertha Barron, Cora Groft, Helen Frahlich, Emma Landis, Edison Brick, Simon Groft, Wilson Brant

McNeal School

The McNeal School was located at McNeal Town along Route 30. The Imgrund School building was moved to McNeal Town to accommodate this "lumbering town." This building later was destroyed by fire.

Mt. Zion School

The Mt. Zion School was located near the crossroads at Mt. Zion. After it was closed in 1942 it was sold and rebuilt into a home in Bedford County.

The pupils attending in 1913 are:

Row 1–Foust, Harry McVicker, **Earl Manges**, Irene Benning, Walter McVicker

Row 2–Robert Keller, Jennie Benning, Mildred Powell, Ethel Clites, Lula McVicker

Row 3–Clarence Sarver, Florence Clites, **Thelma Manges**, Ardella Benning, Marie McVicker, Cora Clites, William McVicker

Row 4–George Keller, Edith Clites, Harry Benning, **Lillian Shaffer**, Marcy Benning, Russel Keller, Nelle Walker, teacher

The names in **bold print** were visitors.

Pine School–1908

This picture was taken at the Pine School located approximately two miles south of the crossroads of Route 31 at Dividing Ridge. As the slate states the picture was taken in 1908. This school was also closed in 1942.

The pupils are:

Row 1–Teacher–Lottie Hillegas, Myrtle Coughenour, Albert Miller, Nellie Deaner, Grace Deaner, Lillie Deeter, Wesley Deeter, Ord Miller, Elmer Coughenour, Ira Coughenour

Row 2–Spergon Deaner, Sam Deeter, Grace Deeter, Elizabeth Miller, Bertha Miller, Etta Miller

Row 3–Russel Deaner, Elsie Deeter, Pearl Miller, Ollie Poorbaugh, Ruth Miller, Carrie Deeter, John Hillegas

Suhrie School—1914-1915

The Suhrie School was located approximately two miles northwest of New Baltimore. After closing in 1942 it was remodeled and is now the residence of Mr. and Mrs. Robert Sarver.

The pupils in 1914 are

Row 1–Donald McVicker, Romayne Smith, Grant Wambaugh, Larry McVicker, Pearl Felton, Kathleen Fochtman, Florence Buratty

Row 2–Margaret Smith, Zita Buratty, Margaret Fochtman, Helen Harbrant, Irene Felton, Clarence Smith, Lawrence Buratty, Clarence Fochtman, George Restly, Paul McVicker, John Brittlebrum, Edmond Fochtman, Robert McVicker

Row 3–Mark Restly, Helen Smith, Lula McVicker, Frances Harbrant, Bertha Will, Regina Harbrant, Clara Felton, Mary Restly, Virginia Buratty, Florence Will, teacher

Werner School

The Werner School was located between Mt. Zion and New Baltimore on the Newland farm. It was closed in 1920. This picture was taken prior to its closing. The pupils are:

Row 1–Marcy Benning, Bill McVicker, Marian Shaffer, Jennie Benning, Lulu McVicker, Ardella Benning, Marie McVicker, John Jordan.

Row 2–Emma Tipton–teacher, George Wyand, Mary Fisher, Lillian Shaffer, Paul Firley, Kathryn Shaffer, Jennings Shaffer

Row 3–Gregory Will, Gertrude Wambaugh, Cecelia Firley, Grace Jordan, Nellie Shaffer, Bernadine Will, John Fisher

Row 4–Paul Fisher

Churches (Key)

1–Sarver Community Church
2–St. Lukes (Mountain) Reformed Church
3–Custer Brethren Church
4–Mt. Zion Lutheran Church
5–Mt. Zion Reformed Church
6–Trinity Lutheran Church (Glen Savage)
7–Mt. Olive Lutheran Church

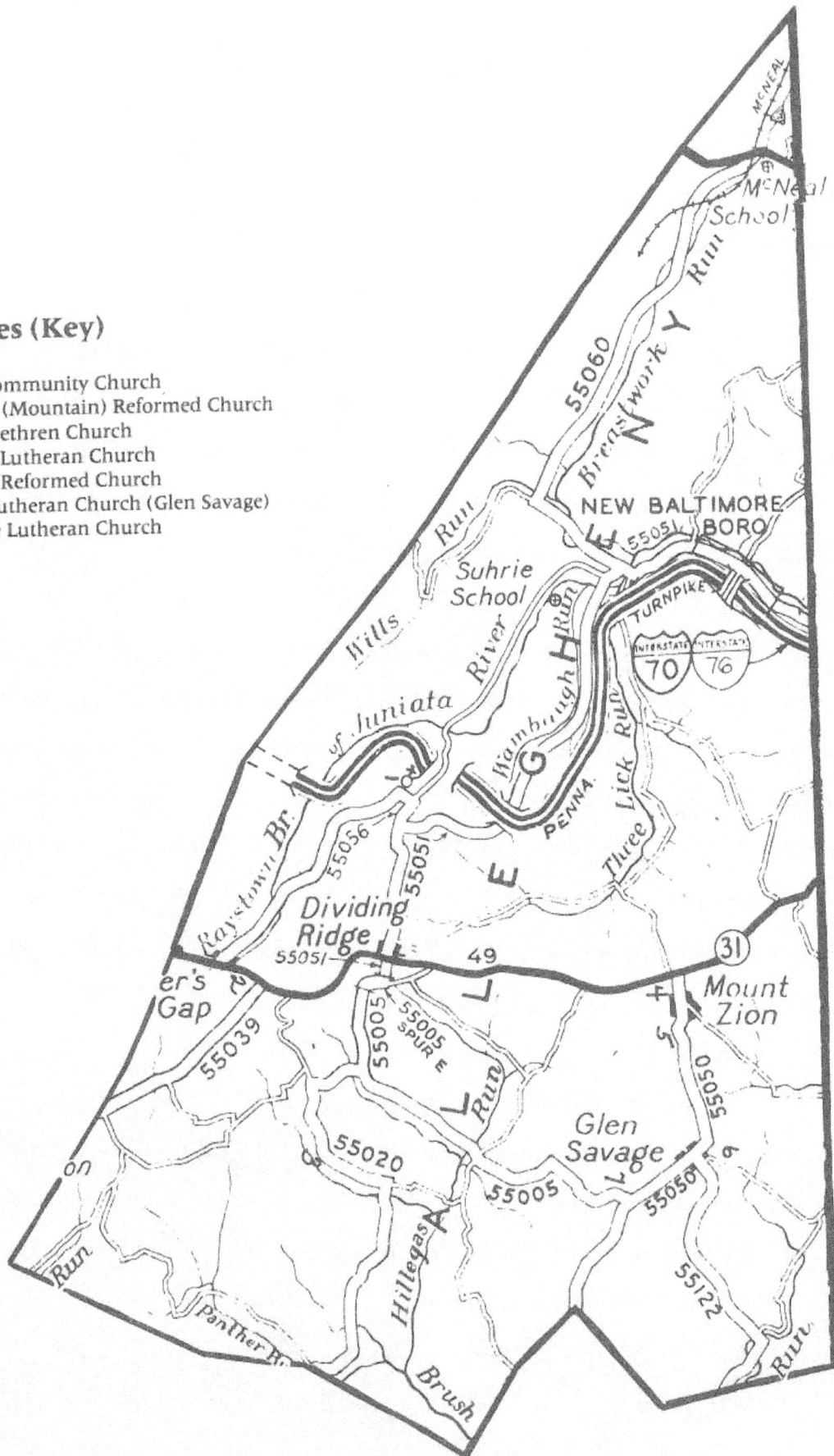

Custer Meetinghouse

This was sometimes called "Custer Schmaltz Thal." Elder George Custer held services here as early as 1738 when he settled in the area with Elder John Keagy who went on to what is now Meyersdale, Pa. Meetings were first held in the open fields or woods, where the members sat on boards between stumps and stones. Later they met in the barn and still later in the house. This was the house of Samuel Custer. In 1880, there were about forty members in this church. The same elders who preached in Switzer Schoolhouse preached at the Custer meetinghouse. They were Daniel K. Walker, Samuel Reiman, and W. G. Schrock. Baptisms were administered below the blacksmith shop in the small stream. The work ceased there in about 1885.

In 1880 the Progressive Brethren of Berlin built a neat white frame church just below the blacksmith shop in the meadow at the turn of the road where Elder Henry Holsinger preached many times. Due to the description of this location, it is assumed that this same church was known as the Custer Brethren Church, where a J. L. Bowman also preached. The land on which the church was built was donated by Mrs. Samuel Custer. Sunday school was held here until 1924. The local Grange also held meetings here until 1931.

After the Grange became inactive the building fell to disuse. It was then torn down by John Custer. It was agreed when the land was donated that it would revert to the original owner when the building was no longer used for church purposes.

Mt. Zion Churches

Early history tells us the first church located at Mt. Healthy, later known as Mt. Zion, was a Dunker or Brethren Church. About 1850 a church was erected at Mt. Zion by the Lutherans, Methodists, and United Brethren, known as the Union Church. It was a frame building, and cost about six hundred dollars. The first minister of the United Brethren was Rev. John Sidman. The first trustees were: John Black, of the Methodists; John Ware, of the Lutherans; and William Barick, of the United Brethren. The Lutherans had a membership of about twenty, and the United Brethren about thirty. The Sabbath school was under the control of the United Brethren, and numbered about forty pupils.

There were two doors in this church—one for the men to enter and one for the women—consequently, the men sat on one side and the women on the other.

In 1909, after the services were discontinued here, this church was bought by James Tipton, for $120, who later sold it to James Ware. He moved the building a short distance east along Route 31 to be used as the residence of the James Ware family. In 1913 Emma and Blair Powell bought it. Over the years it has undergone change and is now being remodeled by John and Carol Kalaha.

Lutheran Church

St. John's Evangelical Lutheran Church at Mt. Zion was built by Alex Coughenour in 1892. The Mt. Zion and Mt. Olive churches were affiliated with the West End charge of Bedford County, later uniting with the Schellsburg charge. These two churches, being only a few miles apart, always had the same minister coming from Bedford County.

When the Mt. Zion Church was dedicated there were one hundred and twenty-seven members with Rev. G. W. Stroup as the first minister. The first to be baptized were Ollie Coughenour and Naomi Beck. There was never a wedding ceremony performed in this church.

With the country population decreasing over the years, the Mt. Zion congregation became too few in number for regular worship services to be continued. The church closed in approximately 1945 or 1946. Most of the members were absorbed into the Mt. Olive congregation.

The Mt. Zion Church is now owned by the Mt. Zion Cemetery Association with the income from a trust fund used for the maintenance of the building. Most of the original furnishings still remain in the church including the pot-bellied stove.

Mt. Zion Lutheran Church

Reformed Church

The Mt. Zion Reformed Church was also built in 1892 just on the opposite side of the cemetery from the Lutheran Church. This was a very modern church for that period with stained-glass windows and a furnace. This church was affiliated with the Bedford County Reformed Churches, with the ministers coming from Bedford County.

In the 1920 to 1925 era the congregation had financial difficulties. Rev. George Ely was the pastor. The church was sold to James Tipton, and the land returned to the farm from which it was acquired, which was the James Tipton farm. The furnishings were all sold. The present owners are Lee and Lorene Hoppert. The building is used for storage.

Old Mt. Zion Reformed Church

Trinity Evangelical Lutheran Church, Glen Savage

Early records date back to 1790, and since they were written in German, it is difficult to ascertain just how the congregation began. The earliest family names which may be considered those of charter members of the Glen Savage Church are Bruck, Felton, Hartge, Hoppert, Schafer, and Schiller. The congregation was organized with a nucleus of 10 voting members.

It seems land was given to Frederick Hartge, as a trustee for the church, in 1841. The Glen Savage Church, known for years as the German Lutheran Church, was originally a member of the Allegheny General Lutheran Synod.

Some years later, when dissatisfaction arose, some families withdrew to affiliate with the Missouri Synod Lutheran congregation known as "The Union Church" at Pine Hill near Berlin.

Around 1860, these particular families withdrew from the Pine Hill Church to establish the preaching of the gospel in the area of Glen Savage near the town of Fairhope. Here they organized a congregation affiliated with the Lutheran Church, Missouri Synod, known as Trinity Evangelical Lutheran Church, and conducted their services in the schoolhouse.

Conrad Schiller, father-in-law of Lewis Hartge, donated land for a church and cemetery to Trinity congregation in 1870, according to the records. However, no deed is available to verify this date, which must have been earlier, for during the excavation for the basement under the original log church in 1966, the cornerstone was found dated 1863. The logs for this church, which cost $500, were furnished by Conrad Bruck.

Trinity's first pastor was Rev. A. M. William Koehler, who served from 1866 to 1870, followed by Rev. F. Dreyer, who preceded a 28-year pastorate which ended in 1898.

During the pastorate of Rev. H. Steger, 1899-1903, the

Glen Savage Missouri Lutheran Church

church changed its appearance with the addition of a new entrance, which included two Sunday school rooms, a steeple, and bell tower. The latter gave the building a churchly appearance. The original log church and new addition measured 20 by 30 feet and was covered with uninterrupted siding in 1902.

Early records show that the same minister also served St. John's Church at Johnsburg, where a log church was built in 1787 and replaced by a frame church in 1863, as well as a congregation at Salisbury probably in existence for only a very short time.

The services were in German until before World War I, when one service each month was in English.

Gradually two services, then three services, were conducted in English each month, but it wasn't long until English was used entirely.

Early records show that the mission budget of the Eastern District of the Lutheran Church, Missouri Synod, subsidized Trinity and St. John's congregations for many years. Monies given for mission purposes by congregations of the district helped to support the ministry here because the congregation was always small in number.

A theological student, Rev. Vicar F. Trauterman, who served in 1912 and 1913, organized Trinity's first Sunday school on January 5, 1913.

Forty children and adults attended.

Three weeks later Trinity's first Bible class was founded for the 48 confirmed members. Ever since then, these groups, including weekly vacation Bible school, have used materials for Christian education supplied by the offices of the Lutheran Church, Missouri Synod.

Because of the dwindling membership at St. John's Church at Johnsburg, it seemed that the need was for the pastor to relocate at Glen Savage, where the membership was larger. During the pastorate of Rev. John W. Rabold, 1923-27, the two congregations decided to purchase a new parsonage on the corner of the Fairhope and Church roads.

The sanctuary was redecorated in 1931 during the pastorate of Rev. Theodore Ernest, 1929-37. The Eastern District Mission Board helped the two congregations to purchase another parsonage in Berlin in 1936. Shortly afterward, the Glen Savage parsonage was sold to Mr. and Mrs. John Coughenour. It is now occupied by Mrs. Ruth Bruck.

By the close of the pastorate of Rev. Arnold C. Schaller in 1941, St. John's Church at Johnsburg had ceased to

function as a congregation. In 1940 the joint parish dissolved and the building fell into disuse.

In 1940, the Rural Electric Association power lines made possible the wiring of Trinity Lutheran Church for electricity.

Rev. Hugo Fickenscher served the congregation from 1941 to 1945. During his pastorate, the Eastern District advised Trinity to form a joint parish with St. John's Lutheran Church, the Cove, in Accident, Md., which still exists.

During the 11-year pastorate (1946 to 1955) of Rev. Martin Franke, the church acquired from James O. Gooden, in 1948, additional land to enlarge the cemetery.

The second addition was made to the church in 1952. The basement under the 1902 addition was excavated making possible Sunday school and social room facilities.

August Woida refinished the altar, pulpit, lectern, and pastor's chair from the vacated Johnsburg Church, which were installed along with new pews at Trinity Church.

The exterior physical features changed with the moving of the entrance from the front of the church to its side.

The following year, the basement was finished to accommodate Sunday school and social rooms. In March, 1954, a dedication service was conducted for the newly remodeled church.

During the pastorate of Rev. Harry Droutz, 1956-61, the organ which was donated by Mr. and Mrs. William Felton when electricity was installed was replaced with a new electric organ dedicated for the same use in 1958.

Rev. Arthur M. Bicker served the congregation from 1962 until 1967 when he died of a heart attack following the Easter service.

In 1966, the basement was enlarged by excavating under the entire church.

Rev. David C. Pardeich of Pittsburgh supplied the congregation from 1967 until January, 1968, when the Rev. August Kreutz began and continues his ministry.

During the vacancies in the years 1937 to 1969, Rev. Carl Dauphin of Accident, Md., supplied the congregation many times.

Although Trinity Evangelical Lutheran Church, Glen Savage, has never enjoyed a great increase in numbers in either its membership or Sunday school, it has been blessed with members and pastors who by the grace of God have been faithful to the pure Word of God and the Lutheran Confessions and practices.

As to Trinity's future, we know that it can still serve as an instrument of the Triune God in educating and training people for this life and that which is to come. We know that God's promise is always true and kept, "Where two or three are gathered together in My name, there am I in the midst of them."

Pastors Who Have Served Trinity, Glen Savage, Pa., since 1866

The picture was taken about 1914 at the church.
Row 1–Clara Felton (child–Merle Sarver), Clara Hartge, Nora Felton, Olga Grenke, Lucy Bowers, Lizzie Hartge, Pearl Hoppert (child–Herbert Bruck)
Row 2–Daisy Sarver, Pearl Felton, Amelia Woida, Helen Grenke, Olga Grenke, Orpha Hoppert
Row 3–Tillie Sarver (three Sarver Children), Rose Sarver, Mrs. Mary Felton, Mary Hartge, Mrs. Ed. Bruck, Mrs. Lewis Hartge, Mrs. Andy Frazier

1866-1879	Rev. A. M. W. Koehler
1870-1874	Rev. F. Dreyer

1875-1898	Rev. Carl Lauterbach	1927-1929	Rev. Erwin Tieman
1899-1903	Rev. H. Steger	1929-1937	Rev. Theodore Ernest
1903-1905	Rev. William Knoke, Jr.	1937-1941	Rev. Arnold Schaller
1906-1909	Rev. J. Koerber	1941-1945	Rev. Hugo Fickenscher
1910-1911	Rev. W. A. Aufsing	1946-1955	Rev. Martin Franke
1912-1913	Rev. Vicar F. Trautermann	1956-1961	Rev. Harry Droutz
1913'1915	Vicar Martin	1962-1967	Rev. Arthur M. Bicker
1915-1921	Rev. F. W. Klemm	1967-1968	Rev. David C. Pardieck
1921-1922	Rev. C. A. Hinney	1968-	Rev. August Kreutz
1923-1927	Rev. John Rabolt		

Mt. Olive Lutheran Church

The Mt. Olive Church is located approximately two miles southwest of the village of Glen Savage. The first church at Mt. Olive was a log building. This was also known as the Shaffer Church. It was replaced by a frame building and I quote:

"The building of the Mt. Olive Church was commenced the latter part of August in the year of our Lord one thousand eight hundred and seventy six and was finished January the 16th, 1877 and was dedicated the 4th of November, 1877 by Rev. D. S. A.Tomlinson."

Building Committee

John Giger

Daniel W. Coughenour

Israel Burkhart

This entry was made Feb. the 4th, 1880, by Samuel W. Coughenour.

The following five quotes were also taken from the early records of the Mt. Olive Church:

"Preached my first sermon in Mt. Olive Church, March 25, 1877, Monday forenoon, very disagreeable day. Raining and snowing. Was taken to the church by Mr. Samuel P. Walker in a little two-horse wagon."

D. S. A. Tomlinson

"Rev. Joseph R. Focht took charge of the West End Charge on the 29th day of March 1885."

"Rev. Cyrus Focht took charge of the West End Charge June 9, 1889, and had only four months as he had to return to the seminary at Gettysburg to finish his studies."

"Rev. Ira F. Brame preached his first sermon in Mt. Olive Congregation on July 13, 1890."

"Rev. G. W. Stroup took charge of the West End Pastorate Jan. 10, 1892."

Other ministers who served Mt. Olive were:

Rev. G. D. Gross-May 1904, 1905, 1906

Rev. G. L. Courtney-Dec. 1908, 1909, 1910

Rev. Geo. Trostle-June 1912, 1913

Rev. W. G. Slonaker-May 1914, 1920, 1921

Rev. C. P. Bastian-Supply

Dr. L. P. Young-Supply

Rev. G. H. Seiler-Supply

Rev. W. G. Slonaker-June 1924 to April 1929

Rev. C. P. Bastian-Supply

Rev. H. M. Petrea-Aug. 1930 to retirement July 1945

Rev. Frank Herzel-Oct. 1945 to Dec. 1948

Homer Duppstadt-Supply

Rev. James M. Scharf-April 1952 to retirement June 1969

After 1961 for a period of time Mt. Olive was a part of the Bedford County Area Lutheran Ministry, consisting of a large number of churches with only a few ordained ministers. Most of the regular worship services were conducted by students or retired ministers. After another reorganization it became part of the southern parish with less churches to serve, and the pastors were Rev. Hebel, Rev. Stouffer, and Rev. Putman.

Raymond Wissinger served as minister for several years followed by Homer Duppstadt, who is now serving the congregation. At present the church building is being enlarged.

Mt. Olive Lutheran Church

Sarver Church

Sarver Community Church

The Sarver Church is located approximately two miles north of the crossroads of Route 31 at Dividing Ridge. In March 1905 the foundation for the church was dug out by John Glessner, Andy Glessner, Edward Glessner, and Joseph Glessner at a cost of twenty-five cents per hour. The carpenter, Henry Meyers, was the construction boss.

Twenty-four pews were purchased for one hundred dollars, and are the same ones being used today. Oliver Meyers made and donated the pulpit. The dedication of the new church was in the fall of 1905.

The Sarver Church was a member of the "United Evangelical Church" until October 14, 1922, when this group united with the "Evangelical Association," taking the new name: "The Evangelical Church." In 1946 this church united with the "United Brethren in Christ," taking the new name: "The Evangelical United Brethren Church." At different times other churches have been on a charge with Sarver: Berlin, Bittner, Camp Run, and Meyersdale—all closed.

Sometime later there was another merger with the Methodist Church. The Sarver Church continued with this merger a short time. In 1972 it separated and became an independent church known as "The Sarver Community Church," and still continues to hold services.

Some of the ministers who served the Sarver congregation over the years were: Rev. A. F. Richards, Rev. Don Joiner, Rev. W. C. Sell, Rev. Harry B. Greer, Rev. C. W. Evans, Rev. A. G. Meade, Rev. C. W. Raley, Rev. G. O. Bishop, and Rev. W. M. West.

St. Luke's (Mountain) Church

St. Luke's Reformed Church was organized January 15, 1861, under the leadership of Rev. F. A. Edmonds, pastor of Trinity, Berlin. The site selected for the building was along one branch of the headwaters of the Juniata, and the full name accorded to the church was "St. Luke's German Reformed Church at Juniata Turn." Its location may be further identified by being only a short distance from the summit of the Allegheny Mountain, near White Horse Inn, a hostelry famous in earlier days.

The building, a simple colonial type, was erected in the summer of 1861. The exterior was painted white as was also the interior woodwork and the pulpit, which was sufficiently commodious to support a Bible and an ornamental oil lamp on either side. The church was dedicated in October 1861. In addition to the pastor, Rev. F. A. Edmonds, the following ministers were present and took part in the service: William Conrad, D. H. Reiter, B. Knepper, and E. R. Eshbach.

At the organization meeting were present: James G. Glessner, Jacob B. Hillegass, Jeremiah Glessner, John L. B. Miller, John Hoyle, Henry Deeter, John Heckman, W. A. Brandt, W. Glessner, and George Glessner.

From this number they elected Jacob G. Glessner, elder; Jacob B. Hillegass and Jeremiah Glessner, deacons; John L. B. Miller, John Hoyle, Jacob B. Hillegass, trustees; Jacob B. Hillegass, John Heckman, Jeremiah Glessner, and John Hoyle, building committee; Jeremiah Glessner, treasurer.

The first communion record, June 8, 1862, contained the names of 28 members—13 male and 15 female. On the day prior eleven persons united with the church by confirmation: Jas. Alex Hillegass, Wm. Spencer, Wm. Hillegass, Geo. A. Brandt, Jacob Heckman, Margarette Heckman, Hannah Smith, Cordilla Brandt, Maria Ringler, Polly Brandt, Ellen Hoyle; four were received from the Evangelical Lutheran Church: Harry Miller, Levi Hoyle, Susanna Dieter, Amy A. Glessner; from the Evangelical Church: John L. B. Miller.

Under date of December 3, 1862, is found in the early minute book an interesting account of the accusation of Elder Henry Miller. The accused elder did not appear to answer charges preferred against him, but the consistory found him guilty, removed him from office, and suspended him from the communion of the church.

The congregation enjoyed a steady growth and after fifteen years had a membership of approximately 100. By 1886, St. Luke's had a membership of 125 members, when some 20 were dismissed to the newly organized Trinity congregation at Roxbury. The loss of these members was a severe blow to St. Luke's, which it never fully overcame. A decline set in and in 1915 reached its lowest point with 54 members.

During the pastorate of Rev. James B. Musser, the old church was razed and a new building, thirty by forty feet, took its place. This church was constructed by Alex Coughenour and Harry Glessner. The cornerstone was laid June 12, 1921, the pastor preaching the sermon. Deposited in the cornerstone were the following articles: New Testament, Heidelberg Catechism, historical sketch, one-dollar bill. Dedicatory services were held October 2, 1921, the pastor consecrating the church, and Rev. E. P. Skyles, a former pastor, preaching the sermon. The building cost, exclusive of much donated labor, about $2500.

Of late years the congregation has had its ups and downs. In 1932, Classis, ill advised, dissolved the congregation; but at a special meeting a few weeks later rescinded its action. While the congregation is a part of Glade Charge, it has been served by supply pastors since 1934.

The ministers who served from 1940 are:

1940-44	J. Keller Brantley
1945-47	Arthur J. Miller
1948-53	Alvin E. Master
1954-58	Dale E. Boyer
1958-60	No minister–supply pastors
1961-67	George B. Halteman
1967-69	No minister–supply pastors

No great project was undertaken from 1940 to 1950 other than the necessary minor repairs. In 1950 the church was wired and electricity was obtained. From 1951 through 1956 the basement was completed, and finished for Sunday school classes to meet in and use; the floor and pews were refinished; the chancel in the main auditorium was refurnished. The interior and exterior was kept painted as the need arose. In 1964, the committee priced and selected carpet, which was installed wall to wall in the entire auditorium.

During the 60's the Synod was urging all the small

St. Luke's (Mountain) Church

churches to merge into one large congregation, but with the Glade Charge, of which the Mountain Church was one of four churches, this did not meet too well and received opposition. After the departure of Rev. Halteman, 1967, the church officers again brought up the idea of a merger, but it was not to take place immediately. After a lengthy discussion for and against the merger, the Sunday of Jan. 3, 1969, was designated as the day for a vote to decide on a merger, but no closure. After the tally of votes that Sunday, there wasn't another service held in the Mountain Church, even though it was not to be considered a vote for closing at that time. The officers discontinued the worship services immediately.

Allegheny Township Cemeteries

Mt. Zion Cemetery—John Black donated ground about 1848. 359 graves.

Imhoff Cemetery—Allegheny Township near the village of Dividing Ridge on Daniel Hillegas farm in a field south of the Old Pike and adjoining the line of the W. A. Miller property, south of the buildings about 15 rods. 13 graves, oldest 1828.

Dorsey—On farm of Henry Weidner, north of the buildings about 15 rods in the fields above orchard. 7 graves, oldest 1840.

Shaffer—Shaffer Lutheran Church about a mile west of the village of Glen Savage. 93 graves, oldest 1842.

Priest Carmelite Cemetery—New Baltimore. 2 graves, oldest 1893.

Edward Grenke Farm—In orchard above house. 10 graves, oldest 1871.

Mountain Cemetery—St. Luke's Church. South of Route 31 near White Horse. 85 graves, oldest 1860.

Glen Savage—In village of Glen Savage. 54 graves, oldest 1873.

Brant Cemetery—On farm owned by Daniel Sweitzer,

in the field a few rods east of buildings and south of White Horse Tavern on Route 31—about one mile and a half. 3 inscribed graves, 17 uninscribed graves, oldest 1863.

McIntyre Cemetery—On McIntyre farm. South of White Horse Tavern. In a field about one and a half miles west of the buildings. 3 graves, no inscriptions.

Deeter Cemetery—On McLuckie Farm at the edge of the woods east of the buildings near an old lime quarry, and not far from St. Luke's Mountain Church. 5 graves, oldest 1783.

Miller Cemetery—On the farm now owned by Dalton Miller.

Sarver Cemetery—Located at the Sarver Community Church. Another located north of the Sarver Church in the woods.

Deeter Cemetery—On the old Deeter farm at Deeter's Gap, marked by a millstone.

There are many other burial plots, some marked and some not, located on various farms in the township.

Did You Know?

Pearl Coughenour Glessner taught school at the Felton School in 1902. This was her first year of teaching. Her salary was $22.50 per month. Her room and board was $7.00 per month. Another expense was her stockings which cost her ten cents per pair.

The second year, 1903, Pearl taught the Hillegass School, where she earned $35.00 per month and paid $7.00 per month for board.

Some of the duties of the teacher were building your own fire and cutting the kindling. On Friday evening coal was carried and kindling cut for Monday morning. During the week the fire was covered with coal to keep it burning until the next day.

Drinking water was carried by the bucket with one dipper for drinking shared by all.

Pearl was permitted to whip her pupils with a stick if punishment was needed. However, Pearl "spared the rod" and chose memorizing of poems and talking to the children as her method of discipline.

Water was carried from the creek to scrub the school floor about three times a year. The children shared the chore of scrubbing.

Fox-in-the-morning and ball were popular games played at recess. The girl wearing the largest apron was chosen catcher. The apron was used in place of a catcher's mitt. Another favorite sport at recess was the rolling of cornsilk into cigarettes and smoking in the outhouse.

The same clothing was usually worn the entire week. Sometimes the apron was worn on Monday to keep the dress clean. It was removed about Wednesday if sufficiently soiled and then just the dress was worn. Occasionally the dress was worn several days until soiled, then a clean apron worn the rest of the week to cover the dress.

A mother of twelve remembers the expense of each baby! Compare with prices of today!

Year			
1906 — first child	(midwife)	$1.00
1908 — second child	(midwife)	1.50
1910 — third child	(midwife)	2.00
1911 — fourth child	(midwife)	2.00
1913 — fifth child	(midwife)	2.00
1914 — sixth child	(midwife)	2.00
1916 — seventh child	(doctor)	10.00
1920 — eighth child	(doctor)	15.00
1922 — ninth child	(doctor)	15.00
1923 — tenth child	(doctor)	15.00
1927 — eleventh child	(doctor)	15.00
*1930 — twelfth child	(doctor)	35.00

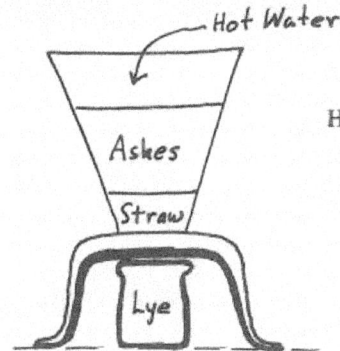

Rock-a-bye Baby

*All the children were born in Allegheny Township except number 12, who was born in Maryland.

Ash Hopper

Hot Water

Ashes

Straw

Lye

How to Make
Lye
For Soap

Ashes should be from hickory or hard wood.

Making Soft Soap

¾ Lye
¼ Fat
Put lye in iron kettle. When lye is boiling, put in fat (tallow, rinds, cracklings).
Cook until it turns thick.
Put in crocks to store until ready for use.

The Burst Family Orchestra, a group of local performers, appeared at a picnic at the Custer Church in 1907. The team of white horses and probably the wagon were owned by Henry Miller. The entertainers are as follows: Charles Deeter, driver; Milton Deeter, George Lane, Chalmer Deaner, Ralph Groft, and John Lane.

In 1905 a front quarter of beef sold for four cents per pound—the hind quarter for five cents per pound. Eggs sold for eight cents and sometimes six cents a dozen. One pound of coffee was eight cents. A yard of gingham, thirty-six inches wide, sold for five cents per yard. Sugar was a special order at four dollars per hundred pound. In 1910 a wooden barrel of flour cost seven dollars.

A meeting was held in the Mt. Zion School prior to 1940 to discuss the possibility of furnishing Allegheny Township with electricity.

Some of the men pictured who attended this meeting are Blair Powell, Andy Frazier, Roy Coughenour, and Richard Deaner.

A Cabin for $50!

By Ellen Rebecca Fenn
Washington, Iowa

Those faced with ever-higher costs of building homes can take heart from the summary below. Although it won't bring down today's costs, it is food for thought from olden times and may make us wonder if what we are experiencing today may seem like small potatoes to our descendants someday!

In 1890, the cost of building a pioneer's cabin (material only) of 10 by 12 feet was less than $50. Broken down here are the costs of "necessary" materials:

500 feet of 1-inch board, 16 feet long, for sides, ends, and gables	$9.00
275 feet of 1-inch boards, 16 feet long, for roof	4.90
209 feet of 1-inch boards, 12 feet long, for ceiling	3.60
230 feet of matched flooring, 16 feet long	4.60
17 pieces of 2 by 4, 16 feet long, and 6 pieces of 2 by 4, 12 feet long	4.62
1 window (4-light), 12 by 26 inches, including frame	3.00
300 pounds of number 1 tar paper for roof and sides	9.00
75 pounds of plain building paper for lining	1.88
200 lath for battens on roof and sides	.80
25 pounds of spike nails	1.50
Tacks for putting on lining inside	.50
Galvanized sheet iron for stovepipe, top to roof	.75
Door trimming	.75
Door frame lumber, 20 feet	.50

Entire cost of material	$48.90

The instructions accompanying the list of materials read:

"Anyone who can saw a board or drive a nail can put it up. If it is hired done, it should not cost over $12.00.

"To build, throw up a bank of earth about 1 foot high and 14 by 18 feet across. That thrown out of the cellar, which is 6 by 8 feet, can be used for banking."

These instructions may or may not be clear for today's carpenter, but they served well enough for the pioneer, no doubt, or we wouldn't be here to read about it! (Information from the American Agriculturist, November 1890.)

A Log Home

Instead of a log cabin this would probably be called a log house. The cost of constructing this house would undoubtedly compare to the cost of the log cabin.

This was the home of Adam and Mazie Werner located south of Route 31 on White Horse Mountain. This log house has been replaced by a new house which is the home of Karl and Marcelene Brick.

The Cider Press

Allegheny Township was not particularly noted for growing apples, but cider and apple butter were important contributions to the family larder (a pantry where meat and foodstuffs are kept). Cider and apple butter, which is made by boiling cider and apples together, aren't the only products derived from apples. As cider ages it changes into vinegar, which was and still is a widely used product.

An old beam type cider press was located on the Milton A. Hillegas farm near Dividing Ridge and was in operation as late as 1948. A huge, hewed, log beam supplied the pressure to squeeze the juice from the apples. The lever in the foreground has a seesaw motion to raise and lower the beam by hand. A platform is located near the opposite end of the beam, and the cider runs from there into barrels. At some presses the cider drained through rye straw into a wooden tank. This long rye straw made an excellent strainer. The straw and crushed apples, known as pomace or "pummies," were fed to the cattle.

In some instances the huge beam was mortised into a tree. Such a tree is still standing on the farm of Lee and Lorene Hoppert at Mt. Zion. The large oak tree had a hole completely through the center. Over the years it is gradually closing.

Hickory Rocking Chairs

Hickory rocking chairs have been built and used for many years. The more recent ones made in Allegheny Township were by Gust Woida, August Woida, Lee Woida, and Eugene O'Neil.

Although each individual has his own method of making rocking chairs, the fundamentals are basically the same. Hickory is cut usually during the fall and winter months. If it is cut after the sap comes up in the tree in the spring the bark will come loose when it is heated. Only small hickory trees are used, the largest being from 1¼" to 1½" in diameter. The smallest tree used would be no less than ½" in diameter.

After the hickory is gathered it should be dried for several weeks. The hickory pieces for the legs are then thoroughly heated in boiling water until it becomes pliable. It is then placed in a jig where it is bent and shaped. There it is left stand for about six weeks in order that the shaped pieces will not straighten.

Lumber such as dried oak, cherry, or ash is cut into boards. From these boards the rockers, slats, and seats are sawed. The slats which form the back of the chair are also heated in boiling water and placed in a jig to be bent into shape. The slats should remain in the jig for approximately one week. Wood filler is applied to the rockers, back slats, and seats of all open-grained wood.

The large circle of hickory used on the back of the chair is boiled and bent into shape by hand as it is needed for each chair. The smaller circles and half circles are heated, bent, and tied with twine to dry into shape. All knots on the hickory are trimmed, rasped, and sanded until smooth. The chair is now ready to be put together. As each piece is added to the chair it is sanded smooth. After the chair is completed it is varnished and ready to use.

Pine Valley Homemakers

The Pine Valley Homemakers Club of Allegheny Township has been organized for approximately twenty-one years. The Home Economist from the County Extension Office works with the group giving very informative homemaking material including recipes, household hints, shopping tips, and sewing lessons to name only a few. The Pine Valley Homemakers Club has an average membership of twelve to fifteen ladies, who usually meet once a month to learn a new craft or to do something creative.

The group also does some community service work. They make items for the guests at the Somerset County Home for the Aged in Berlin, such as bibs, lap robes, and gowns. Bandages and pads have also been made for the American Cancer Society. The ladies often participate in the annual County Homemakers Fair with displays and demonstrations.

One highlight of the year is the Pine Valley Christmas party, including a covered-dish meal and gift exchange with lots of homemaking discussions.

Take Me Back to Long Ago

When Dr. Shaw came across White Horse Mountain to
    doctor the sick,
When he trusted Old Dobbin, so faithful and slow,
He was lazy but steady, as sure as the fate,

He wasn't compelled to wear a license plate,
And though fleetless and speed, sometimes he would
    lack
He took him to the country, and brought him back.

If the roads were all muddy and slick from the rain,
He never would stop to put on the chain,
And when he was driving the old horse about
He never was known to have a blowout.
No tacks ever punctured stout inner tubes
As he jogged along the green country roads
And his spark plug never was known to go wrong
And each cylinder hit as he jogged along
His clutch never slipped, and there wasn't a hitch
And he never was known to slide in the ditch,
His bearings never were known to be loose
And his battery always had plenty of juice.
He always was ready from his nose to his flank
And never stopped to put gas in his tank,
He traveled along in the darkest of night
Without having to wear a pesky taillight.

No cop ever pinched him, or had a fine to pay,
Because he lacked license plates in front and behind.
But we long for those days when we had fewer cares
Before everything went for repairs,
Before everyone stepped hard on the gas,
And all of them tried each other to pass.
Oh how we long for those days of the surrey and chassis
And people of yore with the old-fashioned ways,
When the saddle and bridle were not obsolete
Before the time came, when the people, alas
Used their feet only to step on the gas.
But in 1905 Dr. Shaw got his first car in Berlin,
He still crossed the White Horse Mountain to doctor the
    sick.

Written by Emma Robb - age 83

The Country Store

At the bottom of the Allegheny Mountain
Albert Miller had a country store.
He sold candy for a penny
With his name above the door.
Over the same counter
You could buy sugar, coffee, or butter,
Axle grease, candy, or kerosine,
Spice by the berry, powder, or ground,
Crackers or cookies by the pound,
Salt by the barrel,
Prunes by the box.

You paid a dollar for a pair of shoes
With a free pair of socks.
Those days are all over,
But I never forgot
How a dollar was something
One seldom ever got.
I am telling you, friend,
As I've said before,
I would like to go back
To that old country store.

Written by Emma Robb - age 83

Bicentennial Wagon Train

In June 1976 the Bicentennial Wagon Train moved through Somerset County. The Pennsylvania Bicentennial Wagon left Pasadena, California, after participating in the Rose Bowl Parade on New Year's Day, 1976, and traveled continuously. Other wagons joined along the way. On June 20, 1976, the Bicentennial Wagon Train, consisting of approximately thirty-five wagons and many horses and riders, traveled from Somerset east to

233

the Mt. Zion area in Allegheny Township for their night's encampment.

The Bell Telephone Pioneers of America, Evergreen Council, Greensburg, Pa., planted a Colorado Blue Spruce Tree at each encampment. This tree was planted on the lawn of Kenneth and Charlene Norris.

The pioneers of America traveled westward to establish homes and develop this country. The National Bicentennial Wagon Train traveled eastward to Valley Forge to celebrate the two hundredth anniversary of the United States of America.

Allegheny Township Today

Today farming and lumbering are still important to the livelihood of the people of Allegheny Township. With lots of mountainous area and small streams, hunting and fishing are both quite popular.

One of the largest and most modern maple syrup evaporating plants is located in the township north of New Baltimore. It is owned and operated by B. F. Walters of Somerset. There is also a country store in con-

nection with the maple syrup industry. Mr. Walters is involved in farming, with the complete operation being known as "Mountain Meadow Farms."

Over the years changes have taken place. Many small farms are no longer in operation. Also, quite a few people are employed in other areas to earn their living but continue to live in the township.

New Baltimore Borough

St. John's Church
New Baltimore, Penna.

New Baltimore Committee

Father Robert C. Flaherty, O. Carm.
John Will
Mary Hankinson - co-chairman
Mary Ellen Hankinson - co-chairman

Contributors

John Fochtman
John Hankinson
John Restley
William Flamm
Ray Hankinson
Jeff Lamens

A History of New Baltimore, Pennsylvania

In the latter part of the eighteenth century, Michael Riddlemoser, a resident of Baltimore, Maryland, a man of some wealth and evidently of an adventurous spirit, came westward from Bedford through Harman's Bottom. This territory later was known as Moserburg, no doubt in honor of the founder, and afterward as New Baltimore, after Baltimore, Maryland, through which port most of the immigrants came. For small sums of money Mr. Riddlemoser purchased tracts of land from those who had patented claims, and finding tracts unclaimed, obtained patents for them.

As there were already a few scattered families of Catholics in what is now St. John's Parish, New Baltimore, and as this section lay midway between the Pittsburgh Pike (Route 30) and the Glade Pike (Route 31), then the main arteries of travel, Mr. Riddlemoser thought it an excellent location for a Catholic settlement and college. The land, covered with virgin forest, was well watered and healthful. Bears, panthers, wolves, and deer were plentiful and the mountain streams abounded in fish, especially brook trout.

Mr. Riddlemoser selected a site for a church and plotted a town adjoining the church property. He likewise surveyed and plotted locations for a college and convent, but this part of his dream was never realized, at least in the sense conceived by him. His plan may be called a dream, for Father Lambing says, "No sooner were the foundations of the settlement laid than plans were formed, as we learn from an article in the Bedford Gazette, for the erection of a Catholic university. The size and style of the buildings were specified and expectations were excited that were never realized."

Having returned to Baltimore, the zealous promoter was anxious to see the settlement grow and sent all immigrants he could from Baltimore, Maryland, where so many of the German and Irish landed. He promised them a Catholic church building as soon as a sufficient number would warrant the expense. To satisfy their religious obligations they were compelled to go to Bedford,

St. John's Catholic Church

View of New Baltimore before the turnpike was built

Borough of New Baltimore

then only occasionally attended by a priest (very likely Father Gallitzin). The immigrants were poor and very few had horses, oxen being generally used in farming. Yet, strong in body as well as in faith, walked fasting, to Bedford, twenty miles distant, in order to receive Holy Communion.

Difficulty in the practice of their religion was only one of the hardships, which the New Baltimore settlers, like all pioneers, had to endure.

The nearest flour mill was in Pittsburgh; some of the pioneers made occasional trips there, packing their grain and flour on horses. Nearly two weeks were required to make the trip. To satisfy their need, Riddlemoser erected a waterpower grist and sawmill on the Raystown branch of the Juniata River, making full provisions for the water rights of the mill which was operated until 1934. It served the community for many miles around for over a century. The log house he erected for the Miller family is still in good repair and is a historic landmark. It was erected in 1820. In the same year the first grocery store of the settlement was opened by John O'Neil, in a room of the Miller house; and a beginning was made to erect a church.

Riddlemoser began the erection of a stone church building 25 by 30 feet, in 1820. It stood just about two rods west of the center of the old cemetery. The building progressed very slowly and was not finished until the spring of 1824. However, it was not dedicated until January, 1826, the Reverend Thomas Heyden of Bedford officiating at the ceremony. A rectory of logs was erected some time later, being located north of the old church, about where the sanctuary of the present brick church stands.

On October 4, 1823, Mr. Riddlemoser conveyed one hundred acres and ninety perches to Anthony Lucken, Barnabas Riffle, Sr., and Jacob Riffle, for the consideration of one dollar, as trustees, for the use of the Roman Catholic congregation and for the officiating priest therein "who shall at all times have the privilege of residence thereon, receiving all the rents and profits for his own use and by disposing of same during his Minority (sic) as he may think proper, provided always that such priest shall be a regular member of the Roman Catholic Church and his appointment be approved and sanctioned by the regular Bishop of said Church for the State of Pennsylvania or that district in which said land is situated."

Moreover, on May 25, 1829, he conveyed land from Jeremiah Parker to Anthony Lucken, Jacob Riffle, and Patrick Rice as trustees, fifty acres for the express purpose of establishing and supporting a Roman Catholic school. Also, three acres, "which shall be leased, or rented to some person or persons, who shall found or erect thereon a Roman Catholic College to be used and applied to that use alone." Also, thirty lots of ground in Mosersburg and other land, altogether 2,460 acres and 132 perches. The same is to be leased to parties for 99 years, renewable forever for the benefit of the pastor of St. John the Baptist Church. The lease rent is due annually on April 1.

The history of education and the school in New Baltimore is clouded in some obscurity. Whoever is responsible for the history of New Baltimore found in the "History of Bedford, Somerset and Fulton Co., Pennsylvania," says, "At New Baltimore the first school was organized in the Catholic Church in 1830. A schoolhouse was built in 1863. S. M. Topper was the first teacher in this building. The citizens of the Borough generally are interested in the school."

Mr. Lucken says, "A school was opened during the summer of 1874 and was taught by Father Joseph Walsh. The school had an enrollment of 39 pupils." This was a parish school, and the parish records show the tuition to have been fifty cents a month.

"In 1884 a parish hall was erected on the corner of South Street and the Alley in the church meadow. It was used for the parish recreational affairs and also as a school room. In the summer of several years a parochial school was held here and was taught by Mary Callahan and later by Alice Callahan. It usually had an enrollment of about forty pupils. In later years it was also used for public school classes. When Father Theodore became pastor (1890), he decided to establish a parochial school with nuns as teachers. As nuns were permitted to teach in the public schools at that time, they would teach public school in winter and a short term of parochial school in summer. Four Benedictine Sisters were secured and the former home of Michael and Anna Krone was purchased as a convent. The church hall being used that time as a church, classes were held in the Topper storeroom, which was not in use, the store having moved elsewhere. Later classes were held in the hall. The school was attended by ninety pupils.

"About the year 1895 a law, known as the Garb Bill, was passed by the State Legislature, forbidding teachers to wear a dress indicative of religious belief. This placed a double burden on the people of the parish. The financial condition of the parish made the upkeep of both public and parochial school impossible. After about five years the parochial school was closed and the convent building sold." Since then the children have attended public

Grade school

239

Gristmill

school in town until it was destroyed by fire in the spring of 1958. After the fire the children completed the school year having their classes in the rooms in the basement of St. John's Church. Since the fall of 1958, all the school children from New Baltimore (grades 1 through 12) have attended classes at Berlin Brothersvalley Schools.

In its early days New Baltimore was an almost self-contained and self-sufficient community, every kind of trade and calling being represented. At one time there were in the territory of New Baltimore parish several grist and sawmills, wagon and blacksmiths' shops, a cooper's shop, four distilleries, etc. Special mention must be made of the furniture and altar-building establishment of Henry Engbert, which in its day supplied many churches in the Diocese of Pittsburgh with equipment. The woodwork, altars, and pews in the New Baltimore church are specimens of its work. All the woodwork in St. Brigit-St. Benedict the Moor Church (near the Arena), Pittsburgh, with the exception of the altars, comes from New Baltimore.

Although it can be safely said that New Baltimore substantially realized the dreams of its founder, it has not realized the dreams of many who came later on, and who saw in modern inventions and in the growth of American cities, a like future for New Baltimore. True, at its inception it possessed avenues of approach equal to

Furniture and altar manufacturing shop

those of other places in the country; but the new means of communication, so powerful in shaping the development of America, never touched New Baltimore and in fact left it almost inaccessible. The first blow to New Baltimore's chance of greatness was the building of the Pennsylvania Canal which drew nearly all travel from the pikes near New Baltimore. The next great blow was the failure of the South Penn. Railroad to pass through

240

John Werner's Cooper Shop

Main Street of New Baltimore

Another view of New Baltimore's Main Street

Mountain View Hotel

bringing with it opportunities for employment and, eventually, further development of communication and travel to the people of New Baltimore. The parish church of St. John the Baptist became known as "The Church of the Pike" because of the accessibility to it from the turnpike by way of the stairs leading from the level of the turnpike.

The history of New Baltimore and the parish church of St. John the Baptist intertwine so that one includes the other. The church or parish was established in 1820 as a part of the Diocese of Philadelphia and the priests from Bedford were the first to minister to the needs of the people. In 1830, New Baltimore became a part of the Diocese of Pittsburgh and in 1901 a part of the present Diocese of Altoona-Johnstown. Until 1850 the parishioners were ministered to by visiting priests. In 1850, the parish was designated as a residential pastorate. In 1850, Father Joseph Theresius Gozowsky, O.C.D., became the first resident pastor. In the next twenty years, ten different priests served as pastors. During the pastorate of Father Patrick Brown, beginning in 1869, a mission was established at Sand Patch, Somerset County, to serve the religious needs of the workers of the Baltimore and Ohio Railroad during the building of its Connellsville division. In 1870 the Carmelite Fathers were assigned as pastors of St. Johns.

Father Norbert Baush, O.Carm., was the first Carmelite pastor. His first project was the building of a three-story brick rectory, forty feet by forty, to replace the old log rectory which had become dilapidated. With the coming of the Carmelite Fathers, the parish became more united and conditions more stable and in time many things were done in the parish and town.

In 1880 a steeple eighty-four feet high was erected, the bell hung therein, and the old belfry near the sacristy was raised. A new two-story barn was erected about the same time. An addition was made to the cemetery about 1882. In 1884 a parish hall was erected at the corner of South Street and alley in the church meadow.

In 1887 the Carmelite students of theology came to New Baltimore to continue their studies. The Carmelite

New Baltimore as planned. New Baltimore, situated at the foot of the great grades through the mountains, was expected to furnish the best location for necessary railroad yards.

Then, in 1940, came a change. The Pennsylvania Turnpike was constructed along most of the path of the original roadbed of the old South Penn. Railroad. As a result it passed through the borough of New Baltimore

New Baltimore after the Pennsylvania Turnpike was built

students remained until 1910 when they were moved to Chicago. Students, as novices, returned to New Baltimore in 1936. For the next thirty-two years many young men of the Carmelite Order learned to pray and to become a religious in the hills of New Baltimore. The novices moved away, again, in 1968.

In 1890 the present-day church building was begun and finished. The interior, however, was completed only in 1894, when the addition to the monastery was completed. The work of restoration and beautifying of the church building was done in the spring of 1972. This followed the construction of the new parish hall which was begun in 1968 and dedicated in 1970. The most recent development has been that of of a playground for the parish and community on the grounds near the parish hall.

While the population of the parish of St. John the Baptist consists of more than 180 families and over 650 souls, the population of New Baltimore borough itself is 79 families and 232 men, women, and children.

Postmasters at New Baltimore

Post Office Established on October 12, 1876

Postmasters	Appointment Dates Through September 30, 1971
Gregory Hankinson	October 12, 1867
Miss Anne Hankinson	March 20, 1872
William Gillespie	May 1, 1872
Francis J. Gillespie	May 3, 1875
William Gillespie	February 24, 1879
George E. Hufford	October 10, 1881
John M. Topper	September 8, 1885
John Ross	July 11, 1890
Bernard Wolfhope	May 18, 1893
Francis V. Topper	June 22, 1895
Abraham P. Riffle	December 6, 1900
Joseph Topper	July 13, 1915
Miss Sarah Hankinson	February 21, 1920
Miss Josephine M. Engbert	June 10, 1935 (Assumed Charge)
	June 12, 1935 (Acting)
	October 5, 1935 (Confirmed)
John J. Hankinson	February 1, 1948 (Assumed Charge)
Mrs. Regina Hankinson	August 5, 1948 (Confirmed)
	September 11, 1948 (Assumed Charge)
Edward J. Will	April 1, 1968 (Assumed Charge)
	July 31, 1971 (Appointed)

Post office of 1908

Present-day post office in New Baltimore

Present St. John's Church and Carmelite Monastery

Covered bridge in New Baltimore built in 1879

World War I Veteran, Henry Hankinson

Hankinson's Market, present-day store

Lamens' Garage owned and operated by Roger and Jeff Lamens

Oldest resident of New Baltimore - Mr. Henry Hankinson and wife

New Baltimore Restaurant of George Hankinson

New Baltimore borough occupies a picturesque location on the upper waters of the Raystown branch of the Juniata River in the foothills of the Allegheny Mountains. The town retains a population of over two hundred, 99 percent of whom are members of the Catholic Parish of St. John the Baptist in the Diocese of Altoona—Johnstown. Most of the people of New Baltimore are of German origin whose forebears came to the United States seeking religious freedom.

Anthony Luken was one of the earliest settlers in New Baltimore, who settled there about 1820. Among early settlers were Henry Wolfhope, Francis Weber, Abraham Riffle, Peter Topper, Wendelin Werner, and Gregory Hankinson, most of whom settled in the village or its vicinity between 1830 and 1840.

New Baltimore was incorporated in 1874. Adam George was the first burgess. Those who have filled the office since then are: Adam George (two terms), Peter Bridge, Christian M. Stouffer, Wm. Wolfhope, W. A. Garman, F. A. Warner (two terms) J. W. Dull, F. A. Warner, A. P. Riffle (two terms), F. A. Warner, Joseph Topper (two terms), F. A. Warner (three terms), Martin Dull, J. J. Gardill, F. A. Warner (two terms). Joseph Topper

The present members of the New Baltimore Borough Council are James Lynch, mayor, John J. Hankinson, president, Donald L. Lynch, secretary, Margie

Hankinson, treasurer, George F. Will, Harold Will, O'Connell Will and Patrick J. Stoe.

Reverend Father Robert C. Flaherty, O.Carm., is the Pastor of the Parish of St. John the Baptist, New Baltimore, and the Prior, i.e., Superior, of the Carmelite Monastery, New Baltimore. Other members of the Carmelite Community include Reverand Father Zachary H. Monet, O.Carm., who has charge of the Mission of St.

Gregory, MacDonaldton, Pa., Reverend Wilfrid A. Smith, O.Carm., and Reverend Father George D. Egan, O.Carm., who are retired and Brother Stanislaus Reybitz, O.Carm.

References: The Sword (Carmelite Fathers Publications)
            Vol. III (1939)
            Vol. IV (1940)

Northampton Township

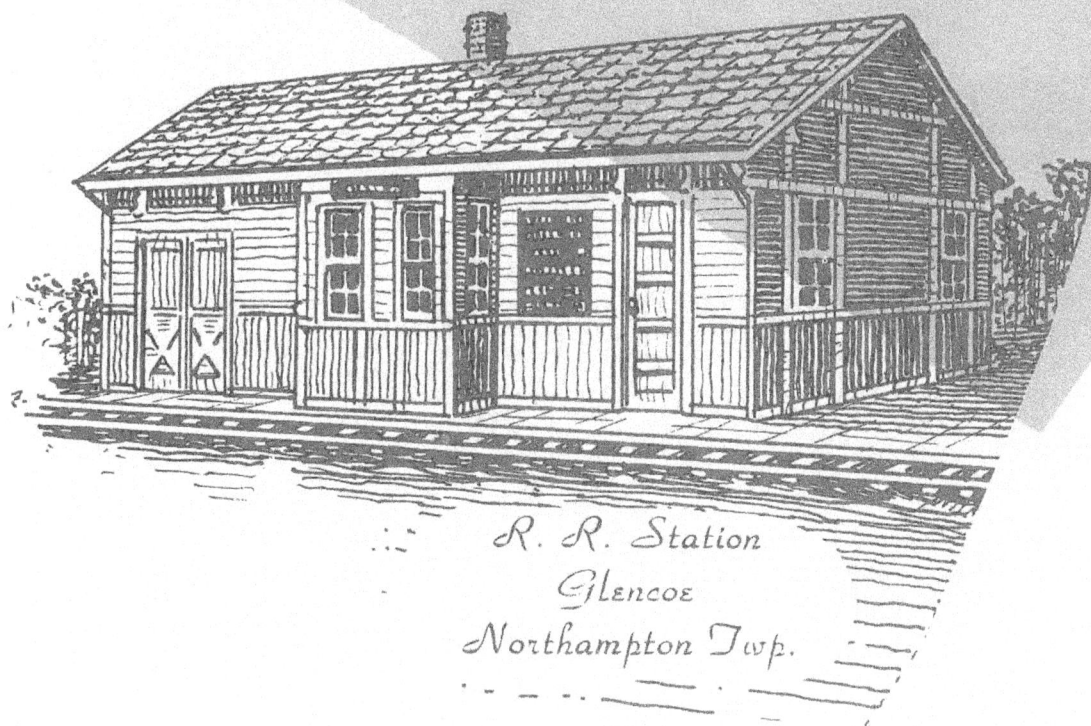

R. R. Station
Glencoe
Northampton Twp.

Northampton Township Committee

Marjorie C. Hay - chairman
Carl A. Hay
Jubal E. Werner

Contributors

Mary Hartman
Hulda Raupach
Mabel Snyder
Leo Bittner
Robert Cook

Northampton Township

Northampton Township was formed in 1851 out of a part of Southampton Township. Like all the other parts of Somerset County that lie east of the Allegheny Mountain, the township is rough and mountainous.

Some of the first settlers of the township were Phillip Poorbaugh, (earlier spelling Burbach), Benjamin Critchfield, Christian Albright, Jonathan Boyer, Jacob Coughenour, Henry Mull, and Jacob Flickinger.

Phillip Burbach (descendants later chose the spellings of Poorbaugh and Purbaugh), one of the earliest pioneers, immigrated from Germany. He came to America on the ship "Recovery," which arrived in Philadelphia on October 31, 1771, where he signed the Oath of Allegiance to Great Britain on the same day. The journey to Somerset county was through valleys, across un-bridged streams, and over hills. One had to be on guard day and night. The region where Phillip settled was rugged and mountainous and required great courage and determination on part of the settlers to clear the land and make it fit for cultivation. Among these hills the settlers built their homes and cleared the land, sowed, and planted.

Phillip Burbach, a Revolutionary War veteran, was a farmer and in 1793 he received a warrant for 710 acres of land in Northampton Township. All of the original grant, though divided, is still under cultivation.

The first schoolroom was held in his residence in 1796. He employed a German schoolteacher, Charles Peterman, and all the neighborhood children were invited to attend classes. This was the nucleus of our present school system.

The first record of a school building indicated the erection of one in 1816 on an adjoining farm of Phillip Poorbaugh, the Bridegum School. This school was closed in 1924.

In 1774, Jonathan Boyer got a tract of land. The agreement stated that if any gold or silver was found on this parcel of land, the sovereign of England would retain one fourth of it. As was often customary, the owner was buried on his own property, due to lack of established cemeteries. Boyer was buried here, along with eight other bodies, on what is known as the Conrod Werner Farm. This tract of land is now owned by Mary E. Werner. The Brushcreek School is built on this tract. The school was built in 1876. The ground was obtained by a lease and agreement. When the school was discontinued, the land reverted back to the owner of the farm.

The school was closed in 1941. The building still stands and is in good condition. There are two scholars still living who attended school here before 1900. They are Mary Deist Ackerman, 84 years old, and Wilson Martz, 96 years old.

Jubal Werner, 81 years old, started to school here in 1901. The first Brushcreek School was built sometime around 1840. It stood somewhere in the area where Melvin Cook now lives. It was also used as a place of worship before churches were built. It was torn down in

First Brushcreek School and house of worship before churches were established—sometime in early 1800's.

Brushcreek School, built in 1876.

Bauman School

the early 1900s.

The Bauman School is still standing. It was built in 1875 on the property now owned by the Charles Merrill heirs. There are still three persons living who attended school here before 1900. They are Ora Bauman Zimmerman, 89 years old, Irving Ackerman, 85 years old, and Harry Ackerman, 83 years old.

The third school still standing is the Philson School. This school was built at a place called Roddy's, along Laurel Run Creek near Wills Creek and the B & O Railroad. Jubal Werner taught school here in 1914-15. When there were no more scholars it was later moved to Philson. Glencoe, Wagaman, Brushcreek, Bauman, and Philson were all closed in 1941, when they consolidated with Berlin-Brothersvalley.

The historic Wills Creek, which rises in Larimar Township, flows through almost the entire length of the township from west to east. The railroad also follows the same stream, and the building of the railroad somewhat enhanced the value of the land in this township. It is believed that there were already sawmills of the old-fashioned type in the township, but about 1845 Henry Thomas Weld, an Englishman by birth, acquired holdings of timberlands that covered about twelve thousand acres. He built a sawmill of a different type. The mill, of course, derived its power from Wills Creek. This mill was operated by Mr. Weld for probably more than forty years, and quite a village—known as Southampton Mills—grew up around it.

Mr. Weld also built a gristmill that was operated by water too. It was later known as Earl's Mill, then Altfather's, and finally Cook's.

There was also a gristmill on the Brushcreek, known as Deal's Mill. It was built by a man named Wysel. A portion of the millrace can still be seen. It was built before the Civil War. There was also a sawmill at Deal's Mill.

The first B & O Railroad came into existence in 1865. The first train made its run in September, 1869. The railroad crosses the township from east to west. The two engineers who ran the survey for the B & O Railroad were Glen and Coe, thus the name Glencoe. It is a small town in the southeastern part of the township, along the main line of the B & O. The town was laid out by David Hay and Hiram Findlay in 1870.

The hotel in Glencoe was built by David Hay in 1874. Samuel Witt was the first landlord and Joseph Sheets, the first proprietor. It was a thriving business for many years due to the building of the railroad. It gave employment to many men, and families moved into the village. John Kessler later purchased the property and operated the inn, later leasing it to U. S. Gallagher. William Christner was the next proprietor in 1901. Charles Hoos took charge of the hotel in 1903 and Arthur Sharp of Salisbury was proprietor from 1906 to 1909. Again, Mr. Kessler conducted the hotel until 1911, when George G. DeLozier of Sand Patch purchased the business and property from Mr. Kessler. Mr. DeLozier was manager and proprietor of the hotel until 1918, when he closed the hotel and purchased the I. D. Leydig Store. This ended the business and many people moved away in search of jobs. The building was torn down in 1944.

The Glencoe Post Office was established in 1881 and S. P. Poorbaugh was the first postmaster. Now, in 1976, the post office is still in operation and Orlene Raupach is

Philson School

Wills Creek and B & O bridge below Glencoe

Steam engine—passenger train

Small village of Glencoe

Residence and store of I. D. Leydig, later residence and store of G. G. DeLozier. Taken 1919.

the postmistress. The first mail was delivered on horseback on what was known as the Old Cumberland Mail Road from Cumberland to Mt. Pleasant in the early 1800s. It passed through the township, starting on top of Savage Mountain to Glencoe, then up the east side of the Allegheny Mountain to Brothersvalley Township.

Glencoe post office with Laura Martz, postmistress, and George Cook, assistant rural mail carrier. Taken 1937.

Glencoe Hotel: Whipp, J. K. Kessler, Kate Smith, Mrs. Samuel Smith, J. L. Snyder, Elliard, Jonathan Martz, Mrs. J. K. Kessler, Jim Snyder, Soloman Martz, Noah and Mrs. Martz, Mollie Martz

The oldest house in the township still stands, but no one lives in it. It is on the farm owned by Leora Deist. There are a number of log houses in the township with portions of frame built to them.

In 1905, the Somerset Oil and Gas Company drilled a well near Philson's station in search of oil and gas. The well was sunk to a depth of 3,000 feet and then abandoned. Salt strong enough to float an egg was obtained from the well, but the company was not seeking salt. About a half mile away is another abandoned well at which salt was manufactured about 1850. A kettle that was used for the boiling of salt is still in existence.

There also was a mineral spring at one time on the farm of Alfred Broadwater, now owned by Richard Colliver.

The township had a distillery in the late 1800s on the farm owned by Nelson Bittner. It went by the name of Reese Distillery.

Before the township was formed, people had to go to Kennel's Mill to vote. Until a permanent election house was established, voting took place in the summerhouse on the John Poorbaugh farm, now owned by Samuel J. Poorbaugh.

Sometime in the 1800s we had the following tradesmen:

Chauncy Stoner - carpenter and blacksmith. He built the Conestoga wagon, which is on display at New Centerville.

Augustus Dom - maintained the first store in 1869

Henry Spangler - carpenter

W. H. Shoemaker - undertaker. He built caskets in what is now the Glencoe Post Office.

From the 1903 Somerset County Directory we have the following as contractors and builders:

W. H. Gaither - Glencoe

Frank Scheller - Johnsburg

The following were general merchandisers:

I. D. Leydig - Glencoe

Eli Martz - Glencoe

C. S. Martz - Glencoe

W. H. Miller - Johnsburg

The following were lumber dealers:

Charles and George Scheller - Johnsburg

The following were ministers:

J. D. Hunsecker - Glencoe

Henry Steager - Johnsburg

There was one physician:

Levi Weaver - Glencoe

Later in the 1900s we have George Elrich as the undertaker and casket maker.

Blacksmiths were:

Jacob Emerick

Harvey T. Meyers

Conrod and William Shiller

Gideon and Irene Werner

County Commissioner - **Samuel Wesley Poorbaugh**

Squire of Northampton Township - **John Miller** - Johnsburg

A Civil War veteran is buried close to the Glencoe U.C.C. parsonage. It is on the ground owned by Eugene

The old Tidenburg house and farm presently owned by The Merrill Family of Berlin.

The Bauman brothers and sister. Harry seated fourth in front row had the Conestoga wagon built for him by Chauncy Stoner.

Glessner. There is a veteran's marker there. Also, several persons are buried across from the John Leydig residence. Several stones were there at one time but they were destroyed.

The village of Johnsburg dates back to about 1866, when the German Lutheran Church was built. John M. Steif built the first house and opened a store in 1868. A post office was established in 1871, which is no longer there. The church still stands.

The area of Northampton Township is 21,552 acres or about thirty-three square miles. It contained 52 farms and had a population of 485 persons in 1930. The 1975 census show a population of 381. This consists of 98 school-age children, 32 preschool age, and 68 retired persons. There are 28 farms in the township.

The following organizations are held once a month in the township.

4H Group - Leader - Mrs. Roy Ogburn

Homemakers Group - Leader - Mrs. Walter Stahl

Christian Fellowship

1928—April 27-29. The late deep snow.

1930—The great drought.

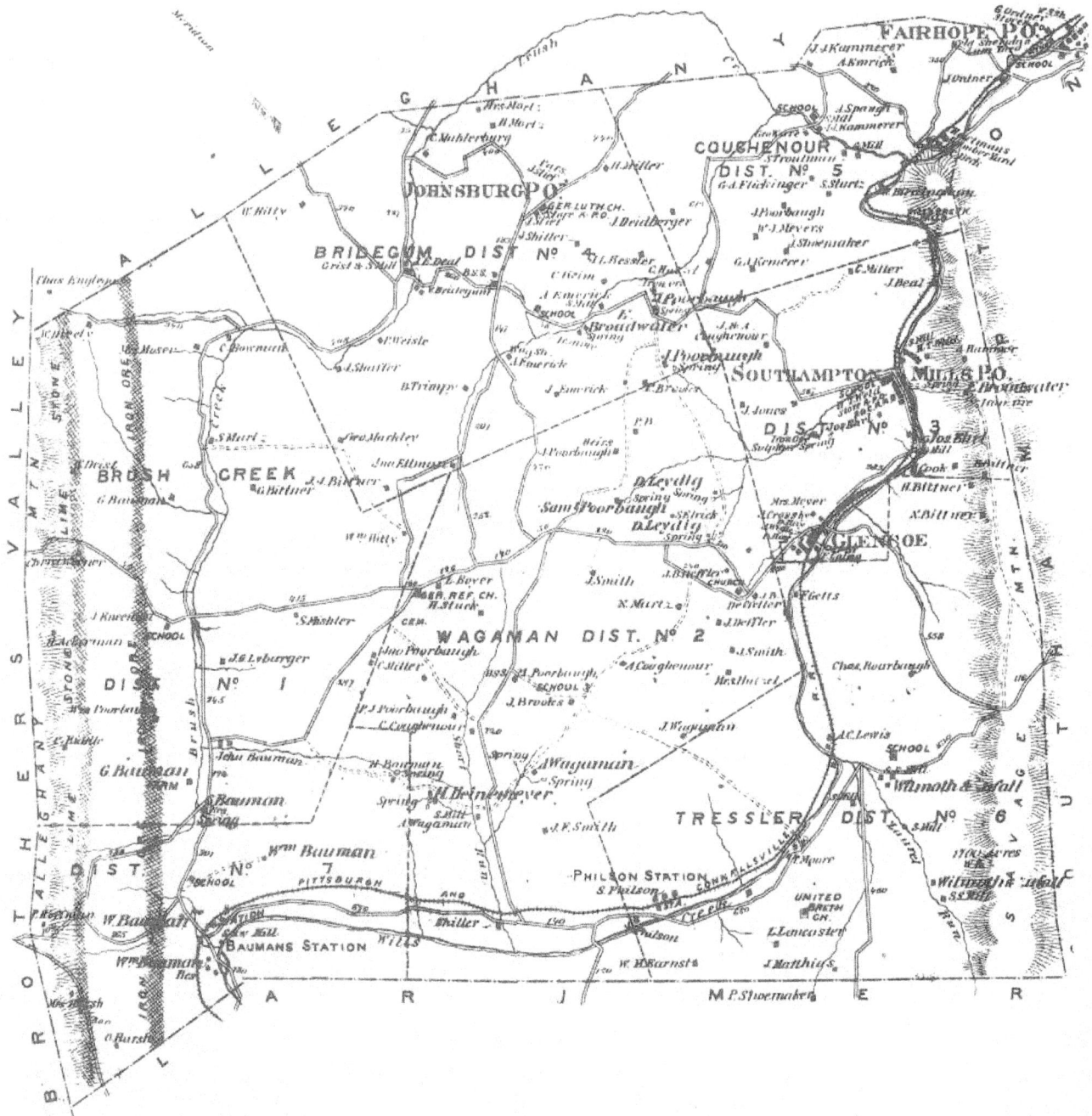

Map of Northampton showing school districts (1876)

The first schooolhouse was built on the farm of Valentine Bridegum, and in it a German school was taught in 1816. The township (then included in Southampton Township) adopted the free schools in 1835.

Tabular Statement for the year ending June 2, 1873: Northampton Township had six schools, five months of school, five male teachers and one female. Average salary for male was $23.80 a month; female: $22.00 a month. Expenditures for teachers' wages for the township for the year: $698.50.

Professor J. B. Whipkey was county superintendent of schools from 1875 to 1881.

Tabular Statement for the year ending June 5, 1882: Average months taught were five. Number of pupils attending: 155. Total expenditures: $1,534.27.

Second Annual Report of the Superintendent of Common Schools of Township, year end 1889, J. M. Berkey, County Superintendent.

School	Teacher	
Southampton	Mary L. Yeager	$24.00
Bridegum	C. C. Heckle	$23.00
Wagaman	G. H. Bauman	$23.00
Brushcreek	H. W. Boyer	$24.00
Smoky Hollow	H. C. Keihm	$24.00
Rhoddy School	B. F. Wagaman	$23.00

Rhoddy School was built in 1889 at a cost of $500.

The teachers received an aggregate increase in wages over the previous year. This was equivalent to an increase of sixty-seven cents in the average monthly salary of each teacher.

School directors for the year beginning June 3, 1889, for the township were:

Henry Martz, Johnsburg
John H. Miller, Johnsburg
George Market, Johnsburg
Christian Werner, Berlin
William Jackson Meyers, Glencoe
Samuel Poorbaugh, Glencoe

Glencoe covered bridge. The only one the township had. It was built in the 1800's and torn down in August of 1956.

William Hosselrode and his ash wagon. He hauled the ashes from the B & O water tower to the the township roads.

Village of Glencoe in 1919, showing main line of B & O

A B. & O. wreck on Roddy's Curve near Glencoe which happened on December 12, 1912, at 12 o'clock midnight. The train's brakes failed and the whole train wrecked, killing several men. It took months before the wreckage was cleared away.

Glencoe B & O Railroad station with J. L. Snyder, station agent. He worked for the B & O for 44 years, 42 of them in Glencoe.

Maple Products Years Ago

Let us first think about the maple syrup after it has been boiled from maple water into maple syrup. Almost every person who had a few sugar maple trees made maple sugar and syrup. In the beginning, very little syrup was made since it was very hard to preserve, usually only enough to last for two or three months; but sometimes it would keep until midsummer. Most of the syrup was stored in open wooden vessels or jars and the syrup would form its own mold. As long as this mold remained blue, the syrup would keep. However, if it turned gray, the syrup had soured. Tin cans or syrup cans did not come into use until about 1890 and were crude-looking cans which held one gallon. These were used more generally until about 1916 when 50-gallon drums were used. The syrup was then graded according to quality beginning with number one and on down because hundreds of gallons in these cans were shipped out of the area. The price per gallon at that time was about 40¢ and now it ranges from $10 to $12 per gallon.

Maple sugar: People who made maple syrup and had more than they could use in a short while would make some of it into sugar cakes and crumb sugar because in this form it could be stored longer. It could then be converted into syrup again should the need arise. Most of the cakes were made into half-pound and one-pound cakes, which were easily kept in a dry place.

There was a time when a lot of the syrup was made into cake sugar. This was kept in wooden buckets and each held about 40 pounds and lasted for about three seasons. The cake sugar was the easiest way to keep the syrup and was also the best method to preserve the syrup. Today it is still a real novelty.

Many farmers made sugar to help with expenses of running their farms and for those "little extras." These would be the farmers having a lot of sugar trees, sugar keelers, and men to take care of them.

I remember when no less than 20 to 25 persons tapped trees for syrup and sugar. There were 10 persons along Brushcreek who had camps. We, the Werners, had 1,150 keelers; the Mulenbergs, 750 to 800; the Fred Millers, 1,000; Walt Lanes, 750 or more. The more maple trees you had, the nicer the sugar and syrup. A hard maple never produced a good sugar or syrup.

At one time the Berlin merchants were the leading sugar and syrup buyers around. Mr. Charles Cook shipped carload after carload of maple sugar. Salisbury was also a loading place for maple products at this time. Brothersvalley, Stonycreek, Allegheny Township, and Northampton Township were also great shippers of these products at this time.

I, myself, made many hundreds of pounds of crumb sugar in my time—as high as 300 pounds in one day. However, that time has gone by—I couldn't do it today!

Jubal E. Werner
Northampton Township

Valhalla Sugar Camp

Cook's Store

The store was originally a frame building alongside of the present site, and was operated by James and Ella Bittner, mother and stepfather of the Cooks. In 1933, after the death of James Bittner, it was operated by Bob and Newton Cook. The present building was built about 1949. Since the death of Newton Cook, in 1953, it has been operated by Bob and Alice Cook, the present owners, who live in the apartment above the store and service station.

Cook's Store

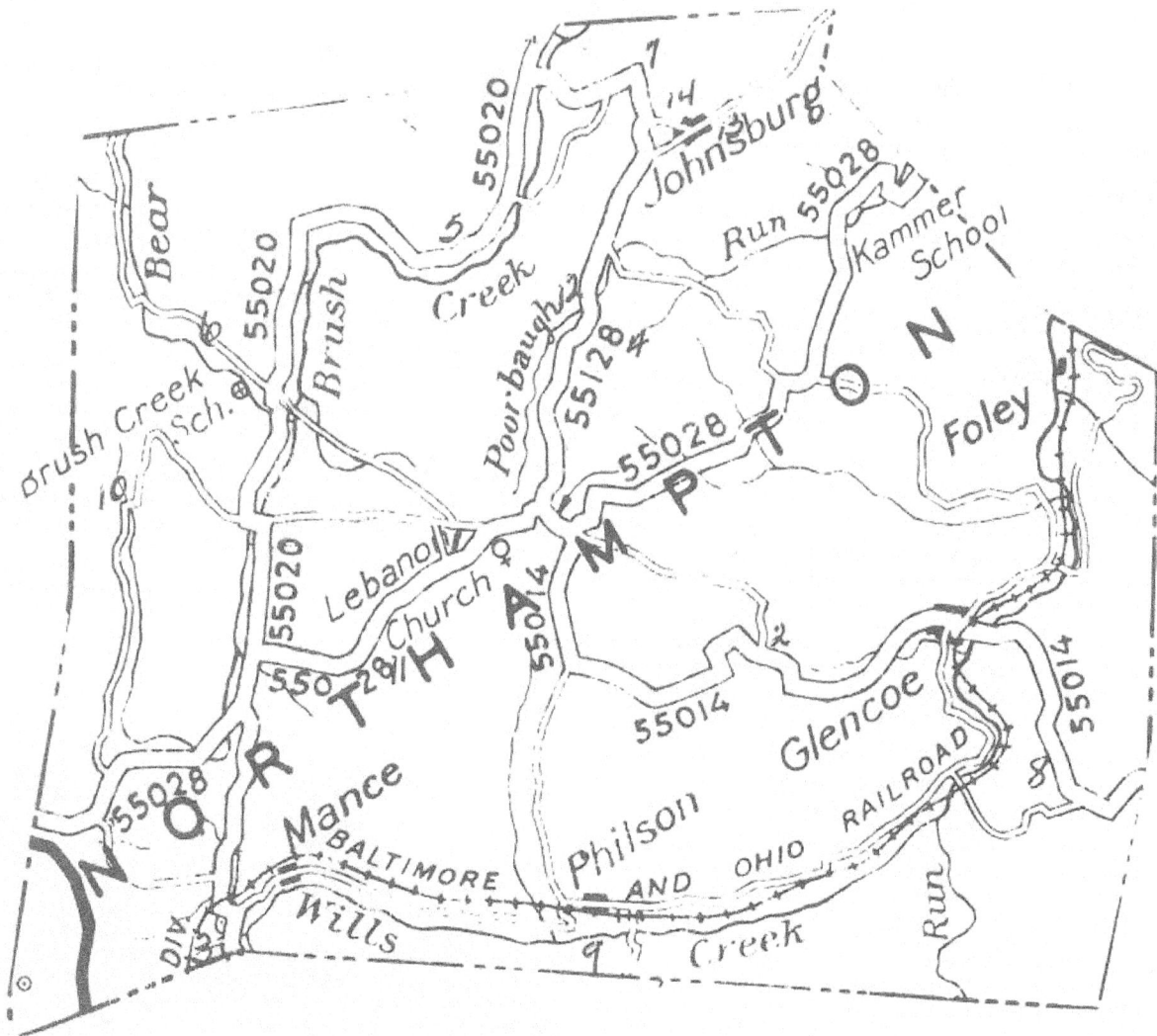

Northampton Township Cemeteries

The following burial grounds are numbered to correspond with numbers shown on map of Northampton Township, and shows approximate location.

1. **Mt. Lebanon**—Oldest 1857.
2. **Fichtner**—On farm presently owned by Dale Hartman. In field about 10 rods south of buildings. 23 marked graves, oldest 1863.
3. **Bowman**—On Peter Felker farm presently owned by Leora Deist. About 60 feet north of buildings off the road leading to Mance. 17 graves, oldest 1832.
4. **Poorbaugh**—On farm presently occupied by Larry Emerick. Located on top of hill along private road that leads from main road to farm buildings—is about midway. 8 graves, 7 fieldstones and unmarked. Marked grave that of Philip Burbach. His grave oldest, 1812. Pvt. Co. 8th 3rd Batt., Pa. Militia, Revolutionary War. Plaque at his grave gives his history.
5. **Weisel Burial Ground**—On Kimmel Farm, Northampton Township, Brushcreek. In a field a few rods above the house. 7 graves, oldest 1853.
6. **Boyer**—On Conrad Werner farm 50 rods north of buildings, in field next to sugar grove. 9 graves, oldest 1849.
7. **Martz**—On Henry Martz farm presently owned by Bertha Beck Estate. Northeast of new cemetery at Johnsburg, about one quarter mile into field. 19 graves, fieldstone markers, no inscription. Said to be Daniel Martz family and Mull family graves.
8. **Meyers**—On B. F. Bittner farm presently owned by Shaffer Bros. Graves one half mile from buildings on lower side of road leading to Glencoe. 7 graves, oldest 1863.
9. **Holley**—On George Holley farm, presently, a part of Game Lands #82 and bought from Stanley Lepley. About one mile southwest of Philson Station. 33 graves, oldest 1864.
10. **Ackerman**—On William E. Ackerman farm presently owned by Margaret Merrill. Northeast of George Ackerman buildings in a field near sawmill site. 3 marked graves, several not marked, oldest 1866.
11. On M. H. Bowman farm presently owned by Daniel Bowman. Northeast of buildings to the right of the road

going to Mt. Lebanon. Near the Herbert Laughery line fence. Said to contain 3 graves. No markers near an apple tree. Said to be Geimer people who were found frozen to death. Information from Mrs. Conrad Werner. M. H. Bowman said they were Breneman people.

12. **Bridegum-Mulls Congregation**—23 graves, oldest 1848. On Elwood Leister farm. Picture in this book.

13. **Johnsburg Cemetery—Old**—Near the Johnsburg German Lutheran Church. 26 graves, oldest 1865.

14. **Johnsburg Cemetery—New**—At German Lutheran Church in Johnsburg. 85 graves, oldest 1848.

12. **Cont.-Bridegum Cemetery**—On Moses Leister farm presently owned by Elwood Leister. North of the buildings at the edge of the woods on top of the hill, to the left of an old abandoned road. There was at one time an old church building. This was known as Mulls Church many years ago, then as Bridegum. This congregation now known as Mt. Lebanon. 78 graves, oldest 1838.

Broadwater—The W. J. Broadwater farm presently owned by Don Williams. Cemetery was a half mile southeast of buildings of the hill. 8 graves, oldest 1873. All moved to I.O.O.F. Cemetery in Berlin.

Jacob Martz was born in 1777 and died in 1845. He was the great-great grandfather of Mrs. Earl Boyer. From 1802 to 1842 he had a game report of killing 42 deer, 1 wolf, 3 bear, and 1 turkey. He was married to Mary McDalena Dughman, who lived to be 103 years, 1 month, and 13 days old.

Mr. Martz wrote his own will. It is recopied below as he had written it. The spelling is also as it was in the original will. He was from Southampton Township, which later became Northampton Township.

Last Will and Testament of Jacob Martz

In the name of God amen I Jacob Martz of Southampton Township Somerset County and State of Pennsylvania Being weak in body but of perfect mind memory and understanding thanks be given unto God. Calling unto mind the mortality of my body and knowing that is appointed for all men once to die do make and ordain this my last will and testament that is to say principally and first of all I give and recommend my soul into the hand of Almighty God that give it and my body I recommend to the earth to be buried in a decent Christian burial at the discretion of my Executors hereinafter named nothing doubting but at the general resurrection I shall receive the same again by the Almighty power of God and as touching such worldly estate wherewith it hath pleased God to bless me in this life I give demise and dispose of the same in the following manner and form viz;

First: I will unto my two sons Henry and Richard Martz, three tracts of land the one is my old home place containing one hundred and thirty seven acres and the other tract adjoining the old tract which is called the saw mill tract containing sixty four acres and the Tract called "Kerns" tract containing one hundred and thirty eight acres besides ten acres which I except for Jonathan out of Kerns tract; for this three tracts of Land the said Henry and Richard shall pay the sum of five hundred and sixty three dollars unto my heirs for the before mentioned three tracts of Land in payments as follows and to the Heirs as follows herein after named.

First my will is that the said Henry and Richard shall pay unto my son John Martz the sum of two hundred and fifty dollars one year after my death this shall be Johns whole portion of my real estate and this shall be Henry and Richards first payment for the Land.

Secondly my will is that Henry and Richard shall pay unto my daughter Polly Leidig the sum of twenty eight dollars and twenty three cent to be paid to her two years after my death and I also will unto the said Polly Leidig a note that I hold against Daniel Leidig amounting two hundred and twenty one dollars and seventy seven cents which note and the Land payment from Henry and Richard will amount to two hundred and fifty dollars this shall be the said Pollys share of my real Estate.

Thirdly my will is that Henry and Richard shall pay unto my Daughter Hannah Fichtner the sum of two hundred and fifty dollars to be paid to her three years after my death this shall be the said Hannahs share of my real Estate.

Fourthly my will is that the said Henry and Richard shall pay unto my daughter Catharine Boyer the sum of thirteen dollars and fifty cents to be paid to her four years after my death and I also will unto the said Catharine the notes I hold against Daniel Boyer amounting to two hundred and fifty dollars this shall be the said Catharine share of my real Estate.

Fifthly my will is that the said Henry and Richard shall pay unto my son William Martz the sum of one hundred and twelve dollars and twenty seven cents to be paid to him five years after my death and I also will unto the said William the notes that I hold against him amounting to one hundred and thirty seven dollars and seventy three cents which notes and the land payment from Henry and Richard will amount to two hundred and fifty dollars this shall be the said Williams share of my real Estate.

Sixthly I will unto my son Daniel Martz the sum of two hundred and fifty dollars of the notes that I hold against him and the balance of the notes if there is any he shall pay to my Executors hereinafter named this shall be said Daniels share of my real Estate.

Seventhly I will unto my son Jonathan Martz three tracts of Land the one tract where Jonathan lives on is alled "Bouchman" Tract containing seventy six acres and ten acres which I bought of Charles Gaumer and ten acres out of the Kerns Tract which is before mentioned where Jonathan begun to clear this three tracts of Land the said Jonathan shall have at the rate of two hundred and fifty dollars which shall be the said Jonathans share of my real Estate.

Eighthly I will unto my son George Martz a Tract of land called "Aleghany Tract" adjoining lands of John Hoyman and Jacob Emrich heirs containing one hundred and twenty four acres the said George shall have the said Tract of Land at the rate of two hundred and fifty dollars this shall be the said Georges share of my real Estate.

Ninthly and Lastly I give and bequeath unto my wife Magdalin all my personal property household and kitchen furniture farming utensils cows horses sheep hogs wagons and all the moveable efects that I own at my death; she may do with this property what she thinks is best to her she may see what she dont need or keep it as long as she lives and after her death the remainder of the property and her estate shall be divided amongst my ten children in eaquel shares My will is that Henry Martz and Richard Martz must furnish my wife Magdalin with the following articles yearly during her

life viz five Bushels of Wheat five Bushels wrye and Buckwheat one hundred weight of Pork half Bushel of salt twenty pounds of shuger five pounds of coffee sufficient fire wood halled and cut tatoes as many as shee needs and all other vigitables that she needs for cooking and one room in the house and to feed the creatures all what is on the place Ha Ha

And I do hereby utterly disallow revoke and disanul all and every other former testaments wills legacies bequests and executors by me in any wise before named willed and bequeathed ratifying and confirming this and no other to be my last will and testament and I make and ordain Henry Martz and Richard Martz Executors of this my Last will and Testament. In witness whereof I have hereunto set my hand and seal this twenty fourth day of October in the year of our Lord one thousand eight hundred and fourty four.

Jacob Martz (Seal)

Signed sealed published pronounced by said Jacob Martz as his Last will and Testament in presence of us who in his presence and in the presence of each other have hereto subscribed our names.

Peter Boyer
Jesse Boyer

Johnsburg Church

The German Lutheran Church in the village of Johnsburg was built in 1866. The first pastor of the church was Rev. Lauterbauch, a German, who also lived in the area.

Germans were instrumental in founding the community and in the erection of the church, which was conducted in their native tongue and for their own people.

Adhering to their native tongue and customs, early services in the church were conducted in German, and later, monthly, one of the four scheduled services would be conducted in English.

Legend has it that the church was established for the German people, and they wished to remain as such. Outsiders frequently attended and were permitted to remain, but were not herded into the fold, nor induced to continue attendance.

Ministers of the church who succeeded the original pastor included a Rev. Prosser and a Rev. Curber. The later pastors also served other parishes and lived in Glen Savage, rather than in the Johnsburg parsonage.

The church parsonage was across the road from the church. It is now owned and occupied by Mrs. Edison Brick, the only person living in the village at this time.

Glencoe Church

Glencoe congregation was organized early in 1887 by Rev. C. H. Reiter, then pastor of the Wills Creek Charge. The same year a church was built costing about $2,500, and was dedicated to the worship of God. Rev. A. J.

Heller, Rev. A. R. Kremer, D.D., together with the pastor, were present at the dedication. The congregation was organized with about 30 members, according to the statement of elder John T. Leydig. The early records of the congregation were burned in a fire that destroyed the home of Stephen Broadwater in 1900, who was secretary of the congregation at that time. David Hay and wife gave the lots of ground for the church and the parsonage.

According to statements of older members, the congregation was a flourishing one, though comparatively small. Elder Leydig states that at one time the membership numbered about one hundred. The Sunday school was also flourishing and continued to grow for some years. This congregation had the pleasure of entertaining Classis at one time.

The officers in 1898 were: elders, Dennis Leydig and W. T. Hensel; deacons, S. R. Leydig and Jesse Smith. The pastor was Rev. John D. Hunsicker.

On the membership list of 1898 were the names of 75 persons. Among these we note the following family names: Bittner, Broadwater, Crosby, Coughenour, Leydig, Miller, Martz, Hosselrode, Poorbaugh, Raupach, Snyder, Steif, Stoner, Saylor, Smith, Trautman, Webreck, and Wagaman. These are quite familiar names throughout Somerset Classis.

During the years 1900 to 1910 many of the members left this community to find employment elsewhere, and the congregation suffered greatly in the loss of membership. The 1906 report to Classis carried the names of 51 members, and a Sunday school enrollment of 72 scholars.

In 1902 the number of members participating in the communion services numbered 45. For several years a decline is noted, then it rose again until in 1916 it reached 50. From then on there is a steady drop until it reached twenty-nine.

About the year 1928 a new roof was placed on the church building, and in the winter of 1937-38 the interior of the building was redecorated.

During vacancies in the pastorate the congregation had been served by the following pastors as supply: Revs. E. P. Skyles, D. N. Dittmar, H. D. Gress, G. A. Teske, H. L. Logsdon, and N. S. Greenawalt.

From its organization in 1887 to the present time the church has been a part of the Wills Creek Charge, and has been served by the following pastors:

Pastors

C. H. Reiter	1887-1888
J. B. Stonesifer	1889-1890
A. C. Snyder	1891-1896
J. F. Bair	1897-1898
J. D. Hunsicker	1898-1904
C. G. Shupe	1905-1908
A. S. Kresge	1913-1917

W. M. Ruprecht	1917-1918
W. H. Miller	1919-1923
N. S. Greenawalt	1925-1927
J. E. Gindlesperger	1928-1947
J. E. Dobbs	1949-1962
Milton Kerr	1963-1964

From 1964 the Glencoe Church had students from Lancaster Theological Seminary until the merger took place in October 1969, which the Glencoe congregation voted against. Rev. Fred Seese was then called and has been the pastor of this church since.

During the year 1970, the coal furnace was removed and an oil furnace system was installed. The exterior of the church was painted and the interior was redecorated. A new cement porch and other improvements were added later.

In April 1975, the Glencoe United Methodist Church, which only had a few active members remaining, joined with the Glencoe Ref. U.C.C. Church. A special service was conducted when the members, building, and contents were transferred, uniting the two churches.

Worship services are held regularly, and there are special services at Christmas, Easter, etc. Officers are: **Elders**: H. C. Raupach, William Raupach, and Mrs. John W. Hartman. **Deacons**: Stanley Smith, Jack Keller, and Ray Landis. **Trustees**: Mrs. Helen Smith, Robert Bingman, and H. C. Raupach. There are 44 members. Sunday school is held every Sunday with Mrs. Helen Smith as superintendent. Donnie Knotts and Kenneth Leydig are the assistants. The 90th anniversary of the church is in the planning for 1977. A homecoming service is held each year when former members are honored.

Glencoe United Methodist Church

About 1909 members of the Evangelical faith decided that a church was needed in the village of Glencoe, located along the Baltimore and Ohio Railroad in Northampton Township, about 20 miles southeast of Meyersdale.

The original founding committee included Eli Martz,

Solomon Martz, Jonathan Martz, William Bittner, Hiram Bittner, William Hutzel, William Cook, and George Cook. The land was purchased and a foundation laid, 28' x 38'. By autumn of 1910 the new frame building was completed and painted white, and had a seating capacity of 85. The church was dedicated in October 1910 debt-free.

The pastors serving the Glencoe Church since its beginning were: Thomas B. Hovermale 1910 (?); A. F. Bender 1912 (?); L. B. Rittenhouse, 1913 (?); A. G. Meade, 1913-1915; C. E. Miller 1915-1917; T. O. Tuss, 1917-1920; A. F. Richards, 1920-1923; A. G. Meade, 1923-1925; DeVaux, 1925-1927; C. W. Evans, 1927-1930; C. W. Raley, 1930-1931; A. M. Gahagan, 1931-1935; Wm. West, 1935-1940; G. O. Bishop, 1940-1941; C. C. Callahan, 1941-1942; Harry B. Greer, 1942-1946; A. F. Richards, 1946-1952; Donald Joiner, 1953-1954; Walter C. Sell, 1954-1957; Earl Meyers, 1957-1965; Paul Snyder, March 1965 - .

This church was first known as Glencoe Evangelical Church, and was a part of the Meyersdale-Olivet Charge. After mergers in 1946, it became the Evangelical United Brethren. In another merger several years ago, it became part of the United Methodist Church. At this time it was also transferred to the Somerset Charge, with Pastor Rummel as overseer.

For many of the 60 years of its existence, the church continued to grow. Many revival services were held, sometimes for a two- or three-week series, with special evangelists being present. Oftimes there was a full house. Families would come by sledloads. Those were the winters when snow would be on the ground two feet deep, most of the winter. Then there was the New Year's Eve Watch Meeting, a community affair which everyone attended. Sometimes there was standing room only.

Times have changed. The railroad was the main support of many families. The younger folks have gone elsewhere to find jobs; the older folks have passed to the Great Beyond. With a decline in population, membership also declined. Mr. Charles B. Bittner, who was a lay leader from the inception of the church, became too ill to carry on the work. Services have not been held since September 1973.

In July 1974 a proposal was made to the Glencoe Reformed United Church of Christ to unite with this group; when voted upon, this was unanimous with both churches.

There was both sadness and gladness at the closing of these church doors. For the faithful few, there was gladness to know there still remains one little country church, wherein the people can still meet to worship God.

The first part of the service was held at the United Methodist Church. A hymn was sung and lay leader Charles B. Bittner gave the invocation and read the specially prepared service program of "The Order of Taking Leave of the Church." Rev. Charles Rummel and Pastor William Snyder also took part in this service.

The procession then left and proceeded to the Glencoe United Church of Christ. Mrs. Mavis Nunamaker led the group, carrying the pulpit Bible. The Bible was later presented to the Reformed United Church of Christ as a token of unity. Collection plates and church records also were transferred.

The vacated building will be used as an educational building and social room for the united group or Reformed United Church of Christ.

Mt. Lebanon Congregation, 1873-1973

The Mt. Lebanon congregation was formed as a merger of five different groups of Reformed people who had each been holding services in their own area. Two of these groups were already absorbed by some of the others when plans were made to build a new church building in a central location. The three remaining groups uniting in 1873 made definite plans for the building of the church at Mt. Lebanon. These groups of Reformed people were as follows:

South Mills Group—This group was located one mile north of Glencoe and was served by Rev. Benjamin Knepper. The congregation worshiped either in the old schoolhouse, or in a store building, or in a private home.

A. Wagaman's Group—This group was also served by Rev. Knepper and worshiped in a schoolhouse located near the intersection of the roads leading from Mt. Lebanon to Philson.

Mull's Church Group—This group had its beginning very early in the 1800's, probably between 1805 and 1813. This group worshiped in a church located about 1½ miles southwest of Johnsburg, and about two miles northeast of Mt. Lebanon.

Fichtner Church Group—The Fichtner Church was

located at the intersection of the roads leading to Glencoe on the farm now operated by Dale Hartman.

Brushcreek Group—This group worshiped regularly in the Brushcreek School and served the people of the Brushcreek area.

Thus Mt. Lebanon was formed by a group of people worshiping in different places who joined their churches in order to be stronger in their ministry to the Lord. A committee representing all five groups was appointed to consider the building of a church. The committee prepared a subscription paper with the following heading: "We the subscribers promise to pay the sums entered to our names for the purpose of building a Reformed church on the land of Levi Boyer on the hill of the Old Cumberland Road". This paper was signed by fifty-three persons, subscribing the sum of $1,078. Sometime during the early winter of 1873-74 a building committee was chosen.

On June 10, 1875, the cornerstone was laid under the direction of Rev. L. D. Steckel, the pastor. About $760 was raised on the occasion, with a large subscription list recorded. The service of dedication took place late in the fall of 1875, and the following ministers took part: Revs. L. D. Steckel, Benjamin Knepper, C. U. Heilman. H. F. Keener, A. E. Truxal, and William Rupp. About $500 was raised at this service. The building cost $2,469.90 when completed. It was a one-story building with a balcony in the rear. The exact date of the dedication is not recorded, but it was likely in November, 1875. The committee held a meeting at the church on November 8, 1875, and again on November 16, when they named the church Mt. Lebanon.

The first Confirmations in the new church building took place on December 11, 1875. Harriet Malinda Wagaman was confirmed and Susan Catherine Wagaman was received by baptism and confirmation. The first infant baptism was held on October 22, 1876, when Rev. L. D. Steckel baptized Virgie Meyers, daughter of Mr. and Mrs. W. J. Meyers.

The Mt. Lebanon congregation became a part of the Dale City (Meyersdale) Charge on April 17, 1876. The Dale City Charge consisted at that time of the following churches: Dale City (Meyersdale), White Oak, Greenville. The charge was formed in 1873 with Mt. Lebanon being added in 1876 and Fairhope in 1880. In 1881 Wills Creek Charge was formed with Mt. Lebanon and White Oak becoming the principal congregations. For a time Hyndman and Fairhope were a part of the charge but eventually transferred to another charge. Glencoe and Greenville (St. Marks, Pocahontas) were added and for most of its history Mt. Lebanon was part of the Wills Creek Charge, which included White Oak, Glencoe, and St. Mark's (Pocahontas).

During the last part of the nineteenth century and the first of the twentieth century, Mt. Lebanon continued to prosper under the guidance of the following ministers: Rev. S. T. Wagner, 1882-84; Rev. C. H. Reiter, 1885-88; Rev. J. B. Stonesifer, 1889-90; Rev. Addison Snyder, 1891-96; Rev. John F. Bair, 1897-98; Rev. J. D. Hun-

sicker, 1898-1904; Rev. C. G. Shupe, 1905-08; Rev. A. S. Kresge, 1913-17.

During the early part of 1915, during the pastorate of Rev. Kresge, the church building underwent extensive repairs. New windows and pews were installed, and the interior and exterior were redecorated at the cost of about $1,800.

The church was then served by the following ministers: Rev. M. W. Reprecht, 1917-18; Rev. William H. Miller, 1919-23; Rev. Norman S. Greenawalt, 1925-27; Rev. J. Earl Gindelsperger, 1928-47.

Early in the year 1934, during the pastorate of Rev. Gindelsperger, the church building was again remodeled. A new hardwood floor was laid, and changes were made to the exterior as well as the interior. A rededication service was held on Sunday, April 15, 1934. Also in 1934 the Reformed Church merged with the Evangelical Church in a national merger of the two major denominations. Mt. Lebanon became the Mt. Lebanon Evangelical and Reformed Church.

During the decade of the 1930's, during the pastorate of Rev. Gindlesperger, the congregation prospered and grew. The church was, in many ways during these years, the center of life in the community. There were not yet the distractions and multitude of other activities that were to intrude in people's lives as the pace of the world speeded up during the following decades. It was a good time for the church.

In 1940 electricity replaced the battery system of lighting in the church building. The early 1940's also saw many of the young men of the church leave to make their contribution in the war that had engulfed the world. The honor roll of these veterans still hangs on the wall to remind all of their distinguished service.

Rev. Gindlesperger left in 1947, and for a period of time the church was served in supply capacity by Rev. Ira R. Harkens, minister of Trinity Church in Berlin.

In 1949 a basement was dug out under the church to

serve as a kitchen and social room, and for Sunday school classes. The improvement was dedicated on June 9, 1949, in a service led by Rev. Harkins. Rev. Harkins served as supply until the Rev. J. Earl Dobbs was called to the Wills Creek Charge in 1949.

In 1957 our denomination was involved in another national merger. The Evangelical and Reformed denomination merged with the Congregational Christian church in one of the largest mergers in Protestantism. The new denomination chose the name "United Church of Christ," and so Mt. Lebanon now became Mt. Lebanon United Church of Christ.

The end of 1950's and the beginning of the 1960's saw a new burst of energy for remodeling and building. The interior of the building was remodeled in 1958 and aluminum siding was installed on the outside in 1960. In 1961 a beautiful picnic pavilion was built between the church and the cemetery. This pavilion became the center for summer social affairs for the congregation.

In 1962 Rev. Dobbs retired from the ministry and was appropriately honored with a "Rev. Dobbs Day" in appreciation of the fine work he and Mrs. Dobbs had done over the years they were with the congregation. In November 1963 Rev. Milton R. Kerr assumed duties as minister but left after serving less than a year.

It was difficult during these years to get ministers, especially ones willing to serve a rural four-point charge. Again supply was secured during the interim from Trinity U.C.C., Berlin, as Rev. Randell Heckman filled in when needed. It was then decided to hire a student from the Lancaster Theological Seminary to supply until an ordained minister could be secured. James Bennett came in June 1965 and supplied the charge until June 1967 when he was ordained and called to a church elsewhere. The work, however, was picked up by another student, James Killian, who came in June 1967 and served during his senior year at Lancaster. Mr. Killian was granted a license by the Somerset Association to perform all ministerial functions for the charge. He too left after ordination and call to another congregation in June 1968. Again, though, the work was picked up by a seminary student, Terry Foor, who came in June 1968, and who was also licensed by the Association.

During the summer of 1968 joint worship services were held between Mt. Lebanon and Glencoe on one end of the charge, and Pocahontas (St. Mark's) and White Oak (Grace) on the other. The joint consistory of the four churches began to talk about the possibility of merging the four in one church. In August 1968 representatives of the four congregations, along with the student supply minister, Terry Foor, went to the Penn West Conference office in Greensburg to talk to Rev. Horace Sills, newly elected Conference Minister. Rev. Sills agreed to help the churches in their discussions concerning the possibility of merger.

Much work was done, and many meetings were held during the fall of 1968 and the winter and spring of 1969. The issue of merger was debated in all the churches, with all the information being supplied to each member of the four churches of the Wills Creek Charge. A commitment was obtained from Terry Foor, student supply minister, that he would remain as regular pastor if the merger succeeded, and the church desired to issue a call.

On Sunday June 29, 1969, a vote was held in each congregation on the question of merger. Two of the congregations, Mt. Lebanon and Pocahontas (St. Mark's) voted to merge, with the other two, Glencoe and White Oak, voting not to merge. It was decided at a joint consistory meeting that afternoon to proceed with the merger of Mt. Lebanon and Pocahontas and to open a charter membership list. Those wishing to join the newly merged church had until October 12 to join as charter members.

On Sunday, October 12, 1969, a service of merger was held in the morning, formally joining the Mt. Lebanon and Pocahontas congregations as one. The service was celebrated with Holy Communion served by Rev. Horace Sills, conference minister, and Terry Foor, student supply. That afternoon in a congregational organization meeting, the new congregation chose the name: New Hope United Church of Christ. A constitution and bylaws was adopted, church officers were elected, and Terry Foor was called to be the minister. Rev. Foor was ordained into the Christian ministry on March 15, 1970.

At the service of merger in October 1969 there were 120 charter members of the congregation. Since that time New Hope has grown to a membership of 190. Rev. Terry Foor left the congregation in June 1974. The New Hope United Church of Christ is now served by Rev. William Moser, who came to us in August 1974.

Mt. Olivet Church

The early history of the Mt. Olivet congregation was connected with the Salisbury Circuit, and was served by the pastors of that work. In 1874 part of the work separated from the Salisbury work, and was called the Southampton Circuit. The members of the Evangelical Association in Northampton Township worshiped for many years in an old log church about 1½ miles east of the present church, and also in what was known as the old Brushcreek schoolhouse, about 1½ miles west of the present site.

In March 1882 the members of the church began to make preparations for the building of a church to the glory of God and the conversion of souls. On August 11, 1882, the cornerstone-laying service for the new Mt. Olivet Church was held. The land on which the church was built was donated by Levi Boyer, and most of the labor and some of the material was donated by the members. The approximate cash cost of the church was $1,000. The trustees at that time were: John Wagerman, Matthias Poorbaugh, Levi Boyer, William Dively, Noah Martz, Sampson Martz, and Samuel Mishler. The carpenter was Franklin Forney of Berlin, Pa.

The church building is 28' x 42', of frame construction. The seating capacity of the sanctuary is 168. There are no separate rooms for classes, but there is a full basement which is used for Christian education and class meetings. This basement was added with construction beginning in 1959. On August 9, 1959, the relaying of the cornerstone was held. Later, a new roof was put on, a new heating system was installed, red carpet and tile flooring was installed, and interior walls were remodeled. New choir seats and pews, new entrance doors, cement steps and walk were added and also a concrete block refreshment stand for picnics and family gatherings was built. Finally, shrubbery was planted around the church. The total cost for this remodeling effort was $7,152. The service of dedication was held on November 10, 1963.

In 1966 the ceiling of the basement was sealed with suspended tile blocks, and the walls of the basement painted, costing $1,057.38. The Ladies Aid Society of the church paid half the cost. Homer Cook was Sunday school superintendent and the trustees were: Noah Ludy, Grant Ackerman, and Harry Smith, Jr. In 1967 the young people of the church bought a new altar, an altar scarf, a brass altar set of two candleholders, two flower vases and a cross, a large Bible for the pulpit, and a Baptismal bowl. The outside of the church was given a new coat of white paint, with the labor being donated by Harry Smith, Sr., Harry Smith, Jr., James Smith, Bob Cook, and Pastor Paul Snyder. In June of that year, the Ladies Aid of the church had a well dug on the church ground, 244 ft. deep, drilled by Steve Svonavec of Friedens, Pa. The drill bit was donated by Edward Baker, a member of the church. An electric pump was installed, and the water was piped into the church basement and to the refreshment stand. Simon Weaver was the plumber, and with the help of other church members, the labor was all donated. The youth group bought Bibles to be placed in each pew. The dedication for these improvements was held on March 23, 1968.

During the summer of 1968, the church had the Keystone Lime Company of Springs cover the church parking lot with black top, at a cost of $150. New hymnals were bought and placed in each pew. The youth group bought an electric organ for the church, and Alvin Summy was hired to put in a new suspended ceiling in the church and all new windows. The cost was $1,214.57. The Ladies Aid Group paid part of that bill. Three of the new windows were donated in memory of departed loved ones: one for Wm. and Carl Smith, donated by the brothers and sisters; one in memory of Mable Dively Smith, donated by her husband, Harry Smith, Sr.; and one in memory of Ella Cook Bittner, donated by her children. The members also painted the interior of the church. The rededication services for these

improvements was held on May 4, 1969. Paul Snyder was pastor, Harry Saylor was the Sunday school superintendent, and the trustees were Grant Ackerman, James Smith, and Harry Smith, Jr.

In October 1969 a new heating system was installed in the church basement. The old coal furnace was taken out and a new oil burner installed, with an underground fuel tank. The total cost of the new furnace was $856.12. It was installed by Simon Weaver and the pit for the fuel tank was dug by Noah Ludy, both men donating their labor. In June 1970 the Ladies Aid group of the church had a new pavilion added to the picnic area next to the refreshment stand. Robert Mays was the contractor. By borrowing $600 from the church treasurer, the Ladies Aid was able to pay the full amount. The Ladies Aid then held festivals, bake sales, and rummage sales, and by November of the same year were able to repay the $600 to the church.

In September 1971 the youth group bought a new piano for the church at a cost of $695. A large artificial palm was donated by the family of Harry Smith, Sr., in memory of their mother, Mrs. Mabel Smith. In July 1972, the United Methodist church of Salisbury closed and donated various items to the other churches on the charge. Mt. Olivet received an almost new pulpit, altar, and lectern for the church, two tables, chairs, sink, water heater, refrigerator for the basement, and an outside bulletin board. Also at the same time, the Ladies Aid had spouting installed around the picnic area and the pavilion. Harold Bittner of Berlin did the work at a cost of $149.

The summer and fall of 1973 saw a lot more improvements at the Mt. Olivet Church. The outside steps to the basement were closed in. The basement was then partitioned off, and a nursery was built in the other part. Paneling was put on the walls of the nursery and on the walls of the two rest rooms that were built. Also, carpet was installed in the nursery and on the inside steps leading to the basement. Noah Ludy dug the footer and installed the septic tank, Simon Weaver did the plumbing for the rest rooms, and also donated one of the commodes. John Long of Berlin did the carpenter work and the carpeting. Philip Martz did the electrical work. The total cost of these improvements was $1,341.91. Tom Smith was the Sunday school superintendent, and the trustees were Irving Smith, James Smith, Glenn Deihl, Kay Ackerman, and Alice Cook. Also the same year the Ladies Aid had a cement floor put in the pavilion and the sides closed in with cement blocks. Robert Mays did the cement work at a cost of $1,380.23. In the fall of 1974, the Ladies Aid had the old tile flooring covered in the church and new wall-to-wall carpeting installed.

The present Sunday school enrollment is 89, with an average attendance of 53.

The ministerial records are in doubt, as well as the dates. Below are listed some of the ministers and dates of service: W. A. Rininger, A. B. Day, A. J. Beal, Soloman Caton, Samuel Milliron, H. M. Cook, Samuel Baumgardner, W. A. McCaully, J. C. Powell, N. F. Boyer, N. U. Kelly, M. R. Tyson, A. G. Meade, M. V. B. Devaux, C. W. Evans, J. M. Gahagen, Charles Calahan, G. O. Bishop, W. M. West, J. H. Wise, C. W. Raley, A. F. Richards, D. J. Joiner, 1953-1954; W. C. Sell, 1954-1957; E. E. Meyers, 1957-1965; Paul Snyder, March 1965-.

Fairhope Township

Pack Saddle
Fairhope Twp.

ROBINSON

Committee

Jeannine Cummins
Cinda Emerick

Much appreciation is extended to all who contributed information about the early history of Fairhope Township.

Alice Maxwell Merritt
Harry Lowry
James Emerick
Alvin Custer
Gilbert Barnhart
Theodore Finney
Rozella Shroyer
Ellsworth Shumaker
Karl Davidson
Edith Deeter
Florence Poorbough
John Day
Lester Foust
Herman Hutzell
William R. Thompson
Mrs. Eber Cockley

Brush Cr.

55005

Emerick School

55122

Shaffer's

N. E S W

FAIRHOPE

55005

• 55005

Fairhope

Wills Cr.

Williams

55024

Fairhope Township

The last township formed in Somerset County and the smallest is Fairhope Township. It was composed from segments of Allegheny, Northampton, and Southampton townships and is comprised of 8,409 acres or thirteen square miles.

A prime mover in the formation of this township was Jacob Kammerer. The other townships bitterly opposed the newly created township, but the petition was approved in 1891, after the end of the Civil War.

The prospects for a railroad in the area had "fair hopes" of the citizens, thus giving it the name. Later, a main line of the Baltimore and Ohio Railroad was constructed, and trains stopped regularly in the village of Williams, at the Williams Station. Today, however, that station no longer stands and the trains make no stops here. Further up the tracks, the trains go through the Falls Cut Tunnel, built in 1897, to lend access through the sides of the mountain. Troops were used in 1917 during World War I to guard the Falls Cut Tunnel.

Williams became the community where the brickyards were located. There was the Savage Fire Brick Company, which had invested several hundred thousand dollars for developing the brick industry; and also in operation at one time was the Welsh, Cloniger, and Maxwell plant. Several hundred men were employed in the brickyards, and families were drawn into the area, creating a small settlement of homes along the banks of Wills Creek. This group became the population sufficient to justify petitioning the court for the formation of Fairhope Township. With fine deposits of clay and a railway system making regularly scheduled stops in the area, the two brickyards in Fairhope Township once did a flourishing business.

Tunnel (Falls Cut)

Fairhope Village

Troops guarding tunnel

Fairhope Area Schools

There were four schools within Fairhope Township. They were as follows: Williams, which was erected near the banks of Wills Creek and near the brickyards. This served the community of persons who lived in that vicinity and were employed by that industry. This school was torn down in the 1930's. However, the other three schoolhouses—Emerick, Kammerer, and Fairhope—are still standing and in use as homes—with the exception of the latter, which was still being used for teaching until the 1960's and is presently used as a community center.

Fairhope School

Old Fairhope School group

Emerick School

Side entrance to old Fairhope School

Kammerer School

Jacob Kammerer

Jacob Kammerer was born on October 18, 1842, and died in the year 1917. He married Elizabeth Ann Johns, who was born December 25, 1844, and died February 15, 1922. They were the parents of ten children.

Jacob had very little formal education, possibly attending a few months for only two or three years, since it was so far to travel to school and the books had to be purchased. However, he was very enthusiastic about all of his children attending and completing school. He served on the school board for many years, working hard to get free schoolbooks for the children, and giving land for the Kammerer School to be built.

He became a man of much discussion when he worked very hard to develop the last township in Somerset County—Fairhope Township. He donated land from his farm not only for the Kammerer School, but the Kammerer Cemetery and the covered bridge also were located on his land.

Seated: Jacob Kammerer, born October 18, 1842, died 1917. Wife, Elizabeth Ann Johns, born December 25, 1844; died February 15, 1923. Standing (left to right): Margaret Elmira, born February 27, 1887, married James Carringer; Emma Rebecca, born August 22, 1872, married Charles C. Burkhart; Sarah Hannah Louise, born April 5, 1880, married Harry E. Tressler; Charles Wesley, born May 27, 1875, married Mary Grace Fleck; Jennie Leota, born July 5, 1884, married Herman G. Lepley; Elizabeth Lucretia, born April 4, 1883, married John A. Wisner.

271

The Fairhope Post Office

Mail service for the Fairhope area was moved from the Glen Savage Post Office to the Fairhope Post Office in 1906.

William Caton served as a mail carrier for one or two years, and carried the mail by horse and buggy.

David U. Foust also carried mail by horse and buggy until March 4, 1927.

Ross Emerick served as substitute mail carrier, who used the first automobile for deliveries.

Homer Cummins was employed for postal service from approximately 1928 to 1947.

James Cummins delivered mail from 1948 to 1971.

Presently delivering mail to the Fairhope and surrounding areas is Warren Warner, who began carrying the mail in 1972.

Other local men who also served as substitutes on the mail route were Wesley Deeter, Oren Bruck, and Gary Baker.

Mr. and Mrs. Joseph Lowry were owners of a general store in the village of Fairhope. Mr. Lowry was also postmaster at the same time. Two daughters of Mr. Lowry later served as postmistresses. Ella Lowry served until her death and her sister Ruth Lowry then served until her death.

Old Fairhope Post Office

David Foust - mail carrier

Lowry

James Cummins - mail carrier

New Fairhope Post Office

Gristmill

On a triangular strip of land purchased in 1856 by Mr. Solomon Troutman, and still standing today, is a gristmill, situated along Brush Creek. This is now the property of Mr. Karl Davidson of the Washington, D.C., area.

Polly Ann (or Mary) Troutman, his wife, helped to work the mill, and later took over the operation when her husband became too ill with tuberculosis, which he contracted from being in the dust made by the mill operations.

Another local resident, Sarah Troutman Bittner, worked clearing rocks from the wooden trough which left water from Brush Creek run down and turn the wheel.

A piece of silk bolting cloth, purchased in Germany, was used to sift the ground flour. As payment for services obtained at the mill, each patron was charged one tenth of each bushel of wheat ground into flour.

When flour was not being ground at the mill, another product, chestnut shingles was also made there.

Mrs. Troutman took in boarders to help earn money to pay her taxes, and the ministers who traveled in and through the area stayed at the home beside the gristmill.

In walking distance from this site, church meetings were held on the Jacob Kammerer farm in their sugar camp area.

Still standing today and in use now for a country home by the Davidsons is a two-story log home. Mr. Davidson plans on restoring the old gristmill in the future.

Gristmill

Loghouse

Pearl V. Emerick

"P. V." Emerick was born on September 24, 1889, and is the oldest female resident of Fairhope area. She lives in her own home in the village of Fairhope and is surrounded by beautiful flowers and large vegetable garden, which she tends herself each year.

On her birthday in 1910, she married George Valentine Emerick, who is now deceased. They set up housekeeping and raised their children on the Frank Emerick farm, where her son, Elwood Emerick, still lives today.

Busy as a mother and housekeeper for David Foust, she also was midwife for many of the women in the area. When asked how many children she has delivered, she answered that she did not keep any record of how many deliveries she has made, since she performed this service for folks who may not have been able to afford the expense of hospital services.

Besides gardening and canning her fruits and vegetables, she walks to the Fairhope Community Church, where she is a member and attends very regularly.

Farm of Emerick's

Pearl V. Emerick

Fairhope Township

At one time Fairhope Township was a very prosperous place with three brickyards known as Fairhope Brickyard, Maxwell Brickyard, and Williams Brickyard. Coal and clay mines in the area employed many people. Several sawmills were located in the township. Many people were employed by the Baltimore and Ohio Railroad which ran through the heart of the community of Fairhope.

There were six general stores operated by Richard Emerick, Simon Poorbaugh, Lou Emerick, Joseph Lowry, Charles Boyer, and Charley Coughenour.

At the present site of the post office Simon Poorbaugh operated a feed store. Mr. Poorbaugh was also in the lumber business. He built a wharf in this area that was used as a loading dock where farmers brought their crops in and loaded them on freight cars to be shipped to all points. Many mining props, railroad ties, and other products were shipped.

A small building was erected by Weld and Sheridan as an office for their lumber business back in the 1800's.

This same building was later used as an office for a visiting doctor whose name was Dr. Pond. He came from Meyersdale by train to attend people in the Fairhope area.

Before this building was torn down it was used as an election house for the Fairhope Township voters.

Feed Store

Old Election House

Paradise Valley Sportsmen's Club

Begun in 1961 by twelve members, the Paradise Valley Sportsmen's Club has grown to an annual voting membership of over 350, plus some thirty lifetime members. In 1966, under the direction of Elwood Norris and Arthur Mangne, the building presently housing the club was built two miles south of the village of Glen Savage on Route 55005. All labor and many building materials were donated by various club members.

The present officers of Paradise Valley are Theodore Robb, president; Ralph Robb, vice-president; Stanley Norris, secretary; and Elwood Norris, treasurer. The club makes itself felt in a wide variety of community activities including wild game feeding, which is paid for by membership fees, shooting matches, the Shaffer Run children's fishing contest, the annual Hunting and Fishing Day banquet, and many square dances and covered-dish dinners. The dates and times of club activities are announced publicly in advance of their occurrence and anyone wishing to attend these events is cordially invited.

Sportsmen's Club

Mr. and Mrs. John Day

John R. and Hannah Hutzell Day celebrated their 60th wedding anniversary on July 16, 1976. Mr. and Mrs. Day were married on July 16, 1916, at the Baptist Church of Cumberland, Maryland, by Rev. York. They are the parents of 12 children, and have 57 grandchildren and 52 great-grandchildren. The Days reside at R. D. 1, Fairhope, Pennsylvania.

Mr. & Mrs. John Day

Church History

The Fairhope Community Church, located in the village of Fairhope nine miles east of Glencoe, received its charter March 1, 1965.

Before that time the congregation was known as the Union Gospel Mission, when, during the pastorate of Rev. C. W. Evans, the church building was purchased from the Pittsburgh Synod of the Evangelical and Reformed Church.

The Reformed congregation had its beginning when Rev. Benjamin Knepper began preaching at Fairhope in June 1878. He continued as pastor until 1880 when the congregation was annexed to the Dale City (Meyersdale) charge and Rev. L. D. Steckel served until 1881.

The next year the church was transferred to the newly formed Will's Creek charge with Rev. T. S. Wagner serving from 1882 to 1884.

In 1890 the Fairhope and Hyndman congregations were placed with the Cumberland mission and this arrangement continued during the pastorates of the Reverends E. E. Weller and A. S. Glessner.

Old Fairhope Church

Supply Point

In 1896 the congregation was placed in the newly formed Hyndman charge and a few years later it became merely a supply point with Rev. Calvin Skyles as first supply pastor in 1907.

The congregation was barely able to maintain its existence by 1908 when a petition by some members of Classis took action to reorganize the congregation in June with Rev. Mr. Skyles and A. E. Truzal acting as a committee of Classis. At this time Jesse W. Deremer and Solomon Shumaker were elected elders. W. H. Smith and W. H. Suder were elected deacons.

Rev. J. C. Knaple, appointed as supply pastor for the congregation, continued to serve until 1909 when the

Fairhope congregation was placed in the Hyndman charge under the pastorate of Rev. D. N. Dittmar, 1909 to 1911.

The following were confirmed on the day of organization: William H. Baker; Susan and Lucinda Carter; Effie J. and Mary DeVore; Mr. and Mrs. James Deremer; Olie, George W., and Robert Emerick; Mrs. Cora and Lanie Kennell; Mrs. Lydia E. Martin; and Mrs. Clinton Smith.

Mrs. Jennie Barclay was received by letter. Those received by statement of faith were: Mr. and Mrs. Wm. H. Suder and Joanne Emerick. Mrs. Margaret Carder was received by renewal of faith.

Medal for Work

David U. Foust, who became a member in 1909 and was an elder for many years, received a medal from the state Sunday School Association for 50 years of Sunday school work. He was born on March 5, 1856.

About 1910, the Fairhope Church was again placed in the Will's Creek charge where it remained until the pastorate of Rev. A. S. Kresge, 1914-15, when it was returned to the Hyndman charge. During the pastorate of the Rev. A. J. Herman, 1915-1917, interest waned and church services were practically abandoned.

The congregation was placed under the care of a supply committee which was granted $100 to carry on the work. By 1930 the congregation had dwindled to about

David U. Foust

Fairhope Church

Group at Church

eight and ceased to function. The officers at that time were D. U. Foust and A. W. Markwood, elders; and W. H. Shumaker and Henry Logue, elders.

Church Built in 1903

The Fairhope Church was built in 1903 by the United Brethren people. In 1908 the building was repaired and enlarged with six feet added to the sides and a pulpit recess in the rear.

The Reformed congregation rented the building from the United Brethren people in 1913 and four years later bought it. It was repaired and rededicated shortly afterward.

The congregation seemed to prosper when the brick works production was up. The community, however, has always found it hard to maintain a church.

A congregation was again established under the pastoral care of Rev. Luman O. Evans, who served from 1941 to 1960. Rev. C. W. Evans initiated the purchase of this Reformed Church by the Union Gospel Mission on March 22, 1956, for $200.

Rev. C. W. Raley served the congregation from 1961 until his death in 1964.

The church was once more reorganized in 1964 and renamed Fairhope Community Church.

Rev. Leroy E. Logsdon, present minister, assumed the pastorate in 1964. In June of that year Rev. Karl Shuck began to share the pastorate and continued in that capacity until February 1969.

The membership was established in February 1965 with 20 persons. In August of that same year, the church became affiliated with the Bedford-Fulton County Christian Churches, a local conference of self-governing independent churches. The church has enjoyed continuous growth since 1965 with a current church membership of 107 persons and a Sunday school enrollment of 147.

To meet the needs of the growing congregation, the church facility was enlarged on three occasions. In 1969 an addition measuring 28' by 24' was made to provide space for Sunday school classes. In 1971 the main auditorium was extended 24 feet in order to enlarge the vestibule and to accommodate additional pews. In August of 1976 the Sunday school area was once again enlarged with a 28' by 24' addition to the facility at a cost of approximately $15,000.

The congregation of Fairhope Community Church has a missionary vision and actively supports foreign missionaries through O.M.S. International, Incorporated; Sudan Interior Missions, and North Africa Missions. These organizations represent missionaries in North Africa, France, Republic of Niger, Brazil, Haiti, Japan, China, Spain, Taiwan, and Ecuador. This congregation also provides support to the local Union Rescue Mission in Cumberland, Maryland.

277

In April 1974, the Fairhope congregation, along with Faith Community Church of Hyndman, Pa., assumed full support of Pastor Leroy Logsdon, who requested early retirement from the Celanese Corporation supervisory staff after 40 years of service in order to enter full-time Christian service.

The church program provides a variety of activities. Sunday services include morning worship and Sunday school and evening worship. Church-sponsored buses run from Hyndman and Glen Savage to the Fairhope Church for Sunday services. The midweek prayer meeting and Bible study service is led by the pastor's wife, Mrs. Catherine Logsdon. Other highlights of the church year include revival services in the fall and spring and vacation Bible school in the summer. Church-supported missionaries on leave from their assignments frequently visit the church and report on their work, adding enrichment to the church program.

Fairhope Community Church, a Bible-believing church with a fundamental doctrine, is independent and not affiliated with any major denominational conference.

Fairhope Community Church—1968

Alex Ohler Property

Now the property of Alex Ohler, this once was owned by Ross M. Sarver. Built in 1910, the lumber was sawed by Henry (Doc) Miller for the buildings.

There was a house, blacksmith shop, and an icehouse. The ice was cut in the wintertime at the Kammerer Bridge from Brush Creek. It was hauled to the icehouse, where it was stored in sawdust. This served the surrounding area with ice.

A wooden platform was built on the lawn and square dances were held there.

Ross Sarver also served the Fairhope area for several years as constable.

Shumaker Place

Solomon Shumaker lived on the Shumaker place, which he called "The 80 or 90 Acres," with his wife, Sarah Rebecca Perdew.

Josiah Emerick, a homesquatter, took thirty of these acres by living and working on the land.

Solomon Shumaker was a blacksmith, carpenter, and also the local undertaker. For this latter occupation, he would measure the corpse with a string, choose a switch from a bundle that he kept for this purpose, and then cut the switch to the length of the person for whom he was making the coffin. He kept several coffins hanging on metal hooks on the walls.

On October 21, 1918, Solomon and Sarah's baby son died of the flu and on October 22, Sarah also passed away. The child was placed at his mother's knees in her coffin for burial. In just one week, the flu epidemic had taken thirteen lives and still spread from home to home, claiming victims.

Story on Shumakers

In 1939, Ruth and Ellsworth (Gig) Shumaker of Fairhope took their children blackberry picking. Mrs. Shumaker carried a stick, which she used as a cane to help her travel over the rough terrain, and she would poke it into the brush to scare out wildlife or snakes.

The group had their buckets filled and had started towards home when Mrs. Shumaker came upon a bush full of plump berries, and she stopped to pick these also, first poking her stick into the bushes. She felt something strike her leg, and realized that she had been bitten by a copperhead snake.

Her husband tied his handkerchief around her leg for a tourniquet and they helped her to the nearest house, the home of Oliver Emerick, where she was taken by car to Dr. John Topper's office in Hyndman, Pa.

As he had no serum for this snakebite and could not obtain any, Dr. Topper prescribed an onion poultice to be applied and three pints of whiskey to be taken internally. Mr. Shumaker thus sat by his wife's bedside and with a tablespoon, managed to coax all three pints of liquor into her. As she was then breast-feeding their baby, Ethel Mae, at the time, it was necessary to wean the child.

With the help of the family and Goldie Emerick, a neighbor, Mrs. Shumaker survived this dangerous experience, and in June, 1976, the Shumakers celebrated their 50th wedding anniversary.

Indian Legend

On the top of a mountain overlooking Fairhope and the railroad, there is a rock called "The Umbrella Rock," due to its shape.

Above or behind this rock, an Indian named "Crow" allegedly mined gold nuggets from the earth, which he made into buckles for belts and shoes and sold.

"Crow" was later found in the White Horse Mountain area, sitting against a fence post, with a bullet through him. The exact location of his digging site died with him and still remains a secret to this day.

Home Remedies

To bring down the swelling and help the pain, egg whites were stiffly beaten and applied directly to the cheek for treatment of abscessed teeth.

Mud was applied to a bee sting or insect bite. This drew out the poison and kept down the swelling.

For brightening the walls of the homes, clothes bluing was added to whitewash and applied to the walls, providing soft color to the decor.

Bridges

There are three bridges of interest in Fairhope Township. The former iron bridge located in the village of Fairhope was an old railroad bridge bought by the county from the Baltimore and Ohio Railroad Company. This bridge was torn down at Cook's Mills when they had a single track and brought to Fairhope before the turn of the century. In 1961 it was torn down and a modern bridge was erected in its place.

Kammerer covered bridge was named for the founder of that area of Fairhope Township. This bridge burned down.

Pack Saddle covered bridge, spanning Brush Creek, is noted for its beauty. Many artists come to this area to paint pictures of this bridge. It is kept in good shape.

Old Iron Bridge

Pack Saddle Bridge

photo by Jan Gleysteen

Modern bridge

Kammerer Bridge

Fairhope Brickyard

George Birchnal was owner of Fairhope Brickyard. Silica brick and building bricks were manufactured in this plant. Many bricks were shipped by railroad to Pittsburgh and Johnstown steel mills. Many people in the area received their livelihood from this brickyard.

Fairhope Brickyard employees

Fairhope Brickyard

World War I

Living in Fairhope Township is Alvin Custer, who was born in 1895. He is the only living resident who served in World War I.

When Mr. Custer was age eleven, he contracted spinal meningitis and was treated for this by Dr. Large of Meyersdale.

Later, at the age of 22, he enlisted, on September 18, 1917, to serve in the military service for the United States in the war against Germany. He was stationed at Camp Lee, Virginia. During his military service, he became ill with tuberculosis and was admitted to a hospital; he then was discharged from the service.

At the age of 81, Mr. Custer is still active on his small farm near the Pack Saddle covered bridge over Brush Creek.

Baltimore and Ohio Railroad

Many train wrecks were recorded on the Baltimore and Ohio Railroad. People came from near and far to see these wrecks.

In June of 1949 there were 17 railroad cars derailed causing much damage to the track and cars plus the loss of the contents of the railroad cars. It took many men days to clear the track and clean everything up.

Village of Williams

The village of Williams, located two miles east of Fairhope, at one time had a railroad station, a brickyard, store, post office, church, school, and numerous houses.

The brickyard manufactured fire bricks. Coal and clay were obtained from the mountain back of the brickyard. There was an incline with a drum and steel cable for hauling the coal and clay to the brickyards. The load coming off the mountain pulled the empty car back up the mountain for reloading.

This village and brickyard were torn down during the 1930's. This was owned by Savage Fire Brick Company.

Williams Church

Williams Brickyard

283

Williams School at Mines

Williams School

Maxwell Brickyard

Welsh, Cloniger, and Maxwell owned a brickyard near Williams in Fairhope Township. This brickyard played a great part in making bricks for the Falls Cut Tunnel in 1897, also for Sandpatch Tunnel in 1913. Many bricks were used for paving, sidewalks, and buildings throughout the tri-state area.

Building brick and also fire brick were manufactured at this brickyard. This plant operated with a steam engine boiler.

Joseph Maxwell was the employer at this brickyard. The employees were paid $.13 an hour wages.

The Maxwell Brickyard also crushed stone for brick silica. This plant was unpopular, however, as the dust caused emphysema of the lungs and many died young in life, due to working under these conditions.

The bricks were stacked to dry and later loaded onto the railroad cars to be transferred to the various points of sale.

This brickyard was destroyed by fire in 1917. All that remains today are the skeletons of the factory structures which are remembrances of the time of prosperous industry for this area.

Mr. and Mrs. J. S. Maxwell

MAXWELL, BRADLEY & CO.,

MANUFACTURERS OF

All Kinds of ◆ Fire Brick

AND **TILE,** FOR

Rolling Mills, Furnaces, Glass Works & Coke Ovens,

OFFICE AND WORKS, · · · · Layton's Station, Pa.
PITTSBURGH OFFICE, · · · · at Gas Works, 2d Ave.

JAMES H. WELCH, General Agent.

Maxwell's Card

Maxwell Brickyard and Employees

Maxwell Brickyard

Maxwell Employees

Maxwell Brickyard Employees

Maxwell Clay Tipple

287

Fairhope Township Cemeteries

The Burkhart Cemetery is located on the old August Grenke farm in the township of Fairhope. It is located in the second field above the buildings, on the left road leading to the back fields. It contains sixty graves, with fifty of these graves uninscribed. The oldest grave is dated 1837.

The Kammerer Cemetery is located on the Jacob Kammerer property, which is now owned by Mrs. James (Rozella) Shroyer. The location of the cemetery is east of the buildings, about 10 rods. It contains 182 graves, with the oldest being 1852.

Community Activity

The Happy Hollow Homemakers held their first meeting on January 13, 1971. It was held in the old one-room school in Fairhope, now known as the Community Building. There were eight persons attending. An election of officers was held and they were chosen as follows:

Sylvia J. Kennell - President
Hazel Shroyer - Vice-President
Florence Day - Secretary/Treasurer

Over the years, the club membership has increased to sixteen persons, losing a few of the beginning members, and gaining some new ones.

The club attends the Annual Homemakers' Fair and have a table displaying the crafts they have made.

They have learned various and useful things from their meetings, such as sewing, drying flowers, needlecraft, cooking, making jewelry, painting pictures, and, in general, having a very nice day once a month when they meet together. A covered-dish luncheon is served, with each member contributing her favorite recipe.

The 1976 officers for the club are:
Helen Baker - President
Phyllis Bishop - Vice-President
Sylvia J. Kennell - Secretary/Treasurer

More Photos

The Emerick residence—one of the oldest in the township

The Shumaker residence in 1916

Mr. and Mrs. Joseph Lowry, owners of the general store and post office (August 18, 1929)

A clay mine crew at Williams, Pa. Kneeling, left to right: Layton, Hays Plumer, Layton, Knute Henry, Harry Burley, Clinton Ritchey, Harry Shaffer, Pete Giffon, Dick Nevil, Joe Moyer. Standing: (unknown), McDonald, Henry Smith, Andy Emerick, Jim Noel, Charley Ranker, Jake Day, Joe Deneen, Shanon Smith, Cal May, Andy Rice, Chiny Beals, Simon Smith, Pete Troutman, Tommy Hartland.

To the right was wooden stairs built down the hillside to the gas pumps that you would pull into, honk your horn, and sit and wait till Salmon or Lucy Bittner could come down to pump your gas. String music was popular to all the folks in the area.

Fairhope Township's oldest married couple, John and Hannah Day, and their 12 children.

Present day Berlin, Pennsylvania

Present day Berlin, Pennsylvania

Geneva Altfather

David and Kathryn Bell

Harold and Harriet Bittner

Lester and Eleanor Bittner

Buhl and Pearl Black

Otis and Vella Bockes

Ronald and Frances Bockes

Robert and Nancy Brant

Robert and Eleanor Brick

Mrs. Evelyn Bridegum

Thomas and Leanne Calvert

Paul J. Coleman

Harold and Catherine Croner

Mrs. Hazel Dickey

A. S. Dudley residence

Edgar and Nora Emerick

William and Ruth France

Clarence and Ruth Gindlesperger

Donald and Dorothy Groff

John H. and Evelyn Hartman

John W. and Mary Hartman

Mrs. Edna Hartman

Carl and Marjorie Hay

Carl Jr., and Betty Hay

Jess Mae Hillegas

Ralph and Ruth Hillegas

S. Richard and Rheta Hillegas

Eugene and Dorothy Johnson

Walter A. Johnson

James and Dorothy Killius

Paul and Marian Klose (Recent home of)

Mrs. Bertha Landis

Mrs. Margaret Logue

Jacob and Violet Ludy

Harvey and Mary Martz

Charles and Libby Merrill

Charles A. Merrill residence

William and Nancy Merrill

Nevin and Delores Mitchell

Mrs. Pearl Mosgrave

S. Garner and Marian Pritz

John O. Ream and Louise

William and Vicki Stifco

Charles and Mary Esther Smith

Harry and Mildred Smith

Mrs. Frances P. Stuck

Mrs. Dora Stutzman

Ernest and Dorothy Suder

G. Richard and Shirley Wetmiller

Clyde and Mildred Zorn

Donald and Betty Cober

Gregory and Jeffery Croner

Richard and Helen Croner

Tommy and Nancy Croner

Donald and Edna Deist

Leon and Elmira Knepper

Edwin and Marcella Landis

Charles and Colleen Maust

Paul and Emma Pritts

John O. and Pearl Stoner

Richard and Rose Ann Webreck

Calvin and Mary Elizabeth Will

Dorothy and John Edward Hay, Larry and Gail Hay